Visualizing Deviance

The news – what we are told daily by newspapers and radio and television news – shapes our understanding not only of world of events but also of the nature of our society. The decisions made by journalists as to what is newsworthy therefore play a significant role in determining social values. In this provocative analysis of how these decisions are made, the authors suggest that in Western societies, the essence of news is its emphasis on social deviance and control.

Journalists, in their use of particular, regular sources as their 'authorized knowers,' decide what constitutes deviance. As this carefully documented study demonstrates, their definition is very broad: it goes beyond such serious forms as criminal acts to such behaviour as straying from bureaucratic procedures and violations of common sense knowledge. This definition, absorbed as it is by huge audiences, has tremendous influence; journalists become key players in constituting visions of order, stability, and change, and in influencing control practices that articulate these visions.

The study is based on extensive, long-term field research in print and broadcast news organizations, including interviews with newsroom personnel at all levels. It combines unique and rich data with a theoretical sophistication to create a revealing analysis of a critical aspect of journalism, one that has important implications for the study of communication, sociology, and criminology.

RICHARD ERICSON is Professor at the Centre of Criminology, University of Toronto. He is author of *Reproducing Order: A Study of Police Patrol Work* and co-author, with Patricia Baranek, of *The Ordering of Justice: A Study of Accused Persons as Dependents in the Criminal Process.*

PATRICIA M. BARANEK is Assistant to the Vice-President, Business Affairs at the University of Toronto and former Research Associate at the Centre for Criminology.

JANET B.L. CHAN is a doctoral candidate in the Faculty of Law, University of Sydney.

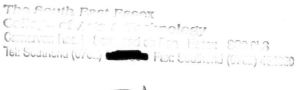

Visualizing Deviance:
A Study of
News Organization

RICHARD V. ERICSON

PATRICIA M. BARANEK

JANET B.L. CHAN

OPEN UNIVERSITY PRESS

MILTON KEYNES

First published in the United Kingdom in 1987 by
Open University Press
Open University Educational Enterprises Limited
12 Cofferidge Close
Stony Stratford
Milton Keynes MK11 1BY
England

ISBN 0-335-15515-4
ISBN 0-335-15514-6 Pbk.

In memory of
John William Ericson, 1919–1986

Contents

Acknowledgments

As with most cultural products these days, this book would not have been possible without the good will and direct assistance of a large number of individuals, organizations, and institutions.

Our greatest debt is to the many journalists who tolerated our presence while they worked. They demonstrated intelligence about their work on the many occasions when we were unable to comprehend it fully. They showed admirable patience when we were lacking in tact and were naive, when our reach exceeded our grasp. We wonder how many academics would tolerate someone peering over their shoulder while they were talking on the telephone, thinking, and writing. We hope that with this book journalists will also come to understand what we do, and benefit from it.

The necessary financial support was provided by two agencies. The Social Sciences and Humanities Research Council facilitated our work through two research project grants (Nos. 410–83–0748 and 410–84–0004) and through a Leave Fellowship (No. 451–84–3311) granted to Richard Ericson. The research has also benefited from the Contributions Program to the Centre of Criminology, University of Toronto, of the Ministry of the Solicitor General, Canada.

Institutional and personal support was provided generously by the Director of the Centre of Criminology, Professor A.N. Doob. Of particular importance was his willingness to assist in gaining access to news organizations and other field locations. A former director of the Centre, Professor J.Ll.J. Edwards, was also extremely helpful at a delicate point in negotiating research access. As true academic leaders, professors Doob and Edwards regarded it as their duty to facilitate our intellectual curiosities and research explorations, even when none of us had a good sense of what might eventuate.

We are equally grateful to Mr John McFarlane for facilitating research access. As a leader in journalism, he helped us to enter a new world. In the process he demonstrated a commitment to the value of scholarship and to our peculiar needs as academics.

Several people contributed during the research process. Geoffrey Townsend was a research assistant at the formative stages of the project, and Sophia Voumvakis was most helpful in organizing the data for this and related projects in their later stages. Ideas for theorizing were sparked in conversations with Professor Clifford Shearing, our colleague at the Centre of Criminology, and with Professor Nico Stehr, while he was Eric Vogelin Professor at the University of Munich. In drafting this manuscript, Richard Ericson benefited from the scholarly environment that he enjoyed as an Overseas Fellow of Churchill College, Cambridge, and as a Visiting Fellow of the Institute of Criminology, University of Cambridge.

Seven scholars have contributed significantly to this book by providing detailed comments on an earlier draft. These include three anonymous reviewers for the publisher, as well as Professor Stanley Cohen of the Hebrew University of Jerusalem, Professor Mark Fishman of the City University of New York, Professor Peter Manning of Michigan State University and Oxford University, and Professor Paul Rock of the London School of Economics and Political Science. Their efforts at pointing to deviant features of the earlier draft proved again, however painfully, that designations of deviance are instrumental in bringing about both order and change.

In the production of the manuscript we were assisted by the word-processing skills of Marie Pearce, the index preparation of Dianna Ericson, and the copy editing of Beverley Beetham Endersby. Our editor, Virgil Duff, has an impressive range of experience in academic publishing, from which we continue to benefit.

As a cultural product this book will become a reality that is more than the sum of its parts. Our remaining desire is that this reality will be experienced deeply and widely, thereby justifying the efforts of everyone who helped us to make it.

RVE

PMB

JBLC

PART I

Theoretical Considerations and Research Approaches

1

Deviance, Knowledge, and News

Introduction

VISUALIZING DEVIANCE

This book is about social deviance and how journalists participate in defining and shaping it. Thinking and research on social reaction to deviance have concentrated on the more obvious agents of social control, such as police, prosecutors, judges, and prison officials. Journalists have not been studied as active participants in social reaction to deviance, which is surprising because, as we document here and in two companion volumes (in preparation), deviance and control are the core ingredients of news; and, as others have documented (e.g., Graber, 1980), most people derive their understanding of deviance and control primarily from the news and other mass media.

In terms of their ability to choose what to convey, and the huge audiences to whom they convey it, journalists possibly have more influence in designating deviance and in contributing to control than do some of the more obvious agents of control. In effect, journalists join with other agents of control as a kind of 'deviance-defining élite,' using the news media to provide an ongoing articulation of the proper bounds to behaviour in all organized spheres of life. Moreover, journalists do not merely reflect others' efforts to designate deviance and effect control, but are actively involved themselves as social-control agents. As such, journalists play a key role in constituting visions of order, stability, and change, and in influencing the control practices that accord with these visions. In sum, journalists are central agents in the reproduction of order.

In order to understand this characterization of journalism, it is necessary to undertake a detailed examination of journalists' methodology. This methodology is captured in the concept of visualizing. Visualization – making something visible to the mind even if it is not visible to the eye – is the essence of journalism as a method. The news brings to mind events in the world through the accounts of journalists and their sources. These accounts visualize what happened, why it happened, what it was like to be involved in the event, what is likely to happen next, what should be done about it, and whether any or all of this is good or bad. Using their sources, journalists offer accounts of reality, their own versions of events as they think they are most appropriately visualized. The object of their accounts is rarely presented for the viewer, listener, or reader to contemplate directly. This is so even in television news, where the pictures are most often of the reporter and his sources giving a 'talking head' account. Rarely shown are the documents, behaviours, or other objects that are the subject of the account. And even when they are shown, it is usually to represent indexically or symbolically, rather than iconically.

Deviance refers to the behaviour of a thing or person that strays from the normal. Here we are including as deviant not only serious forms of abnormal behaviour such as criminal acts, but also such behaviour as straying from organizational procedures and violations of common-sense knowledge. Deviance in myriad forms is the essence of the things or persons journalists concentrate on in producing the news. Thus, our focus extends beyond the popular diet of crime stories, especially with elements of violence and sex. Crime stories actually constitute a small proportion of news content, even in popular news outlets. Rather, we understand crime as but one of many clas- sifications of deviance decided upon by journalists in conjunction with their sources. In keeping with the concerns of journalists we have studied over many years, we are focusing on what is seen as deviation in all aspects and spheres of organizational life: the doctor who fails to follow hospital procedure and harms a patient; the hospital procedure that fails to control a threat to the health of patients; the company that fails to protect the interests of its investors; the government that fails to provide regulations that would control the com- pany's use of investors' assets; the police department that unjustly targets a minority group that seeks to maintain its own cultural identity; the politician who uses his office for personal gain; the government agency that does not enforce the law against an organization responsible for polluting the envi- ronment; and so on, as far as is allowable by organizational access, reporting imagination, and cultural criteria of rational acceptability.

Conceived in these broad terms, deviance is *the* defining characteristic of what journalists regard as newsworthy and, as such, becomes inextricably linked with journalists' methods. Deviance and control are not only woven into the seamless web of news reporting, but are actually part of its fibre: they define not only the object and central character of news stories, but also the methodological approaches of journalists as they work on their stories.

They not only constitute the essence of what is deemed to be newsworthy to begin with, but also enter into choices, from assignment, through the selection and use of sources, to the final composition of the story.

Visualizing deviance and control serves the several functions of the news. It allows journalists to act as watchdogs, policing organizational life for deviations from their conceptions of the order of things. In turn this watchdog role allows journalists to bring into relief the normal or expected state of affairs, acknowledging order and contributing to community consensus. The focus on deviance is also a primary vehicle for entertaining the consumer and evoking emotive aspects of human interest. Visualizing deviance is a matter of the heart as well as of the head, sustaining the interest of the audience whatever the thrust of the news story. In the process, journalists become part of the phenomenon they report on, enacting their organizational environment as an agency of stability, reform, and change.

In summary, an examination of the role of journalists in society is coincident with an inquiry into the nature of social deviance and control. This coincidence is made more evident in the following preliminary statement of our conception of deviance and outline of journalism as an occupation.

THE NATURE OF SOCIAL DEVIANCE

It is now conventional sociological wisdom that deviance requires social reaction (Durkheim, 1933, 1938; Mead, 1918; Lemert, 1951, 1972; Becker, 1963; Erikson, 1966, 1973; Matza, 1969; Ericson, 1975; Ben-Yehuda, 1985). Deviance is not inherent in a person or his specific acts, but in the social reaction to the person and his behaviour. Furthermore, since deviance is socially defined it is culturally relative. What is designated as deviant in one time and place may be ignored or seen as acceptable in another time and place. A century ago, in Canada, the distribution and use of heroin was not controlled by law, and the arrival of new shipments from the Far East was advertised prominently in local newspapers. In some countries today, heroin distribution is legal for particular purposes such as medical use.

The truism that deviance is a matter of social reaction has the corollary that rule violation must be visible, a matter of public knowledge (Becker, 1963). In the process of being made public knowledge, the designation of deviance, and the control of the deviant person that comes with that designation, have functional aspects for society. Deviance, through the process of labelling and control, can contribute to social stability and provide for social change. This statement requires elaboration, since it initially seems counterintuitive to assert that acts of wrongdoing are of positive benefit to the community, and contradictory to claim that the benefit can be in the direction of either stability or change.

Durkheim (1933: esp. 70–110) provides the starting point for our theoretical discussion of how deviance contributes to social cohesion and the 'collective conscience.' His ideas are in accord with those of other writers in the early part of this century. For example, Mead offered the following formulation:

> While the most admirable of humanitarian efforts are sure to run counter to the individual interests of very many in the community, or fail to touch the interest and imagination of the multitude and to leave the community divided or indifferent, the cry of thief or murder is attuned to profound complexities, lying below the surface of competing individual effort, and citizens ... separated by divergent interests stand together against the common enemy ... The criminal does not seriously endanger the structure of society by his destructive activities, and on the other hand he is responsible for a sense of solidarity, aroused among those whose attention would otherwise be centered upon interests divergent from those of each other. (1918: 590)

More recently, Erikson (1966: 13) introduced his classic empirical study of the social functions of deviance by stating '[D]eviant behavior is not a simple kind of leakage which occurs when the machinery of society is in poor working order, but may be, in controlled quantities, an important condition for preserving the stability of social life. Deviant forms of behavior, by marking the outer edges of group life, give the inner structure its special character and thus supply the framework within which the people of the group develop an orderly sense of their own cultural identity.'

Deviance has also been conceived as a functional mechanism of social change, although this aspect has received much less emphasis. As inevitable and vital components of society, deviance and control sustain social awareness and a flexibility for society to adapt to varying conditions. Durkheim (1938: 71) provided the classic statement that 'Crime implies not only that the way remains open to necessary changes, but in certain cases it directly prepares these changes. Where crime exists, collective sentiments are sufficiently flexible to take on a new form, and crime sometimes helps to determine the form they will take.'

In this process deviance and control are entwined with morality. Morality as a process involves the use of evaluative dualisms (e.g., good-evil, brave-timid, free-enslaved) to assess objects. Morality motivates humans to achieve particular goals and identifies the legitimate means to achieve them (Merton, 1957). The significance of the various ethical considerations that constitute morality is represented symbolically in the public culture of official documents, news media, drama, professional literature, novels, and so on (Gusfield, 1981). The perpetual public conversation about morality, deviance, and control in these media draws the contours of the moral boundaries of society. There is an ongoing articulation of who and what are in and out of bounds and the current state of the elasticity of the boundaries (the extent to which the moral territory is expanding or tightening up).

The abilities to stretch and to contract the moral territory are not equal. Morality is bound up with power (Giddens, 1976), so that there is structured inequality in who has a say in the definition and control of deviance. There is a 'hierarchy of credibility' (Becker, 1967), establishing who is authorized to say what is good and bad and what should be done about it – those elevated in that hierarchy are assumed to know better. Thus, there is a nexus among morality, power, and knowledge.

> In complex societies, the distribution of deviant phenomena is closely linked
> to the distribution of power and life-chances ... A stratification system can
> also be viewed as a moral system: a major organization of beliefs about the
> rights, duties and moral properties of the members of a society ... A system of
> control based on authority rests, in part, on a recognition of the *moral* right of
> the authoritative to make decisions ... Thus, in a stable, but unequal society
> class position is often identified with moral position – the higher one's position
> in a stratified order, the greater is one's moral worth. (Rock, 1973: 47; see
> also Foucault, 1980)

Deviance and control are not marginal to society, but rather of central significance. They are key elements in everyday life, used by all of us to define who we are and what we might become. This is increasingly so in modern, complex societies because moral boundaries are equivocal and constantly shifting in accordance with ongoing negotiation among different interests (Strauss, 1978). The nature of these negotiations – who participates in them, what is at stake, whose definitions prevail, and who is affected by them and how – is an essential topic for social research, as it contributes to an understanding of social stability (our sense of order) and social change (our sense of progress).

It is here that we locate the significance of journalism. Journalists provide a daily 'common-sense' articulation of deviance and control processes and their implications for boundary-maintaining and boundary-changing functions. As central agents in social-reaction to deviance, journalists draw on key spokespersons in the hierarchy of credibility to publicize what they think are the most significant problems of deviance and what should be done about them. In their discourse of threats, dangers, and precursors of change, journalists sharpen our senses about order and progress. All the negativism of this discourse, all the bad news, can be read as serving the good purpose of contributing to our abstract visions and practical templates of social stability and change.

Today we no longer parade deviants in the town square or expose them to the carnival atmosphere of Tyburn, but it is interesting to note that the 'reform' which brought about this change in penal policy coincided almost precisely with the development of newspapers as media of public information ... [N]ewspapers (and now radio and television) offer their readers the same kind of entertainment once supplied by public hangings or the use of stocks and pillories. An enormous amount of modern 'news' is devoted to reports about deviant behavior and its punishment: indeed the largest circulation newspaper in the United States prints very little else ... [These reports] constitute our main source of information about the normative contours of society. In a figurative sense, at least, morality and immorality meet at the public scaffold, and it is during this meeting that the community declares where the line between them should be drawn. (Erikson, 1973: 29)

In chapter 2 we elaborate upon the place of journalists at the fulcrum of deviance-defining activity. However, at this juncture we need to make some preliminary statements about the nature of journalism as an occupation.

THE NATURE OF JOURNALISM

In discussing the nature of deviance we have already indicated a lot about the nature of journalism. The defining characteristic of journalism is that it visualizes deviance and control as these relate to visions of social order and change. The journalistic search for procedural strays and signs of disorder is a means of charting the consensual boundaries of society and acknowledging order. Importantly, it is also a means of pointing to directions for reform, change, and progress. This aspect of journalism has been overlooked by most contemporary analysts of the news media. News of deviance is a discourse of failure and, as such, is essential to imagining what might be better – the discourse of progress. Contemporary news-media analysts have also failed to explicate how journalists, as they contribute to this discourse, function, themselves, as agents of control. Journalists become part of the control institutions they report on, affecting social relations there with ramifications for future control initiatives.

As is true for every other agency involved in the business of social control, journalism has its own preferences and procedures. There is a preference for some 'readings' of deviance over others, with attendant implications for control practices. The topics of deviance and control to be addressed, the labels to be applied, the people who are authorized to act as the deviance-defining élite to give the labels their adhesive properties, and the preferred control solutions are all created from a much wider, indeed infinite, universe of possibilities. This creative work is done within a system of procedures that allows journalists to make their choices seem obvious and routine.

Our research inquires into the preferences and procedures of journalists. We wish to understand how journalists understand, their 'knowledgeability' (Giddens, 1984), and the understanding this produces of deviance and control, order and change. In order to make news, journalists must interpret reality and tell stories, as opposed to simply reflecting reality or gathering facts. However, the creation of news is not therefore a matter of the personal whim and fancy of the journalist. Rather, it is a matter of systemic relations among journalists and their sources. It is a product of the cultural and social organization of news work, not of events in the world or the personal inclinations of journalists.

News sources are extremely important to this process. Sources themselves function as reporters in the sense that they prepare accounts already tailor-made for both their own purposes and the journalist's purpose of news communication. As we document, news organizations become a part of source organizations, and news can best be seen as an ongoing communication among journalists and influential sources (Tuchman, 1978). This situation leaves the vast majority of citizens as mere spectators to the processes of deviance designation and control represented in the news. Moreover, it is extremely difficult for anyone outside the deviance-defining élite to penetrate its inner circle and sustain competing or alternative accounts (Gitlin, 1980).

The cultural and social organization of news work narrows the news aperture, so that the news is ideological or 'partial' knowledge in two senses. First, it is partial because it gives preferred readings to the ideological messages of particular source organizations, either by omitting altogether the ideological messages of other organizations that have something to say on the matter or by relegating them a less significant status. News represents particular interests, allowing accounts of justification, excuse, and apology to selected individuals, organizations, and institutions. Journalists' 'words are also deeds' (Wittgenstein, 1972: 146), enacting a view of the world partial to particular sources and their versions of reality.

Second, this same methodology also makes news partial knowledge in the sense that it is 'a procedure not to know' (Smith, 1974; Tuchman, 1978; Fishman, 1980). The very act of discovering and construing events in the world in journalistic terms blinds the journalist and consumers of his product to other ways of seeing. The result is not the whole truth but truth reduced to the genre capacities of the newspaper article or broadcast-news item. This result is nicely summarized in Lec's (1962) observation that 'The window to the world can be covered by a newspaper.'

In large urban markets the institutional environment of the news media is complex. There are a large number of news outlets operating in three different media (newspapers, television, radio). Each outlet has at least some constraints and facilitaters peculiar to its own operations and is competitive with the other news outlets. Furthermore, there is a myriad of different source organizations in various institutional spheres. These organizations have varying needs for news access in terms of their own internal criteria and constraints. Some news beats are relatively closed to all but official regions and forms of disclosure (e.g., the courts), while others are relatively open, with sources competing vigorously for news access and disclosing damaging information about their opponents (e.g., government legislatures) (Ericson et al, forthcoming a).

In our research we set out to document that, with a large number and range of news outlets and source organizations in a particular market area, there is more openness and variation than suggested by recent analysts of the news media. Sources, reporters, and editors have more freedom, autonomy, and play in creating news than others have suggested. They need a frame for their stories, but there are multiple frames among which to choose. Their occupational environment is characterized by interorganizational, interpersonal, and ideological conflict, a view that is in sharp contrast to the normative consensus portrayed in the existing literature.

These are not light matters. Many people, academics in particular, are inclined not to take the news media very seriously. Yet in terms of the number of people they reach and the intensity with which they are consumed (Royal Commission on Newspapers [RCN], 1981), as well as their importance to other control agents in a range of institutional spheres, the news media are one of the most important and powerful institutions in society. As such, the news media are deserving of very serious attention indeed, which includes academic scrutiny of their preferences and procedures.

We begin our inquiry by fleshing out the fundamental points raised in this introduction. In the remainder of this chapter we contemplate the nature of news as knowledge, and what is known about news from existing research literature. In chapter 2 we give further consideration to the nature of deviance and its place in the news. We show that the dominant place of deviance in the news has been acknowledged by others, but there is a need to systematize this knowledge to underscore its salience. With this task completed, pertinent research questions can be asked and the appropriate research design specified, the topic of chapter 3.

The discussion in part I of this book allows us to place our work in the traditions of media studies, and to draw on the strengths and point to the weaknesses of those traditions in justifying our own research. We show that an adequate understanding of news requires consideration of fundamental issues in the nature of knowledge, social organization, and communication. Once due consideration has been given these issues, we can initiate the empirical investigations reported in parts II and III of this volume, and in the two companion volumes in preparation.

News as Knowledge

THE KNOWLEDGE SOCIETY

An understanding of news as knowledge involves the understanding of the society in which news is produced and used. We begin with the consideration that we live in a 'knowledge society' in which the production of information and its conversion into knowledge is a primary activity and knowledge is a key aspect of organizational power and social stratification. The place of news work and news will become evident as we proceed to document the features of the knowledge society.

Knowledge can be conceived of as the belief that something is real – has a being independent of volition – and that it possesses certain characteristics (Berger and Luckmann, 1966: 13). As the 'objectivated meanings of institutional activity' (ibid: 70), knowledge is not a matter of true belief but of whatever people take to be knowledge, regardless of validity. Knowledge is an essential component of culture: the shared understandings that people use to engage in social activity. It is the fibre out of which are woven the 'webs of significance' (Geertz, 1973: 5) that constitute the cultural context within which action takes place. It contributes to the flow of social activity by allowing predictions about the collective or organized actions of others (Becker, 1982: 522).

Information and knowledge do not simply lie around like pebbles in the sand, waiting to be picked up. They are always and inevitably a matter of interpretation, given meaning in the context of their use. Thus we differ sharply with statements such as the following one by Bell (1985: 17): 'Information is news, facts, statistics, reports, legislation, tax-codes, judicial decisions, resolutions, and the like, and it is quite obvious that we have had an "explosion" of these ... But that is not necessarily (or even usually) knowledge. Knowledge is interpretation in context, exegesis, relatedness, and conceptualization, the forms of argument.' News and other 'information' designated by Bell *are* knowledge, in his own sense that they have been interpreted in context and given particular meanings. They may be given different meanings as they are transformed and used in additional contexts, but that does not make them 'knowledge' in the additional contexts as distinct from 'information' in the original context. They are knowledge in all contexts, in the sense of being given an objectivated, real meaning that is used in action and has social consequences.

People's actions can only be understood in terms of their knowledge-ability. Knowledge is both tacit, that which allows actors to get on with their activity, and discursive, that which they use to account for their actions in discourse (Giddens, 1979, 1982, 1984). The active production of knowledge is fundamental to the reproduction of society, since social order is possible only because there are shared symbols for collective action.

Furthermore, knowledge is a social and public mechanism for ordering the world, and thus is an instrument of social control and a condition for social order. As Geertz (1973: 46) has observed, 'Undirected by culture patterns – organized systems of significant symbols – man's behavior would be virtually ungovernable, a mere chaos of pointless acts and exploding emotions, his experience virtually shapeless. Culture, the accumulated totality of such patterns, is not just an ornament of human existence but – the principal basis of its specificity – an essential condition for it.'

Contemporary society has been characterized as a knowledge society because so much time and energy are expended on the production of symbols and their transformation into knowledge (Bell, 1973; Böhme, 1984; Stehr and Böhme, 1986). Social order can be conceptualized as an organization for the transformation of knowledge (Thompson, 1967; Coon, 1969). The primary resource of this society is knowledge. The primary mode of production is communication (the transformation and reception process) within communications systems (the organizations and institutions within which transformation and reception take place).

It has been estimated that by the mid-1970s approximately 50 per cent of the members of the U.S. labour force could be classed as information workers, and that 40–45 per cent of Canadian workers could be so classified (RCN, 1981d: 9). Of course these statistics are difficult to verify. Certain occupations are clearly distinguishable as being exclusively concerned with information and knowledge, for example, those of educator and journalist. Other occupations involve information work as a primary, although not exclusive component, for example, police. Most police activity consists of searching for and checking information on citizens and converting that information to organizational knowledge by writing occurrence and investigation reports. Indeed, police spend more of their time writing accounts of their activities than they do on the activities themselves (Ericson, 1981, 1982). Moreover, in the last two decades there has been an expansion of activity of security-service police or 'information police,' whose task is penetration of organizations to set up surveillance mechanisms that allow gathering of information that can be registered and ultimately converted into knowledge for use in controlling the organization concerned (Marx and Reichman, 1984; Marx, 1985). Jean-Paul Brodeur (1983: 513–14) quotes the head of a French police agency as saying that the task of the members of his force is 'police journalism on behalf of the state,' indicating that all organizations and all activities are potential candidates for their information work.

The primary goal of knowledge production is control of the environment and those who people it. It is to render them knowable, to make them more predictable. All organizing is related to inputs that are not self-evident, deviant happenings that represent a change, difference, discontinuity, or equivocality (a suggestion of multiple meanings) that must be understood, rectified, and incorporated into activity (Weick, 1979). Hence knowledge is the 'raw material' of organizing, and communications systems the vehicle for connecting people to the changing, equivocal environment in the constant search for a workable level of certainty (ibid; also Smith, 1980: 317).

Weber observed that doubt is the father of all knowledge. We apparently live in a very doubting society, as enormous human and material resources are spent on the production of knowledge to assist in the 'policing of organizational life' (cf Reiss, 1983). This policing is not exclusively a government task. As Warshett (1981: 180) observes, corporations increasingly attempt to control markets and other aspects of their environments through 'discretionary intelligence operations,' diverting economic resources from the production of goods and services with use-value to the production of information with no direct use-value. Moreover, since the demand for such information is elastic and insatiable, and the goal of control unrealistic, 'efforts to attain such control only feed the demands for further investment in information' (ibid).

The desire for control and command of the environment is *the* feature of the 'information revolution' (Smith, 1980: 20). However, there is an unequal ability to acquire and use knowledge, and to prevent its acquisition and use by others, so that conflict and power characterize the knowledge society.

> Conflicts over secrecy – between state and citizen … or parent and child, or in journalism or business or law – are conflicts over power: the power that comes with controlling the flow of information. To be able to hold back some information about oneself or to channel it and thus influence how one is seen by others gives power; so does the capacity to penetrate similar defences and strategies when used by others. True, power requires not only knowledge but the capacity to put knowledge to use; but without the knowledge, there is no chance to exercise power. To have no capacity for secrecy is to be out of control over how others see one; it leaves one open to coercion. To have no insight into what others conceal is to lack power as well. Those who are unable and unwilling even to look below the surface, to question motives, to doubt what is spoken, are condemned to live their lives in ignorance, just as those who are unable to keep secrets of their own must live theirs defenceless. (Bok, 1982: 19–20)

The knowledge society is an administered society in which authorization gains primacy over allocation and centralized, bureaucratic control of information and knowledge is a medium of domination (Giddens, 1979). Authorized bureaucracies are able to more routinely penetrate other organizations for the acquisition of knowledge, and to register and store it for eventual use in administration. As Foucault has argued, 'The exercise of power over the population and the accumulation of knowledge about it are two sides of a single process: not power and knowledge, but power-knowledge' (Sheridan, 1980: 161–2).

Attached to concrete power interests, knowledge is ideological. It is 'partial' in the double sense of being a limited way of seeing and of supporting particular interests. Ideologies have the power of simultaneously producing discourse and limiting discourse through distortion and occultation (Sumner, 1979; Gabel, 1984). All signs or symbol systems are ideological because they are entwined with the social practices, including power relations, in which they are produced. Knowledge of ideology, itself a form of power, therefore requires knowledge of the conditions of its production and use.

The knowledge/power relation means that contemporary society is socially stratified in terms of knowledge (Böhme, 1984). Knowledge is a form of 'cultural capital' (Gouldner, 1979), a central definer of social membership along with the more traditional components of labour and property. Knowledge provides a structural principle for social hierarchy. It also provides a principle of class-structure formation, the 'new class' who derive their labour and property membership from the production, distribution, and administration of knowledge (Berger, 1977; Konrad and Szelenyi, 1979; Gouldner, 1979). Knowledge in turn is also a basis for social exclusion, for the distribution of social influence and personal life chances. Seemingly more democratic than real capital, knowledge as cultural capital is especially effective in reproducing class position and privilege (Bourdieu and Paseron, 1970). Knowledge also provides a principle for social cohesion and integration; as pointed out earlier, the integration of organizations and institutions, of social order itself, is dependent upon the knowledge of those who participate in it.

At this more concrete level of organized activity, the division of knowledge corresponds roughly to the division of labour in society. It is therefore a part of the roles which people perform, especially in professional and bureaucratic organizations. The knowledge society is characterized 'by entrusting the accumulation and classification of information to willing bureaucracies, state or corporate. This could lead to greater social and economic divisions and less freedom for the individual' (RCN, 1981d: 101).

Most of this 'signwork' (Manning, 1986) is second-level production. That is, it entails taking symbols, information, and knowledge produced in other organizational settings and transforming them into forms suitable for the organization's purposes. Rather than directly dealing with nature, it involves interpretations of interpretations of other knowledge producers in other organizational settings.

A lot of this work is directed towards building an image of the organization within its wider environment in order to maintain or enhance its legitimacy and spheres of influence. As Meyer and Rowan (1977: 341) state, 'the formal structures of many organizations in postindustrial society (Bell, 1973) dramatically reflect the myths of their institutional environments instead of the demands of their work activities.' In seeking isomorphism with organizations in their environment, members of a given organization use external, symbolic criteria of evaluation. These help to legitimate the value of their organization and its structure. 'Many of the positions, policies, programs, and procedures of modern organizations are enforced by public opinion, by the views of important constituents, by knowledge legitimated through the educational system, by social prestige, by the laws, and by the definition of negligence and prudence used by the courts' (ibid: 343; see also Manning, 1982).

JOURNALISM AND THE REPRODUCTION OF KNOWLEDGE

Journalism has a unique position in the knowledge society, which makes study of journalists' practices and products an excellent vehicle for understanding the properties of that society. News discourse is one of the important means by which society comes to know itself. Studying the ways in which journalists make sense of the world is a significant means of achieving understanding of society.

Journalism has all of organized life, all of society, as its sphere of operation. There is no major institution, and few large organizations, that remain untouched by the reporting of journalists. Only the public police and social scientists share with journalists this total organizational field of operation. While their mandate to probe and expose may have less general legitimacy than that of the public police, journalists almost certainly have greater legitimacy than social scientists. All other organizations and occupations work within much more restricted spheres, and generally with more highly specialized bodies of knowledge.

The news media, and in particular the newspaper, have traditionally sought to include information on a full range of organizations and transactions which seem to relate to everyday life. As Kazin (1973) observed, 'The world as our common experience is one that only the journalist feels entirely able to set down.' As modern society has become bureaucratic and pluralistic, the news media have attended to an enormous range of subsystems and organizations. They express 'multiculturalism' in the form of what they think is salient in the multitude of organizational 'microcultures' in society. The news organization is a hub, repository, and active agent of organized life. It is 'an institution for the collection, storage, and dissemination of all kinds of information from hundreds of different microsystems that exist within its sphere. It is, as it were, a library of human activity. More than that, it acts as an information broker to society' (Smith, 1980: 11). Beyond the information-brokerage aspect, journalists are 'chief knowledge-linkers, translating and interpreting what politicians, philosophers, and scientists conceive. That is, knowledge – in its most elementary form – is mass media created and disseminated' (Phillips, 1977: 63).

As information brokers and knowledge linkers, journalists are a classic instance of what we noted as a key feature of work in the knowledge society. They engage in reproducing the knowledge of their sources, governed not by the laws of nature but by the laws of social constructs. Their work, and their creativity, comes from refining, reformulating, recirculating, and reordering knowledge: discovering 'ways to burrow into the abundance rather than augment it, to illuminate rather than search' (Smith, 1980: 326). This enterprise is not substantially different from those of other 'cultural workmen' (Miliband, 1977), such as academics who write literature reviews of the type you are reading.

In effect, sources are also 'reporters,' choosing, shaping, and defining occurrences in their organizational world to turn into events for possible news-media use. Roshco (1975: 66ff) points out that the more 'institutional' the reporting – in the sense of covering key bureaucracies and sources – the greater the dependence on sources who are reporters but not journalists. This situation, and the dilemma it creates, was expressed well by a former managing editor of the Toronto *Globe and Mail*:

> [O]ur function is to make society understandable to readers, to try to figure out what's going on, to try to make some sense out of it ... [but] [t]here is so much information now that nobody can master it all and explain it all and digest it all. Yet, we're supposed to be a major force in trying to sort it all out, and say: 'In all this welter of material, this is what's important, and this is what you should focus on and this is what we think is important as news. And you ought to be concerned with it.' That means developing some reporters and editors with a different kind of skill than they used to have. Skills at sorting out the morass of information. That's number one ... Nobody has the resources, except government now, to gather the data and to interpret it [sic] and to formulate policies. The kind of resources that are necessary to dig up that kind of information, organize it, and come out with government programs – the resources you need are enormous. So how do we, as a newspaper, begin to come to grips with a very basic social program when (a) the government won't give us the basic data that it is making its decisions on; and (b) we don't have the resources to duplicate what government studies show. And nobody else has the resources, either. (Keillor, 1982: 16)

Journalism is a trade of rendering fact and making representations. In this respect journalism is similar to other cultural trades such as science, law, ethnography, and art. However, each of these trades has a different way of 'propound[ing] the world in which its descriptions make sense' (Geertz, 1983: 173; see also Putnam, 1981). In the case of journalism, the trick of the trade is to translate the specialized knowledge and concerns of sources into the locutions of the readership or audience. Journalism seeks common-sense understanding by reducing one type of reality to its own way of construing the world, thereby producing common social knowledge and cultural values.

The common sense which journalists convey is the type of wisdom that everyone requires to get on with social activity. As defined in the 1726 *Secret History of the University of Oxford*, cited by Geertz (1983: 93), common sense is 'the ordinary ability to keep ourselves from being imposed upon by gross contradictions, palpable inconsistencies, and unmask'd impostures.' As Geertz (ibid: 85–91) points out, common sense has the properties of being natural (inherent, intrinsic to reality); practical (sagacious or having practical wisdom); thin (simple and literal); immethodical (as the world is intractable and, inconsistent, common-sense wisdom is ad hoc, a 'potpourri of disparate notions' needed to capture the plurality); and, accessible (anyone can grasp it and embrace its conclusions). These characteristics make common sense seem so obvious that it is difficult to reflect on it, let alone analyse it. Nevertheless, it is a crucial body of thought that is relatively organized, providing the authoritative stories necessary to comprehend and enact the everyday world (ibid: 84; see also Holy and Stuchlik, 1983: 50–4).

The journalist reproduces the common sense out of the specialized knowledge of sources. 'In fact this active and creative work of the news media is their distinctive feature – their special job among the various institutions in society' (Hartley, 1982: 105). In particular the journalist addresses authorities who are distant from the rest of us, and does so on our behalf. The journalist stands in for the people asking tough questions of sources. These questions are framed so as to translate sources' politically interested views into a seemingly apolitical, no-nonsense, common-sense view of everyone (Brunsdon and Morley, 1978).

Commentators have stressed the growing power of those who possess specialized knowledge within the specialized division of labour and organization of the knowledge society (Stehr and Meja, 1984). However, there is also considerable power available to those who are in a position to translate this specialized knowledge into locutions that are generally accessible. Chief among agents of translation are journalists, as they purvey a common-sense wisdom that incorporates the knowledge of a wide range of experts, bureaucrats, and specialists of all types. Moreover, in the process of providing knowledge of what is of relevance to others in a range of organizational settings, journalists also provide knowledge about who are the key power holders, the 'authorized knowers,' in the knowledge society. This, too, is a crucial element of the practical wisdom needed to conduct our lives. 'Knowledge of *how* the socially available stock of knowledge is distributed, at least in outline, is an important element of that same stock of knowledge. In everyday life I know, at least roughly, what I can hide from whom, whom I can turn to for information on what I do not know, and generally which types of individuals may be expected to have which types of knowledge' (Berger and Luckmann, 1966: 61).

Journalists exist to offer the notions and visions of 'well-placed persons who are in a position to give official imprint to versions of reality' (Goffman, 1983: 17). However, journalists themselves also 'enjoy social arrangements of institutional authority' (ibid) to imprint versions of reality. Indeed journalists enjoy a particularly strategic position as the daily translators of organized life. An inquiry into the nature of ideological work and the ways in which particular ideologies are reproduced and sustained can be located in no better place than in the practices of journalists. Journalists as cultural workmen provide a means of unpacking the nature of communication, and of culture, in the knowledge society. They provide an excellent substantive focus for what Holy and Stuchlik (1983: 103) have identified as a crucial area for research: 'There are probably many ... reasons why specific ideological representations are maintained. The more general the notions are, the more complex and sinuous is the way in which they enter into the ongoing social interactions between individuals and groups. A more systematic empirical investigation of this complexity is, in our view, one of the urgent tasks facing future anthropological fieldwork.'

Knowledge of News

ORGANIZATIONAL CONTEXTS OF NEWSMAKING

It is well established that reality is a result of cognitive processes of interpretation, and social processes of construction. This is true of formal and empirical scientific discovery (Bloor, 1976; Mulkay, 1979; Brannigan, 1981; Knorr-Cetina, 1981), of sociological discovery (O'Neill, 1981), of the way police make cases (Ericson, 1981; Marx, 1981), of writing novels (Knight, 1980), and of making news (Roshco, 1975; Tuchman, 1978; Fishman, 1980). All of these activities are forms of action with attendant symbolic and rhetorical features, used to discover knowledge and settle problems by constructing views which satisfy their respective criteria of rational acceptability (Putnam, 1981: 130).

In the case of science, this point was succinctly made by Heisenberg (1958: 58): 'What we observe is not nature itself, but nature exposed to our methods of questioning.' This point has been taken up by philosophers and sociologists of science, who argue that the view of Merton (1973) – that science is a special form of knowledge not subject to the same social and cultural organizational processes as other forms of knowledge – is doubtful and that research should be conducted on the assumption that scientific knowledge is produced and established by the same processes as other cultural products. Knowledge in science is established by processes of negotiation, interpreting cultural resources in the context of social interaction. Scientific knowledge does not consist of definitive statements about the physical world, but rather of *claims* which a particular group judges to be adequate in a particular context. 'There is, then, at least a *prima facie* case in favour of the thesis that "objects present themselves differently to scientists in different social settings, and that social resources enter into the structure of scientific assertions and conclusions" ' (Mulkay, 1979: 95).

This statement is applicable to newsmaking. The news process does not entail the reporting of a self-evident reality; it involves using organizational resources and occupational routines of the craft to make news. This process is 'the act of structuring reality, rather than recording it' (Smith, 1978: 168). The basis of this act is news discourse which, like any type of discourse, is not about objects but rather constitutes objects or objectivated meanings. To reverse a popular phrase, the reporter sees it when he believes it in the terms of news discourse. This, of course, means that it makes no sense to say that the news is new, because news always implies the existence of a past that is framed in terms of news discourse.

The reality offered by the news is thus embedded in the knowledgeability or ways of knowing of news workers, and the ways they formulate their knowledge in language. News language, 'like any other language ... both frames and accomplishes discourse. It is perception and it guides perception; it reconstitutes the everyday world' (Tuchman, 1978: 107). This relationship between language and reality inevitably entails a blurring between fact and interpretation, between hard (factual) news and soft (commentary, opinion) news (Glasgow University Media Group [GUMG], 1980: 406). What are reported as facts in the news are interpretations framed by the apparatus of reporting. As sociologists of the ethnomethodological school have pointed out, even what are taken as basic primary facts oscillate by context, situational contingencies of interaction, and 'indexicality' (meanings attributed apart from the context in which the fact is produced). In this view, fact, values, and what passes for knowledge are entwined with cultural and social apparatuses, and fact is always ambiguous and problematic.

These properties of newsmaking explain why its practitioners have difficulty articulating what news is and how they decide newsworthiness (e.g., Tuchman, 1978; Smith, 1981). They can recognize it when they are engaged in the work, but they become inarticulate when they attempt to describe it apart from doing it, except by saying they have a 'nose for news.' 'News as a working term can be defined only as an actual organization of relations between the work of the reporter, of the editor, the production process, circulation, etc. of the newspaper. It is a term that is part of the work and does the work in talking about the work' (Smith, 1981: 327).

News workers have a working ideology which simultaneously enables them to get the job done and to publicly legitimate what they do as a 'profession' (Chibnall, 1977: chap. 2; Tuchman, 1978; Schlesinger, 1978). News is 'the manifestation of the collective cultural codes of those employed to do this selective and judgmental work for society' (GUMG, 1976: 13–14), and the images of news content are 'prefabricated according to internal, journalistic criteria' (ibid: 139). Understanding the working ideology is thus crucial to understanding the ideology that is reproduced as a result of the work. Again, any attempt to understand the process of reproduction requires explication of the knowledgeability of actors as they make choices in their social and cultural contexts (Giddens, 1982, 1984).

The source organizations that routinely provide events for journalists to report on operate in the same way. Sources choose among occurrences in the world and construe them in terms which suit their vocational and organizational purposes. Their work too is carried out according to a working ideology, as occurrences in the world are construed, chosen, and made into organizational property, worked on by many and scrutinized by still others, ultimately becoming an 'event' that may be of public interest and deemed newsworthy by journalists. Long before the reporter has an 'event' to possibly report on, that 'event' has been through the manufacturing process of the source organization. In this respect sources join with journalists as newsmakers, transforming occurrences as amorphous happenings in the world into a meaningful structure that has potential as a news event (Molotch and Lester, 1974).

A source organization is also composed of a series of cultural divisions or microcultures, and the organization may wish to keep some of these divisions and some of their practices out of the purview of the public culture. Many acts which are privately observed may be publicly condemned, and there is an active effort to ensure that public life does not mirror private behaviour. Instead, the public culture is produced as a reality in its own right, with source organizations endeavouring to maintain a public image that they are doing things more or less in the terms 'the public' expects them to be done. Maintaining this image requires an enormous amount of ideological labour. The source organization has to develop means of patrolling the facts, of keeping things unknowable from outside. The power of secrecy is a complex and crucial component of organizational power (Bok, 1982). The organization must also devise means of implanting reality, actively putting objectivated meanings into the environment which provide the framework for perception and negotiation (Weick, 1979: 165). This is an important component of showing that the organization knows what it is doing, of displaying the authoritative certainty that will demonstrate public accountability and minimize calls for further accounts (justifications, excuses) of its activity.

A key to the production of organizational ideology in these terms is the maintenance of front-region and back-region divisions (Goffman, 1959; Giddens, 1984: 122–6). 'The maintenance of differentiations between the ''publicly displayed'' aspects of social activities, and those that are kept hidden, is a major element both of the ideological use of symbol-systems by dominant classes or groups, and of the response of those in subordinate classes or positions. All the more discursive types of ideological phenomena have ''display settings'', often of a partially ritualised kind, which readily lend themselves to front/back divisions' (Giddens, 1979: 191). Hence source organizations structure written documents as news releases, organize media rooms within their buildings, and hold meetings and news conferences as 'display settings' within which to keep up the front.

This ideological labour is greatly facilitated if the organization can invoke systems of rationality that are generally available in society as legitimaters of particular practices. Chief among these in contemporary society are law and science, which routinely authorize a range of practices (Ericson and Shearing, 1986). Both law and science offer particularly convincing ways of construing fact according to apparently neutral, general, and universal criteria. As Gusfield (1981: 28) argues in regard to science as rhetoric, 'Science, scientific pronouncements, technical programs, and technologies appear as supports to authority, and counterauthority, by giving to a program or policy the cast of being validated in nature, grounded in a neutral process by a method that assures both certainty and accuracy.' This means that, in practice, invocations of science, or law, are truisms; the need for additional discussion or further accounts is usually circumvented. Gusfield's (ibid) analysis of the use of law and science as rhetoric in the drinking-driving debate in the United States illustrates this point brilliantly. Furthermore, because this knowledge is so specialized, it is often the case that only specialists can have an authoritative voice on matters of public importance. As Gabel (1984: 30) observes, the resolution of many public issues, such as the problem of energy, can only be 'voted' on by those with specialized knowledge; therefore, 'the scientific and technical knowledge of the elite takes on an ideological function since it becomes the instrument for maintaining a privileged position.'

What is really happening in the world is a matter of what journalists and their sources attend to. It is, of course, possible to compare the reality so produced with other measures of reality obtained by other methods. However, such a comparison tells us nothing about the knowledgeability that goes into the work of journalists and their sources. As Fishman (1980: 12) argues in his study of news creation regarding a crime wave against the elderly, it would have been possible to compare the reported news incidents with an independently conducted victimization survey using refined social-scientific techniques. If the victimization survey concluded that crimes against the elderly were decreasing, one might conclude that the news was distorting reality. 'But news organizations did not first know the real situation and then distort or reflect it through the newsmaking process ... whether victimization was increasing or decreasing was irrelevant to the methods journalists used to detect crime and assemble the crime wave. For a wave of publicity to have existed there need only have been *some* incidents on the streets and considerable concern about them among those sources the media relied upon' (ibid; see also Tuchman, 1978: 177ff).

Another reason why the news is not a veridical account is that the journalist is part of a system of regular sources that he plugs into for information. At the 'nth' level of knowledge production, the 'newspaper is not a mirror of reality, but a realization of the potential of its sources ... its chief characteristic lies in the selection, arrangement and reformulation of information passing to it through regular channels' (Smith, 1979: 182). Rather than being a mirror of reality, the news media are a 'mobile spotlight' (Gitlin, 1980: 70). Focusing on particular people, organizations, and troubles, they create the sensation of being in a hall of mirrors.

Many theorists engaged in cultural analysis have rejected the Mannheim formulation that culture and ideology are a reflection of the social, and that they can be measured scientifically. They take the view that the cultural is a sphere of reality in its own right, with its own rules, patterns, and relations (e.g., Jackson, 1981; Wuthnow et al, 1984). The cultural is independent of, yet very interdependent with, the social and, thus, the mirror-image view 'is rather too primitive a conceptual apparatus' (Geertz, 1973: 169). For example, Barth (1975) has shown in his study of the Baktaman of New Guinea that the different grades of male society have logically interrelated symbols, yet for each grade there is different meaning of symbols and a different relation to other symbols. Barth's work illustrates that a symbol has meaning only as it is given a meaning by particular people and is perceived as such by particular other people, and that people of different statuses can perceive different meanings in the same symbol.

On the practical level of news work, journalists and their sources use social and cultural resources together as they turn occurrences into events for public use. The interrelation between the social and cultural is illustrated by Schlesinger's (1978) analysis of television-news production. Television-news work is socially organized to be reactive, with journalists responding to newspaper stories, planned events (meetings, press conferences), and recent emergency events (e.g., police, fire, and ambulance 'chasing'), by taking visuals and talking-head accounts from authoritative sources. Rarely is independent investigation or elaborated interpretation undertaken. This is so because of organizational features such as time, resource limitations, medium constraints, legal constraints, and the need for source co-operation. However, this approach also complies with the working ideology regarding fairness, objectivity, and impartiality, which constitutes good reporting as that which includes an authoritative account from each side involved. 'Organization and ideology are in fact mutually reinforcing' (ibid). Moreover, organization and ideology link with the wider society and culture. Authoritative sources who hold key roles in large bureaucracies are routinely locatable and available to give established, dominant views of events and issues.

Some have argued that the source organization can become the primary definer and the news organization be left as the secondary definer to reproduce and recirculate the symbols put on offer by its sources (Hall et al, 1978). In extreme cases little more than the 'bureaucratic propaganda' of source organizations may be being transmitted (Altheide and Johnson, 1980). Again, this situation is not the result of a conspiracy but of routine social practices and firmly held cultural beliefs general to the society and/or specific to the organizations involved. The product consists of images of authorized knowers performing their roles in bureaucratic settings, representing institutional order in terms of both social hierarchy and cultural knowledge that is ideological.

News organizations and source organizations overlap, and in some respects become *part of* each other. Reporters develop regular relationships with sources, share in their organizational cultures, and often even occupy space within the walls of the organizations they report on. Sources reciprocate in various ways, are invited to meet with editors and management, and are asked to write or produce features or columns for the news organization. A fluidity develops across organizational boundaries, as the reporter finds a niche *within* the source organization. As Weick (1979: 88) instructs about organizations and their environments generally:

> Most 'things' in organizations are actually relationships, variables tied together
> in systematic fashion. Events, therefore, depend on the strength of these ties,
> the direction of influence, the time it takes for information in the form of dif-
> ferences to move around circuits. The word *organization* is a noun, and it is
> also a myth. If you look for an organization you won't find it. What you will
> find is that there are events, linked together, that transpire within concrete
> walls and these sequences, their pathways, and their timing are the forms we
> erroneously make into substances when we talk about an organization. Just as
> the skin is a misleading boundary for marking off where a person ends and the
> environment starts, so are the walls of an organization. Events inside organiza-

tions and organisms are locked into causal circuits that extend beyond these artificial boundaries.

Of course walls do make a difference. They represent in a concrete manner what is in the front region and public and what is in the back region and private. For example, the fluidity of activity between police organizations and the organizational life they police is restricted by walls and the institution of privacy itself. However, police organizations are much more 'open' than, say, prisons. The police have press rooms, prisons do not. Journalists often succeed in penetrating the physical boundaries of the organizations they report on, sometimes routinizing this type of fluidity by obtaining an office within a beat organization. Of course this situation may be an important control device for the source organization, relegating journalists to their proper place as a subunit or subfunction of the organization. More important is the fact that journalists can transverse, affect, or at least touch the symbolic boundaries of source organizations by obtaining their documents and verbal accounts from members. Source organizations engage in 'inscription,' transforming events or objects into documentary form (Goffman, 1974; Latour and Woolgar, 1979). This documentation can be done in written or verbal communication. In either case, it offers an account to others that the organization is acting in an accountable manner. 'The process of inscription is of special significance at the boundaries of an organization or discourse, where ''environing'' actualities are ''converted'' into the conceptual and categorical order of organizational or discursive courses of action' (Smith, 1984: 13). The reporter picks up these symbols of order of the organization he reports on, and communicates them in the news product. Since this news communication entails a transformation of the source-organization symbols, it is perhaps more accurate to say that images of the source's organizational order are conveyed in the news product. Moreover, since 'communication and decision making are inseparable' (Tompkins and Cheney, 1983: 124; see also Simon, 1976) the news organization is also indicating aspects of the decisions and decisional premises of source organizations.

Weick (1979) instructs that organizations are not simply after orderliness in their relations with other organizations. To be adaptive, organizations must allow for fluidity, situational contingencies, and equivocal meanings. This is especially the case for news organizations, which deal with a wide range of sources and obtain highly mediated and equivocal communications from them. '[O]rganizational processes that are applied to equivocal inputs must themselves be equivocal' (ibid: 189). Thus, it is important for journalists to at least sustain the belief that they are not working in a rigid production system, and that they are relatively autonomous from both their editors and their sources in ferreting out 'news.' A belief in 'a nose for news,' and nothing else, as a basis for action, expresses the journalists' need for fluid interchanges in their organizational environment. 'Processes have to become disorderly if the disorder in information is to be registered accurately' (ibid: 243). Just as the policeman says that in spite of all the technological and legal apparatuses in his work, his craft is, after all, based on common sense, so the journalist relies on a sense of disorderly processes to order his work. 'Equivocal processes are rather untidy, they often work at cross purposes, and they often have the appearance of being wasteful and inefficient. Those seeming inefficiencies testify that the process is *working*, not that it has registered discontinuities, and it preserves them for further sense-making. The disordered process preserves the independence of its sensing elements; in this way, the disordered process preserves more of the fine grain in the enactments' (ibid: 192).

To be adaptable, 'the organization either has to use old interpretations in the selection process but produce continually novel enactments, or it has to produce routine enactments under the control of tradition and precedent but use continually novel interpretations to make sense of those standard outputs' (ibid: 222–3). The news organization tries both. Novel enactments are made less difficult by the fact that journalists have a wide range of organizations and activities to become involved in and report on, and by the fact that many sources are only too willing to co-operate with the publicity process. Novel interpretations in the process of routine enactments are also quite possible. However, the bulk of research effort on the news process indicates that the news is 'eternal recurrence' (Rock, 1973a) because both enactments and interpretations are routine.

A large source bureaucracy has multiple subunits and processes, and these may be working in terms of different goals and interests, and be characterized by conflict on the level of everyday work and contradiction on the level of organizational structure. When several large bureaucracies make up an institutional context (for example, the many police forces, courts, and prisons at various levels of jurisdiction and government), and when various institutional spheres are in turn linked (for example, under government and state), the conflicts, contradictions, and complexities multiply. In this respect, the exceptional caution of Murdock and Golding (1979: 33) demands respect; one should avoid 'collating these institutions into a shopping list of undifferentiated state agencies with the same functions and roles whenever and wherever found, and ... evacuating sociology by presenting the mass media as a simple relay system for the direct transmission of a ruling ideology to subordinate groups. Such institutions do play important roles in legitimizing an inegalitarian social order, but their relationship to that order is complex and variable and it is necessary to analyse what they do as well as what they are.'

News organizations have been depicted as having similar working ideologies, practices, and products (Black, 1982: 94). Journalists are depicted as being committed to the dominant order and having a professionally shared means of interpreting the world (Chibnall, 1977; Tuchman, 1978). Different news organizations structure content in similar ways within the same medium (ibid; GUMG, 1976, 1980) and even across different media (Hirsch, 1977: esp. 14; Schlesinger, 1978; Tuchman, 1978; Graber, 1980). The product is substantially closed in terms of dominant ideology: 'Apparatuses of cultural production rarely thrive on ideological pluralism today, as in the past' (Sumner, 1979: 228). Recently some theorists and researchers have begun to examine popular and quality news outlets as to whether they are more 'open' or 'closed' in terms of the range of sources, ideas, formulations of problems, and contradictory messages (e.g., Murdock, 1982; Schlesinger et al, 1983; Voumvakis and Ericson, 1984). This research, which matches the use of openness and closure by analysts of popular and high culture more generally (e.g., Eco, 1981), is still nascent.

A marked tendency in ethnographies of news organizations is to emphasize the homogeneity of journalists within the organization in terms of professional ideology and practice. There is virtually no attention to the fact that within a news organization, as in all bureaucracies, there are many conflicts among subunits and levels. The organization is better depicted as having a myriad of 'microcultures,' and as being characterized by 'multiculturalism' (Goodenough, 1978). Similarly, a large-scale organization is a group of groups (Simon, 1957).

Occupations and organizations vary substantially in the degrees to which they engage in the social construction of reality. The work of some organizations brings them closer to nature, or objects immediately produced out of nature, while other organizations are at the other end of the continuum in that they process symbols at an 'nth' level of production. As Weick (1983: 18) suggests, 'What we may need to talk about are ratios of constructed reality to preexisting realities. People in news organizations deal with a higher ratio of constructed to preexisting realities than do technicians in a hospital emergency room ... and both have higher ratios of constructed to preexisting realities than does a locomotive engineer.'

Furthermore, all social constructions start with 'grains of truth that are enlarged into constructions by interdependent actions' (ibid). For example, the journalist takes versions of truth formulated by different sources relating to an event or issue he is covering, and creates additional objectivated meanings by juxtaposing them in the published text and placing them in a wider frame with a lead. In turn other journalists may take this text and report aspects of it as truth, and also add to it by further questioning of the same sources or interviewing further sources for their text. Source organizations with an interest in the matter may do the same. 'The point is that small objective details provide an excuse for constructions, but things do exist.

Constructions do not materialize out of thin air. Clear documentation of how, when and where reality construction gets started should reveal that subjectivity and objectivity are blended at the start and that their relative influence over understanding varies as a function of context' (ibid: 18–19).

SOCIETAL CONTEXTS OF NEWSMAKING

The organizations and processes involved in newsmaking do not exist in a vacuum, but contribute to, and are shaped by, a wider institutional and societal order. Consideration of how this macro level relates to the mecro level of organizations, and to the micro level of interaction, is necessary to complete our overview of newsmaking. The actions of journalists and sources presuppose the existence of institutional and societal frameworks, and these frameworks in turn presuppose the organizing activities of human subjects. Neither human actors nor the social, cultural, political, and economic orders they construct have primacy; rather, each is constituted in the process of human activity (Giddens, 1984).

The product of knowledgeable actors making choices is an organizational or system pattern. This pattern in turn intersects with a host of other organizational systems in the society, and the background structures to which they relate collectively. The ways in which social, cultural, political, and economic structures relate to organizational systems and to everyday human transactions are enormously complex and not easily rendered in the traditional terms of micro and macro analysis (Knorr-Cetina and Cicourel, 1981), or by simply adding emphasis on the organizational or 'mecro' level (Ericson, 1982). It does seem, however, that research on the news media is a fruitful substantive means of exploring and charting this complexity. News organizations produce and reproduce accounts of relations among authorized knowers in bureaucratic roles, and these accounts convey aspects and images of social, cultural, political, and economic order. Studying how this is accomplished can inform us about general processes in the reproduction of society and their implications for stratification and legitimation. For example, news-organization material restraints, conflicts, values, ideologies, interests, rules, and goals of the work situation can be related to the market situation, politics, dominant culture, and social relations and regulations that pertain to source organizations and the society as a whole.

The central point is that the wider societal forces do not simply impinge on news organizations and source organizations and make their activities preordained. These forces themselves are constructed out of human activity. Indeed, the news media have a key role in creating public consciousness of, and belief in, a rational and ordered society which in turn gives faith that efforts at constructing social order will work (Douglas, 1971: 308).

Given that ownership of, access to, and use of news media are not uniformly and generally distributed, aspects of power are a primary consideration. The news media join with other major cultural institutions in society, including law and science, in constructing an order that is consonant with the needs and interests of dominant groups (Gramsci, 1971). They can act as a powerful force, forging particular versions of community through their communications. 'The history of the mass media shows clearly enough that such control is regarded as a valued form of property for those seeking political or economic power' (McQuail, 1979: 90).

As Black (1982: 259) points out, Miliband's (1977) distinctions about the functions of the state – fostering law and order, consensus, economic advancement, and national interest – can be seen also in terms of the functions of the mass-media institution. Indeed, one needs to look no further than legislation governing broadcasting to discover the way in which the state defines broadcast media as essential to its functioning. For example, the Canadian Broadcasting Act directs all broadcasters to 'safeguard, enrich, and strengthen the cultural, political, social and economic fabric of Canada.' Moreover, the Canadian Broadcasting Corporation (CBC), in putting forward definitions of its role in support of application for renewal of its broadcasting licence from the Canadian Radio-television and Telecommunications Commission (CRTC), claims that this clause in the Broadcasting Act provides the context for its mission to express the 'Canadian identity; or "reality", and to "contribute to the development of national unity" ' (CBC, 1978: 34). Indeed, this document is full of testimonials to the CBC's role in reproducing order. Assertions are made regarding 'what the CBC is really all about: the creation of a national consciousness' and that it is 'a central concern of national policy ... one of the most powerful weapons available to us in our struggle for national survival.' This document compares the CBC's ability to keep the nation on the rails with the development of the Canadian Pacific Railway a century before. Its values are those stated in the Canadian constitution, 'peace, order, and good government.' It seems to elevate the role of the CBC in this respect to the level of *the* traditional symbol, the Royal Canadian Mounted Police: 'For years ... the CBC has been a living institution in Canada, a symbol of Canadian nationhood, a central constituent in the cement which binds this country together' (ibid: 365). Far more is involved here than reporting who was murdered on the next block last night, or how many penalty minutes were handed out in the local hockey game. The CBC is an expression of 'common experience' of the highest order, along with 'parliamentary government ... an integrated economy ... and common institutions of transportation and communication – institutions which are at once the lifelines and the symbols of nationhood, not merely the vehicles for moving materials and messages' (ibid: 366).

These assertions are not isolated. In their more routine articulations of the organization's role, CBC officials make similar statements; for example, 'We're fighting a battle for the existence of Canada, and the CBC is at the heart of it' (Steed, 1982: 10). The Davey Committee (1970) emphasized the importance of the media in producing Canadian consciousness, and their *obligation* to promote Canadian distinctiveness from the American reality.

While the situation may be different for the newspaper industry, which thrives economically on private ownership, important print organizations such as the Canadian Press wire service also explicitly state their obligation and dedication to contributing to national unity (RCN, 1981c: 41). Furthermore, the issue of whether there should be a newspaper act similar to the Broadcasting Act, favouring government regulation over private corporate monopoly, has been seriously addressed and promulgated by the Royal Commission on Newspapers (1981).

In summary, the ideological labour of reproducing social, cultural, political, and economic order is not simply a matter of vacuous theorizing by academics interested in the political economy of the state. It is a matter of major concern to the state, as evidenced in existing and proposed legislation, official documents and reports, and statements by senior officials. Moreover, laws and policies at these high levels actually direct or encourage journalists to work on behalf of established order. Journalists are officially defined as crucial agents in the reproduction of order, 'called upon to *fashion* a broader Canadian consciousness' and 'an instrument for the defence of our identity as a nation – of the cultures which make up that identity, of the common cultural characteristics which form an *invisible thread* throughout Canada' (CBC, 1978: 37; emphasis added). To continue these metaphors of the clothier, it should not be surprising if we find that journalists tailor their news accounts accordingly.

These official pronouncements of the role of the news media accord generally with the views of social analysts on the cultural functions of the news media. For example, Fiske and Hartley (1978: 88) argue that television functions as a 'cultural bard,' to 'articulate' the prevailing cultural consensus about the nature of reality and the reality of nature; to 'implicate' citizens in dominant values; to 'celebrate, explain, interpret and justify' the cultural centrality of authorized knowers; to 'assure' the culture of the efficiency of its ideologies; to 'expose' any inadequacies in the ideologies of assurance; and to 'convince' users of television of their place in the culture and thereby 'transmit' a sense of membership or collective identity. Other broadcast media, as well as print media, have a similar bardic function, providing knowledge of the character, status, and role of key actors in their respective spheres of social organization, and rendering 'readable' their contributions to social, cultural, political, and economic order. The news media contribute importantly to the 'public culture' (Gusfield, 1981) in this way. They also provide cultural knowledge that can in turn be used in the realm of the private, a filter through which social forces and interactional contingencies can be grasped and used as resources.

Obviously, the news media are only one institution in society which attempts to provide a general, universal, and stable 'symbolic canopy' in face of cultural pluralism (Berger and Luckmann, 1966: 103). The law is similarly directed (Ericson, 1985), as are science (Gouldner, 1976; Habermas, 1970) and religion (Geertz, 1973: chap. 4). For example, what Geertz says about the institution of religion relates directly to what news-media analysts have said about the institution they study. Geertz (1973: 90) defines religion as '(1) a system of symbols which acts to (2) establish powerful, pervasive, and long-lasting moods and motivations in men by (3) formulating conceptions of a general order of existence and (4) clothing these conceptions with such an aura of factuality that (5) the moods and motivations seem uniquely re-alistic.' The impact of religion in sustaining a dominant value system depends on visualizing the good and the bad in its formulations, and using this to frame the meaning and factuality of events in the world.

> The force of a religion in supporting social values rests, then, on the ability of its symbols to formulate a world in which those values, as well as the forces opposing their realization, are fundamental ingredients. It represents the power of the human imagination to construct an image of reality in which, to quote Max Weber, 'events are not just there and happen, but they have a meaning and happen because of that meaning' ... the tendency to desire some sort of factual basis for one's commitments seems practically universal ... religion, by fusing ethos and world view, gives to a set of social values what they perhaps most need to be coercive: an appearance of objectivity. (ibid: 131)

The news media have been shown to use the symbols of the dominant culture in a similar manner, focusing on deviance or 'bad news' as a means of establishing a 'consensual paradigm' for society as a whole. Sociological research on the news media has concentrated on showing how this occurs, and has speculated on its effects (Young, 1981; for more detail, see chapter 2).

Contemporary society is characterized by the need for 'legitimation work,' to develop ways of linking new trends and meanings to existing disparate institutional processes. This need is particularly acute as religious and other traditional, community-based systems of meaning recede, and the state must develop new mechanisms for the establishment of a stable symbolic canopy (Carnoy, 1984). Law has become an important mechanism in this regard (Ratner and McMullan, 1987), especially all-encompassing legislation such as the Canadian Charter of Rights and Freedoms and the law that flows from it (Ericson, 1985). The media, too, are a particularly important institution in this regard because their efforts are directed at the entire range of organizational and institutional spheres in society, translating the activities and concerns of those spheres into a culturally common sense. The news media report on and enact the meaning systems of legal, scientific, religious, family, and other institutional spheres. Hence, 'the media have not simply supplanted the priest, the patriarch, the little old woman and the minor intellectual: they have, in both fictional and factual output, taken them over, and *used* them in a mediating role to construct cohesion out of the fragmented "facts" of life' (Hartley, 1982: 104).

The news media thus depend on, and contribute to, the dominant cultural ideology and its expression in the moral terms of 'bad news.' This ideology sets the terms and limits of public culture. News workers encode in terms of 'preferred codes,' and those 'which appear to embody the "natural" explanations which most members of the society would accept,' so that troublesome social problems are placed 'within the *repertoire* of the dominant ideologies' (Hall, 1979: 343). There is a range of ideologies which fit culturally held conceptions of being universal and natural, and news workers take these for granted, as do most other members of the culture. Encoding thus takes place within a limited repertoire 'and that repertoire (though in each case it requires ideological "work" to bring new events within its horizon) will have the overall tendency of making things "mean" within the sphere of the dominant ideology' (ibid). Similarly, decodings of news content 'will tend to be "negotiations" *within* the dominant codes – giving them a more situational inflexion – rather than systematically decoding them in a *counter*-hegemonic way' (ibid). Encoders and decoders are both involved in a social process in which the dominant cultural ideology links the 'facts' of the news to the background assumptions which make the facts understandable (Gouldner, 1976: 111; GUMG, 1980: 402). In a manner which few newsmakers or members of the public are probably aware of, this involvement has the ideological effect of reproducing hegemony.

So goes the theorizing. The fact that the reproduction of hegemony is a real function, and presumed effect, of the news media is suggested by both historical and contemporary research. For example, in the early 1800s 'useful knowledge' newspapers were established to educate the working class in terms of middle-class values (Asquith, 1978: 106). These declined by mid-century, and were replaced by popular newspapers which visualized crime and disaster as a vehicle of moral education. Popular newspapers developed after the British government repealed stamp duty tax, partly on the justification that newspapers were vehicles for fostering the obedience of citizens and a national consciousness and identity. In the words of Gladstone, 'The freedom of the press was not merely to be permitted and tolerated, but to be highly prized, for it tended to bring closer together all the national interests and preserve the institutions of the country' (quoted by Curran, 1978: 58). Another spokesman referred to 'public journals' as 'a police of safety, and a sentinel of public morals' (ibid: 60). Other historical examples abound, such as the role of *Time* and *Reader's Digest* in America in the 1920s as vehicles for transforming middle-class values into lifestyles (Bell, 1976: 77).

Contemporary research has shown how dominant ideology articulates with news work on the level of routine practice (Chibnall, 1977; Tuchman, 1978; Fishman, 1980); in dealing with political movements (Gitlin, 1980: esp. chap. 10); and, in routine reporting of industrial strikes (GUMG, 1976, 1980, 1982). In particular, there are conventions of using authorized knowers which assure the dominant view of what appears to be the case. There are also conventions of staging language use which structure reality in the terms of the dominant culture.

The fact that factual meanings are made variable according to the cultural context in which they are transmitted is nicely illustrated in statements of practice by Radio Canada International. 'For example, a news story on unemployment in Canada cannot be reported in quite the same way to Africans or Latin Americans as it would be reported to Canadians or most Europeans. Being unemployed can involve quite a different level of hardship in a poor country than it does in Canada. Many other terms – ''poverty'' is another good example – have relative meanings in Canada and abroad, and these must be taken into account as a matter of daily routine' (CBC, 1978: 360).

The dominant cultural ideology is politically constructed and has political effects. We have already noted that the state is involved in engineering consent through broadcasting legislation, directives, and procedural rules. There are many other areas of law which relate to news operations. For example, in Canada, newspapers are subject to a large number of regulations and regulatory bodies, including those pertaining to criminal libel and contempt; monopoly and conspiracy to restrict trade; advertising; taxation; foreign investment; national security; marketing; provincial business regulation and trade and commerce; postal service; copyright; electronic communication; federal and provincial professional regulation; incorporation; and human rights (RCN, 1981: 41–2). Through such legislation the state has many forms of power and potential for direct control over newspapers, although arguably fewer than is the case with broadcasting.

Issues in the political and economic control of the news media have been debated for a long time. In the emerging state of the seventeenth century, there was controversy over state control of printing, as there is today about state control of broadcasting (Smith, 1978: 156). In Canada, control of the press shifted from the state to political parties, and more recently into the hands of monopoly capital (Rutherford, 1982; Cayley, 1982a). At the time of the founding of the Canadian state, newspapers were explicitly political 'rags,' asserting the political views of opinionated gentlemen. Political patronage was taken for granted both by the government and by opposition parties and interests (RCN, 1981: 136–7). The same situation prevailed in Britain (Curran, 1978; Smith, 1978, 1980); for example, the Foreign Office provided an annual subsidy to the *Times* of London in exchange for support of its policies. Political patronage began to dissipate from 1910 and into the 1920s, as about one-third of the newspapers in English Canada folded. The businessman, as monopoly capitalist, took over from the individual publisher as opinionated gentleman. However, political-party control and patronage continued to a lesser extent over the subsequent decades. 'In the 1930s, the deficits of a daily newspaper in western Canada were met by the country's prime minister, R.B. Bennett. It was not until the 1960s that the Union Nationale party in Quebec relinquished control of its newspaper, *Montréal-Matin*' (RCN, 1981: 137; see also RCN, 1981b: 112 regarding the political origins of *Montréal-Matin*). In Britain, even the seemingly more neutral output of Reuters was tied closely to government concerns and interests (Boyd-Barrett, 1978). However, as in Britain (Seymour-Ure, 1974) political-party affiliation and patronage in Canada declined greatly after the Second World War, and by the 1960s it was unbecoming to state a political affiliation even if a political-party bias could be read in from time to time (RCN, 1981b: 12). By this point monopoly capital had a firm grip on the Canadian newspaper 'industry.' As Rutherford (in Cayley, 1982a: 140) observes, in comparison to previous state and political-party control, this 'doesn't make the press more free; it simply implicates it in a different system of social control.'

In the present era, monopoly chains produce over three-quarters of all newspaper copies in Canada, and newspapers in general derive over three-quarters of their revenue from advertising (RCN, 1981). Advertising usually constitutes 60 per cent of space in a newspaper, not counting travel, leisure, entertainment, sports, and other 'news' sections which relate directly to the interests of advertisers (Smith, 1980: 11; RCN, 1981: 69). Research on Canadian élites demonstrates that the news-media élite and the economic élite are one and the same, and in turn are linked to the major sources of advertising revenue (Clement, 1975: esp. 297, 325–8, 342; regarding the United States, see Dreir, 1982). The dominance of monopoly capital and advertising control has been of increasing concern to the Canadian state in the past three decades, as evidenced by the Davey Senate Committee followed by the Kent Royal Commission on the newspaper industry. Put most bluntly, the Kent Commission cited with approval the Davey Committee view that 'the economics of advertising ultimately determine all other decisions basic to the operation of a newspaper' (RCN, 1981: 69).

Although broadcasting has more direct government control via legislation and a regulatory agency (Canadian Radio-television and Telecommunications Commission), and direct government ownership via the Canadian Broad-

casting Corporation, it too is greatly influenced by the economics of advertising. The 'ratings game' to build audiences and thereby attract advertisers
for news as well as entertainment programming is paramount, largely over-
coming active efforts to insert personal touches or ideological preferences
(Gitlin, 1983). Even the Public Broadcasting Service in the United States is
dependent upon government legislation and named corporate sponsorship, so
that high-culture drama is emphasized and politically relevant programming
is minimized (Monaco, 1981: 405–6). The combination of limited capacity
for broadcasting, attendant government regulation, and advertising as *the*
source of revenue means that broadcasting gravitates to the mass audience
rather than to specialist audiences.

To be sure, the Canadian Broadcasting Corporation does address minority
audiences statistically, especially on FM radio in programming for high-culture
interests and on AM radio in information programming. Furthermore, cable
television offers a variety of specialized content for those willing to pay.
However, network television is the epitome of *mass* media: instead of each
television station being available for choice in a vast marketplace of ideas,
each television station tries to provide the marketplace *itself* by offering a
potpourri of news as well as entertainment items that will appeal to the broadest
mass possible.

Arguments abound that this situation has sharply curtailed the range and
representative capacity of political discourse in the news media. To Curran
(1979: 177–8), it 'introduced a new system of press censorship more effective
than anything that had gone before. Market forces succeeded where legal
repression had failed in establishing the press as an instrument of social
control.' This does not mean that politics is evaporating via the extraction
procedures of monopoly capital. What it does mean is that the political role
of the news media has changed in the context of contempory politics. P.B.
Waite, in *The Life and Times of Confederation*, states that at that time in
Canadian history newspapers 'had in fact the same characteristics as politics
itself' (quoted in RCN, 1981: 136). They still retain the characteristics of
politics, but of course politics itself has changed along with economic, cultural, and social dimensions of Canada. Politics has become a prefabricated
'spectacle' (Lasch, 1979: chap. 4), with 'fragmented conversations' (Postman,
1985).

The contemporary polity in Canada is characterized by features of the
knowledge society we outlined earlier. We live in an administered society in
which close to one-half of the gross national product (GNP) goes to the service
sector at multiple levels of government. Governments are committed to policing all aspects of organized life, including self-monitoring. Thus, distinctions between public and private corporate spheres are diminished to the extent
that it is perhaps more appropriate to speak of the 'public household' which

distributes entitlements within an elaborate apparatus of penetration, surveil-lance, information, registration, knowledge, and administration. 'It is the polis writ large' (Bell, 1976: 252; also O'Connor, 1973).

The news media are part of this apparatus and bound up in its contexts of organizing. The knowledge they seek and the knowledge they communicate in this respect is inherently political. 'All knowledge is political not because it may have political consequences or be politically useful, but because knowl-edge has its conditions of possibility in power relations' (Sheridan, 1980: 220). For example, the selective use of authorized knowers and their accounts in official bureaucracies is bound up with the nature of power and authority in contemporary society. 'Every time journalists treat bureaucratic accounts (such as case histories) as plain fact, they help an agency make the reality it wants to make and needs to make in order to legitimate itself. Thus, not only does routine news provide ideological accounts of real people and real happenings, it ends up legitimating institutions of social control by disseminating to the public institutional rationales as facts of the world ... Ultimately, routine news places limits on political consciousness' (Fishman, 1980: 138).

The news media also 'underwrite' the state by the use of language, presuppositions, and limitations to argument which are within the dominant political mode of the state (Curran, 1978; Hall, 1979). An essential element in politics is the language and other symbols used to legitimate decisions which relate to power moves (Edelman, 1964, 1971; Connolly, 1983; Shapiro, 1984). The news media, *within* the prevailing terms of the state, are a key terrain for the negotiation of meanings for political purposes. Again, as is true of religion, the words chosen are also deeds, giving preference to par-ticular meanings over others and ultimately presenting '*evaluative* differences as differences in *fact*' (Hartley, 1982: 24).

The modern political temper redefines all existential questions, turning them into 'problems' and then seeking control over their solution. The control over problem definition and solution is in turn a primary vehicle for the assertion of claims to authority. In particular, there is a close association between what a particular interest group sees as the locus or cause of a problem; their attribution of causal responsibility; their preferred political solution; and their attribution of political responsibility (Gusfield, 1981).

As we emphasize and document in subsequent chapters, more than any-thing else they do the news media attend to the definition of social problems and the preferred solutions of accredited bodies. When there is a problem – ranging from urban riots in Britain (Tumber, 1982: esp. 40ff), to violence against women in Toronto (Voumvakis and Ericson, 1984) – politicians, police, religious leaders, pollsters, professional experts, citizen-interest lead-ers, etc., offer a cause of the troubles that is predictable in terms of their political cause (see generally, Ericson, 1977). On a more general level, this tact can be appreciated by the observation that when there is an assassination, or assassination attempt, in the United States, the American news media and their accredited knowers medicalize the problem by casting the culprit as someone in need of psychiatric custody and care, whereas similar acts in other countries are depicted by the same news operatives as the work of criminal terrorists.

The advantage of the news media for promoting one's cause is that they have the aura of being somewhat removed, a third party. Moreover, by translating them all into the common sense, the causes which are conveyed appear naturally to be the case. This makes the news media a much better vehicle of communication than printed or broadcast material put out by a particular interest group to get its message across, because in comparison that material appears explicitly to be bureaucratic propaganda. '[P]ropaganda is contestable, whereas, as common sense tells us, "nature" is not' (Hartley, 1982: 106). Indeed, the news media regularly and routinely promote, marginalize, or exclude political movements as part of their work of validating people, organizations, and institutions. This is not simply a matter of whether or not pre-existing credible sources are responded to; rather, the hierarchy of credibility can itself be structured by the news media as they selectively attend to persons, factions, and organizations in emergent political movements (Gitlin, 1980).

Many who are not regular sources experience politics at best as a spectator sport, and at worst as matter of indifference. The contemporary era is one in which a political leader, such as Reagan in the 1984 presidential election, can claim a landslide victory by gaining the votes of only a quarter of the eligible electorate (50 per cent voted, 50 per cent voted for Reagan). Max Weber (1946: 97) attributes much to the news media for contributing to the lack of participation or interest in politics: 'Our great capitalist newspaper concerns, which attained control, especially over the "chain newspapers", with "want ads", have been regularly and typically the breeders of political indifference.'

The matter is undoubtedly more complicated than attributing the cause of contemporary public uninterest in politics to the mass media. A cogent argument can be made that crucial aspects of politics, economy, and social structure are kept out of media content altogether. Through 'erasure' (O'Neill, 1981a), politics appears as a matter of routine expert and technical administration conducted in the public interest. '[T]he media spectacularization of everyday life functions to hide the real nature of the political economy by treating it in terms of highly cathected scenarios of medical, legal and police work – the television staples – where responsible social agents risk everything in the service of persons and families and their intimate interests in the values of health, law and order' (ibid: 14). This portrayal operates at both the state and market levels, and in O'Neill's view has the effect of legitimizing the political économy and the interests it serves.

> The function of the media at both the state level and the market level is to manage the necessary separation between expert and technical administration processes. on the one hand. and public participation, on the other; this is achieved through the media- fix of turning the political and economic pro-cesses into spectacles while at the same time raising the level of *civic priva-tism* and *depoliticizing the public realm.*
>
> To the extent that the media can be used to manage the legitimation prob-lem at the market level, that is to say. as a commercial communication, then the state use of media assumes a less obvious *propagandistic* function, and appears as a democratic instrument of information: the *right to know*. In turn, the media generally assume an apparently *benign* function in filling the leisure time of a highly privatized mass democracy. (Ibid, emphasis in the original)

The extent to which 'the people' are outside of the sphere of authorized knowers who are regulars in the news media is indicated by contemporary styles of journalism. Especially on broadcast media, the journalist stands in as a regular and familiar representative of the people, asking tough questions of the authorities on behalf of the rest of us. The journalist appears as a no-nonsense person of common sense, and even adds personal views which rely on 'the people' understanding and nodding that 'of course' it is so. The people, depoliticized and even apolitical, provide the reference group for all that is done by journalists in questioning political authority on their behalf.

Exchanges between journalists and authorities are not simply passive or idle banter. The media institution itself is part of the authoritative apparatus, and as such it is directly involved in and interested in policing the organi-zational life of those it reports on. No longer acting in the name of opinionated gentlemen or political-party interests, but rather on behalf of the whole society, what is variously called fourth-estate, investigative, or adversary journalism has come to the forefront. The political role of the news media is no longer a matter of damaging opinion per se, but of information that can be damaging to particular people, organizations, and institutions. The capacity to do damage has been enhanced, or perhaps only made possible, under conditions of local monopoly and/or corporate power of the news outlet. This type of journalism 'is based on an adversary notion of the position of the press, a term that embodies a complete internalization of the political and social universe of journalism. The reporter puts himself in the place of a statutory authority or acts as a goad to statutory authority. There is an assumed permanent rela-tionship between journalism and political bureaucratic power comparable to that between a law-enforcement agency and the criminal classes' (Smith, 1980: 30–1).

Journalistic policing of organizational life concentrates on political and governmental bureaucracies. Private corporations are rarely subject to journalistic policing for wrongdoing or mismanagement as compared to public bureaucracies (RCN, 1981b: 21, 1981e: 45). Corporate business coverage is often relegated to a special business section for consultation by interested businessmen. More generally, when private organizations are discussed it is with a more favourable tone than discussions regarding public organizations, even when the two are involved in similar activities (e.g., a Crown corporation and private corporation in the same economic sector) (Winter and Frizzle, 1979). This apparent partisanship may be related to the fact that the media élite and economic élite are one, and the media work to reflect the ideology of the economic élite (Clement, 1975). Moreover, private corporations supply the advertising revenue which provides the major source of income for news outlets, and news outlets are thereby constrained not to offend the hand that feeds (Singer, 1986).

As Black (1982) observes, it is perhaps understandable that the owners of watchdogs will not set them loose on their friends. Instead, they train them on governmental power as it relates to private interest: whether government laws and agencies are operating fairly and justly in areas which affect most of us (e.g., criminal justice, health, education, welfare) as well as areas precious to private industry (e.g., too much government interference). More broadly, explanations for wrongdoing or mismanagement, or even everyday criminal acts by citizens, are kept at the level of personal failure rather than organizational, institutional, or societal failure. The government exists to develop knowledge, to be used in rationalization and administration, on behalf of the private sector. In turn the private sector uses its various knowledge outlets, including the news media, to be watchdogs of government and to influence and shape their processes of rationalization and administration.

One complication with this view is the fact government itself has become the biggest single advertiser. In 1984 the Government of Canada was the leading advertiser at $95.7 million, the Government of Ontario was sixth at $32 million, and the Government of Quebec was fifteenth at $17.7 million (Singer, 1986: 8). All levels of government are increasingly spending the people's money to convince the people that they are *witnessing* instances of democracy. For example, it is estimated that the federal government's Canadian Unity Information Office spent more than $30 million of the people's money advertising the virtues of the Canadian constitution, while provincial governments spent millions more, often offering views against the federal government (Johnson, 1982).

In a knowledge society, where symbols become a paramount vehicle for mediating reality, government action increasingly takes the form of words rather than any other deeds. Nevertheless, the very same news outlets which carry the advertisements criticize the governments which advertise. Indeed, one significant reason for government advertising may be the fact they are unable to have their 'bureaucratic propaganda' transmitted in the ways they want via regular news items. It may also be necessitated by unfavourable coverage, where advertising becomes the only vehicle for setting the record straight. Furthermore, the Canadian Broadcasting Corporation's radio and television journalists routinely police official bureaucracies at all levels of government, including self-policing of the federal politicians and federal-government bureaucracies of which their corporation is a part. The matter of which organizations are subject to adversary journalism, on what topics, with what tone, and with what effect, is complex, and is addressed in our empirical research.

News organizations have long been recognized as a crucial link between culture and politics. In the political theorizing of the last century, newspapers and other vehicles of publicity were seen as indispensable to democratic government (e.g., Bentham, 1843; Mill, 1962). In contemporary society, broadcast-news corporations contribute to the justification of their existence by the same notions, including the fact that they are *part of* the political process. For example, in their 1978 application for licence renewal, the CBC cited the Annan (1977) report on the British Broadcasting Corporation: 'News and current affairs programs are at the interface between broadcasting and politics and are at the centre of controversy.' The CBC also cited the 1974 decision by the CRTC to renew its licence: 'The Corporation's News and Public Affairs Activities place it at the very centre of the issues, problems and conflicts affecting contemporary society.' They went on to claim that, 'We stake everything – indeed the whole notion of democratic society – on the rational dialogue of an informed public. Only the media can reach the mass of population to provide the information base required for that rational dialogue.'

As a *part of* politics, the news media have the characteristics of politics and contribute to political processes. Politics is 'one of the principal arenas' in which culture, 'the structures of meaning through which men give shape to their experience,' unfolds (Geertz, 1973: 312). The principal activity in this arena is the construction of the view that the authorities have not only an extensive reach over affairs of state, but also an authoritative grasp. To accomplish this, politicians and their senior officials are required to mystify, to have 'a deep, intimate involvement – affirming or abhorring, defensive or destructive – in the master fictions by which [social] order lives' (Geertz, 1983: 146; also Gusfield, 1981).

The news media are important players in the political arena, helping to construct the ideology which makes autonomous politics possible. Politicians and journalists share in the construction of ideology by framing the public culture in terms of the 'five Ws,' or as the privately controlled Canadian Television Network expresses it, 'W5.' This is the culture of investigation, of adversariness, of policing organized life. 'The enfoldment of political life in general conceptions of how reality is put together did not disappear with diagnostic continuity and divine right. Who gets What, When, Where and How is as culturally distinctive a view of what politics is, and its own way as transcendental, as the defense of "wisdom and righteousness", the celebration of "The Daymaker's Equal", or the capricious flow of *baraka*' (ibid: 144).

The state, its politicians, and its official agents are culturally bound to appear right and just, to achieve legitimacy (Habermas, 1975). The state's claims to legitimacy – to be a corporate body acting in the name of society and making decisions which purport to affect the whole society in the public interest – ultimately depend on culture. As such, the state is dependent upon agencies of cultural production, including the news media, for the construction of legitimacy and the achievement of consent. Indeed, many news organizations also purport to be a fourth estate, or in the case of the CBC a 'Fifth Estate,' operating on behalf of the whole society in the public interest. As such, the news media are a crucial ingredient of politics. They take events out of the stream of political life and translate them into the stable beliefs of culture. In joining the 'chaos of incident' to the 'cosmos of sentiment,' the news media help the population to obtain 'the politics it imagines' (Geertz, 1973: 311–13), and the state to maintain the stability required for its routine efforts at reproducing order.

NEWS ORGANIZATION, COMMUNICATION, KNOWLEDGE: A MODEL

Our discussion of the organizational and societal contexts of newsmaking is summarized in schematic form in figure 1.1 (adapted from various models presented by McQuail and Windahl, 1981). Occurrences, amorphous happenings in the world, are attended to by source-organization members and some are selected for further attention within the source organization. The occurrence may be worked on by many source persons in various organizational roles, and one possibility is that an occurrence may be given a meaningful structure as potential news. This is done in accordance with news factors such as timing, professional values and organizational interests, media outlets, ability to give an account that satisfies news-media criteria of rational acceptability, and other elements common both to sources and to journalists as newsmakers. It is also accomplished under various organizational pressures specific to the source organization, e.g., material and technical resources, freedom of information, and organizational visibility. Through these processes, the source organization eventually transforms the occurrence into an

Figure 1.1
The contexts of newsmaking

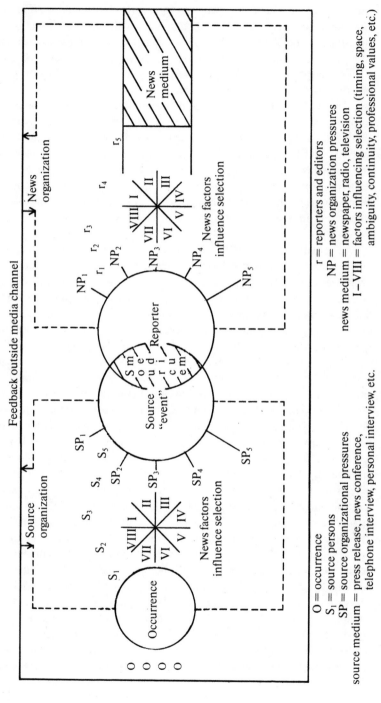

O = occurrence
S_i = source persons
SP = source organizational pressures
source medium = press release, news conference,
telephone interview, personal interview, etc.

r = reporters and editors
NP = news organization pressures
news medium = newspaper, radio, television
I–VIII = factors influencing selection (timing, space,
ambiguity, continuity, professional values, etc.)

event which is potentially available to the reporter as news. This can be communicated through a variety channels to the media, from the highly structured (official reports, news conferences, news releases), to the less structured (personal or telephone interview), to the unstructured (reporter acquires documents or otherwise learns of event by chance or on proactive initiative within the source organization).

The reporter, his colleagues, and editors in turn face pressures and selection factors within their news organization (timing, space, material and technical constraints, professional expectations) which relate to how they translate and transform the source event into published or broadcast news. The news item in turn may occasion feedback into the news organization by response from the general public, persons involved in the matter reported on, or reporters and their texts from other news organizations. The news text also enters back into the source organization, possibly influencing social relations there.

In actuality, there may be several source organizations whose event material is used for a particular news item or related series of news items. Moreover, there may be several news organizations connecting with these same source organizations simultaneously, and with one another in the sense that they rely upon one another's news texts for their own story developments. Furthermore, social, political, economic, and cultural elements articulate with these transactional, organizational, and institutional processes of newsmaking.

Weick (1983: 28) has placed the study of 'newswork as organizational prototype' at the top of his research agenda for scholars of communication, emphasizing that news organizations are an important substantive vehicle because they highlight and accentuate the processes of reality creation and knowledge formation in all organizations. 'So, while communication does not now have a prototype, newsmaking could supply one' (ibid: 15).

Journalists and their sources are moving syntheses of their organizations and their experiences. Their acts of organizing consist of processing each other's signs, and in the process communicating in a way that creates and recreates their respective organizational structures. They develop speech or textual communities which share socially constructed systems of meaning that assist in the work of interpretation, taking action, and connecting episodic action in an orderly manner (Bailey, 1983; Weick, 1979). In this respect organization is a metaphor for collective co-ordination of activity, for negotiating order (Brown, 1978; Strauss, 1978; Manning, 1982; Smircich, 1983). The order that evolves from these processes spirals 'upward' as many organizations become involved, to the level of institutions (both the media institution and the various societal institutions, such as law, family, science, etc., they report on), and in turn to the societal level. This spiralling entails 'the articulation of organizational and institutional models, in which mass media organizations *qua* organizations play a far larger role than they are usually accorded in case studies of single newsrooms, entertainment and production units, or occupational communities' (Hirsch, 1977: 16–17).

Knowledge links organizational processes to institutional and societal levels. Researchers on the news media need to go beyond a focus on selection practices to study the kinds of knowledge the media deal with and convey before the broader cultural and societal implications of news work can be established (Tuchman, 1981). How do people with different orientations and different purposes accomplish understandings about one another and about things? This issue accords with recent concerns and research directions in the sociology of knowledge. For example, Abercrombie (1980) calls for attention to precisely how knowledge and ideologies are transmitted in the everyday life of organizations; to how knowledge differences divide groups (as a corrective to the focus on unquestioned common knowledge by theorists such as Schutz and Berger and Luckmann); and to consider that the ideologies of different groups can distort in different ways (see also Stehr and Meja, 1984).

Senior media spokespersons (e.g., Robert Fulford, cited in RCN, 1981b: 35), and academics (Black, 1982: 5) have commented on the lack of detailed and systematic research on the news-media institution. Hoggart (GUMG, 1976: Foreword) states the need for 'much closer and more varied analysis of the process by which "the agenda" is set up, of what really happens, deep down and inside, and of the degree to which it is or isn't preordained. From that we can move on to what also and no less needs doing – to analyzing what really are the relations, direct or indirect, explicit or implicit, between the television people and the authorities – government, business, the trade unions.' There is a need to search for knowledge differences as well as uniformity, to at least consider news organization, source organization, and media differences in news products and their uses. In undertaking this search, emphasis must be given to the complexity of the news process, starting with the source construction of occurrences, and ending with how the news product flows into the news and source organizations and orders relations there. We need to know whether this is a fairly discrete communication process, or whether there are many communication sub-processes which require explanation in their own terms.

The detailed research agenda required for such analysis is presented in chapter 3. Before proceeding to that point, however, it is necessary to address in greater detail the fact that the news media are primarily oriented to visualizing deviance and control. There is a need to document and consider explanations of this fact, for it relates directly to our discussion of organization, communication, and knowledge in the construction of institutional order and social change.

2

News of Deviance and Control

The Salience of Deviance and Control News

CRIME AND CRIME-CONTROL NEWS

There is a long history of news accounts of crime and crime control. The earliest popular newspapers in the United States, beginning with the New York *Sun* in 1833, established police-beat reporters to offer a daily menu of crime stories (Schudson, 1978; Sherizen, 1978). By the mid-1800s British newspapers also looked to a regular supply of crime stories to offer their readers, and crime, police, and court reporting became institutionalized in some popular Canadian newspapers (Craven, 1983; Rutherford, 1982).

The French concept of *fait divers* sums up this type of news as focusing upon infractions of laws or the 'natural order.' Indeed, news is so synonymous with crime, disaster, or other violations of order that some French-English dictionaries define *fait divers* simply as 'news items.' This emphasis in news reporting led to the formulation of events in terms previously unknown to human cognition: 'the crisis,' 'the horror,' and the 'human story' became everyday 'angles' upon which to 'hook' stories, and the readership (Smith, 1978: 168).

News of crime and crime-control efforts remains a regular feature of both print and broadcast content. The proportion of news space devoted to crime-incident reporting alone has been found to be 4 per cent in English newspapers (Roshier, 1973); 6.5 per cent in Scottish newspapers (Ditton and Duffy, 1982); and 9 per cent for newspapers, 8 per cent for local television, and 4 per cent for national television in Chicago (Graber, 1980: 26). In Canada, 11 per cent of the items on the Canadian Press datafile pertain to the crime/accident category (Royal Commission on Newspapers [RCN], 1981e: 40–1). If items pertaining to aspects of crime control and the administration of criminal justice are considered, the proportion of news space devoted to this sphere increases sharply. For example, Graber (1980: 26) reports that, in Chicago, crime and justice topics averaged 25 per cent of all newspaper news space, 20 per cent of local television offerings, and 13 per cent of national television news content.

Television content other than news also features crime and its control. In the United States, shows featuring crime and law enforcement have averaged between one-quarter and one-third of all prime-time network dramatic shows from 1958 through 1977 (Dominick, 1978; for Britain, see Williams, 1976: 117). Graber (1980: 26) reports that, in the United States, in 1976, 'prime time television featured 20 shows weekly in which crime and law enforcement were the main themes. A total of 63 program hours per week were devoted to these shows, which took up 33 percent of the total program time. The figures for television specials were quite similar.' These figures do not include crime or law-enforcement activities which occur in shows that are not primarily crime dramas.

News organizations have been shown to differ significantly from one another in terms of how much attention they allocate to crime and its control, and in terms of the specific crime and law-enforcement matters they attend to (Davis, 1973; Sheley and Ashkins, 1981; Ditton and Duffy, 1982). Regardless, crime news does not mirror crime and its control. The volume of crime-incident news items does not accurately reflect changes in official statistics on crime gleaned from police sources (Davis, 1973; Jones, 1976). Moreover there is an overemphasis on murder, other forms of serious violence, and offences involving sexual aspects (ibid; also Roshier, 1973; Sherizen, 1978). For example, Ditton and Duffy (1982) found that in six Glasgow newspapers, of both popular and quality orientations, sex crimes were fourteen times overrepresented and violent crimes twenty times overrepresented in comparison to official crime statistics. Similarly, Graber (1980: 39) found: 'Murder, the most sensational crime, constitutes 0.2 percent of all crimes recorded in the police index. In the [Chicago] *Tribune*, it constitutes 26.2 percent of all crime mentions. By contrast, nonviolent crimes like theft and car theft constitute 47 percent of all crimes on the police index, but only 4 percent of all crimes mentioned in the *Tribune*.' A similar focus on murder, violence, and sex is evident in other cultural products, including televised drama (Dominick, 1973; Barrile, 1980) and novels (Knight, 1980).

Research has also demonstrated that the news media focus predominantly on solved crimes (Roshier, 1973), and in particular on the process of capture, arrest, and charging the accused (Sherizen, 1978: 217). Little attention is given to phases of the criminal process after arrest and before sentence (ibid; Dussuyer, 1979; Graber, 1980), and the court cases presented are not representative (Ditton and Duffy, 1982). Prison sentences are overrepresented (Roshier, 1973; Cumberbatch and Beardsworth, 1976; Graber, 1980), although the nature of prison itself, and other practices of criminal punishment, receive very little attention. Again there are parallels with televised drama (Hurd, 1979) and novels (Knight, 1980), in which the police predominate and justice appears summary because the legal process is rarely shown in operation beyond capture of the villain.

Regardless of whether it appears factual or fictional, media portrayals of crime, deviance, and control are consumed avariciously. According to the Royal Commission on Newspapers (1981, 1981a), in Canada at the beginning of the 1980s 98 per cent of all households possessed a television set – as compared to 10 per cent in 1953 – with an average of 1.6 sets per household. A television set was on average played for slightly more than three hours a day, with a similar figure for radio. During weekdays, 90 per cent of Canadians said they listened to at least one radio newscast, with an average of 3.6 newscasts per day per person. During the full week, 94 per cent of Canadians said they watched at least one television news broadcast, with an average of six newscasts per week. On average, there were 0.6 daily newspapers taken per day in Canadian households, down from 1.06 in 1948. A daily newspaper was read at least once during a week by 89 per cent of Canadians, with an average of 6.4 issues per person week. On weekdays an average of 53 minutes a day per person was spent reading daily newspapers, and on weekends this average increased to 66 minutes.

For most people, knowledge about organizations, events, or phenomena with which they have no direct experience comes from the news media. This is certainly the case for knowledge about crime and the administration of crime control. For example, 95 per cent of the panel respondents interviewed in Chicago by Graber (1980: 49–50) designated the mass media as their primary sources of information about crime and crime control. Only in the case of localized crime incidents did people mention neighbours ahead of the media as the primary source of knowledge (ibid: 118). Among media, television was designated as the first outlet for knowledge of crime and justice (ibid). Other research has emphasized the primacy of newspapers as the source of most citizens' knowledge of crime (Croll, 1975).

Public perceptions of the level of crime have been shown to be closer to official statistics than to media accounts (Roshier, 1973; Hubbard et al, 1975), although some research has shown that the public perception is very discrepant from both official crime figures and news-media (especially television) accounts (Sheley and Ashkins, 1978). On other dimensions there are also discrepancies between public perceptions and news accounts in the aggregate. For example, Graber (1980: 68–72) shows that in Chicago the public is more likely than the news media to think of crime in terms of 'street crime' rather than 'white-collar crime,' and to think of criminality as being a result of personal character defect rather than as being related to failures in the crime-control or political systems.

DEVIANCE AND SOCIAL-CONTROL NEWS

It is a basic truism of criminology that designation of something deviant as criminal and responding to it in terms of the system of crime control is only one possible response among many. There may be conflicting views on whether the action is deviant at all, on how to categorize it if it is (e.g., as a medical problem, a criminal problem, or a welfare problem), and subsequently on what are the most appropriate control mechanisms to remedy it.

Whether the matter is ultimately labelled and reacted to as a crime or otherwise, news accounts have a similar structure. They provide 'accounts' – describing, explaining, justifying, and/or excusing unanticipated or untoward behaviour (Scott and Lyman, 1970) – by consulting various documents and sources. These accounts include imputations of deviance, what happened, and what should be done about it. A conclusion is reached in terms of the authoritative definition and resolution of a particular, usually official, source. The formulation of the type of deviance and attendant control response is highly variable, depending on the activities of officials, situational aspects, cultural and political considerations, and sometimes the news-media institution itself. Ditton and Duffy (1982: 13) offer the example of 'a coup in Mauritania that failed, and whose leaders were executed; and a coup in Thailand that succeeded. The successful coup was hardly criminal, as its perpetrators now controlled the state, and hence the legal system. The unsuccessful coup was subsequently treated as a treasonable, and thus criminal offence.'

A substantial amount of reporting consists of accounts of 'policing' undertaken by one organization in relation to other organizations or individuals (e.g., a securities commission investigates irregular trading by a member company of a stock exchange); or, accounts of policing matters internal to a particular organization (e.g., a hospital administration initiates an investigation into the death of a patient) which may or may not eventually lead to policing initiatives from outside that organization (e.g., municipal police or coroner). The news-media emphasis on organized life, and its policing, means that they focus on aspects which violate expectations about organized life or which suggest tendencies towards disorganization, and the social control or policing efforts to deal with these. Furthermore, because news organizations are entwined in the organizational nexus of policing they report on, in some instances they themselves take on a policing (fourth-estate) role with social effects. In summary, the news media give pervasive attention to deviance within, and policing of, organized life, only one part of which is the sphere of crime and crime control.

Events that can be typed as predictable, orderly, and ordinary are unlikely to make the news for just that reason. When organizing efforts appear to be working smoothly news organizations will rarely attend to this fact, let alone attempt to discover why it is so. However, if someone steps out of line, news accounts proliferate. Rudyard Kipling's observations about the news system, in *The Light that Failed*, illustrates this point well: 'there is more joy in England over a soldier who insubordinately steps out of square to rescue a comrade than over even twenty generals slaving even to baldness at the gross details of transport and commissariat.'

A disruption to organized life is often construed in terms of potential further harm, disaster, or crisis. For example, a strike by garbage collectors is framed by the news media in terms of the potential health hazard of garbage remaining uncollected (Glasgow University Media Group [GUMG], 1976: 245). Problems in the market regulation of oil and other forms of energy become translated by government, business, and the media into an 'energy crisis' in which the main culprit is the short-sighted consumer who has been spoiled by cheap energy (Garrison, 1981).

Many other examples of how the news media attend to social problems are now available in the research literature (Hubbard et al, 1975; Cohen and Young, 1981). Since all of organized life is attended to, the news media themselves are also subject to being viewed as a social problem, with attendant imputations about the locus and nature of the problem. The locus of the problem varies from issues of ownership and freedom of the press to effects of content on audiences who consume it. The news media in turn give coverage to these accounts of their own organization and how it fits into their view of their place among other organizations and institutions, and in society.

THE PERVASIVENESS OF DEVIANCE AND CONTROL NEWS

The most cursory inspection of a newspaper or news broadcast reveals that aspects of deviance and control are pervasive. These aspects cut across distinctions of popular and quality news outlets, permeate every section of a newspaper or news broadcast, and punctuate conventional topic classifications of news.

Popular newspapers, and television, are particularly noted for their emphasis on sensational crime, violence, sexual aberrations, major fires, disasters, and other tales of the unexpected that titillate and entertain. 'Quality' news outlets disavow attention to such matters, but this is usually a matter of degree rather than kind (Voumvakis and Ericson, 1984). As the founder of the *New York Times* once expressed it, in referring to the reporting of crime and scandal,

'When a tabloid prints it, that's smut. When the *Times* prints it, that's sociology' (quoted by Sherizen, 1978: 207). Furthermore, it appears that quality news outlets give more attention to deviance and control in spheres (e.g., professional associations, government organizations, and private corporations) relevant to their particular audiences.

The fact that the focus is on classifying deviance and mechanisms of control in any organizational sphere means that news of these aspects appears in every section of the newspaper or news broadcast: city, international, entertainment, business, sports, leisure, travel, real estate, and so on. For example, the Royal Commission on Newspapers (1981c: 36) has observed that international news about Third World countries largely consists of stereotypical stories of riots, scandals, or disasters. The Glasgow University Media Group (1980: 129–30) found that in television reporting of industrial news in Britain, between one-half and two-thirds of all nouns used were 'strike' and 'dispute,' indicating the emphasis on industrial organization *conflict*. An inspection of the sports section of the Toronto *Globe and Mail* on 19 August 1982 reveals seven items relating to crime, deviance, and control in sports:

–   page-one lead regarding a U.S. court award of $850,000 to a National Hockey League player who had been struck by a stick;
–   page-one feature, with two photographs, regarding the association of beer with fan violence and rowdiness at Toronto baseball games;
–   page-one major story regarding the cancellation of a boxing match after a boxer was deemed to be an imposter;
–   page-two major story about riot police being called to a Canada-Yugoslavia basketball game in Columbia;
–   page-three feature column regarding the case of the U.S. court award to the National Hockey League player featured on page one;
–   page-four brief news item regarding a Miami Dolphin football player charged with trafficking in cocaine;
–   page-five major wire story regarding a St John's hockey player who was discharged by a judge on a charge of assault occasioning bodily harm.

To offer an example from broadcast media, the Canadian Broadcasting Corporation (CBC) FM network offers a morning 'high culture' arts and music programme which includes a slot called 'Arts Billboard' that announces major events in the world of art. On 6 August 1982, 'Arts Billboard' carried an item about theft of Peruvian art and its distribution in the United States, and another item concerning theft of art in New York City.

In addition to the fact that aspects of crime, deviance, and control arise in every section of news products, the same issue or theme of deviance and control can cut across the traditional news section or topic classifications. For example, Chibnall (1977: chap. 4) shows how newspapers in Britain created 'The Violent Society' theme by linking deviance in various spheres, including 'militant' industrial action, ordinary delinquency, political deviance, and professional crime. '[I]nterpretations generated in one domain of newspaper discourse (e.g. crime news) can easily be, and have been, transposed through linking concepts (e.g. the violent society) to other domains (e.g. political and industrial news)' (ibid: 75). This means that any effort at classification that separates out crime, deviance, and control from other types of news is very problematic. For example, at the time of reporting of the Royal Commission on Newspapers (1981c: 70–2), the Canadian Press used the following headings for its datafile: 1 / Politics; 2 / Economics/business/production/labour; 3 / Accidents and crime; 4 / Social issues (including 'social problems ... Examples: status of women, system of justice, prison reform, minority rights'); 5 / Arts and entertainment; 6 / Sports; 7 / Human interest; 8 / Other. These are rather arbitrary and pointless classifications. A given news text can include several of these categories, and 'Accidents and crime' and 'Social issues' can cut across all of them. The same point applies to efforts by academics to separate out 'crime news' from news of politics, economics, entertainment, sport, and so on (e.g., Graber, 1980). The *fait divers*, the things visualized to be out of order in all spheres of organized life, are attended to by journalists regardless of any other classifications they themselves manufacture for getting the job done, and regardless of the classifications of academics who wish to understand how the job is done.

Explaining Deviance and Control News

ENTERTAINMENT, AUDIENCE, WHAT SELLS

One of the historic obligations of the news media is to entertain. This obligation is directly related to the need to fulfil the demands of audiences, which in turn are used to increase markets and expand revenues from advertising. Crime, deviance, and control items have served these commercial needs of the news media (Altick, 1970; Schiller, 1981). Asquith (1978: 107) records that,

> Confronted by falling sales from mid-1833, several proprietors of the un-
> stamped made their papers less austerely political, and Henry Hetherington
> promised that his *Twopenny Dispatch* would 'abound in Police Intelligence, in
> Murders, Rapes, Suicides, Burnings, Maimings, Theatricals, Races, Pugilism,
> and ... every sort of devilment that will make it sell' ... John Bell started in
> 1815 to give more space in his *Weekly Dispatch* to reports of murder, rape and

seduction, and in the 1820s the reports of parliamentary debates in the *Morning Herald* were abridged in favour of humorous accounts of police cases, with the result that the paper's sales quintripled in eight years.

Commentators on the contemporary period note that the news media continue to market bad news because it entertains, is popular, and maximizes audiences (e.g., Young, 1981; Murdock, quoted in Alderson, 1982: 22). This situation has been accentuated by the emergence of television news, which is directed to a mass audience whose attention must be held through successive items on the newscast. Television news has a particular propensity to be reduced to the condition of popular entertainment. Indeed, a training manual for CBC television producers declares explicitly that 'news is theatre' (Cayley, 1982a: 136).

There are several points that qualify, and raise the complexity of, entertainment as an explanation of the prevalence of news of deviance and control. First, there is the question of the extent to which this material is genuinely popular, or fed to the masses on the assumption that they are 'cultural dopes' who would be unresponsive to alternatives. Raymond Williams (1976: 114–15), having considered the dominance of crime and illness in television content generally, observes, '[W]e find little that is genuinely popular, developed from the life of actual communities. We find instead a synthetic culture, or anti-culture ... not the culture of "the ordinary man"; it is the culture of the disinherited.'

Second, the theatrical aspects of news may be as much a result of the activities of sources as of journalists. In their efforts to control information, to establish front and back regions of their organizations, to stage news productions through display settings such as news conferences or public meetings, sources do little more than dramatize what they are up to through ritual and rhetoric. They write the scripts, provide the stage, and train their actors for public-culture dramas, while reporters are the audience left to write a (sometimes critical) review of the performance.

Third, entertainment may be only one aspect of what the reporter is attempting to convey in a news item. For example, the reporter may primarily wish to convey information, but feel that the audience will only attend to it if it is related to an interesting bit of crime, an innuendo of deviance, or a hint of hostility among parties concerned.

Fourth, news of deviance and control functions as a morality play, a conflict between good and evil people and forces. It engages the audience by being entertaining and titillating, but also by reassuring insofar as the evil element is condemned and the conflict resolved by authoritative sources (Young, 1974; Chibnall, 1977: 31–3). The link of news as entertainment to its broader social-order explanations is considered in more detail in a subsequent section.

THE ORGANIZATION OF NEWS WORK

Another explanation of the predominance of deviance and control items in
the news is that they fit with the beliefs and practices of news workers. The
need for news workers to transform events into the genre capacities of the
newspaper, or the broadcast news bulletin, means that ' "developments" and
"processes" must always be immobilised and presented in the news in terms
of crisis, novelty or as an important departure from the normal course of
events' (GUMG, 1976: 120). Chibnall (1977: 115–16) summarizes his study
of law-and-order news by arguing in a similar vein that it 'is not a product
of editorial conspiracy, but a reflection of the social organization of reporting,
and the professional imperatives and commercial interests which underlie it.'
While Lester (1980: 989) avoids a conspiratorial view, she does note that in
a newspaper she studied it was explicit editorial policy to report on conflicts,
and then do continuing stories on control efforts to the point of a consensual,
'good' resolution. The editor of this newspaper described the overall goal as
'healing' or 'problem solving' through the three phases of factual reporting,
interpretive reporting, and what-to-do-about-the-situation reporting.

Crime-incident news is particularly suited to the routines of news work
(Chibnall, 1977; Fishman, 1980). The police and courts supply an endless
number of potential items on a regular basis. They are also reliable and credible
sources, whose documentary or verbal accounts can be treated as 'facts.'

Beyond crime reporting, other large organizations, especially governmental bureaucracies which deal with social problems (e.g., child welfare,
energy, health), similarly provide an endless supply of stories, not only stories
about the activities those bureaucracies are designed to control, but about the
procedures and controls within the bureaucracies themselves. The policing of
organizational life itself offers endless possibilities, as journalism participates
in determining who are the proper 'owners' of public problems (Christie,
1977; Gusfield, 1981) and whether they are acting with propriety. 'Every
institution of society contains, it appears, as many morally doubtful elements
as secure ones. Journalism could go on for ever "cleaning up" public life
without ever finding the task completed, while finding its own criteria of
cleanliness constantly changing' (Smith, 1978: 178). Operating with a conception that human rights are related to bureaucratically identifiable rights,
as well as legal rights, reporters organize to report on the organizational
proceedings and procedures of others. 'Reporters clean up and repair flawed
bureaucratic proceedings in their news stories. Their model of cleanliness,
orderliness, and normalcy is a bureaucratic one' (Fishman, 1980: 135).

Crime, deviance, and control news also fits in with the central, conventional features of news stories. It gives the feeling of being directly relevant
because it is timely and concerns events 'close to home.' It accords with the

focus of news on events. It also relates to the personalization of events characteristic of news: the reconstruction of the biography of the accused, the fear and loathing of the victim and victim's relatives, and the sometimes benevolent and always authoritative actions of officials. For many persons in the news, 'Deviance constitutes their very ''news value'' – unless they are legitimate authorities, of course, in which case precisely the opposite rule applies, and their official status is what makes them newsworthy' (Gitlin, 1980: 152). Entwined with this is the 'human interest' element in many of these stories. Criminals are portrayed as heroes as well as villains; victims as blameworthy as well as deserving of empathy; enforcement officials as buffoons as well as admirable elements of humanity who risk everything in the interests of our safety, health, and order. Deviance and control also accord with the news emphasis on conflict and confrontation.

From the viewpoint of writing and editing, news of crime, deviance, and control is easy to process and assists news flow (Gordon and Heath, 1981). Particularly in the case of crime-incident reporting, standard leads can be utilized, and the story is easy to produce within the inverted-pyramid style thus making it easy to meet deadlines and get into print. The use of single credible official sources, or two sides in a conflict within a point/counterpoint format, meets the journalistic criteria of 'objectivity' (Tuchman, 1978) and makes it relatively easy to avoid errors and attendant calls for retraction or legal action.

The routine reliance on official sources – with a conception of human rights as being related to bureaucratically identifiable rights as well as legal rights – reproduces objectivity on another level. The news media share with the law itself as a cultural product 'the mantle of ''impartiality'' ' (Hartley, 1982: 55; see generally Sumner, 1979). The news media can no more maintain their legitimacy than can the law or the state's agents if they appear to be partial to particular interests. They have to speak on behalf of the general public, and appear to be acting in the public interest. Our point here is that by giving such predominant attention to the law and legal authorities, the news media can go a long way towards making convincing the image that they are an objective, impartial, universal, and general voice of the people. They can rely on the same properties in the law as a cultural product to convey the image that they, too, are a neutral, objective arbiter of conflicts in the world.

ORGANIZING AND ORGANIZATIONAL ORDER

In chapter 1 we introduced the idea that all organizing is directed at occurrences which are unexpected, discontinuous, or equivocal (Weick, 1979). In the knowledge society, many large bureaucratic organizations are devoted exclu-

sively to visualizing and controlling equivocality in the environment and those
who people it, and all large organizations employ at least some people who
have this as their exclusive task. It is their job to make sense of organizational
actions and choices by articulating what is anticipated (plans), what is going
on (commentary), and what has gone on (accounts) (Harre and Secord, 1973;
also Weick, 1979: 195). This procedure applies to both intra-organizational
and inter-organizational concerns, and is a necessary part of trying to make
people and their organizations more predictable.

Given that there is nothing fixed or immutable about organizing, life
inside an organization and among organizations takes on the character of
being a negotiated social order (Strauss, 1978). The microcultures within and
among organizations have the qualities of fluidity and flexibility, enabling
ongoing negotiations over things that interest them to take place and creating
some ability, albeit differential, to resist as well as compromise. All of their
efforts at social control – from affixing a classification to the deviance or
problem to accomplishing a remedy for it – are negotiable and involve a
complex interplay of signification (communication of meaning), domination
(power), and legitimation (moral norms) (Giddens, 1976).

> [W]hat the transgression *is* is potentially negotiable, and the manner in which
> it is characterized or identified affects the sanctions to which it may be sub-
> ject. This is familiar, and formalized, in courts of law, but also pervades the
> whole arena of moral constitution as it operates in day-to-day life ...
>
> The 'interpretation' of norms, and their capability to make an 'interpreta-
> tion' *count*, by participants in interaction is tied in subtle ways to their compli-
> ance to moral claims ... The moral co-ordination of interaction is
> asymmetrically interdependent with its production as meaningful and with its
> expression of relations of power. This has two aspects, themselves closely as-
> sociated with one another: (a) the possibility of clashes of different 'world-
> views' or, less macroscopically, definitions of what *is*; (b) the possibility of
> clashes between diverging understandings of 'common' norms. (ibid: 109–10)

Deviance prompts discourse: about the symbolic boundaries between
organizations, about their power relations, and about their norms. It is these
boundaries, power relations and norms which the news media attend to,
offering an ongoing articulation of what journalists and their authorized knowers deem to be out of order and visualize as possibilities for control. Much
of what is reported in this respect involves a source from one organizational
sphere imputing deviance to activity within another organizational sphere,
whose spokesperson is called upon to account for the activity in question.

The account usually entails an excuse or justification of the activity. An
excuse is an account which admits the activity is morally questionable, but
averts imputation of fault or blameworthiness and avoids condemnation or

disapproval (Brandt, 1969). A justification is an account which declares that given the circumstances the action was the right thing to do (ibid). As such, excuses and justifications have to appeal to objectified knowledge held in common by the interested parties, and sometimes a third party involved in the effort to resolve the matter. That is, they rely on commonly held cultural criteria, and on publicity (Hume, 1948; Rawls, 1971). In the publicity offered by the news media, the criteria employed in justification are within the com- mon-sense knowledge of the culture. The everyday articulation by the news media of justifications for deviance and control in organizational life provides us with a common sense that the world is intelligible and accountable.

In providing a justification as opposed to an excuse, the hope is to be 'let off the hook' so that 'there is no charge left, no defective feature of one's behavior, which even looks like a reflection on one' (Brandt, 1969: 339–40). As such, justification is intimately related to the question of motives and to personal moral character. On the question of motives, all actors develop a 'vocabulary of motives' (Mills, 1940) to co-ordinate and control their activities in terms of acceptable grounds for their actions. On the question of personal character, 'an objectively wrong action (or an action in some way out of order) is excused if it does not manifest some defect of character' (Brandt, 1969: 354). In this context, it is understandable that the news media person- alize deviant events and efforts at control. It also becomes clear why source organizations put forward senior, respectable, authorized knowers to *represent* their position. What is regarded as a noble motive, and indeed what is taken to be the truth, is largely dependent on the nobility of the persons in question. Therefore much attention is directed to those persons, their organizational positions and status, and other features of their personal biographies.

News focus on accounts of sources as they face allegations of deviance and efforts at control reveals much about the source organizations' decisional premises and from where those premises are derived. It is also revealing of whom the organizational members involved see as the relevant audiences to receive the account. Furthermore, it provides knowledge about the framework of accountability of the organizations involved (their institutional arrange- ments designed to ensure that the obligations of their members are being upheld), and their account ability (their ability to give accounts that make it appear that accountability has been achieved).

The question of legitimation, the ways in which source organizations, through the news media, are able to justify in a plausible way the activities and functions of their organizations, is also important. The news media are an important vehicle for making *claims* in the public culture that one's organizational activities are right and just, and for gaining *recognition* for being committed to justice and propriety (Habermas, 1975). For many or- ganizations, especially those within the direct jurisdiction of the state, recognition is an important, ongoing political accomplishment, and a dominant political goal. In reporting on the deviance and control efforts of organizations in relation to other organizations in their environment, as well as on the self-policing efforts within organizations, the news media offer a view of the political accomplishments of particular groups in society. This political dimension is another reason for the focus on bad events and the process of making them good, and requires more detailed consideration in its own right.

REFORM POLITICS AND CHANGE

As outlined in chapter 1, social reaction to deviance has implications for reform and change as well as order. By participating in discourses of deviance and control, especially as these are grounded in official bureaucracies, the news media become part of the administrative apparatus for controlled reform and change.

The knowledge society is also an administered society. Professional managers 'run' the political system, transforming existential questions into problems and then searching for solutions to these problems in and on their own terms. Defining deviance and mobilizing efforts at control are central to this form of politics, and the news media participate by picturing politics in this way.

There are many organizations and professions that claim authority over the regulation of social, cultural, political, and economic affairs. Their claims to authority necessarily entail assertions that they are better at doing what they do than other organizations or professions. The definition of 'better' is phrased in terms of the trinity of reform discourse – effectiveness, cost, and humaneness – as each organization or profession in a particular sphere argues that it offers a more efficient and humane system of control and social improvement than its competitors. The state is at the centre of this reform discourse, as its agents define, initiate, and control what are the problems and who is best suited to deal with them. In the contemporary state reform efforts increasingly come from within the state rather than from outside organizations; these outside organizations are left to contract with government, become its paid employees, or otherwise co-exist with state mechanisms if they wish to have an impact (Ericson, 1987; McMahon and Ericson, 1987).

A central thrust of efforts to claim problems as the property of one's organization or profession is to convey the view that things are not quite as they should be and that reform is needed. Reform in this sense is as integral a part of the state's control apparatus as the law, courts, police, and so on (Foucault, 1977). In order to justify control over the property of the public problem, to sustain or enhance resources for control, and ultimately to convey a sense of progress, the organization or profession must constantly traffic in the imagery of failure, of the need for amendments, adjustments, more humane conditions, better facilities, and so on.

Discourses that visualize problems and their solution are a central feature of reform politics, and the news media participate in this 'reform talk' as a major component of their coverage. There would be no greater testimony to a totalitarian state and ideological hegemony than if the news media offered only good news. A better world, a sense of progress, requires a sense of what it is not. It requires bad news. News of deviance and control is political coverage in the broadcast sense. The reform processes of politics and the dimensions of organizational and political power in society are revealed on an everyday basis by the news media. As Black (1982: 142) argues, 'Close analysis of treatment of social deviance would enable us to fill in some more of the features in the mass media pictures of politics.'

As introduced in chapter 1, reporting problems of deviance and strategies of control provides an ongoing articulation of claims to political authority. Control over problem definition and solution is a primary vehicle for assertion of claims to authority, and the news media provide images and information about the authoritative apparatus through news of deviance and control. One significant way in which this is done is the reporting of sources' political causes in terms of the causal attributions they make regarding a problem of deviance and control. There is a close link between what is attributed causal responsibility and aspects of political responsibility (Gusfield, 1981) and this is featured in news accounts of deviance and control.

This process has been documented in studies of 'moral panic' (Cohen, 1972; Fishman, 1978; Pearson, 1983; Voumvakis and Ericson, 1984). A related example is provided in Tumber's (1982) analysis of British television coverage of the urban riots of 1981. The authorized knowers who were cited all offered explanations of the riots that reflected their political causes and the solutions that follow therefrom. The home secretary, followed by a chief constable, other senior police spokespersons, and municipal politicians, blamed the riots on criminal hooliganism and outside agitators. A deputy commissioner of police described them as sheer criminal hooliganism. The Labour shadow home secretary cited bad housing and unemployment as the causes, and similar attributions to social deprivation were offered by Father Joe Daly of Liverpool. Lord Scarman, who was later to head an official inquiry into the riots, blamed unemployment and the fact that it was outside the football season and youths were looking for fights. The prime minister, echoed by her home secretary, blamed parents. Enoch Powell, exclaiming 'You haven't seen anything yet,' said the riots were a problem of race, and Winston Churchill called for an end to immigration. A professor observed that high lead levels make children more sensitive to stress. Mary Whitehouse asserted that the media were the chief culprit. 'All of these views could have been foreseen as the riots inevitably produced entrenched positions and reinforced opinions. Politicians and other opinion-makers retreated in this time of crisis into their well-known ideological positions. They had to respond, the public was demanding explanations. What better way than on known territory – using the riots as justification for previous statements and predictions' (ibid: 44).

Some analysts of the news media have pointed out that, in the aggregate, news accounts of deviance and control contribute to ideological hegemony. The 'definitions of social deviance are essentially expressions of dominant ideology in moral terms' (Sumner, 1979: 4). The range of causes of problems that are legitimate to offer, and thus the political causes that are on offer in the news media, are circumscribed in terms of the dominant ideology. As Young (1981: 242) expresses it, 'a process of ideological inversion occurs; where to the question: why is there problems in capitalist society? We have the answer: because of strikes and crimes, not that capitalism inevitably produces strikes and crimes. The problem endemic to capitalism becomes the blemishes and the solution to the malaise is to remove the blemishes not to change the system.' Furthermore, 'lawandorder' is a preferred solution to problems for a variety of political causes, but it gains no favour as a cause of problems.

There is extensive attention to the procedures of those involved in deviant designation and control. Much of reform discourse and politics is about this. As Habermas (1975) has instructed, the state's legitimacy increasingly rests upon procedures defined within norms of constitutionality, legality, citizenship, and representation. This is indicated, for example, by the Canadian Charter of Rights and Freedoms and its impact on political reform talk (Ericson, 1985). State agents constantly and actively tinker with the details of these procedures, doing the repair work necessary for controlled organizational change.

The police and crime are in the forefront of state control efforts at the level of symbolic politics. The police, as part of the justice system, are within *the* major sphere used by citizens to assess the state as a moral agent. In particular the procedures of the police are a fundamental basis for assessing the reality of liberal democracy (Murdock, 1982: 110; generally, see Jefferson and Grimshaw, 1984). Likewise, criminalizing events or designating them otherwise is a fundamental exercise in political power. It therefore follows that a politically interested news media will focus on crime, deviance, and control, whether it be dramatizing police funerals, representing a debate over criminal-law reform, reporting that a criminal got off because of a police error in procedure, or mentioning the latest murder in the city.

There is nothing new about political authority using crime and punishment this way. What is new is the media of its dramatization. Before newspapers and television there was more live theatre; people attended court and public executions to learn of the majesty, justice, and mercy of central authority (Erikson, 1973; Hay, 1975). Now it is all packaged and reproduced for home consumption, even to the extent of re-enacting 'real' trials using 'real' legal actors. The media have changed; the visualization of crime, deviance, and control for public drama and political instruction has not.

VISIONS OF ORDER AND CONSENSUS

As introduced in chapter 1, another explanation of the predominance of deviance and control in the news is that it constitutes an important means by which our culture constructs a sense of order and consensus. While such news may be entertaining, it also articulates current sensibilities about collective life and the basis of social order. News of deviance and control is included because it is intrinsically instructive about social order, in addition to being intrinsically interesting (cf Box, 1971: 40).

With a highly specialized division of knowledge and a plethora of microcultures in the knowledge society, there is enormous strain between social and cultural spheres and difficulty in integrating them into the common sense. In addition to the fact that constructed versions of reality are readily subject to deconstruction, the material world itself can be experienced as destructive. Accidents and disasters are dominant cultural fears, disturbing meaning and threatening social order in the same way as crime and other forms of deviance. As Wuthnow et al (1984: 27) state with regard to Peter Berger's thought, 'While humans continually strive to maintain their sense of arrangement, this sense is continually threatened by the marginal situations endemic to human existence. Dreams, fantasy, sickness, injury, disaster, emergency, mistake, all reveal the unreliability of the social world; all present a menace of various degrees to the paramount reality of everyday life.'

Faced with fears and foibles, including the fear of foibles, human beings look for mechanisms outside themselves for ordering behaviour. Culture provides these mechanisms, in the form of programs or 'templates' (Geertz, 1973) which offer recipes or instructions for understanding and for action. That which is out of order – from the most explosive eruption to the simply peculiar person – must be accounted for, and culture offers a stream of 'diagnostic symbols' (ibid) for doing so.

Many types of cultural workmen – including, for example, novelists, journalists, and social scientists – are employed to manufacture cultural products which will aid in the diagnosis, and, it is hoped, lead to action. Their actions and their texts, through ongoing 'conversations' with influential members of the culture, provide what Peter Berger calls a 'plausibility structure' (Berger and Kellner, 1964) for that culture. The greater the strength of the plausibility structure they build, the greater the social cohesion and stability.

The plausibility structure is also a reassurance structure, acknowledging the familiar and excluding alternatives. Along with other cultural products, the news attends to what will fit within existing plausibility and reassurance structures, and thus is impelled towards eternal recurrence (myth) and ideological reassurance. It serves to 'acknowledge order.'

The news media thus attend to deviance and control as a way of acknowledging order. Most fundamentally, the news media participate in the constitution of the moral boundaries of the society reported on. News workers, much more than social scientists and other servants of the administered society, emphasize the traditional question in political philosophy of the nature of goodness and decency. As Mary Douglas (1966; also Douglas and Wildavasky, 1982) has stressed, highly organized societies place particular emphasis on the community as a moral territory. The news media take up a central place in mapping this moral territory. They do so by constant reference to the authorized knowers who are well placed in their respective organizations to offer the demarcations of symbolic boundaries, which in turn provide the very basis of cultural classification and order in social life.

The close articulation among cultural signs, moral norms, and power means that the very act of assigning reality to a person, event, process, or state of affairs is infused with moral meaning. The question of classification, of ascribing factuality, is also a question of right and wrong. What is accepted as a factual classification draws the contours of what is possible, and hence also what is a duty or obligation of those in the organizational and institutional spheres reported on. Hence, by their everyday attention to organizational sources, assigning of reality to persons, events, processes, or states of affairs, the news media offer not only cultural facts but also the moral order of things.

This moral component of reality construction is especially evident when things are deemed to be out of place or deviant. As Mary Douglas (1966) argues, every detail of social life, from the world of street crime to the world of household dirt, reveals the infusion of moral and factual construction. This is a normal and functional aspect of society, and it is normal and functional that the news media attend to it.

> The presence of order – society – makes disorder possible. Rules, boundaries, categories, and all sorts of cognitive and moral classification systems create lines that are crossed and categories of things for which there are exceptions. Not everything fits, and what doesn't becomes deviant, odd, strange or criminal. From this point of view crime and dirt are the same phenomena [sic]. Both represent something out of place. For crime, it is behavior that violates the normative and legal order; for dirt, it is a matter which is not in its correct place. When things get out of place the normative and legal order is challenged and society re-establishes that order by taking ritual action. For individ-

uals and crime there is punishment. For dirt there is a clean up (we often speak of 'cleaning up' crime too). (Wuthnow et al, 1984: 88)

The rituals of cleaning up crime and excluding deviants to purify society are not simply based on responding to events in the world. In addition, there is proactive effort to manufacture symbolic boundaries by visualizing deviance and effecting enforcement and punishment. From witch hunts (Erikson, 1966; Bergesen, 1977, 1978), to confining people in asylums and prisons (Foucault, 1965, 1975, 1977), to technological and environmental dangers (Douglas and Wildavsky, 1982), the powerful construe the undesirable and relegate it to the status of social waste. The news media play a central role in these rituals and their effects.

Humans constantly search for a factual basis to their commitments, and the news media provide one mode of discovery through their focus on evil events and the right remedies. Hence, the focus on deviance and control in the news is not just in the interest of control, but also in the interest of reality. It is a mode of reality discovery and affirmation which gives tangibility and detail to otherwise nebulous events. This is well summarized in Kermode's (1966: 18) analysis of the narrative technique of peripeteia – a sudden change of fortune – which is

> present in every story of the least structural sophistication. Now peripeteia depends on our confidence of the end; it is a disconfirmation followed by a consonance; the interest of having our expectations falsified is obviously related to our wish to reach the discovery or recognition by an unexpected and instructive route. It has nothing to do with any reluctance on our part to get there at all. So that in assimilating the peripeteia we are enacting that readjustment of expectations in regard to an end which is so notable a feature of naive apocalyptic.
>
> And we are doing more than that, we are, to look at the matter in another way, re-enacting the familiar dialogue between credibility and scepticism. The more daring the peripeteia, the more we may feel that the work respects our sense of reality; and the more certainly we shall feel that the fiction under consideration is one of those which by upsetting the ordinary balance of our naive expectations, is finding out something for us, something *real.*

Even if something is wholly expected by those in the know, such as massive famine in Africa, when the news media decide to pick it up they present it as an unexpected disaster and then focus on, and affect, efforts at remedy and control. Moreover, whether it is famine, earthquake, strike, or street violence, the developments and processes are framed as a 'crisis.' 'Crisis' is also a means of construing the world, of discovering reality. Crisis, 'inescapably a central element in our endeavors towards making sense of the world,' is 'a way of thinking about one's moment, and not inherent in the moment itself' (ibid: 93–4, 101).

The journalist uses the 'crisis' frame to establish an event as newsworthy and to transform it into news discourse. In turn, the elevation of an event into a crisis provides an opportunity to make explicit and intensive confirmations of reality (Berger and Luckmann, 1966: 175). The crisis formulation quickly establishes the reality of the 'problem' so that particular 'immediate' solutions can be called for and effected. It frequently inhibits the asking of alternative or critical questions. The news formulation is based on limited assumptions and a limited range of solutions. Nevertheless the particular formulation takes on the character of reality, and the preferred solution takes on the character of inevitability. Everything else is made improbable (for examples, see Fishman, 1978; Hall et al, 1978; Voumvakis and Ericson, 1984).

Analysts have stressed that news frames of this type play on a consensus against which deviance is a threat requiring defusion. There is a 'consensual paradigm' (Young, 1981) which is occasionally explicit, but normally implicit, in reporting on deviance and control. '[T]he framework trades on and assumes a consensus of values. There is no way in which "good" and "bad" news can be readily understood if the question "Good or bad for whom?" is admitted' (GUMG, 1980: 145). The accused's crimes cause trouble for his victims, law enforcers, taxpayers, everyone. The striker's wage demands cause trouble for those who wish to work, for law enforcers, for consumers, for everyone. The news media speak on behalf of the public as victims in typing the deviance and deviants as 'hooliganism,' 'violence,' 'psychopathic,' and in proferring preferred 'lawandorder' solutions.

As Young (1981) argues, consensual-paradigm theory sees instances of deviance and control as being selected in terms of their violation of a shared sense of order and justice. The controllers, as 'good guys' who sacrifice their personal lives in the public interest, are stereotyped to the same degree as the 'bad guys.' A 'morality play' is presented, in which the peripeteia device is used to assert the reality of deviance, but then to explain it away and reaffirm consensual reality through cathected scenerios of heroic control agents neatly trimming the blemishes from the otherwise orderly landscape. The believability of this depiction is enhanced by the fact that most citizens have no direct, independent knowledge of the phenomenon reported on or its relation to other aspects of social order. The news media fill in the void with factual detail and a consensual framework, thus giving the public both a factual basis for their commitments as well as a context in which to understand them.

In sum, the paradox of trying 'to force intransigent reality into a consensual mould' (ibid: 242) is dealt with by explaining away the deviance and using it to reaffirm reality in a way that serves to acknowledge order. In Berger and Luckmann's (1966: 132–3) terms, the news media engage in both 'therapy' (using the *legitimations* of the consensus paradigm to assure that deviance remains within institutionally defined parameters and their implications for control) and 'nihilation' (using the same conceptual machinery to *delegitimate* the reality of phenomena or their interpretations which do not fit the consensual paradigm). In nihilation, 'deviant phenomena may be given a negative ontological status, with or without therapeutic intent,' or there may be an effort 'to account for all deviant definitions *in terms of* concepts belonging to one's own universe ... The final goal of this procedure is to *incorporate* the deviant conceptions within one's own universe, and thereby to liquidate them ultimately. The deviant conceptions must, therefore, be *translated* into concepts derived from one's own universe' (ibid).

The use of a consensual paradigm to focus on deviance and control as they relate to social order is not exclusive to journalists as cultural workmen. The crime novelist does the same. This is exemplified by Doyle, who made his Sherlock Holmes stories 'a bridge between the disorderly experience of life and a dream of order, by construing both aspects in a graspable, contained and controlled form' (Knight, 1980: 105). Kuhn (1970) has argued that scientific discovery is sometimes a matter of having symbolically generated expectations fail to match direct observations. In publishing research results, the social-science researcher finds his audience most attentive if what he has to say challenges, or better still *attacks*, their ground assumptions (Davis, 1971). The 'normative paradigm' (Parsons, 1937) in sociology has assumed that all action entails following norms and that what requires attention and explanation is not conformity, but people who apparently do not follow the paths laid down in the normative system. Much of sociology is therefore the study of error, deviance, and abuse from the viewpoint of the analyst's conception of normative order. In interactionist sociology too, the ethnographer looks for the empirical exception to prove the rule, uses his own world to decide what is different or unexpectedly similar in the world under study, and otherwise develops 'knowledge based on incongruity' (Van Maanen, 1979: 548). For example, Weick (1983: 25) advises researchers of organizational communication to focus on their subjects' talk when 'routines fail' because these 'may be the moments when talk has its strongest impact on action. Talk uttered while routines are successful may predict nothing because it resolves nothing.' Such talk when routines fail is also the essence of news of crime, deviance, and social control.

In sum, a range of cultural workmen operate with conceptions of the norm and the anomaly in our knowledge society. They proffer classifications within which people are to think of themselves and of the actions open to them. The more scientifically oriented among them provide an assurential technology aimed at the taming of chance; deviation from the mean becomes the norm. Journalists, novelists, and others are left to comprehend these classifications and translate them into the common sense.

Consensual-paradigm theorists can be criticized for conveying the view that the news media are nearly totally effective in achieving consensus and the reproduction of social, cultural, political, and economic hegemony as officially mandated. In as simplistic a fashion as psychological research on the effects of mass-media content on behaviour, which posits deviance coverage as causing a decline of authority which causes deviance, consensual-paradigm theory posits the opposite, that deviance coverage causes a strengthening of authority which yields consensus. Moreover, in traditional-effects research only the audience is affected and afflicted, whereas consensual-paradigm theory assumes everyone is deceived, including news workers. The news message is portrayed as relatively unambiguous with relatively unidirectional effects, and not varying substantially by news organization or media. As Murdock (1982: 105; see also Schlesinger et al, 1983) argues, in relation to television, it is better to assume that it is 'a complex and conflictual system of representations which is capable of generating a wide range of different and possibly contradictory "effects".' While the news media do have to work within the common sense and popular concerns, this does not necessarily entail uniformity because there are a range of popular issues and ideologies from which to choose. '[P]opular ideologies are *themselves* conflicting and contradictory, and different programmes pick up different currents within them, with the result that crime and police shows display "a variety of hybrid mixtures of a range of authority and outlawry, elaborating in turn a range of popular ambivalences towards bureaucracy, law and state (Gitlin, 1982: 225)" ' (Murdock, 1982: 116).

At the societal level, there are also contradictions among economic, political, and cultural aspects which are revealed in tensions and conflicts at the institutional level. As Bell (1976) argues, Western societies over the past century and a half have constantly experienced contradictions among the economic emphasis on efficiency; the political emphasis on equality; and, the cultural emphases on privatism, self-realization, and gratification (manifested by fascination with consumption, family, and leisure) (see also Habermas, 1975; O'Neill, 1981a). Thus it is possible to argue that predominant attention to news of deviance and control is 'a function of the way in which the contradictions of the system generate bad news: ideals that constantly undermine themselves, quiet dreams that turn into nightmares. The frustrations of the material world, the exasperations of consciousness drive the audience to the media, the media in their desire to maximize audience market bad news' (Young, 1981: 249). There is a complex relation between the social-control and audience functions of the news media. There is a pull towards images of order and consensus on the one hand, to smooth over the social, economic, political, and cultural contradictions and the anxieties they create with the public. On the other hand they have to play to the 'accommodative culture' (ibid) of the audience, who are drawn to bad news because it articulates with their anxieties over societal contradictions, social conflicts, crisis, the unpredictable, and the feeling of coming apart. A society which is oriented to material consumption, equality administration, and public knowledge is impelled to produce bad news.

NEWS AS AN AGENCY OF SOCIAL CONTROL

Historically it was feared that the news media had a destabilizing effect that had to be brought under control. This belief persists to a lesser degree, especially among certain academics and moral entrepreneurs who believe that bad news causes bad behaviour. In the contemporary era an alternative view is that the news media are an agency of social stability. Bad news provides good lessons about collective values and identity. Beyond this educational value news organizations are more directly involved in defining and responding to deviance. They scrutinize and report on the activities of official control agencies, and in the process become part of the control process. They participate in the biases of policing authorities, and augment their power to sanction both positively and negatively through the definition of risk. In doing so they contribute to particular visions and versions of social organization. '[E]ach social arrangement elevates some risks to a high peak and depresses others below sight. This cultural bias is integral to social organization. Risk taking and risk aversion, shared confidence and shared fears, are part of the dialogue on how to organize social relations. For to organize means to organize some things *in* and other things *out* ... We choose the risks in the same package as we choose our social institutions. Since an individual cannot look in all directions at once, social life demands organization of bias' (Douglas and Wildavsky, 1983: 8).

News-media participation in the control of social developments and conflicts occurs both at the symbolic level of media messages and at the instrumental level of the media institution. At the symbolic level, news messages can function as organizers of public opinion, constructing particular realities and nihilating or ignoring others. In turn news messages at the symbolic level can affect the priorities of the organizations involved and place limits on their actions. Thus there is an important sense in which news-media symbols have an instrumental effect. In spanning spheres of reality, symbols 'tangibly impose themselves upon everyday life in their capacity to inspire or to give meaning to individual or collective activity, to delegitimate other activity, and to bring to bear the force of social control. In a word, symbols and symbol

systems provide an important ordering impulse to social affairs and to collective views of the world' (Wuthnow et al, 1984: 37). As with a job description, written law, or administrative rule, news texts are misread if they
are treated only as an account of an event, process, or state of affairs. Their
'organizational force is in part achieved precisely because [they do] not describe any particular ... process but enter into a variety of settings and order
the relations among them' (Smith, 1984: 15). This point relates to the more
general one that language, written or spoken, is not only a means of description
but also a medium of social practice. For example, as Austin has observed,
the words used in the marriage ceremony are part of that ceremony, not a
description of it.

News organizations also have instrumental social-control effects on the
organizations they report on through their reporters' ongoing relations with
regular sources. Reporters have physical and social space at their regular
sources' work place, and develop permanent relations with them. These relations mean that journalists are an everyday fact of the organization's existence, and become an instrument of social control within the organization.
This is not simply a matter of the journalist imposing himself on key informants
within the source bureaucracy, but a situation of mutual interdependence, and
sometimes particular initiative by sources to use the journalist as a conduit
pipe. Beat reporters in particular are pressured by their sources to participate
directly. Participation is encouraged in exchange for information, scoops,
status, or other rewards; because journalists take on the working ideology of
their sources; or simply because it makes the job more interesting. Participation varies by beat; for example, it is most likely on a political beat (Dunn,
1969) or police beat (Chibnall, 1977; Fishman, 1980) and much less likely
on a court beat (Stanga, 1971; Drechsel, 1983).

Symbolically, and instrumentally through symbols and ongoing social
relations, the news media enact their organizational environment and effect
social control there. In the process they are subject to symbolic, symbolic-
instrumental, and instrumental controls through social transactions with the
source organizations they report on. As news organizations watch, they too
are watched. 'The environment that knows it is being watched is thereby
rearranged and gives off different raw data than if it were blind. Under these
conditions it is obvious that the organization sees much of itself in the data
collection effort' (Weick, 1979: 168). News discourse is reproduced, dramatically presenting the control rituals and myths of the organizational environment, and helping to create that environment. News discourse self-
perpetuates in continuous dialectic with the organizations reported on. 'The
consequence of news is more news' (Fishman, 1980: 11). News organizations
accomplish 'discursive penetration' into the source organizations they report
on, but they are in turn penetrated in a 'dialectic of control' (cf Giddens,
1979: 6).

These processes are not equal among all organizations in the environment. We have already considered that news organizations gravitate to state or official bureaucracies more than those in the private corporate sector. They also tend to report routinely and regularly on large organizations. This may be the case because large organizations are more accessible generally. Just as 'the larger the organization within a population of organizations, the more accessible it is to law enforcement' (Reiss, 1983: 86), so it is more accessible to journalists. In turn, realizing this, large organizations are likely to develop specialized units and personnel to deal with the news media so that they provide a regular menu of appropriately tailored newsworthy material for reporters to pick up. The result is involvement with a few large public bureaucracies and their social-control efforts.

There seems to be little doubt that journalists sometimes act intentionally to affect social-control processes in the organizations they report on. This is not surprising if we respect that 'journalism is a practical discipline; its end or *telos* is action, not theoretical knowledge' (Phillips, 1977: 73). Journalists think it is a legitimate role to put right what they see as wrongs, or at least to goad official bureaucracies into doing the same. As Phillips (ibid: 66–7) reports in her survey of journalists' conceptions of their work, 'journalists qua journalists do political work. In the main they recognize this. For instance, 85% of the journalists (n = 157) polled believed that they had written or supervised at least one story which had public policy impact. Further, 83% (n = 162) agreed that "the news media are a powerful force in the community".'

Journalists' belief in their social-control impact is revealed by their decisions not to report. Tumber (1982: 25–6) reports that British television crews covering the urban riots of 1981 had as a 'prime concern' 'the effect that the presence of a camera can have on a situation,' and there were many instances in which this led to decisions not to report. For example, the idea of doing a television piece on Scotland, where there was no similar trouble, was dropped because it 'was regarded as provocative.' The news media in Toronto have a general consensus not to report suicides in the city unless it involves a particular prominent figure or unusual circumstance. Based on a belief that reporting will have the effect of provoking imitation among persons prone to suicide, the news media co-operate with concerned sources such as the Toronto Transit Commission, whose subway lines are interrupted by suicides daily.

While recognizing the active involvement of journalists and sources in processes of social control, it is also necessary to appreciate that some social-control effects may not be intended or anticipated by the authors of a text. A text produced by a journalist and his sources in one circumstance of social and cultural organization may have quite a different impact than intended or anticipated because it enters into new circumstances of social and cultural organization. Indeed, most often the author and his source-informants probably cannot even foresee the ramifications of the text.

One of the main tasks of the study of the text, or indeed cultural products of any kind, must be precisely to examine the divergences which can become instituted between the circumstances of their production, and the meanings sustained by their subsequent escape from the horizons of their creator or creators. These meanings are never 'contained' in the text as such, but are enmeshed in the flux of social life in the same way as its initial production was. Consideration of the 'autonomy' of the text, or the escape of its meaning from what its author originally meant, helps reunite problems of textual interpretation with broader issues of social theory. For in the enactment of social practices more generally, the consequences of actions chronically escape their initiators' intentions in processes of objectification. (Giddens, 1979: 49)

Furthermore, the provision of information by source organizations may often have a less negative consequence than there being no information at all. Without public information, rumour can proliferate and panic responses can run rampant. News-media texts can often dispel rumour and marshall reasoned responses to problems, so that their social-control effect ends up being more beneficial to the organizations reported on than if there had been no reports at all.

With these conditions and qualifications of social-control effects in mind, we can turn to the research literature which indicates that the news media regularly and routinely report on deviance and control in a manner that has social-control effects. This is so in relation to the reporting of individual incidents or cases; reporting on the enforcement activities of regular sources; the reporting of various social movements; and general reporting on social problems, risks, and dangers.

The reporting of crime incidents can have social-control effects. Sumner (1982: 23–4) argues that the coverage of the Toxteth riots in the British national press converged on the need to equip the police with the 'latest' riot gear. Tumber (1982: 35–7) shows the same approach was taken in television coverage. The equipment has since been acquired and deployed in other circumstances, such as the miners' strike of 1984 and 1985. As Sumner (1982: 24) argues, to the extent that the media helped to generate this police 'need' in the public culture, 'the whole thesis that the growth of a mass-circulation press has meant the reduction of the political propaganda role of the press must be re-examined.'

In relation to law-enforcement agencies too, it is often 'critical events' of deviance that lead to new social-control initiatives. For example, Sherman (1983) argues that reforms to control and reduce use of guns by police officers often depend on a dramatic 'critical event' of wrongdoing which the local news media help to determine. This is also the case regarding police corruption more generally (Burnham, 1976; McDonald Commission, 1981; Punch, 1985;

Sherman, 1978;) which requires sustained publicity over long periods as 'a necessary condition for unfreezing the patterns of organizational behavior' (Sherman, 1983: 123).

Court reporting on routine criminal cases has also been shown to influence the cases reported on, and of course there is a substantial body of law of 'contempt of court' designed precisely to control this possibility (Robertson, 1981). Stanga (1971) reports that transactions among journalists, prosecutors, and police were influential in some cases regarding decisions to charge accused persons.

The vulnerability of some source bureaucracies to policing efforts by the news media encourages them to develop elaborate mechanisms to control the message. As Graber (1980: 71) shows in her study of the quality Chicago *Tribune* newspaper, when causes of crime are reported, by far the most frequent attribution is to deficiencies in the criminal justice system (37.1 per cent), followed by political-system deficiencies (20.1 per cent). Source bureaucracies that are the subjects of this respond by co-operative information control. Chibnall (1977) shows how the Metropolitan Police of London came to appreciate the strategic advantages of controlled co-operation after being stung by a series of corruption scandals (see also Jefferson and Grimshaw, 1984). Perhaps the extreme example is provided by the military and Royal Ulster Constabulary (RUC) in Northern Ireland, whose arsenal is not limited to firearm machinery but also a powerful publicity machinery. In early 1976 'the army had over forty press officers in Ulster with a back-up staff of over 100, while the RUC had twelve full-time press officers. Beyond these the Government had another twenty civil servants briefed to deal with the media' (ibid: 177).

Political movements have also been shown to have their activities shaped fundamentally by the news media. Gitlin (1980) has documented how news organizations influenced the political developments of the Students for a Democratic Society movement, and how members of the movement in turn acted upon the public stage constructed for the purpose. He also shows how routine news procedures occasionally amplify deviance to the point that news managers are forced to step in for political purposes to alter the standard frame (ibid: 210ff). This fact that deviance often appears functional to political movements to gain publicity is frequently lost in research which examines apparent unidirectional effects from news coverage to group action. For example, Mazur (1982) draws a parallel with imitation of suicides and argues that when there is news-media attention to nuclear-power issues there is an increase in bomb threats to nuclear-power facilities. He does not emphasize the possibility that bomb threats may be a way for a protest group to sustain publicity or just continue to register the fact of public protest. Perhaps at the extreme of what we are indicating here is the involvement of a news organization in a political movement so that they can have a scoop or inside story. Thus, Toronto radio station CFTR was implicated in a coup attempt on Dominica, apparently in connection with the Ku Klux Klan and criminal 'mobsters' (Moon, 1981). The station knew of the coup plans but failed to inform authorities in the hope of obtaining a 'scoop' once it happened.

On a more everyday basis, news organizations are active in constituting what are social problems and what should be done about them. They do so by focusing upon a few dramatic incidents of criminal victimization of the elderly (Fishman, 1978), children (Ng, 1982; Geach, 1982), or women (Voumvakis and Ericson, 1984) to manufacture a problem in a local community. They do so by ignoring, or selecting stereotypical features of, minority groups, such as women (Butcher et al, 1981; Tuchman, 1981a) the mentally ill (Nunnally, 1981; Fleming, 1983), racial minorities (Hartmann and Husband, 1981), and homosexuals (Pearce, 1981). They do so by focusing upon a particular habit of the populace, such as the use of illicit drugs (Young, 1974).

As an agency of social control, news organizations are bound to report on the social-control efforts of other organizations. In the process they are bound to be part of those same social-control efforts. In the result they are bound to have social-control effects. We have developed a major research program to address these social-control aspects of the reporting process, the products it produces, and its effects upon the source organizations involved. We now turn to an examination of the research questions raised by our discussion to this point, and to the research strategies we have devised to address these questions.

3

Research Approaches

Research Questions and Methodological Requirements

RESEARCH QUESTIONS

Our discussion of how news is organized, of how news-as-knowledge is focused on aspects of deviance and control, and of how the media institution is central to the knowledge society has raised basic issues, concepts, and questions. However, theorizing about these matters can only be advanced through sustained empirical inquiry that is interpretive and critical in approach (Bernstein, 1978; Giddens, 1984).

Our central concerns are how news of deviance and control is produced; how the organization of production articulates with the product; and how the news product plays back into the organizations that report and are reported on. How do sources and journalists as newsmakers in the knowledge society reproduce culture? What is their relation to the texts they produce ('intentionality')? How do the parts of a news text relate to each other ('coherence')? How does a news text relate to other culturally associated texts ('intertextuality')? How do news products relate to other realities ('reference')? (cf Geertz, 1983: 32).

Our discussion in chapters 1 and 2 contains seven major prescriptions for research: 1 / work with a broad conception of deviance and control news; 2 / incorporate all the stages in the news process; 3 / get inside news organizations; 4 / get inside source organizations; 5 / examine the nature of knowledge as produced and conveyed; 6 / consider news-media variation in production and product; 7 / consider news-organization variation in production and product. We shall briefly summarize these considerations and then state the methodological requirements for a research program that can address them adequately.

Deviance and Control. Studying the production and products of deviance and control news is a fruitful vehicle for understanding how cultural workers reproduce order in the knowledge society. Researching deviance and control news in the broadest sense helps us to understand news workers, assumptions about organizational order, social order, and processes of social change. It reveals how reporters work in concert with others whose job it is to police organizational life, symbolically constructing the moral boundaries of stability as well as the reform politics of change. It makes evident how the organizational cultures of reporters and sources intersect to accomplish particular interests in the name of objectivity, neutrality, and balance. In the process the relation between organizational cultures and dominant cultures is addressed. There is nothing like operating conceptions of good and bad to reveal the beliefs, values, and understandings which underlie representations of reality.

News Process Stages. Research must respect the entire news process. The central research question in this respect is the extent to which one can speak of a somewhat discrete process from occurrence, to news event, to news product, to the reception of news by the news organizations and source organizations concerned. Is it a discrete communication process, or are there several different processes along the way, with each one requiring explanation in its own terms because it is associated with a unique set of organizational activities?

This question is a matter for empirical inquiry. Existing wisdom suggests, 'It is relatively rare for original source, mass communicator, and audience member to be united and co-operating in the same activity with a common perception of it at the same time or in a connected sequence' (McQuail and Windahl, 1981: 8). Any text written within an organization is a 'situated production,' 'the concrete medium and outcome' of its work activities (Giddens, 1979: 40–4). The author of the text draws upon the tacit knowledge of his experience to construct the text, especially what sort of account is required to achieve accountability with the 'audience' (organizational superior, client, regulating agency, etc.) to whom it is directed. The author must be studied in this connection, for he as the subject becomes bound up in the text as object (ibid, 1979: 43). This is not a matter of considering the author's personal characteristics and competence alone, but of considering how the individual author's knowledge and practices in producing texts are a property of the organizational relations in which he finds himself.

Furthermore, once a text is produced, whatever meaning it had to the author, or others immediately involved in the account, can 'escape' them as the text is interpreted and used within other contexts of organizational relations. As the text becomes objective knowledge, it is interpreted and used by others in a manner which is external to, and independent of, its creators

(Popper, 1972). Its transformation as objective knowledge, impacting on other persons and organizations, may have been unintended or unanticipated by the author. Additionally, the use of the objective knowledge in the new organizational context may ultimately affect the original author, forcing him to give it new interpretations and to incorporate it for use in further accounts, and so on.

In sum, it seems likely that the social and cultural organization of the reporting process varies at each stage. A particular constellation of social and cultural organization will affect what source activities are considered legitimate news events in the first place; another constellation affects what reporters attend to, choose, produce, and publish; and, yet another constellation relates to what published news items sources and reporters choose from and make further use of within their respective organizations.

Inside News Organizations. Examination of how news texts are situated products of organizational relations, and yet escape authors at successive stages, necessarily entails detailed scrutiny of practices inside news organizations. To what extent do internal social and cultural aspects influence reporters and the directions their news organization takes? To what extent are the news texts produced by journalists, or by their colleagues in the same news organization, used to construct interpretations and meanings about their organization? To what extent are the texts of other news organizations used by journalists to construct meanings and interpretations about their own work and news organization? Other questions flow from these considerations. To what extent and how is competition in the production of news a matter of what is happening among members of a particular news organization? To what extent and how is competition a matter internal to the practice of journalism? As a consequence, to what extent and how does the news constitute knowledge that is essentially internal to the news-media institution? This is the central focus of the research reported in parts II and III of this book.

Inside Source Organizations. The same questions need to be asked of members of source organizations who are involved in the situated production of occurrences which become news events, and whose texts also escape them in the news-reporting process. In particular, what social and cultural processes in their organizations lead them to transform occurrences into news events? What are their strategies and tactics to draw reporter attention to their events and to ensure prominent and favourable publication? What is the influence of news texts in constructing interpretations and meanings within their own organization? How are news texts interpreted and used as a vehicle for further contact and influence with news organizations (e.g., provision of additional information, letters to the editor, efforts at remedy for unreasonable coverage).

(Source organizations are the central focus of a forthcoming companion volume [Ericson et al, forthcoming a].)

Nature of Knowledge. Process and product must both be understood to appreciate the nature of news as knowledge. On the level of process, inquiry must be made into the minutiae of everyday transactions. '[B]y examining routine procedures, it is possible to develop an account of the material and sources used regularly in media production. Such an account is necessary to any sociological analysis of the type of knowledge and culture the media convey' (Elliott, 1979: 159). These transactions bear the imprint of the organizational structures and systems within which news as knowledge is reproduced; indeed, it is these organizational elements which permit newsmakers to define reality in their particular symbolic form.

In Geertz's (1983: chap. 7) terms, the nature of news as knowledge requires 'an ethnography of modern thought.' Thinking must be regarded as a social process as well as an individual one, in which people actively manipulate cultural forms to sustain their activities. An ethnography of thought requires a description of the contexts in which the thought, or knowledge in use, makes sense (ibid: 152; see also Holy and Stuchlik, 1983: chap. 3). The study of news production seems particularly suited to the task because news workers span most spheres of organized life and most aspects of the common sense. News workers' practices and the knowledge associated with them display the very elements which Geertz (1983: 153) recommends should be attended to in an ethnography of thought: 'the representation of authority, the marking of boundaries, the rhetoric of persuasion, the expression of commitment, and the registering of dissent.' More generally, the work of news sources and journalists seems particularly suited to address central theoretical questions about the production of knowledge. These questions focus on 'translation, how meaning gets moved, or does not, reasonably intact from one sort of discourse to the next; about intersubjectivity, how particular individuals come to conceive, or do not, reasonably similar things; about how frames change ... how thought provinces are demarcated ... how thought norms are maintained, thought models acquired, thought labor divided. The ethnography of thinking, like any other sort of ethnography ... is an attempt not to exalt diversity but to take it seriously as itself an object of analytic description and interpretive reflection' (ibid: 154).

The news product has structured features which relate to the news system and to structural resources. Employing Giddens' (1984) conceptual scheme, structure consists of the rules and resources, 'organized as properties of social systems' which knowledgeable actors use in social interaction. ' ''Structure'' can be conceptualized abstractly as two aspects of rules – normative elements and codes of signification. Resources are also of two kinds: authoritative resources, which derive from the co-ordination of the activity of human agents, and allocative resources, which stem from the control of material products or of aspects of the material world' (Giddens, 1984: xxxi). Structure is actually present only when the rules and resources are used. It is a medium and outcome of social practice, and can be enabling or constraining on parties involved in a transaction. Social systems are regularized or recurrent practices, 'reproduced across time and space: power in social systems can thus be treated as involving reproduced relations of autonomy and dependence in social relations' (Giddens, 1982: 39).

A key task for social analysis is to study the 'structuration of social systems.' Methodologically, this entails examining the choices social actors make, do not make, or overlook as they constitute the social system in question. An examination of the full range of the actors' transactions can benefit from both quantitative and qualitative analysis. The social analyst can depict the system by quantifying the outcome of a series of individual choices, thus providing a description of the system which can then be explained in terms of the individual choices of which the statistical pattern is the outcome. For example, one could examine how a newsroom assignment editor creates and participates in a system for assigning reporters to stories (see chapter 6). His choices on a large number of stories in terms of their origin, topics, whether an assignment was made, who was assigned, and the outcome, can be systematically portrayed by statistics, and the patterns produced can be explained by similar detailed attention to the situated context of individual choices that contributed to the pattern.

The overall news product can also be used to descriptively display the system which is structured by news workers. For example, in relation to news of deviance and control, many of the aspects of interest to us can be described statistically through systematic content analysis. What topics of deviance are published or broadcast? What topics of social control are published or broadcast? Who is involved as sources? In what news formats are they represented? Do these vary by different news media? Do these vary by different news organizations within a medium? Having shown the patterns in this respect, the analyst can explain them in terms of the processes of production he has captured via observation, interviewing, and scrutiny of other organizational texts (documents, memos, manuals, etc.).

News-Media Variation. The question of whether all news media are relatively similar in their practices of knowledge production and in the knowledge conveyed is one which is central in the reserch literature. Many persons have called for research comparing media. For example, Fishman cautions that his study of newspapers is limited: 'It remains an open question just how general my findings are with respect to news produced through other forms of mass media (notably television and radio) and news produced outside American society' (1980: 19). On the specific topic of crime news, Garofalo (1981) stresses the need for media comparisons.

Those who have compared media vary in the extent to which they see differences. This variance of course depends on what they have looked for. Those who have studied ethnographically the production process have generally argued that there is little difference across media. This is the impression given, for example, by Tuchman (1978) in her studies of newspapers and television, and the finding of Schlesinger (1978) in his studies of BBC radio and television. Hirsch (1977) goes to the extent of criticizing those who emphasize differences in print and broadcast news, asserting that there are a number of organizational similarities across media. However, some of those who have engaged in systematic analysis of news content have shown media differences. In the area of industrial news, the Glasgow University Media Group (GUMG) has demonstrated alternative priorities and treatments in British national newspapers compared to British national television (1976: chap. 5). In the area of crime news, Sheley and Ashkins (1981) and Graber (1980) have shown divergence in television and newspaper coverage.

News-Organization Variation. An attendant series of research questions concern how news organizations within a medium, or across media, vary. Again research is divergent in this area, and there has been too little research to enunciate general trends. Are any two organizations within a medium more similar in process and product than any two organizations in different media? Or, are two organizations in different media that have a similar orientation and audiences (for example, a quality newspaper and a quality radio station) likely to be more similar to each other than two organizations in the same medium that have a different orientation and audiences (for example, a quality newspaper and a popular newspaper)?

Again, the degree of convergence or divergence is likely to be related to the questions asked. We wish to employ a range of methodologies in relation to a large number of research questions on news-organization similarities or differences in order to present a more complete picture than has been available until now. We now turn to a more specific consideration of the methodological requirements to address the many research questions we have raised in this section.

METHODOLOGICAL REQUIREMENTS

In chapters 1 and 2 we emphasized the limitations of any one way of knowing. The only way to deal with this fact is to employ multiple ways of knowing about the matters under consideration. A combination of social-science research techniques, including observation, interviewing, scrutiny of organizational documents, and systematic analysis of organizational products, is a requirement for a full view of the news-media institution.

There has been a traditional division between those in the humanities, who study individual texts, and those in the social sciences, who study processes of text creation. 'The study of inscriptions is severed from the study of inscribing, the study of fixed meaning is severed from the study of the social processes that fix it. The result is a double narrowness. Not only is the extension of text analysis to nonwritten materials blocked, but so is the application of sociological analysis to written ones' (Geertz, 1983: 32). As argued previously, knowledge can be broadened by appreciating that textual production and texts themselves are part of continuing social processes, in which texts feed back into the production of further texts, and so on. A full range of methodologies are required to capture this process/product relation, including those associated with the techniques of ethnography and those associated with the techniques of content analysis.

Ethnographic approaches which employ observation, interviewing, and document-analysis techniques are essential for our purposes. Whether it is across the world or around the corner, the social scientist is better equipped to convey understanding of his subject matter if he has been immersed in the world of which it is a part. As Runciman (1983: 296–7) asks, 'How can the armchair sociologist presume to pronounce on the experience of people to whom he has never spoken, in whose institutions and practices he has never played a part, and whose manners and mores are far removed from his own?' While ethnographic approaches are no guarantee that understanding will be forthcoming, and while other methods can add to their richness, they are a necessary part of any organizational or institutional analysis.

Nevertheless, some of the more influential cultural analyses of the news media have been presumptuous enough not to include ethnographies of the social relations of production (e.g., Hall et al, 1978; for a critique in this regard, see Sumner, 1981). Some researchers were excluded from ethnographic research by the news organizations they sought to scrutinize, and were therefore left to undertake content analyses exclusively (e.g., GUMG, 1976, 1980, 1982). They at least appreciate the point that ethnographic approaches are a particularly important part of research on the news, and of cultural studies more generally (GUMG, 1980: 407–10).

Ethnographic methods are especially suited to recording 'the cultural' at the level of human activity, allowing 'a sensitivity to meanings and values as well as an ability to represent and interpret symbolic articulations, practices, and forms of cultural production' (Willis, 1981: 3). Indeed, ethnographic methods are essential if we accept that the core concerns of cultural studies compared to behavioural studies are understanding rather than explanation;

the interpretion of significance rather than underlying causal forces; diagnosis rather than prediction; and descent into the empirical world rather than ascent to abstract empiricism and high theory (Carey, 1979: 418–19).

Sociological explanation is best served by quasi-experimental reasoning rather than either deductive-nomological or inductive-statistical reasoning. It is not the empirically common that is important, but whether a phenomenon is revealing about the processes which underlie it, and whether there are systematic relations among diverse phenomena. The search for such phenomena, and for other diverse phenomena that might relate to them, is enhanced by the open methodologies of ethnography more than the closed methodologies of fixed-choice instruments which demand regularities even if they are not there. The ethnographer seeks knowledge about how knowledge is socially distributed in the organization he studies, and then seeks out knowledgeable informants in key organizational positions to begin mapping their social relations of production. At least until a very detailed map has been charted, notions of randomness are not relevant to this process.

Immersion in the organizational culture of one's subjects is also an aid to understanding data of different kinds. Unless the researcher has a fairly extensive grasp of the background knowledge which his subjects have to give meaning to their particular utterances, pieces of organizational 'paper,' and so on, he will be unable to understand his bits of data and how they represent notions held by his subjects (cf Holy and Stucklik, 1983: 56–60). Moreover, once the researcher has acquired such knowledge he can make better sense of data, such as formal interview materials, which are obtained in conditions somewhat removed from the actual setting.

The development of various kinds of data allows them to be put alongside one another for comparison, so that better sense can be made of them than would have been possible with one isolated type of data (cf Weick, 1983: 16). It is of course necessary to keep different types of data distinct, to exercise caution with regard to the 'seeing is believing' (observed data) and 'believing is seeing' (what subjects' present, usually verbally) problems that plague ethnographies (Van Maanen, 1979; Holy and Stuchlik, 1983: chap. 2). However, the fact of having been in the world under study to obtain detailed background knowledge, and the derivation of different types of data through different methods to be compared and contrasted with one another, is the best guarantee of veracity and accuracy known to us.

Researchers 'in organizational communication ... have spent very little time observing and describing the communicative activities of organizational members' (Trujillo, 1983: 73). The ethnographic approaches are the only means of acquiring knowledge in this regard. Moreover, they are especially suited to the study of interorganizational processes since these are usually dependent upon a small number of trusting, reciprocal relations between people strategically placed in their respective organizations. In the case of journalists, the nature of their information source networks and elements of negotiation and reciprocity with sources cannot be gleaned from analysis of news content. For example, court clerks are key informants on the court beat but they are rarely if ever cited in news stories (Drechsel, 1983: 50).

Ethnography is also *the* means for acquiring knowledge about what it is like to be a member of the organization under study. 'The ethnographer becomes part of the situation being studied in order to feel what it is like for the people in that situation' (Sandy, 1979: 527). This is what Runciman terms 'tertiary understanding,' and it is this type of understanding which is partic- ularly needed in the study of cultural production and products (Runciman, 1983: 183–4).

The ethnographer is also well situated to suspend belief in what his subjects take as common place and common sense, and to analyse these common elements as functions of the ideological paradigms his subjects bring to bear on the objects of their world. He can examine at first hand the relation between the observing ideologies of his subjects and the observed appearances of their objects, a necessary step towards appreciation of the ideological effects under study.

While news-media content can be analysed to reveal the conventions of published or broadcast communications, these are not the conventions em- ployed by newsmakers in producing content. Some aspects of newsmakers' orientations can be gleaned from content, but the inferences will be weak without knowledge of the actual methods and activities of newsmakers. Con- tent analysis reveals nothing about critical decisions to report on something: about assignment editors who decide not to give coverage; about sources who decide not to send a release to a news organization, or not to respond to requests for interviews, or to give only selected information; about reporters who decide not to contact particular sources, to abandon a story, to work at making a non-newsworthy event into a newsworthy one, to change an angle; about desk editors who alter a story, incorporate wire material into it, make it into a minor item; about legal advisers who recommend alterations or no publication; and so on. Bias is built into these everyday decisions and eth- nographic methods are best suited to ascertaining the nature and direction of this bias.

Exclusive reliance on content analysis yields a picture of news work as being much more structured and rational than it actually is. Moreover, the rationality presented through aggregate data is certainly not that which informs news workers as they work on a given story. Content analysis is ultimately directed at the communicators' consciousness and intentions, but inferences from content are unsuitable for understanding consciousness and intentions. Quantitative content analysis consists of the counting of appearances, and correlating these, often without any theory about the significance of what is being counted (Sumner, 1979). One way of developing a theory of significance, and therefore of making content studies more than just speculation about repetition, is to examine at first hand the relations among journalists and sources at different levels in various source organizations and news organizations, and working with different media.

Related to the practices of newsmaking, both qualitative and systematic quantitative content analyses are of significance, indeed necessary for an adequate analysis of the news-media institution. Aggregate data on content do show systematically what is published and broadcast and what is not. For example, these data might show that most violent crime reported is 'street crime,' rather than domestic violence, the violence on workers resulting from unsafe working conditions, or the violence on citizens caused by environmental pollution. The reasons for this can then be pursued ethnographically in terms of the social relations of cultural production, for example, is it related to what material journalists are fed routinely from the police and other regular sources? is it related to the values and ideology of journalists and their regular or more influential sources, regarding what is the greatest source of actual risk or public fear?

In terms of our central focus on how the news media report on and contribute to organizational life through accounts of deviance and control, systematic content analysis can be most revealing. By systematically indicating who are the authorized knowers, what organizations they represent, and what are their preferred problems of deviance and their preferred control remedies, a great deal can be made evident about the nature of news ideology and the media institution. As Hirsch (1977: 35–6) observes, content studies 'afford a rare opportunity for researchers to link occupational, organizational and institutional nexes and cross-pressures.' Drechsel (1983: 142) has stated as a future research priority the need for quantitative analysis of deviance and control news content that focuses upon who the sources are and what type of information is attributed to them. (This issue is the central focus of the research reported in a forthcoming companion volume [Ericson et al, forthcoming b].)

Content analysis offers a way of knowing that adds to our knowledge of the process/product relation. It is a necessary component of research on this relation although it is very limited in what it can reveal about the social relations of production. At best, analysis of what does not get presented can suggest aspects of the scheme of conceptualization with which information is presented; and, the uses of authorized knowers and organizations in relation to topics within their command suggests the news media's main frames, and where the ethnographer might search to learn the conventions by which they are framed.

The Research Program

We have undertaken a series of empirical studies on news of deviance and control. In the remainder of this book we report on ethnographic studies of print and broadcast news organizations. In a forthcoming companion volume (Ericson et al, forthcoming a) we present comparative ethnographies of court, police, and legislature news beats; a study of news sources based on interviews; and, an observational and content study of the letters to the editor decision-making process. The primary focus in this forthcoming volume is newsmaking from the perspective of regular sources. We document variation in sources' particular requirements for news, and how they organize to deal with the news media in accordance with their requirements. We also underscore the power of the news media. This is revealed in particular by the fact that sources think that remedies for unreasonable coverage are minimal or nonexistent; and, by the fact that the letters to the editors columns, which appear as an opening for a range of opinion, are effectively closed because criteria for acceptance and editing are the same as those employed by editors for other sections of the newspaper. In another forthcoming companion volume (Ericson et al, forthcoming b) we report a large survey of news content. We document how news varies by media (newspapers, television, and radio), orientation (popular and quality), topics of deviance and control, sources cited, organizational settings for stories, and the types of knowledge conveyed. Aggregate patterns in content are analysed with the knowledge gained from the ethnographies presented in the other volumes.

NEWS-ORGANIZATION ETHNOGRAPHIES

The components of the research program reported here were designed to examine the news process from inside out. We sought an understanding of how news is produced by reporters and editors working on assignment from city desks. We present initially a brief overview of the news organizations studied, and then describe salient aspects of the research process.

The Organizations Studied. In-depth ethnographies conducted on a regular basis over several months in 1982 and 1983 were based at the Toronto *Globe and Mail* newspaper and the CBLT television station. This study was supplemented by observation of, and interviews with, journalists from a large number of other Toronto news organizations on a less regular and systematic basis. Since our main sources of data for the following chapters are the *Globe and*

Mail and CBLT, we will provide an overview of these organizations and their place within the local news-media context.

The *Globe and Mail* is one of three large circulation newspapers in Toronto, along with the *Star* and the *Sun*. In 1981 the *Globe and Mail* had 1,100 employees, the *Star* 2,300, and the *Sun* 500. In 1981, among the 26 leading newspapers in Canada, the *Globe and Mail* ranked second in total readership over the course of a week, third in terms of being read 'most often,' and fourth in terms of the number of issues read during a week. The Toronto *Star* ranked first in all of these categories, and the *Sun* fourth in readership, third in being read 'most often,' and second in terms of the number of issues read during the week (Royal Commission on Newspapers [RCN], 1981a: 69). In 1980 the *Globe and Mail* weekday (Monday-Friday) circulation was 287,000, 49 per cent of which was in the immediate Toronto area. The *Globe and Mail* is also a national newspaper, now printed in several cities across the country with the aid of a satellite system, and thus has substantial circulation elsewhere. The Toronto *Star* circulation was 478,000, 79 per cent of which was in the immediate Toronto area; and, the *Sun* had a circulation of 224,000, 85 per cent of which was in the immediate Toronto area. The *Globe and Mail* had 20 per cent of the Toronto area market, the *Sun* 27 per cent, and the Toronto *Star* 53 per cent (RCN, 1981f: 75). The *Globe and Mail* had the largest amount of news space in proportion to advertising space, about 45 per cent, compared to the Toronto *Star* and the *Sun* which each had about 30 per cent (ibid: 76–8).

The *Globe and Mail* is part of the Thomson chain. Along with Southam, Thomson is one of the two large newspaper chains in Canada. The Toronto *Sun* is in a small chain of *Sun* newspapers which started in Toronto, but has since emerged in a few other Canadian cities and expanded into the United States. It is also a partner in a wire service. The Toronto *Star* has no chain affiliation, but is part of the Torstar company which has purchased a number of suburban newspapers in the Toronto area and has other holdings in the culture industry, such as the Harlequin Enterprises Limited, publishers of the romance novel series.

According to the Royal Commission on Newspapers (1981e), the *Globe and Mail* is one of only three or four newspapers which are agenda-setters nationally, the others being the Toronto *Star*, *Le Devoir*, and *La Presse*. It has an élite readership, meaning that it is in perpetual dialogue with the authorized knowers who are regularly cited as sources. Survey research involving interviews with top-level decision-makers regarding news media as sources of information and influence, indicates clearly that the *Globe and Mail* is number one (ibid: 19). The percentage of various élites reporting regular readership of the *Globe and Mail* include federal civil service 98 per cent, media 91 per cent, business 89 per cent, federal parliament 80 per cent, provincial civil services 74 per cent, city councils 73 per cent, law 70 per cent, union leaders 64 per cent, provincial legislatures 60 per cent, and city civil services 56 per cent (RCN, 1981e: 20). It is the prime source of guidance for other news organizations regarding their own priorities, coverage, and comment, and has substantial effect on the priorities of leading wire services such as the Canadian Press agency. It is also the newspaper cited most frequently in federal-government clipping services for their ministries (ibid).

The *Globe and Mail* is explicitly directed at its élite government, business, and professional audiences rather than a mass market. At the opposite end of the spectrum is the Toronto *Sun*, which is directed at popular tastes for lively entertainment and which has been described as the closest thing to television in print. The Toronto *Star* is the only major daily newspaper in the Toronto market which still pursues the mass market.

A senior executive of the *Globe and Mail* whom we interviewed indicated that mass-circulation newspapers are vulnerable, because of fragmentation of interests in the knowledge society, and the specialized information outlets demanded by the diversity of interests. He stated that the *Globe and Mail* had decided to pursue its specialized readership nationally rather than to focus exclusively on competition within the Toronto mass market. Most of the readership buy the *Globe and Mail* as a specialized publication in addition to mass-market and popular newspapers.

> I think, there's no doubt that what has been happening in the information mar-
> ket is that it has been fragmenting and fragmenting and fragmenting again …
> We had two ways to go. We could say, all right, we're going to try and ex-
> pand in the Metropolitan Toronto market and to do that we would have to
> substantially change the nature of the paper. Or, we could recognize that we
> already have a relatively narrow band of people and say let's try and get more
> of the same kind of people in more places instead of saying let's try and get a
> lot more different people in the same place. We decided to try and get more of
> the same kind of people in different centres all across Canada and we went
> national … We went to the national edition without a market survey. We
> thought we knew our audience pretty well and, turns out that we were right,
> they are buying it, circulation has gone up … We have done readership sur-
> veys to see who is reading it … subsequent to starting up the national edition
> and it simply confirmed what we … had thought at the time and that is that
> the people that read the paper have a ferocious appetite for information …
> [O]ur readers, ninety-eight percent of them, also buy a local paper. They buy
> us as a second newspaper.

A former managing editor of the *Globe and Mail*, quoted in a magazine article, defined the newspaper's role in a similar way. In his eyes, the *Globe and Mail* has a special élite audience which makes it comparable to quality newspapers internationally and different from local popular newspapers.

> We're writing for three different audiences. An audience outside Ontario. An audience in Metropolitan Toronto and an audience outside of Metropolitan Toronto in Ontario. And they are three fairly distinct kinds of audiences. But they're all the same kind of people ... We find that the kind of people who want to read us are different from the ones that normally read a local paper, because they want a lot more information on a more international scale than others do. So we tend to end up comparing ourselves with other papers that function at that kind of level, and that would be the New York Times or the London Times or Le Monde or the Wall Street Journal. That's where we make our comparisons. I think it would be an unfair comparison, both to us and to, say, the Calgary Herald, to try to compare the two of us because we're doing two, really quite different, things. (Keillor, 1982: 33)

CBLT is the Toronto affiliate of the Canadian Broadcasting Corporation (CBC). As part of its responsibility to the corporation it operates a newsroom that services not only local news shows, but also the CBC national television-news operations that are based in Toronto. While our focus is on CBLT within the Toronto news-media context, their place within the CBC network is of significance. *Within television*, the CBC is comparable to the *Globe and Mail* in being at the 'quality' end of the spectrum, and in helping to set the agenda for national affairs (RCN, 1981e: 9).

The CBLT newsroom is required to fill several slots during weekdays, but the major show and the one which we focused on was a 6:00–7:00 p.m. program known as 'Newshour.' This show ran for 59.5 minutes, including about 29 minutes of news items as well as sports, weather, and advertising. The second most significant show produced by the CBLT newsroom was 'Newsfinal,' which was 14.5 minutes in duration from 11:00 p.m., with about nine minutes of news followed by weather and sports. The newsroom also serviced a ten-minute newscast at noon on weekdays, two forty-minute news-casts on weekends, and a weekly half-hour show reviewing events in Ontario.

In the Toronto television market, CBLT 'Newshour' competed with three other news shows in the 6:00–7:00 p.m. period: City-TV's 'Citypulse,' CFTO's 'World Beat News' (6:30–7:00 p.m. only), and Global-TV's 'Global News.' On a quality/popular dimension, members of the CBLT newsroom regarded themselves as the quality outlet, and Global the nearest in outlook among the other stations. City was at the other extreme, a popular station that practised 'disco journalism.'

During part of our field-research period at CBLT, their ratings were the highest for the 6:00–7:00 p.m. time period. According to an internal memo of 15 October 1982, referring to summer period ratings in the full coverage area, CBLT had 173,000 viewers, CFTO had 154,000, City 136,900, and Global was a very distant fourth with precise figures unavailable. This memo also noted that '*Newshour* appeals primarily to Adults 50 + with a slight skew to Men over Women. Of the Adults 18 +, 60 per cent are over 50 years. In the general population, Adults 50 + represent approximately 35 per cent of the Adults.' However, when the 6:30–7:00 p.m. time block was considered, the block in which CFTO news was aired, the figures changed dramatically: CFTO had 243,100, CBLT 139,500, and City 117,000 viewers. Another memo, dated 29 October 1982, reads:

GOOD NEWS!!

The ratings for September 20 to October 3rd are out and they show that Monday to Friday on average we have 240,000 viewers. Our high day is Monday – 270,000 people

Tuesday	261,000
Wednesday	264,000
Thursday	218,000
Friday	186,000

(this drop off is traditional and typical of all news programs).

Our back half is not doing so well, and when combined with the first thirty minutes, it drags our hour average down to 194,000. Citypulse hour rate is 182,000. I do not have any figures for Citypulse from 6–6:30. These figures are full coverage audiences, they are published by BBM [Board of Broadcast Measurement]. Global is doing so poorly that BBM only guesses at its share in ratings and does not give total numbers; they are languishing behind Newshour and behind Citypulse. These figures were taken when we had three different lead-ins. It is encouraging to note that our lead-in through the fall sweeps and the spring sweeps will be Three's Company. It, among the three different lead-ins, drew the most people. The figures show that City has a young female audience; ours tends to be an older, male audience.

The importance for ratings of the entertainment shows which precede and follow news shows is a well-known fact of the business (Epstein, 1974). In interview, one of the 'Newshour' producers noted this fact, and said one of the competing stations almost doubled its news show audience figures when it was followed by 'M*A*S*H*.' This producer insisted that an audience survey showed the CBLT audience wanted quality journalism on international, national, and local events (in that order), and that the best way to improve ratings was to improve quality journalism. However, he also indicated that entertainment programming around the show – and even in it – were keys to popularity as measured by the ratings. Hence, two new features were introduced within the show: 'Soap Box,' in which a citizen was given broadcast time to air his views; and 'Choirs,' in which local choir groups sang a song as a nightly feature. He said his hope was that the persons filmed, their relatives, and their friends would watch the show, like it, and decide to continue watching. He compared this technique with the City practice of showing local school and club sports to achieve more audience.

Another producer at CBLT echoed this view, saying he was interested in news, but the news must be packaged in a glittering way so that viewers who have just finished watching Carol Burnett will stay tuned for the news. In noting that 'Newshour' ratings had gone up to 24 per cent of the audience in the previous eighteen months, this producer observed that Kellogg's does not spend most of its money on cornflakes, but rather on the cornflakes box.

A producer stated in interview that CBLT tried to blend 'institutional' news with the 'voice of the people' or vox pop. In this respect, CBLT was a blend of the *Globe and Mail*'s predominant institutional approach and the *Sun*'s predominant vox-pop approach. In the words of this news executive, 'The *Globe* ... is going to spend a lot more time on what's become known in the trade as our institutional news ... where the story isn't people as much as it is rules and documents and technicalities and legalistics. The *Sun* on the other hand is going to be interested in man saves dog ... [W]e are interested in both.' Some reporters with CBLT noted that the institutional emphasis at CBLT had declined with the appointment of a new executive producer, who wanted increasing emphasis on accounts from 'ordinary people' as well as 'official accounts.'

Fieldwork Techniques and Process. The ethnographic fieldwork in news organizations was conducted in 1982 and 1983. It entailed more than 200 researcher days in the field, and a total of about 2,500 hours including the preparation of research notes. We spent 101 days with *Globe and Mail* journalists over a nine-month period, and 86 days with CBLT journalists over a seven-month period. We spent additional days with radio, television, and newspaper reporters from other news organizations, observing their activities and interviewing personnel at various levels. All three authors conducted research in both the *Globe and Mail* and CBLT, as well as with reporters from a number of other news organizations. This system provided three perspectives on each news organization. It allowed the strengths of each researcher to be used to obtain information and insights from journalists which the other two researchers could not glean. On some dimensions it also allowed us to check the accounts of one another.

The basic approach was to ask a reporter if his work on a story or series of stories could be observed. If the reporter agreed, the researcher tried to follow the story to conclusion. With the reporter's permission, copies were made of any newspaper clippings, research materials, news releases, and documents from sources pertaining to the story. Telephone conversations were listened to from the reporter's end, and occasionally on an extension telephone or transmitter. Personal interviews were attended, as well as news conferences, public meetings, courts, public inquiries, political assemblies, political committees, and other settings.

We also examined the work of assignment editors systematically, and observed and interviewed editors and management. The observational study of assignment editors entailed sitting with them as they prepared the daily outlook roster and assigned reporters to items mentioned there. For each story listed the assignment editor was questioned about the origins of the story idea, the reasons for assigning a particular reporter, subsequent discussions with the reporter, and the publication outcome (whether published, played, etc.). The formal open-focused interviews with management were tape-recorded and subsequently transcribed for easy access.

Detailed fieldnotes were written at the conclusion of each day in the field. More than two thousand pages of fieldnotes were indexed by topic for qualitative analysis. The data pertaining to the assignment of stories were systematized and quantified. Also available for subsequent scrutiny and analysis were copies of internal memoranda; draft or filed stories of journalists whom we were observing; assignment outlooks or lineups; television news scripts; and, sources' news releases, documents, official reports, or any other material in connection with a story being studied; journalists' notes and research files connected with a story being studied; and, copies of published newspaper stories studied and videotapes of broadcast television stories studied.

Research on news is as much an organizational accomplishment as the news itself (Smith, 1981: 313). We were subject to a series of organizational constraints which affected our cultural product, namely this book! Without regressing to a full account of the cultural- and social-organization processes by which our research was produced, it is instructive to consider some of the pitfalls and significant gains we experienced in the research process. As Geertz (1983: 56) states, referring to Malinowski's *A Diary in the Strict Sense of the Term*, the fieldworker is not a chameleon 'perfectly self-tuned to his exotic surroundings, a walking miracle of empathy, tact, patience, and cosmopolitanism.' We sometimes found it difficult to tune in to what journalists were up to, to empathize with their approach, to tread carefully enough so as not to offend, to wait until we had a better appreciation or a full story, and to be as *au courant* with the myriad of organized life as they were. It is therefore instructive to discuss some of the journalists' general concerns about our research; their efforts to limit, control, or deny access; their instrumental use of researchers; the practical constraints we faced leading to self-imposed limitations; and, the level of co-operation that was ultimately accomplished.

Journalists expressed concern to us about our interference with the process by which their work gets done. Reporters complained that our presence made it more awkward to work generally. For example, it was difficult for reporters to be constantly giving details of a telephone conversation just completed when we were able to listen only to the reporter's end. It was also difficult for journalists to repeatedly give reasons for their decisions as they were taking them; this was found to be disruptive to their thinking processes. Many found our presence interfered with source interviews or their ongoing relations with sources, and we were sometimes excluded on these grounds. This is a common problem in fieldwork with information workers who conduct inter-views; for example, researchers have been excluded from police interrogations and interviews with victims, complainants, and witnesses on the same stated grounds (Ericson, 1981, 1982). This problem may be connected to a general reticence among information workers to turn over freely the information they obtain through hard work. Some reporters said they, and/or their colleagues, were unwilling to give us names of some sources, or details of what they had to offer, because this was their property. As we found, journalists were often reluctant to share information with their own colleagues, let alone with out-siders whose purposes they were unclear about.

Journalists expressed concerns about how our findings would be used. In this connection, several wanted extra assurance that confidentiality would be maintained and that they would not be identifiable in research reports. Some journalists said they were concerned that their work habits might be communicated to management with the effect that controls would be instituted that would cramp their style. This concern pertained to how they spent their time and paced their work, as well as to questionable practices. On three occasions reporters' sensitivity seemed to reach a peak, as they grabbed the fieldworkers' notes to ascertain what had been written about them.

There was concern about the nature and impact of the published findings. There was persistent concern among several reporters from different news organizations that our work would unfairly expose journalists' practices in a negative light, and generally demystify the occupation. On several occasions they referred to previous research by Ericson (1981, 1982) which had become a matter of public controversy and considerable news-media attention. At an early stage of the fieldwork, a newspaper feature article about Ericson's previous police research, with the headline 'Why the Police Hate This Man,' was put on the notice board in one newsroom. Presumably, this was a reminder that research efforts of this type can generate bad news, at least in the eyes of those who produce such news!

We experienced limitations related to some of these concerns among journalists. This situation is common among all persons who seek information from others. Those with the information try to keep it as their property, or give away only snippets that will not adversely affect their interests. As one reporter observed, we were being treated by reporters in the same way that sources treat reporters. While most reporters believed that some limitations on access were inevitable, they were sarcastic about their colleagues who excluded us entirely and noted the contradiction of journalists' demanding openness among sources but not being open themselves.

Apart from the expected reticence of journalists to give freely of their 'information property,' there were other aspects affecting the level of co-operation. If journalists did not get along with their colleagues who were seen as our sponsors or as encouraging our research, it affected our relations with them. In one news organization an influential, middle-level editor was very resistant to our research. He advised the news organization against our presence in the first place, refused to talk to us or to reporters in our presence, and once walked out of an editorial meeting at which a researcher was in attendance. The fact that he was the editorial boss of many of the reporters we wished to study made it awkward and tense for them, and in some instances they used this as the reason for exluding us either from particular matters or entirely. Over time this led us to accept that we could not capture certain matters involving this person. For example, if a reporter went into this person's office to consult with him about a story we would not follow; we were left to obtain an account from the reporter of what transpired in their meeting.

Patterns developed in our access to news operations. Areas which epitomize public access to the news media, such as letters to the editor, were very open. Topics which indicated a sympathy to victims which would be widely shared, such as features on the issue of rape, were also open. However, some of those who represented the occupational culture ideal of the tough, investigative reporter were the least open to co-operation. There are interesting parallels in efforts to research police investigators (Ericson, 1981: chap. 2): symbols of responsiveness to the public, such as the citizen complaint bureau, are open; investigative specializations which are victim-oriented, such as sex-offence units, are open; but those who represent the occupational culture ideal of the tough investigator, who are perhaps a little devious, but efficient, are least open to co-operation.

We were occasionally excluded from particular interviews with sources because the reporter wanted to 'protect' a source who wished to remain anonymous; because the reporter thought the presence of another person would affect the extent to which a source would be forthcoming with information; and, because it was simply awkward to explain the presence of a researcher or have a researcher lingering. The problem of an additional person present was less acute with television journalists, probably because both they and their sources were used to having film or video crew members accompany a reporter.

We were also sometimes excluded from particular exchanges among journalists. A couple of reporters said they were willing to have us observe them in activities outside the newsroom, but not in the newsroom because they found it 'awkward.' It is certainly awkward to have someone peering over your shoulder while you are trying to write, although in these cases the definition of awkwardness also seemed to include the fact that their editorial boss was not sympathetic to our research. One reporter refused co-operation on a specific story because he said he would also be working on his own union matters during the day and he wanted information about that kept secret. Occasionally reporters excluded us from discussions they had with reporters from other news organizations regarding 'tips' for stories or background information on a continuing story.

As we acquired knowledgeability of what appeared tactful in particular situations, we occasionally excluded ourselves without exchanging words with the reporter. For example, we excluded ourselves from interviews with sources where the matter appeared sensitive emotionally (e.g., the relatives of murder suspects and victims) or politically (e.g., the campaign manager for an election candidate who was demanding a recount because of alleged voting irregularities). We occasionally excluded ourselves from certain newsroom scenes, such as an executive, in the privacy of his office, giving verbal reprimands to reporters we were studying. Often we simply gave a reporter a little physical and social space while he wrote his story.

We also faced practical constraints of time and space which affected the research process. If we had to leave early for personal reasons, we would choose a story to follow, or other research activity, accordingly. On some stories it was quite impractical to follow everything that was being done because there were several reporters involved, covering different angles and conducting different source interviews pertaining to each particular angle. Sometimes it was simply difficult to hear conversation between reporters and sources, for example, when wide shots were being taken for television-news items. Sometimes we expected journalists to change their routines for our research purposes but they had difficulty remembering to do so because of the routines they were used to. For example, we asked the wire editors of one news organization to save all wire copy they perused, but they sometimes continued to throw it in the garbage as was their usual practice.

As we stressed in chapters 1 and 2, the reporter becomes part of the bureaucratic organizations he reports on and contributes to the enactment of activities there. The same is the case for the ethnographic researcher. The researcher can hardly expect a high level of co-operation for his intrusions without yielding to requests for assistance, and eventually offering assistance as a human gesture of reciprocity.

We were called upon to make suggestions pertaining to story ideas, or regarding a particular event which might prove newsworthy. We were asked to suggest possible sources to contact regarding a story being worked on.

Possible story angles were also requested or debated with us, as were ideas for editing written texts, film, and video.

We obliged requests to undertake a variety of pragmatic tasks while out in the field with a reporter. We made contacts with sources because the reporter was otherwise engaged. We were asked to try to overhear conversations to pick up information in group contexts. We were used to call the newsroom for a film crew, and to pass on orders from the journalist to film crews and graphic artists. Occasionally we were asked to participate in the 'staging' of television visuals, for example, posing as a travel-office customer using a credit card for a story on fraudulent uses of credit cards.

We were asked to collaborate in the provision of various types of information relevant to what the reporter was working on. Our criminological expertise was occasionally called upon, even to the point of asking us if we were willing to be a source (we refused). Reporters unfamiliar with the structure and organization of criminal-justice agencies asked us for details relevant to the story they were working on. If we had other capabilities, these too were called upon, for example, Janet Chan twice acted as a Chinese-English interpreter.

We were frequently asked to assist with various information searches undertaken by a journalist. This task included searching documents belonging to a source organization; searching news organization files, library, or film 'stocks'; and, access to and use of the university library. As we acquired recipe knowledge about the news organization and process, journalists sometimes asked us to share it. For example, we were asked by reporters where the news organization filed particular materials. We were asked what past decisions had been taken on a continuing story, and what background information gleaned, by a reporter new to a story that a researcher had been invovled with before. Reporters frequently asked us for factual details they had missed about an event they were covering, in much the same way as they ask their colleagues from other news organizations for the same type of information. Occasionally we handed over our notepads for the reporter to obtain what he wanted regarding names, spellings, and factual details.

The degree and nature of co-operation varied greatly among journalists, and we came to rely upon the more co-operative as key informants. We had a number of such informants in important organizational positions at several levels, thus providing for a range and depth of such data (cf Van Maanen, 1979). Over time, some journalists began to appreciate that we had knowledge of their organization which they themselves did not possess, and they took this as a sign of the extent to which we had been accepted by their peers at different levels. Overall we were given, and achieved, a significant degree of co-operation. Therefore, the onus is on us to use the rich data obtained to advance knowledge of how journalists visualize deviance.

PART II

The News Institution

4

Newsrooms and Journalists' Cultures

Newsrooms

We begin with an overview of news production, and the roles of those who produce the news, as it typically occurs in newsrooms. We consider newspaper and television newsrooms, highlighting the similarities and differences in production and roles between these media.

Our overview of a newspaper newsroom is based on the city news desk at one newspaper. A senior executive described the city desk as '*the* basic department. That's where you put your young reporters. When they get experienced and when they get good, then you move them off on to bureaux so that a lot of the training function is there, most of the investigative stuff is there, a lot of the issue-oriented stuff is there. That's where the generic beats are: health, education, welfare, law, labour.'

At the time of our research there was a city editor, assistant city editor, night city editor, and staff of thirty-six reporters operating from the city desk. Approximately one-third of these reporters were on general assignment, while two-thirds were on special-topic (e.g., law, labour, welfare) or special-beat (e.g., courts, city hall, provincial legislature) assignment. The assistant city editor was the assignment editor, beginning his day at about 10:00 a.m. and staying on until the 6:00 p.m. deadline for filed stories. His hours overlapped with those of the night editor, who came in at 5:00 p.m. to discuss the schedule of stories that had been produced during the day. The reporters also worked from about 10:00 a.m. to 6:00 p.m. According to one editor, anywhere from 15 to 35 stories were filed each day on the city desk. The newspaper's first edition came together at around 7:30 to 8:00 p.m., was into production by 8:30 p.m., and was on the streets between 10:00 and 11:00 p.m. The night editing staff worked on alterations for the morning edition, and their work was usually completed by midnight.

City-desk personnel worked in an open office plan with the exception of the city editor who had a closed office situated alongside the offices of the assistant managing editor and the managing editor. The assistant city editor (assignment editor) was located between a row of desks belonging to city-desk reporters, and another set of desks from which the slot editors worked. Thus, there was open access among assignment, reporting, and editing personnel to discuss story assignments, developments, angles, editing suggestions or problems, and so on.

Our overview of processes and roles in a television newsroom is based on one television station. The operation of this newsroom in most respects paralleled that of the city-desk of the newspaper, covering general assignments as well as the police, court, city-hall, and provincial-legislature beats, and a few specializations (minorities, citizen advocate). At the time of our research the newsroom was headed by an executive producer, and his production team also included a producer, assignment editor, lineup editor, and an assistant producer for the night show. There were a dozen reporters, and about the same number of film or video crew members, although on any given day shift the number was usually fewer. There were also two video technicians and several film technicians available for the editing stages. Additional personnel monitored news-service feeds from VisNews and U.S. television networks, as well as print wire services, to fit items into the lineup with locally produced stories. The two anchorpersons came in mid-day to examine the lineup, prepare for any feature interviews they themselves were to conduct, and to rehearse their scripts.

The assignment editor began his day at about 8:00 a.m., staying on until mid-afternoon at which time he was replaced by the assistant producer for the night show. The reporters and crews came in around 9:00 a.m., and worked until their items were ready for the 6:00 p.m. newscast, which was usually between 5:00 and 6:00 p.m. Each reporter filed one story, although occasionally a reporter ended up not producing a story, and very occasionally a reporter would manage to file two stories.

The newsroom was an open plan, with the exception of administrative officers, the executive producer, producer, and two anchorpersons, who had closed offices. The assignment editor had a desk off to one corner, but the rows of reporters' desks were near and there was easy access for discussion and consultation. The executive producer and producer were directly and actively involved in all aspects of the process, beginning with assignment ideas and preliminary schedule right through to giving studio directions for the broadcast. The crews had separate rooms, as did the film and video technicians who were located on the floor above the newsroom, but they sometimes sat in the newsroom, chatting or discussing ideas with reporters, editors and producers.

The news-production process is represented schematically in figure 4.1. At the hub of the process initially is the assignment editor, whose job does not differ in any significant respect across news organizations and media (for greater detail, see chapter 6). The assignment editor was responsible for developing the schedule of news events to be covered for the day. He assigned reporters to particular items and he was supposed to keep in touch with story developments. Reporters on beats were supposed to call in at least once during the day to indicate what they are working on, their angles, and what and how much they expected to file by the deadline. The assignment editor was also a consultant regarding story angles and developments, and an educator to the inexperienced reporter. The assignment editor worked more closely with the reporter if the reporter was inexperienced, was working on an important or controversial matter, or was involved in an item that originated with more senior levels of the news organization.

The assignment editor attended news conferences, although in the newspaper it was on behalf of the city editor, who sometimes attended himself. The main newspaper conference was in the early afternoon. It was presided over by the managing editor, or the assistant managing editor, in his absence. It was attended by the assistant managing editor, news editor, executive editor, makeup editor, art/photography editor, and editors from each news desk (city, national, international, business, sport, lifestyle, entertainment). Each desk editor circulated his schedule of stories to the others, while the features editor simply submitted a schedule without attending the meeting. Each desk editor was asked to highlight the most significant stories on his respective schedule, and sometimes also made a special plea for prominent play or extra space.

The main purpose of the meeting was to suggest to the news editor what were the best candidates for page one. However, there was also considerable negotiation outside the news conference between individual desk editors and the news editor concerning what should be on page one. The news conference served additionally to inform everyone about prospects for the forthcoming edition, and was a forum for discussion about important continuing stories, story ideas, and story angles. It also allowed the managing editor to enunciate policy, offer criticisms, and make comparisons with competitors.

There were additional meetings later in the day. At 5:30 p.m. the national-edition editor met with some other editors to consider what city stories should go into the national edition. At 8:00 p.m. the managing editor met with some other editors to scrutinize the page proofs, and later the actual copy, to see that there were no major errors or problems, and to consider changes for the later edition.

In the television newsroom there were several meetings during the day between the executive producer and particular persons whose work he had to direct or know about. These meetings were not formal, and much of the work

Figure 4.1
The news-production process

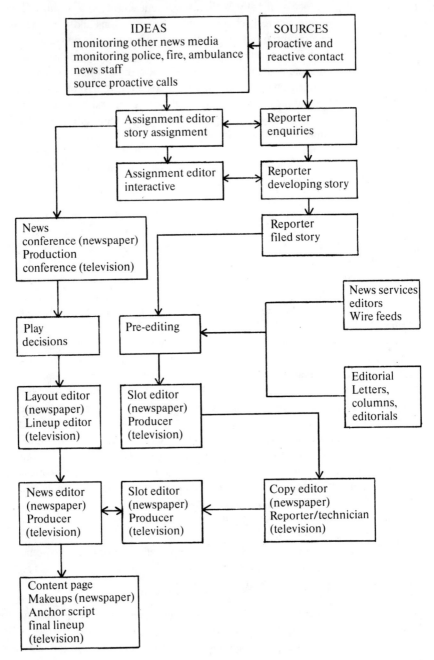

was done by ongoing and repeated consultations throughout the day. The executive producer met with the assignment editor early in the day to grasp the assignment outlook and make suggestions. As the lineup, including news-service material, became clear, the executive producer and producer met with a graphic artist to develop the graphics for the show. According to the artist, the number of graphics averaged about six to eight per show. In our observations, the suggestions for graphics came mainly from the executive producer and producer, who sometimes drew rough sketches for the artist to work from. In the early afternoon a production meeting was held with the executive producer, producer, lineup editor, script assistants, night assistant producer, and film and video technicians. The schedule was distributed at this meeting, and the basic lineup was prepared including decisions about the leading stories and what news-service or 'fire' stories were available as fillers. This was also a key meeting for informing the technical editing staff of what items were from news services, on ENG (video) or DSS (film), so that they could prepare their editing resources accordingly. The executive producer also met with the anchorpersons, consulted with reporters on scripts and film editing, and held planning meetings with relevant staff during the day.

Reporters used interviewing, observational, and documentary methods, with the television reporter having the additional task of acquiring suitable visuals (for details see chapter 7). As just mentioned, in the process of producing a story the reporter consulted with editors or producers. The reporter usually had to make a special plea for greater space in the newspaper (more than 15 column inches), although the newspaper-editing process allowed for flexibility in this respect. In the case of television, a longer item (more than about 90 seconds) could affect whether colleagues' items got into the show and was a matter that required the attention of the lineup editor and producers at the earliest possible stage.

The newspaper story was prepared on a word processor, and the reporter usually took a copy of his filed story for his own records and to compare with what was published. The assistant city editor or city editor checked filed stories for their overall content and watched for anything that might cause legal problems. The slot desk received the filed story on the word-processing system and assigned it to a copy editor. The slot editor worked with the news editor, quality editor, and makeup personnel, tailoring the length of the item to the space available for city-desk stories, including what city-desk stories had been taken for the front page or might be used as fillers elsewhere. The assistant city editor, city editor, and slot editor decided which stories were worthy of the reporter's byline, the most important symbolic recognition of good work available on a daily basis. A night editor was also available to check the copy further, and there were further checks at the night meeting in which the managing editor and other editors scrutinized the page proofs and first printed copies.

The television story was initially prepared in the form of a written script, which was examined and edited by the producer or executive producer. The script included the 'roll-up' or lead of the anchorperson into the story, the reporter's own words, and an indication of where actuality clips or the 'talking heads' of sources were used. It also included an indication of the overall time, and the timing of each segment within the item. Upon approval of the script, the reporter prepared the item in accordance with the visuals he had gathered. In this task the reporter was the producer and editor of his own item, directing the film or video technician to edit as the reporter saw fit. Occasionally the producer or executive producer participated, especially if there was a technical problem or the deadline was approaching. It was possible to continue editing the item right up to show time, and even into the show, as the producer could juggle the lineup to accommodate the need to put the finishing touches on a particular news item. The executive producer and producer controlled the show as a whole, including its themes across items, anchor scripts, and linkages, but the reporter had considerable autonomy in the production of his individual item.

Working Ideologies

In this section we consider the views of journalists on the nature of news as knowledge. What are their views on the nature of reality and the criteria of rational acceptability which journalistic methodology brings to bear on it? In light of these views, what is the meaning of the working ideology of being objective, fair, and balanced in news production and products? To what extent do these aspects of working ideology relate to practices? To what extent do these aspects of working ideology relate to the legitimation of news in the public culture, in the face of practices which diverge from or belie them?

JOURNALISTS AS INTERPRETERS OF REALITY

The Royal Commission on Newspapers [RCN] (1981: 114) tells the story of two weekly newspapers in Mississauga, Ontario, which, upon being merged in ownership in 1981, decided to have one city-hall reporter in common. A newspaper executive is quoted as saying, 'I don't see how stories from two reporters covering City Hall will be different.' The Royal Commission derides this view as an administrative rationalization. However, the newspaper executive may not be expressing an unsound view in the context of contemporary research and thinking on the news media.

If one takes the view that reporters reflect or mirror a self-evident reality, then one must assume that no matter who is looking, similar factual accounts of that reality will be forthcoming. Therefore, the need for different people and news organizations saying the same thing does seem rather wasteful, and perhaps unwise. The mirror-of-reality view continues to be put forward by news-media officials, who recognize that while some selection goes on, nevertheless 'the very purpose of news broadcasts ... is to report on events, to hold up a mirror to the reality of the day' (Canadian Broadcasting Corporation [CBC], 1978: 374). A similar view seems to be prevalent among practising journalists. For example, Fishman (1980: 32–4) depicts the journalist's working ideology in terms of the following assumptions: that events are self-evident; exist independently of their knowers; are not created, altered, or otherwise affected by the process of discovery; and, occur logically and temporally before the event is detected. Tuchman (1978: 99–100) notes that journalists take for granted the distinction between fact and interpretation, between objective reporting and analysis, believing that they are quite separate entities even if they have difficulty articulating the differences.

The response of contemporary news analysts is to say that the news reflects not the reality being reported on, but the social and cultural organization of news work and the frames for news discourse these provide. However, since news organizations and news frames tend to be very similar, two reporters covering the same event, even for different news organizations, will tend to give similar accounts. A great deal of research effort has been devoted to showing that the news must be understood not 'as it happens' but 'as it is reported.' It is the organizational and professional conventions of reporting, operating in a fairly deterministic way, which explain the uniform products of the mass media. Again, the need for different people and news organizations saying the same thing does seem rather wasteful, and perhaps unwise.

Another view is that there will be different accounts given by two different reporters from two different news organizations. This difference exists because the factuality and explanation of all events is interpreted and constructed situationally and contextually according to personal and organizational criteria of value: what is important, the slant it requires, and the wider goals and interests it sustains. Different journalists, and especially different news organizations as they recruit and socialize journalists in their mould, will offer different versions of reality in their news products. It follows from this view that there is a need for different people and news organizations because they will say different things that are useful, and perhaps wise. The journalists we studied generally supported this third view, and incorporated it into their practices.

Among television journalists, there was an explicit view that the job entailed story-telling. They appreciated that their stories had elements of fiction in the original sense of *fictio*, making or fashioning something through interpretation, as well as fictive or fake elements to sustain the dramatic narrative. This view was manifested in the terms used to talk about specific

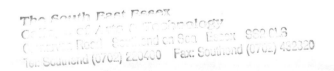

practices. The use of visuals which did not relate directly to what was being presented was referred to as a 'fake.' For example, an interviewee was asked to act as if he was talking directly to the interviewer when he wasn't; stock film of a hospital operation was used with a voice-over for a story about a different hospital operation. Having sources repeat what was supposed to be a natural act in order to obtain better visuals was referred to as 'staging.' 'Staging' sometimes also included the use of newsroom personnel as actors in visuals. As they worked on a story, television journalists and crew members would refer regularly to the ways in which they were constructing the story. Continuing stories, and the techniques for sustaining them, were seen as constituting an ongoing dramatic narrative. For example, a continuing story on a series of deaths, kept alive by emotive interviews with relatives of the victims, was referred to as a 'yarn.' In these respects television journalists seemed fully cognizant of the view that they were making stories, and were apparently in accord with a producer's manual which directed, 'treat news as theatre' (Cayley, 1982: 136).

Another sign that news was constructed interpretively was the concern among journalists for adequate representation of ethnic minority groups and opinions. This concern was of major importance in one newsroom we studied, and some journalists took an active part in raising and addressing the issues involved, both internally and by membership in outside organizations which pressured for change. The concern included a call for more reporters from different ethnic minority groups, and more and better coverage of ethnic-minority issues. Such concerns show a conscious recognition that news events and types of authorized sources are chosen selectively and construed in particular ways, and a belief that interpretive interventions can change what and who are chosen and construed.

Journalists took the view that while one should strive to be fully accurate and complete, it is not possible in practice because only some aspects of events and only some perspectives on those events can be represented. The knowledge conveyed in the news is perspectival, and the perspectives are presented not concretely in the original context of the events, but abstractly in the news context of the events. As a newsroom manager commented to a researcher, after receiving a complaint from a well-known and frequently cited source that she had been quoted out of context, the sophisticated source realizes that whatever is used is out of context. This is inevitable because only brief quotations can be included, and these are combined with other quotations from other persons in other contexts *by the journalist*. In the news, the journalist provides the context and each individual source is likely to have a sense of being taken out of context.

From the journalist's perspective, newsmaking involves construing and constructing factuality at each stage of the process. As a senior newspaper editor observed, in interview, the reporter is inevitably *in* the story from the very beginning, giving facts significance and value:

> The mere choice of deciding what facts to report involves an interpretive process in which you're saying these are the facts. These facts are important because they mean something out of the ordinary that people should know about and so there's an interpretive process that goes on in picking them. From there on in, you're involved in the process of trying to decide how much you have to explain why these particular facts are important and those are judgment calls all along the way ...
>
> [O]bjective reporting generally you think of as being reporting the facts and making sure that both sides are adequately reported. But facts don't mean a damn thing, the streets are littered with facts. We could fill the paper with facts and the damn thing would be totally meaningless. So, what you do essentially is pick and choose which facts you're going to publish and try to attach some meaning to them. Why do you choose these facts? What do they mean? You could have a story saying that two cars are racing down the street, that one of them crashed into a lamppost. So what? You could add more facts and say one of those cars was being driven by a policeman in pursuit. Well, that's fine. You could add more facts saying that it was contrary to the policies of the police department to engage in hot pursuit. You could go further ... and place that within the context of a political debate going on about whether hot pursuit is necessary or unnecessary. The whole process I think, of reporting is investing facts with significance, and trying to decide what are significant and what aren't significant.
>
> Q: Would you try to train your reporters in terms of finding significance?
> A: Oh yeah. You do that every day with stories saying look, your lead is in the wrong place ... We had ... a story about the establishment of a poor house in Sacramento, California. It was a lovely lead which said in the capital of the richest state of the richest nation of the world, a poor house has been established. But ... way down in the story it was pointed out that the reason for establishing a poor house was so that Sacramento county could get out of paying welfare to individuals, and that other counties were keeping an eye on it to see how it worked because if it worked there chances were they would all do the same thing. Well that becomes a very significant story, that, you know, we're back to the Keynesian type ... in the capital of California ... they had established a poor house to get out of paying welfare. Well, I said to the editor, 'Take that paragraph and move it up high in the story. Make it the third paragraph in the story because that is what gives the story its importance and it shouldn't be way down in the story.' I mean otherwise you're just reading about a hostel. We've got hostels here. There are hostels ... all over the place so what's so significant about one being established in Sacramento? Well, the

significance was precisely that, the way they had organized it, ingenious as it was, got the county out of paying welfare and that should be well up in the story. So, it's that kind of process that goes on day after day after day and night after night, that develops them.

This senior editor also stressed that he judged reporters by their interpretive ability in relation to facts, and their skill in signifying a good lead. Realizing that it was an interpretive process 'all the way along,' he placed emphasis on the value of having reporters who were good interpreters of reality.

This does not mean that in their everyday work, journalists were continually conscious of, and reflexive about, the process of construing factuality and constructing reality. They did sometimes experience the matters before them as entailing immediately obvious and evident facts and meaning. Assignment editors and reporters sometimes spoke of a story which could 'write itself' or 'take care of itself.' This meant that any reporter schooled in the organization's news frames and format would immediately recognize what should be reported on and how. It did not mean that the facts were 'self-evident,' but rather 'news-evident' in terms of the criteria learned 'day after day and night after night' in the news organization.

OBJECTIVITY, BALANCE, AND FAIRNESS

Appreciating that their craft is a creative enterprise, journalists recognize the need to be sensitive to the possible impact of their work. If one is telling stories about real people, then the consequences for those people must be taken into account. This consideration is especially salient because news mostly deals with imputations of deviance and efforts at control, and itself can have social-control effects. Journalism has attempted to manage this aspect in terms of notions of objectivity, balance, and fairness at the level of working ideology as well as the level of public legitimacy. Since journalists are interpreters of other people's lives and organizational arrangements, they must strive to be fair with these people and offer an objective and balanced view of their affairs.

There has been considerable research attention given to the notions of objectivity, balance, and fairness in journalism. Phillips (1977: 65) states that in her survey of journalists, 98 per cent 'virtually defined journalism as adherence to the norm of objectivity. From this and other studies, it is clear that the norm of objectivity forms the core of the defining logic and mission of news creation. Further, my research suggests that the daily journalists observed had habits of mind, attitudes, and personal characteristics which depend on, and are structured around, the ideal of objective reporting.' Phillips also says that virtually all of the reporters surveyed defined objectivity as equivalent to balance and fairness (ibid: 68), a fact borne out in the ethnographic research of Schlesinger (1978: 163–4) who observes that these concepts are 'interchangeable, and arise in similar contexts.'

The notions of objectivity, balance, and fairness embody the assumption that journalists are neutral and non-partisan agents who base decisions on uniform technical criteria. The techniques include preventing the intrusion of personal bias; separating fact and opinion; including opposing viewpoints; and constructing texts in a narrative form that brackets out historical or explanatory frameworks which give an explicit interpretive basis (and bias) for construing truth. These techniques relate to the selection and use of sources, the construction of themes in the news, and the format and language of news texts in terms of accuracy and factuality.

Among the journalists we studied, the starting point for an objective stance was a bracketing of one's own judgments prior to interviewing sources and developing other information on a story. In the words of one news executive, 'Objectivity to me means that you don't go in with any preconceived notions.' Like the juror, the reporter was to listen and learn before giving due weight and deciding. Moreover, the journalist was not to give the appearance of having personal interests, or outside organizational ties or affinities, which might suggest that whatever he reported was preconceived or prejudged. A political-beat reporter related to a researcher that he had strong personal loyalty to a particular political party, but said he would be 'finished' in his job if his leanings became known publicly. He noted that his employer expressly forbade reporters to give any signs of political-party loyalty, such as putting election signs on their lawns.

This type of concern seems particularly acute in television. For example, it is CBC policy that 'the Corporation takes no editorial position in its programming' (CBC, 1982: 6). Where anchorpersons or other television journalists had a segment in which they reflected on particular items or events in the news, it was referred to as 'analysis' rather than 'commentary.'

The concern over explicit ties to political or other organizations was also evident in newspapers. One newspaper we studied had an explicit rule that reporters were not allowed to accept any gratuities from sources. Journalists at a newspaper became very upset because of a speech delivered by a senior executive. A news item about the speech was published in the newspaper, in which the executive appeared to be expressing opinions against one of the major political parties. Journalists were concerned that readers would take this item as a sign of the newspaper's bias against this political party, and in particular that it would affect their ability to continue dealing with sources who did not have the same political leanings. Their belief was that if a newspaper wished to have the fullest possible access to authorized knowers with different organizational ties and opinions, then the appearance of neutrality had to be upheld at all levels of the news organization.

Journalists also considered objectivity to include notions of accuracy and balance. As one news executive put it, 'Objective reporting generally you think of as being reporting the facts and making sure that both sides are adequately reported.' In terms of accuracy of facts, it was generally recognized that the way facts are construed and expressed can be infused with value. In a discussion among three reporters in a beat press room, there was general agreement that values fuse with facts in the interpretive construction of news accounts. One reporter offered the example, 'If there are 26 city councillors and 18 are at a meeting, you can either say "8 councillors did not show up for the meeting" or "18 councillors were present at the meeting" and that makes a difference.' A senior executive of one newspaper agreed that facts are construed and constructed variously, and also read variously by different audiences. His position was that reporters should not *intentionally* 'write it so that everyone can read between the lines.'

Accuracy was frequently talked about in the same breath as balance. Seeming to adopt a limited version of Mannheim's view of relational knowledge – that one moves closer to the truth by considering different perspectives on the reality in question – journalists frequently professed the need to seek out and obtain accounts from different sources. In practice, although many sources may have been consulted or cited, usually only two sides were presented. However, contrary to Epstein (1974: 227), this situation was not invariable. It was felt that even two sides prevented journalists from allegations of bias, which was defined as presenting only one side of a story.

The two sides did not necessarily have to be presented in the same story. A television executive said his preference was to 'try and get it within one story,' although the official policy of the station allowed for single views in a single item as long as multiple views were expressed in the aggregate, and this in fact was often the practice in continuing stories. Newspaper editors also had an eye for balance over time. For example, a newspaper reporter told a researcher that after he had done a story on an election candidate that was perceived as critical by one of his superiors, he was ordered to write a conciliatory piece on the same candidate to be published before the election.

In election coverage some systematic, and even statistically based, notions of balance came into play. It was the policy of a television station to do quantitative checks of pre-election coverage to assist in calculating the relative amounts of time given to the major candidates and parties. A newspaper had a policy of counting pre-election letters to the editor in support of each major party, and publishing letters in proportion to the number received that supported each party. However, as an editor told a researcher, the newspaper was known to have a particular affinity to one political party which meant that it received a disproportionate number of letters to the editor in favour of this party. Therefore, a disproportionate number (in relation to opinion polls or election results) of letters were published in favour of this party.

In the course of reporting outside of election contexts, it was generally not a statistical standard that was taken into account, but a sense of fairness and equity. This practice is revealed in a CBC policy manual which states that 'fairness is not to be achieved by a rigid neutrality or mathematical balance' (CBC, 1982: 111). Just as conceptions of legal equality and fairness do not mean that there should be absolute or numerical equality – for example, that persons sent to prison should reflect exactly the demographic composition of Canada – so the journalistic conception is one in which their own criteria of value enter into decisions about what is just, fair, and equitable in the particular context for the particular story before them.

Thus, journalists are judges of 'reasonableness,' just as judges are judges of 'reasonableness' in law. There is evidence of this fact in official statements of principles regarding television journalism, the medium which by some accounts (e.g., RCN, 1981e: 12, citing Smith, 1980: 179) has provided *the* standard for objectivity, balance, and fairness for all news media. For example, the CBC (1982) manual sees fairness in the following terms: 'the information reports or reflects equitably the relevant facts and significant points of view; it deals fairly and ethically with persons, institutions, issues and events' (p. 6). Balance is addressed as follows: 'CBC programs dealing with matters of public interest in which differing views are held must supplement the exposition of one point of view with an equitable treatment of other relevant points of view ... Equitable in this context means fair and reasonable, taking into consideration the weight of opinion behind a point of view, as well as its significance or potential significance' (p. 8).

Beyond the tautology of defining fairness in terms of dealing fairly, and fairness in terms of balance and balance in terms of fairness, these statements reveal some other values by which journalists are to construe the world. They are to decide what is 'equitable,' 'relevant,' 'significant,' 'ethical,' 'reasonable,' 'weight of opinion,' et cetera, and there are no attendant guidelines on how these assessments are to be made.

In the United States and Britain journalists have received more explicit instructions. The U.S. Federal Communications Commission has a fairness doctrine and a fairness primer for journalists, which among other things direct them to exclude communist viewpoints (Epstein, 1974: 63–4). In Britain the Annan Report (1977) on broadcasting emphasized the need to take into account the range and weight of opinion, and to appreciate that it changes. However, this approach is to be taken because 'the broadcasters are operating in a system of parliamentary democracy and must share its assumptions. They should not be expected to give equal weight or show an impartiality which cannot be due to those who seek to destroy it by violent, unparliamentary or illegal means' (ibid: 268).

Similar criteria of value are echoed in the British Broadcasting Corporation (BBC) journalists' policy manual. For example, in the BBC document *Principles and Practice in News and Current Affairs*, as cited by Schlesinger (1978: 165), it is stated that 'there are some respects in which the BBC is not neutral, unbiased or impartial. The BBC cannot be neutral in the struggle between truth and untruth, justice and unjustice, freedom and slavery, compassion and cruelty, tolerance and intolerance. *It is not only within the Constitution it is within the consensus about basic moral values*' (emphasis in Schlesinger). As Schlesinger (1978: 170) goes on to observe, 'the ostensibly unattached BBC man does have a political commitment: impartiality is itself predicated on the existence of the present British political system and its underlying social and economic order, and the BBC is required to sustain it. In this sense, impartiality and the domain assumptions it contains are closely akin to the supposed neutrality of the civil service – and this comparison, as will be seen, is by no means fortuitous.'

As we considered in chapter 1, Canadian broadcasters are legally bound to uphold social, cultural, political, and economic order. Here as elsewhere in Western democracies, broadcasting institutions 'are legally committed to controlling the knowledge of their audience' (Seaton, 1980: 92). Through the legislation of morality, and through the enunciation of moral concepts in policy manuals, broadcasting journalists are told that objectivity, balance, and fairness are a matter of correct moral judgment in the particular reporting contexts in which they find themselves.

In summary, television journalists were directed to be particular about the sources they selected and the weight they gave to their opinions. They were also told to put value to their facts according to journalistically and organizationally shared criteria of rational acceptability. They were to shape what citizens needed to know, who was authorized to tell them, and what should be said. To repeat the words of a former CBC president: 'Programming cannot be limited to what the largest audience wants to know; it must include what the public is entitled and needs to know' (CBC, 1982: iv). When journalists have an explicit mandate to decide what the public needs to know, it should come as no surprise when researchers document that while more than one side may be presented, they are usually given differential status and legitimacy in the particular story and in the aggregate (Glasgow University Media Group [GUMG], 1976, 1980, 1982).

Objectivity is problematic because truth does not lie in facts themselves, rather the journalist must seek the truth by interpreting and evaluating the facts. It is also problematic because the 'strategic ritual' of objectivity (Tuchman, 1978), whereby truth is taken to reside somewhere between what two opposing sources say about a matter, can be a way of avoiding the truth or constructing damaging untruths, as U.S. journalists discovered in the McCarthy era. Some journalists we studied made statements that objectivity in this sense was 'dangerous,' and asserted that their mission was to be 'fair, but not objective.' Fairness meant giving a source an opportunity to explain his position, and to address any aspersions cast upon him by another source.

Ultimately, like good moral philosophers, journalists realized that the criteria of value they employed depended on the concrete case and were a matter of shared wisdom on the job as well as hierarchical direction and control. As Bok (1979: 82n) has observed generally about those faced with moral choices, 'You cannot always make a choice, or expect others to make it, which achieves both the fairness and the beneficence you desire. Moral principles, just like length and weight, represent different dimensions by which we structure experience and can therefore present conflicts in concrete cases but never in the abstract. It is for this reason that the search for priority rules among moral principles in the abstract is doomed to fail; one might as well search for such priority rules among pounds, yards and hours in the abstract.'

Many believed that others' views – those of other journalists and sources – are more biased than those nurtured in one's particular news organization. For example, during a policy seminar for a television station's journalists, discussion arose over the quality of international news coverage. The station had been relying heavily upon freelancers, and feeds from other television networks. The freelancers were depicted as being credible reporters, but probably subject to personal bias. One response was that the organization needed more of their own reporters in key international settings, although it was recognized that it is impossible to have your own reporters 'everywhere.' The management response was that the editor was supposed to control what was on the air and if there was a perception of bias he could have the original reporter's words voiced-over to 'wipe out bias.' Another person stated that radio reporters do not have that option, and raised the question of whether an entire report should be thrown out because of a line that manifested bias. Again the 'ideal' alternative suggested was to have 'our own people in the hot spots of the world' to ensure that there was no bias.

Inside news organizations, there was ongoing and active negotiation over the limits of the permissible. Editors in particular played the role of 'bias police.' Significant differences and conflicts were common, as one would expect given that the principles involved only became manifest and reflected upon in the concrete case. If a reporter seemed to be in regular difficulty regarding accounts which his colleagues viewed as being biased in the wrong direction, they too attempted to bring his work and accounts into line. A case example illustrates some of the issues, conceptions, conflicts, and tensions involved.

The case under discussion involved the revealing situation in which the story itself focused upon the credibility of accounts of organizational actors, in this case the police. Following a well-publicized trial that included allegations about police fabricating evidence, a reporter decided to write a feature article on the topic of police perjury. He wished to focus on the extent and dimensions of the practice, and on police motives in doing it. To this end, he interviewed and cited eight prominent and credible defence lawyers who were of the opinion that some police evidence in court is 'shaded' or 'fabricated.' The first draft of the story was presented to his editors, who told him to provide more balance, including more from the police side.

A filed story of 58 column inches was provided, posing the lead question 'Do some policemen shade or fabricate evidence to secure evidence?', and the lead answer 'a number of defence lawyers are saying: yes, some police do.' The article reports that, according to some lawyers, the police motive is to secure convictions or protect themselves or their colleagues. Furthermore, some lawyers believe 'the legal establishment is willing to turn a blind eye to it.' 'Police spokesmen' are said to deny the existence of perjury, pointing to the very low rate of legally proven cases against them, and lawyers are quoted regarding the difficulty in proving legally that a police officer has committed perjury. A lawyer attributes part of the problem to the fact that the Crown attorneys function as police agents and allies rather than as independent reviewers of the police case. Different lawyers are quoted, speaking about the problem in different contexts, including the taking of statements and situations where the suspect has been 'roughed up.' Lawyers and a police spokesman are quoted on the subject of the legality of police practices of deception and lying in obtaining certain kinds of evidence, such as incriminating confessions from a suspect.

The filed article was acceptable to the reporter's desk editors, but it was eventually rejected at a higher level. One editor said the rejection decision was taken entirely by a superior. The reporter said this editor had told him that had the story been written on the basis of a news release from the Criminal Lawyers Association, 'We would have printed it right away.' A senior editor said that the article was rejected because it was too broad in the sweep of the allegation, lacked detailed substantiation, and entailed a complex philosophical argument about the nature of giving accounts, lying, and deception. As such, it was unfair and lacked balance.

A: [The story] began by asking the question, 'Do police lie sometimes?' I think when you're dealing with a question like that, you have to be very, very, very specific and it's a question of fairness, again ... this time the police force. You may have people say, as we had some lawyers saying in that story, 'Well yeah, they colour their evidence.' Well every one of us colours our evidence in court. Every single one of us tries to put the best face on whatever it is.

Q: In terms of one's interests?

A: Sure, one's own self-interest. And I think that's what this particular lawyer was trying to say. Well, to take that kind of a situation as support for the proposition that police lie, to my mind takes it out of context. So much so that ... it's not accurate, it's not fair. Again, the argument against that is that the police have a greater duty to be accurate in their statements and not to try and colour. And that's true, but ... all that means is that you have to spend that much more care in making sure that the proposition is taken within the context. It's a very, very delicate thing to do ... [A]nd a reporter worked very hard on it. He worked with the best of intentions. The end result was that I didn't think that we had been specific enough, detailed enough, contextual enough, to publish the story.

Q: What would have made it more specific?

A: Specific instances.

Q: Actual cases?

A: Actual cases with lawyers being very detailed about what they meant. Pushing them very hard to examine the differences between colouring ... of testimony by other people. When you raise the question 'Do police lie?,' you're asking the question, 'Have you got a corrupt force? Are policemen corrupt?' And you've got to be very, you know, it's like saying, 'Are political scientists corrupt?' Are you corrupt? Is political science your field or is it sociology?

Q: Sociology.

A: Are sociologists corrupt as a group? Well Christ, that gets into such a very big definitional problem, that you've got to be very, very, very precise ... It's like saying, 'Are all reporters biased? Do all reporters lie when they write?' Well, I mean I could make a case for saying that every single reporter lies.

Q: Yeah, I don't think I would use the word lie, but I like ...

A: Well, tells something that isn't true. Bias is an easier example because everybody's heard of biased, in his writing.

Q: Versions of the truth.

A: Sure ... Lie means deliberate falsification, knowing that it's false and intending to mislead. I mean that's, you know, major, heavy stuff. Well, if you can deal just with that, o.k., but if you start, then you get into big lies and little lies, dark lies and white lies. It's just a ... mine field really.

Such honesty in recognizing that a news organization cannot deal with matters in a fair and balanced way takes into account other organizational constraints, including the law and ongoing relations with sources. This particular editor had a reputation for being conservative. In his words, 'When in doubt, leave it out.'

The fact that considerations of objectivity, balance, and fairness are situational and contextual was evidenced by the fact that they yielded to organizational constraints in particular cases. Normal expectations regarding objectivity, balance, and fairness sometimes evaporated in face of the journalist's desire to reduce the work involved in producing stories; deadlines; problems with technical resources; or the need to edit a story to a reduced length to fit the space available. We will draw upon examples to illustrate how these practical considerations were linked to the notions of objectivity, balance, and fairness.

In the context of writing a story about the financial estimates of a particular government ministry, after the minister had read a prepared statement, a reporter decided to obtain some background information about one program within the ministry's portfolio. The reporter called a researcher from one of the Opposition parties for this background information. He said he selected this source because this person used to work in the ministry program the reporter was interested in. When asked if he would quote this researcher directly in the story regarding the information from him that was used, the reporter said he would not because if he did he would have to worry about balancing his story by obtaining accounts from spokespersons for the other major political parties.

It was sometimes difficult to contact a source who represented the other side, and a decision had to be made regarding whether publication should be delayed or a story should be published with the possibility of a follow-up story from the other source at a later date. For example, within three hours of air time for a newscast, a reporter was assigned to a story involving a case of police misconduct. He was told that a representative of a civil-liberties organization was bringing the case to the attention of the police public complaints commissioner, and that according to a police association spokesperson, the police officers involved were suing the newspaper which had made the matter public. The reporter decided to interview the civil-liberties representative, followed by a reaction from the police public complaints commissioner. He obtained the former interview, but was unable to interview the commissioner because no one returned the telephone messages he left. The reporter proceeded to select a thirty-second clip from the interview with the civil-liberties representative, and prepared a script for the anchorperson to use in conjunction with it, and these alone constituted the item.

In television-news production, technical-resource constraints were also a factor. For example, a reporter interviewed a lawyer about a law society practice directive against lawyer price-cutting in the area of legal services for real estate sales. The reporter and crew returned to the newsroom after this interview, planning to have lunch and then go out in the afternoon to interview a law society spokesperson about this matter. She made several calls to the law society, but had difficulty contacting a spokesperson and her crew was assigned to another reporter. Later in the afternoon when she was ready to go out with her crew, they were not available and the item included only clips from the lawyer.

If a television reporter was working with a film crew rather than video crew, the time needed to process the film was also a factor. For example, a reporter originally planned to interview a provincial-government spokesperson after obtaining an interview from a municipal-government politician expressing concern that provincial regulations apparently allowed the sale of municipal voters' lists to commercial firms. However, given the fact that he was working with film and the deadline was approaching he dropped this second actuality clip.

The time available for a broadcast item, or newspaper space for a story, was also a factor affecting the balancing of accounts. For example, a newspaper reporter was covering a Supreme Court of Ontario case involving one of the first tests of the Canadian Charter of Rights and Freedoms. His story emphasized the submissions and perspective of the defence lawyer, whom he interviewed twice while the Crown attorney was not interviewed at all. Indeed, the initial filed story made no reference to the Crown attorney, but within a few minutes of filing it the reporter was told by an editor to add something about the Crown attorney's arguments and he sat down to do so. In the published story, however, the two sentences added about the Crown attorney's position did not appear, apparently edited out to keep the story to the available space.

JOURNALISTS AS INVESTIGATORS

Journalists also conceive of themselves as investigators. This conception incorporates both means and ends. The means are similar to those of police investigators, finding out ways to penetrate organizations to obtain information even if trickery or deception are necessary. The end is the policing of organizational life, ferreting out injustice and forcing accountability. Investigative exposés 'give journalists the sense that they are autonomous actors in touch with the finest traditions of their craft – crusaders in the cause of truth, protectors of the people's freedoms rather than mere functionaries of a production process which panders to consumer wants' (Chibnall, 1977: 161–6). Chibnall adds that journalists' sense of significance of this work is reinforced if there is an indignant response from the sources involved.

The belief that they are investigators allows journalists to sustain a sense of individualism: that they have the freedom to use all known investigative techniques to construe the truth and produce the great story. The feeling of individualism persists even in face of the reality of using the interview method predominantly and producing the usual story. This feeling is so strong and persistent that it takes on a mystical character, crystallizing in the myth of investigative reporting. In the myth of investigative reporting methodologies and goals are one: the range of undercover investigative techniques of the reporter-as-detective are entwined with the uncovering of wrongdoing and its 'trial' in the news-reporting process.

A handbook for television journalists recommended a broad conception of investigative journalism: 'While all journalism is, in a wide sense, investigative, the term can be particularly applied to the vigorous, intense examination of institutions or activities which concern public policy or touch upon the lives of a large part of the population. Investigative journalism should examine issues for their importance and should not be exclusively concerned with the revelation of errors, injustice, or wrongdoing.' However, journalists in the television newsroom had a narrower conception. They imagined investigative journalism simply in terms of the uncovering of wrongdoing.

In reality there was little to satisfy their imagination. There were no teams for extended investigations. The only teaming of reporters was to cover a major disaster (e.g., a highrise fire) or a major event (e.g., an election, a parade for the local football team). A few individuals tried to sustain what they regarded as investigations, amidst the daily demands of spot-news production. A reporter conducted 'stake-outs' at a bank that seemed to be the type of bank that had been targeted in recent robberies. One reporter constantly referred to an investigation he was doing into illegal prostitution and gambling establishments. This included sitting parked outside these establishments in his own vehicle, and in his own time apart from his regular shift. The reporter said that the key to his success in obtaining a story was to somehow get inside these prostitution and gambling 'dens' to secure visuals. His explicit goal was to make the facts of this deviance visible to the eye, and of course to capitalize on the subsequent investigations by the authorities in response to the evil he had ferreted out.

At best, television reporters managed occasionally to insert some of their investigative imagination into the reality of routine stories. They gave off signs of their investigative work, at least letting the public know how they wanted to appear. For example, after the bombing of a building, an organization claiming responsibility sent copies of a letter to several news outlets. The letter was received in the television newsroom, but because of inefficiency in the station's mailroom it had been delayed. A producer wanted a reporter to do a story in connection with the newsroom receiving this letter, even though the existence and content of the letter had already been reported by other news organizations that apparently had more efficient mailrooms.

The reporter proceeded to construct his story in terms of three elements: 1 / the receipt of the letter in the newsroom and handing it over to the police; 2 / a break-in at the building the previous night, which police said was unconnected to the bombing but the reporter interpreted as a sign of 'security problems' there; and 3 / the wider issue of the availability of dynamite for purchase. The receipt of the letter was the lead segment, and was constructed in terms of how the news organization was collaborating with the police in the investigation.

Anchor Roll-Up: Metro Police have received new evidence that ties the group Direct Action with the bombing of Litton Systems. A letter arrived in our newsroom today from Direct Action. In it was an exact copy of a warning letter used at the bomb site. [names reporter] reports

Reporter: [visual of the envelope and postmark]
The communique came in a plain white envelope, dated October nineteenth [this was 22 October]. The postal code M4L 3T0 indicates it was mailed in downtown Toronto/
[visual of the reporter in the newsroom pulling the letter out flipping through it. Even though the letter had been handled by many people in the newsroom at this point, the reporter was shown handling the letter with a pair of white gloves]
Inside, the nine-page letter that was released earlier this week, plus one more page/
[visual of a page with bold heading: 'Danger Explosives' followed by a graphic of a van and box, zoom to the box containing dynamite]
It was a copy of a warning taped to a box left in front of the van containing the 550 pounds of dynamite/
[Front shot of the reporter, wearing white gloves, flipping through the letter. Visual of 'Danger Explosives' bold heading on letter, out of focus; Vistas of 'Fifteen to 25 minutes'/'Two detonators'/'Do not enter or move the van'/ 'Phone police immediately']
It warns 'the dynamite would explode fifteen to twenty-five minutes after the van was parked,' that there were two detonating systems and that the van was boobytrapped. It instructs Litton Security to call the police/
[Graphic of box containing dynamite]
An unarmed stick of dynamite was taped to the top of the box. The warning states the stick of dynamite was there to confirm the act wasn't a hoax/
[Shot of a policewoman with the reporter. She had been filmed showing the reporter her badge, and then receiving the letter from the gloved hands of the reporter. She was not wearing gloves]
We turned over the letter to the police as evidence in the case.
[continues with elements (2) and (3) noted above]

The reporter who did this story was working on continuing stories related to the bombing. At the forefront of this story was the imagery of not only reporting on the investigative work of others, but being part of the investigative process. It was evident that the reporter wished to visualize that the evidence had been *handled* properly, and that this was an important collaborative step with the authorities. This visualization was sustained in face of the fact that what was on offer was essentially old news.

In the newspaper newsroom the definition of investigative reporting was focused more on the methods, although it was still connected with uncovering wrongdoing. A senior newspaper executive emphasized that reporting always entails looking for what is wrong so that controls can be improved, and using whatever techniques might allow the matter to be sustained. He indicated that what is regarded as investigative is usually a matter of the time and resources devoted to it, but that in terms of using standard journalistic techniques to visualize deviance all reporting is the same.

A: [In investigative reporting] there's just an enormous amount of leg work that has to be done. It sounds awfully exciting, cops-and-robbery sort of stuff, but the weeks and weeks and weeks and weeks and months of labour, piecing together this little bit of information with that little bit of information, you never see that. I can tell you from having done some of it myself, the business of going over the records and searching back, it takes a certain kind of person who's prepared to do all that day after day after day – you know if you're doing research how boring it can get. It takes somebody who has a penchant for accuracy. You have to be deadly accurate because almost inevitably you're going to end up with defamatory statements and those defamatory statements are going to be libellous unless you are absolutely right and can prove it, and if you can't, you're going to be looking at tens of thousands of dollars in lawsuits. It requires somebody with, usually with a high level of analytical skills who can go through complex problems and issues and arrive at, and separate, the important from the unimportant. And then it's awfully nice to have someone who can write clearly about complex things. Now, that said, there are different kinds of investigative stuff. And the term gets used very loosely. Watergate I guess is the prime example of investigative journalism. Well that's not a case which involved a great deal of research, involved some, but primarily it involved digging away at the people, getting the people to answer questions ... I want us to take a look at what happens to people of limited intelligence who are not retarded in the adult years. We have set up, we have a whole apparatus for handling people with learning who are retarded. In between there are a hell of a lot of people with, say, minimal brain damage. We've been getting some studies lately ... linking violent crime among males to brain damage of one sort or another. There haven't been very many linkages made with women but from what I can make out a lot of them end up on the street ... in prostitution, that sort of thing ... what happens to them? What resources have we got to deal with them? There are group homes but how many of them get into that? Basically talking about the kind of people that need some level of supervision in their lives in order to be able to function ... Now is that investigative reporting? Investigative reporting tends to be imbued with the possibility of uncovering scandal of some sort. Uncovering wrongdoing. I think that's too narrow a definition ... I think you can take this example as investigative journalism and that's the kind of stuff that has always been done traditionally.

Q: So it's more a matter of the method rather than, say, trying to uncover particular things? It's a methodology?

A: Generally speaking you're trying to uncover a situation of some sort. What the hell is happening? What's going on? What's the situation? Where you have to go out and do a fair amount of leg work to uncover what the hell is going on.

Q: But you're going to ask those questions in most situations or most stories. So is it a matter of length: that it's an extensive questioning? Or is it a matter of methodology?

A: No, it's a matter of the amount of time and effort you have put into it. The degree, and I guess, time ... See, I would think that particular story [on what happens to people of limited intelligence] is going to take somebody the better part of a month to do. On the other hand we've had stories take six months. We've just gone through one that's taken ... ten weeks with four people, would be forty weeks for one person ... in man hours you'd be talking about the better part of a year.

In these terms, investigative reporting is no different from other types of reporting except for aspects of intensity (more personnel, time, and technical resources committed) and scale (aimed at righting more significant wrongs).

In the newspaper there was concerted effort to have teams work on something over time, for example, on continuing stories related to deaths of babies on the cardiac ward of a children's hospital, and on continuing stories related to possibly illegal financial transactions involving major corporations and trust companies. However, these were exceptional; did not seem to involve exceptional methods; and in the eyes of some reporters involved, fell short of their ideal of what investigative reporting should be.

Particular individuals in the newspaper newsroom were seen as full-time investigative reporters. While some looked up to these investigative reporters, others stated that their methods were no different. A reporter talked about a colleague who was a 'star' investigative reporter. He noted that his colleague actually did very little investigation. Rather, he relied upon the cultivation of contacts or 'deep throats' inside source organizations to supply basic information which then was pursued otherwise. The resultant material was displayed to the public as if it was obtained following exhaustive and exhausting investigations.

In fact what was most often pointed to as an instance of investigative journalism was a reporter working on a continuing story who was keeping abreast of developments through the assistance of key informants. These were usually known informants who favoured particular reporters because they had proven fair and helpful in previous dealings and reports. For example, in the case of the baby deaths on the hospital ward, some reporters cultivated the victims' parents as sources to learn of developments and to use them publicly to pressure the authorities into disclosure. In general the secret source finds it easy to maintain secrecy since the reporter himself is motivated to collaborate in order to sustain his investigative mystique. The reporter can convey the image that his work was accomplished by long, hard, diligent investigation, rather than by sporadic tit-for-tat chats on the telephone lasting a few minutes.

The limitations on long-term and intensive investigative reporting are threefold. There is the problem of scarce resources in the news organization. There is the enclosure by sources over access to information. And, there is self-enclosure by journalists themselves, who often do not bother to use approaches that lie beyond their own methodological limitations and criteria of objectivity, balance, and fairness.

Limited news-organization resources curtailed serious investigative work. This was especially the case in the television newsroom, where the dozen or so reporters were needed to supply a story a day to keep the show filled. It was simply too costly to assign reporters to something that took them a long time to develop and had no predictable payoff compared to tapping regular sources for a daily supply (see also Epstein, 1974: esp. 24, 36–7).

Sources are another major limitation. Ongoing relations with regular sources mean that reporters are typically precluded from even contemplating more thorough searches for information using methodologies other than interviewing. Those involved in the detection trades have four basic modes of discovery (Reiss, 1983). They can establish a mode of regularized *inspection*. This is usually available to reporters only in the forum of public hearings (e.g., courts, legislatures), which are also open to other members of the public and which usually entail no special privileges of access to back-region proceedings. They can establish means of *surveillance*, looking for deviations from regularized conduct by continual and systematic observation. Reporters are limited in the ability to use this approach because of the spatial limitations on back-region access, the legal and ethical limitations on what would be reportable, and the resource limitations of the newsroom. A third mode is *auditing*, making efforts to aggregate data and match information to detect abuse. This is an increasingly common mode for police and other government and private regulatory agencies (Marx, 1984). It is open to journalists as long as they can obtain access to the data, controlled by other organizations, that will allow them to calculatingly use other people's calculations. Finally there is *investigation*, 'a search for evidence that a particular violation has taken place' which 'often depends on finding ... residues and traces' (Reiss, 1983: 92). Investigation is extremely difficult to accomplish for members of one organization attempting to operate in and against another organization. This is as true for police officers or detectives as it is for journalists (Ericson, 1981, 1982). In large organizations the policing trades typically rely more on inspection, surveillance, and audit than on investigation (Reiss, 1983: 93). The police are at least backed up by enabling legal powers and technological capacity to enter and police organizational life (Ericson and Shearing, 1986). The journalist is in a much more limited position with respect to investigation, as well as in auditing, surveillance, and inspection.

Hence, 'the journalist's investigative methods are primarily interview methods' (Fishman, 1980: 92). While the lack of investigation may be lamented by journalists with reference to the excessive resource commitments required (RCN, 1981: 15–16, 83ff), they are more structurally limited in terms of social, cultural, and political restrictions on penetrating organizational life as embodied in the institution of privacy and articulated in the law. The 'investigations' of reporters are carried on in the context of laws and other structural impediments that are essentially controlling and limiting, while the state's policing authorities have a legal and structural framework that is enabling in design and effect.

Journalists' powers of investigation are also circumscribed by aspects of their own working ideology. The investigative quest accords with the view of journalists that they are interpreters of reality, but it can conflict with notions of objectivity, balance, and fairness. In many instances, and certainly not limited to cases that are designated as investigative stories, the reporter in fact learns far more than he is able to report because of objectivity, balance, and fairness criteria. Moreover, the 'strategic ritual' of objectivity – with the focus on accounts from sources in a point/counterpoint format – means that reporters often report source statements which they are doubtful about in the context of other knowledge and interpretations they have but cannot report directly (cf Fishman, 1980: 87–8; Chibnall, 1977: 36–9). Some journalists expressed to us their perception of a division between what is known and the appearances that are presented in news accounts. Some saw this as a source of cynicism among journalists, and said it made them fall into the conventions of routine news work.

Looked at another way, reporters become conventional because of their reliance upon sources for 'hard facts.' This reliance creates a disinclination to pursue other methodologies. 'A "hard fact" appears to be information delivered as being disclosed by an "unimpeachable source". The validity of sources is again the prerequisite of journalistic intuition, it seems. Any form of conjecture or an investigative approach would "soften" a fact' (GUMG,

1976: 67). The disinclination is strengthened further by the point/counterpoint format, in which one source is used to visualize deviance, and the other source is used to counter that this vision is impaired or is being looked into out of the public eye. If the reporter then initiates his own investigation by using other methods, on behalf of the public eye, he undercuts the value of the point/counterpoint format.

In summary, journalists sometimes go to elaborate lengths to *show* that they are investigators on behalf of the public eye. This much is demanded by their working ideology. However, their private eyes usually look no farther than what a source says in interview. This much limits them to telescopic vision.

OCCUPATIONAL IDEOLOGIES AND PUBLIC LEGITIMACY

In addition to having a bearing on practices, the working ideologies of journalists form part of an *occupational* ideology, a basis for justifying the news product publicly in order to achieve and sustain legitimacy. The major vehicle for sustaining legitimacy is making claims around procedural conceptions. As Habermas (1975) has argued, in contemporary society bureaucratic organizations of all types focus their claims to authority and legitimacy around procedural conceptions.

In the case of journalism, legitimacy is based on procedural conceptions that news is produced in accordance with objective, balanced, and fair criteria. These conceptions have many legitimacy functions for journalism within the wider public culture, and amount to journalism's *claim* to authority. They allow journalists to avoid offending important segments of the mass public. As Smith (1980) and Phillips (1977) have noted, the notion of objectivity only arose with the development of newspapers directed to the *mass* market, and was furthered by television's orientation to the mass audience.

Objectivity claims allow journalists some insulation from charges of error or bias made by sources and the general public. They protect against opening the can of worms associated with admitting that reality is constructed and truth problematic. Like scientists (Mulkay, 1979; Mulkay and Gilbert, 1983) or policemen (Ericson, 1981, 1982; Ericson and Shearing, 1986) journalists must espouse an empiricist view publicly even though they hold a view privately that their decisions are equivocal and context-specific. They realize that this is necessary to sell what is at the very core of their product – authoritative certainty. A conception of objectivity also allows journalists to take topics, sources, story lines, and forms of rhetoric that are based in particular interests, and to translate them to appear as being in the general public interest, thereby reproducing dominant ideological meanings (Hall, 1979: 343).

In the case of journalists, objectivity takes on increased importance in the face of other elements in their work. It is a means of easing selection of sources and stories for the routine production of news in face of limited organizational resources. It is also a means of dealing with the fact that journalists lack specialist knowledge of the matters they report on, and therefore do not have the option of invoking specialist knowledge as a claim to authority as some professions do.

Smith (1980: 169) has commented that the public-culture role of objectivity in journalism is as 'a refuge, not the result of a quest.' At least publicly, journalists' claims to professionalism focus on the procedural means, with little articulation of substantive goals other than to be serving the general public interest as a source of authoritative information and as a watchdog of government. At least officially the journalist is to appear as a disinterested professional. In Elliott's (1978: 184) view, the 'disinterest in ends leads to a concentration on means. The "bland professionals" of the popular press are the "intellectual eunuchs" of broadcast news.' The trick of the trade is for the reporter to make the news so that 'the audience is not only agreeing with the point of view that he has put into his report but actually doesn't think he has put anything in at all' (Cayley, 1982: 132, citing Stuart Hall). At least in the eyes of commentators, 'Television *appears* to fully realize the myth of objectivity. It takes the consumer right to the event. He sees it, doesn't he? He hears it, doesn't he? Now the consumer is himself the reporter and that's a horrible belief because of course what the viewer often forgets, even subconsciously forgets, because television undermines his defences, is that it's organized ...' (Cayley, 1982a: 141, citing Paul Rutherford).

Survey research in Canada (RCN, 1981) and elsewhere does indicate that viewers attribute greater believability to television than to newspapers (e.g., GUMG, 1976: 1–5; CBC, 1978: 379; RCN, 1981: 35–6). However, the more general question that is begged in relation to all news media is, who is taken in? Who really believes that the journalist has not 'put anything in at all,' that the broadcast or print content is a window on the world without any frame?

A survey reported by the Royal Commission on Newspapers (1981a: esp. 51, 57) indicates that Canadian newspaper readers are not taken in even though most of them have only one mass daily in their local market. In this survey, on a scale of 0 (poor) to 10 (excellent), newspapers were rated as only slightly better than average (5) to good (7) on a number of dimensions relevant to our present discussion. To the question does the local daily newspaper clearly separate facts from opinion, only 8 per cent rated it as 'excellent' and 48 per cent as 'good,' with an average score of 5.3. To the question is the daily 'fair and balanced in its coverage,' 9 per cent rated it as 'excellent' and 55 per cent as 'good,' with an average score of 5.8. To the question does the daily have a 'variety of opinions on controversial issues,' 12 per cent rated it as 'excellent' and 45 per cent as 'good,' with an average score of 5.4. Asked if there is an overall 'high level of reporting and journalism,' 13 per cent rated their daily as 'excellent' and 54 per cent as 'good,' with an average score of 6.0. Asked if the local daily gives its readers what they want, 13 per cent rated it as 'excellent' and 55 per cent as 'good,' with an average rating of 6.0.

Furthermore, readers surveyed were very ready to identify the interests associated with the daily newspapers they read. In response to the question, 'which one group's interests do newspapers tend to represent most?' the groups mentioned were government (45 per cent), advertisers (20 per cent), businesses (19 per cent), their readers (6 per cent), politicians (4 per cent), and a variety of others in smaller proportions (13 per cent). Most regular sources also believe the news media slant, distort, and are unfair, and that there are few effective remedies for the source who suffers in the process (Ericson et al, forthcoming a).

The fact that news texts are open to different readings as they enter into different organizational environments with different interests and goals ensures that the effort to traffic in conceptions of objectivity, balance, and fairness is always problematic. Indeed the view that the journalist is not in his product, that he is an automaton always operating with the right calculus of objectivity, fairness, and balance, can be pushed too far. It can create an impossible mandate that contains the seeds of delegitimation because it is belied so blatantly in public experience with news content, and sources' experience with both news content and newsmaking practices. It also creates tension for working journalists, who see public articulation of their news organization's procedural criteria as a means of protecting the organization's 'corporate ass' when something goes wrong, while leaving the individual reporter involved fully exposed.

This point is illustrated from our observations of a news organization's policy seminar, its written policies, and interviews with journalists about policies. The policy seminar focused on a recently published policy handbook that was to stand as an official summary of principles and rules previously stated in different forms. This handbook stated the role of journalists as agents of the public; articulated principles of objectivity, fairness, balance, accuracy, taste, etc.; and stated rules pertaining to the use of particular techniques, such as the requirement of going to a senior-executive level for authorization to use hidden microphones, bodypacks, or cameras.

At the seminar there was great concern among journalists that the written policies were idealistic rather than in accordance with the realities of newsmaking. Journalists felt the organization could not admit publicly what was routine practice, and that in formulating these written policies its intention was to protect itself rather than journalists on the line. The tone was established by the first question from the floor, as a journalist asked, 'How can we get these policies changed?' He gave an example of a rule he wanted changed, but was told it could not be changed because it was an edict reflecting the corporate view.

A discussion ensued about a rule that prohibited the publication of election polls commissioned by the news organization a specified number of days before an election. A journalist demanded a rationale for this rule, and was told it was necessary to maintain the organization's status as 'observer' rather than 'player.' Another journalist pointed out that they were allowed to publish polls done by other organizations. He argued this was peculiar since these polls may be suspect, and at least with its own polls the news organization could control quality. The executive response to this was that these other polls were published and have to be referred to as part of election-campaign coverage.

A reporter voiced his concern about a rule which required authorization from a senior executive for the use of specified questionable techniques. He said journalists try the front door first, and then the back door if necessary. He said his team routinely used bodypacks and concealed cameras to be 'as unobtrusive as possible' so that better quality could be attained in interviews. He stressed that quick decisions had to be made on the spot, and it would be awkward to contact the senior executive as specified in the rule in order to obtain permission. He charged that the rules offered protection to the public and management but none to the reporters, and argued that if management wished to keep the rules they should a / make sure that home telephone numbers of senior executives were available so that consultations could take place at all times of the day or night; and b / ensure that no reporters are criticized afterwards for letting a story go because of the inability to use clandestine techniques. The suggestion was made that reporters should be encouraged to obtain the information and then leave the decision about what could be used to their editors.

In actual practice this last suggestion was sometimes followed. For example, a common technique was to have a tape-recorder or even television camera running when the source did not know it and was chatting informally. If this produced some juicy information for a story, a more senior person would be consulted for a decision about its use, and take responsibility for any repercussions.

In interview a senior person in the news organization that had released the new policy handbook expressed the view that it was a public-culture handbook open to interpretation depending on the circumstances. For him it was the journalistic goals of his newsroom that were paramount, and ways would be found if official procedures got in the way.

A: [Those rules] have also been around since the beginning of time, but, you
     don't ruin your integrity when you do something against policy. You know,
     what's the old line about rules are made to be broken? I mean, these are very
     common-sense things. You just have to instinctively know when you have to
     bend a rule or break a rule in order to achieve something.
Q: You look at that, presumably, in the context of the value of the information
     and the story?
A: Exactly. Exactly.
Q: Why would they bother to put out a policy book like that?
A: ... it is a motley band of individual stations and individuals but in the final
     analysis ... it's all supposed to be run by one person and although ... the cor-
     poration is set up so that all authority travels down from that one person, in
     fact, it doesn't operate like that, but because in theory it operates like that, in
     theory there should also be a single policy.

This person indicated that he would support his subordinates in situations
where important goals superseded the means. He also underscored the general
sentiment of reporters at the policy seminar that their goals were often paramount over the means. In general journalists in this newsroom did not want
to become what Elliott (1978: 184) has termed 'bland professionals' and
'intellectual eunuchs' who ritualistically conformed to procedures designed
for public-culture consumption rather than the practice of journalism.

The importance of journalists' interests and goals has been underem-
phasized in the research literature. This literature generally portrays the newsroom as a homogeneous place with few overt conflicts, as reporters go about
doing what is expected of them in terms of the 'strategic ritual' of objectivity
(Tuchman, 1978; see also, e.g., Chibnall, 1977; Schlesinger, 1978; Fishman,
1980). However, both individual and organizational goals of journalists must
be kept in mind, a matter we return to in the next section. Journalists work
to receive economic reward (e.g., money, status, recognition), to control their
social environment (e.g., use techniques to ease work, to make the work
interesting), to pursue cultural interests (e.g., advancing particular themes or
ideas, selecting topics of interest), and to convey political views (e.g., by
focusing on possible deviance in targeted organizations and promoting the
favoured control remedies of selected sources). Similarly the news organization has economic (profit-making), social (effective organization and management), cultural (promoting collective values and identity), and political
(both partisan and general public-interest) goals. Some of these substantive
goals may articulate with the procedural goals of using proper techniques and
being objective, but they may also conflict and pose contradictions. These
conflicts and contradictions are a significant component of the newsroom
environment, and journalists certainly do not follow the rituals of the norms

laid down among their own peers or at the level of the formal organization. This fact is documented and given emphasis in subsequent chapters.

Having outlined some focal dimensions of the craft, we need to consider how the journalist learns the craft and how norms and values relate to the choices he takes.

Learning the Craft

Our discussion to this point raises the question of how journalists learn the procedures and goals of the occupation, so that they can bring off a published story and recognize that it was done competently. The answers to this question must address the different sources of knowledge pertaining to news work, how they are acquired, and how they relate to news judgments.

The reporter must learn to organize himself to the point where his activities become habitualized. Habitualization narrows choices and makes routine action possible. Of course the news organization itself is structured to produce habitualization, canalizing the reporter's curiosity into the grooves of the occupation.

Organization requires the reproduction of consensus among those required to co-ordinate their activities on the production line. Without a degree of working consensus among managers, editors, and reporters it would be impossible to produce the broadcast show or newspaper. 'The essence of news judgement is that it is consensual. Consensus minimizes the need for discussion and speeds routine role-performance. The daily, time-pressured routines of news-gathering and production can be conducted only because most news judgements, if reviewed, would be concurred in by peers and superiors' (Roshco, 1975: 105). The news organization tries to effect a consensus via effective practices of recruitment, training, supervision, editing, rotation, procedural manuals, and so on. This is an ongoing process, as problems emerge, contradictions are revealed, and conflicts erupt.

FORMAL TRAINING AND SPECIALIZED KNOWLEDGE

One potential source of occupational socialization is formal training. This occurs in universities and community colleges, or in seminars developed by the news organization. It pertains to either the practices of journalism, or to specialized knowledge about the topics journalists report on.

While some journalists we studied had university or community-college education in journalism, it was not greatly valued by them, or by their peers who lacked such qualifications. The common view was that journalism is a trade that must be learned on the job, and if one is going to bother obtaining higher education it is better to obtain a broader liberal education. One journalist, who depicted formal journalism education as 'trade school,' noted that journalism schools are inhabited by former journalists who pass on their old, tested, pragmatic ways of doing the job rather than foster a philosophical and analytical approach. Another journalist, who had a graduate degree in a social science, and who had also completed one year in a graduate journalism course, said he found that course 'useless.' It was his opinion that the job cannot be learned in an academy, but skills must be acquired on the job. He said news organizations need to hire smart people and train them to sharpen their instincts about news, rather than hire journalism students in the hope that they might be smart.

Journalists also stated that they had no *formal* training on the job, or structured guidance. Many of the younger journalists found this to be a source of anxiety, as they struggled to please but received many disappointments when editors rejected their stories or seemed displeased. This problem was mentioned repeatedly by journalists in one news organization studied, who felt in a position of dependent uncertainty in relation to their editors.

The role of specialized knowledge in reporting, acquired through higher education or professional training, has been described as 'one of the great unresolved conflicts of the newsroom' (RCN, 1981b: 63). We found that the matter was resolved quite clearly. Most reporters did not have advanced specialist knowledge. If they did have advanced specialist knowledge, they were not usually assigned to topics or beats in which they could make use of it.

There was agreement among newspaper and television executives interviewed that, from their management viewpoint, specialist knowledge is required only in certain areas of economics and business coverage. Even then, in the words of a newspaper executive, 'I'm not saying that that background has to be academic.' In coverage of criminal justice and legal issues, there was no need for someone trained in law, social science, or criminology.

A reporter said that he was given three days to prepare for his assignment to the court beat. He said he did a little reading, talked to reporters who had previously been on the beat, and observed a few cases, over the three days. A news executive, who had a university degree in law, was asked whether it would be advantageous to have legally trained reporters covering legal topics. His answer was an emphatic no.

A: [W]hat you train them [lawyers] in is a thought process which is almost the antithesis of good reporting. Lawyers, by definition, have to deal with an issue. Their job is not to deal with ... broader issues. It is absolutely impossible to write a story that any two lawyers would agree on. They deal in qualifiers, always, and you can't put the qualifiers in, you can't put all those qualifiers in ...

To be a lawyer, what is important is the issue. Every little fact has to be just so and you build and you construct it on that. You have to know precedent and cases and how and why and you can't let yourself get caught up in the sweep of things or you end up with gaping holes in your case. And it really does create a thought process that is quite the opposite. Generally speaking, lawyers cannot write. They're trained to write for the law ...

Q: More generally, do you see it being better that someone has the qualities of a reporter that you mentioned and therefore can be used flexibly in the organization, to move from desk to desk and assignment to assignment?

A: Well, it's awfully useful to have people with, who can be generalists ... [Even if someone had a PhD in economics I] wouldn't let them report on economics for three or four years. I'd have them out chasing fire engines and police and work up, and go through the whole range of reporting. At four or five years down the line, you might find you've got one hell of a good person ...

At this juncture in the interview this executive discussed the fact that reporters assigned to beats in other cities in Canada or internationally must be good writers and able to cover a wide range of topics. They do not have to be experts in local politics or foreign affairs, but rather persons with a nose for significant trends or developments in any sphere of life, able to translate it into an interesting story that articulates with the common sense of the readership. This was indicated, for example, by the reassignment of a journalist working in the sports section of a newspaper to the bureau in China. He had a reputation as a first-rate writer of interesting stories, which was required of anyone with the China assignment. Another journalist who had held the China posting had prior to that been a regular writer for the entertainment section of the newspaper. The newspaper executive underscored the need for a generalist by using the example of a posting to London, England.

I mean he has to be all over that EEC [European Economic Community] stuff as well as ... cover the theatre, the House of Commons, the Irish situation and what the hell's going on in Europe, the EEC, sports, to cover the Olympic games, to be able to do skiing and the world ski championships, soccer ... [Y]ou really have to go the route of running the full gamut of reportorial experience in order to gain the breadth that would make you among the best ... You could become a very good economic reporter or you could become just a superb writer. Able to do anything and with particular strengths than somebody else. That's the person ... you would love to have ... if you've got somebody with a PhD in economics, eventually five years, six years, seven years, eight years down the line, he could work extremely well for you in London provided he can also write about [many other things] ...

The generalist is obviously preferred in the newspaper, and even more so in the television newsroom. In one television newsroom we observed, a reporter who had graduate education in the social sciences, and read avidly, was the subject of frequent teasing and jibes. His ambitions to cover matters with greater breadth and depth were regularly undercut by his superiors who directed him to 'keep it simple.' For example, one morning several reporters were assigned to cover aspects of a major continuing story involving a series of complex, possibly illicit financial transactions. The reporter in question eagerly informed the assignment editor that he could bring to bear some research he had been doing on the matter, but the assigment editor kept telling him to forget it and concentrate on a point/counterpoint interview format, using two politicians with opposing views on how the matter should be controlled.

Being a generalist is not only a matter of being able to cover a variety of topics. It also entails having experience on a number of news desks and learning the particular methodology and presentational style associated with the desk. For example, writing for a 'travel' or 'homes' section requires an approach that is very uncritical of the related industries, because these are essentially advertising sections in which the stories themselves are a form of advertising and one does not wish to bite the hand that feeds. In contrast, writing for the sports section frequently includes throwing barbs at the personalities involved and trying to manufacture controversy in a bombastic manner. What is said about the coach of the local team, or about Harold Ballard or George Steinbrenner, would be totally out of place and probably treated as libellous if it were said about the local chief of police or about the mayor.

There are different methodologies even on the same desk, with some reporters being expected to do more hard-hitting 'investigative' pieces, others being expected to develop specialization by sustained work on one topic area with carefully cultivated sources, and still others being expected to do 'fire chasing' stories, updates,and human-interest stories. From the perspective of management, depth and breadth mean having worked across a number of desks using a range of these styles, rather than having specialist knowledge and long-term experience in any one of them.

The availability of generalists has a number of advantages to the news organization. There is the economic advantage of not having to hire a range of specialists. Generalists can be shifted to other assignments in the face of such contingencies as holidays, cutbacks brought about by decreasing advertising revenue, and special assignments where teams of reporters are required. As Tuchman (1978: 67) reports, 'Specialties are ignored when necessary. Everyone must be capable of doing everyone else's work ... For all recognizably newsworthy stories to be covered, each specialist must be a generalist, and vice versa.'

The de-emphasis on specialist knowledge also means that reporters have no special claim to news-relevant knowledge that is not also available to their supervising editors. Supervising editors are assumed to know as much as reporters, thus allowing them a control over the decisional autonomy of their subordinates which would not be possible if their subordinates could claim specialist knowledge.

The lack of specialized knowledge has a double edge regarding relations with sources. If a reporter has specialist training and knowledge he may become too personally involved in the area because of his professional affinity with sources. The lack of specialist knowledge may allow him to maintain a detached stance and attitude that are more in accordance with the occupational ideology of journalism. However, the lack of specialist knowledge can make the reporter more dependent on his sources. Reporters observed that if one works on a specialist topic such as legal issues, but without having had specialist training in law, then one has to depend on sources for ideas, quote extensively from them, and be cautious about interpretation. This gives sources much greater control than if one has the specialist knowledge that would allow more independent judgment as to what is a significant idea, and more ability to interpret what has been said about it. We observed instances where a reporter obtained a professional's document pertaining to the matter reported on, but was unable to understand it and in consequence had to interview the professional who prepared it in order to understand it and translate it for the purpose of news discourse. In these instances professionals were asked to translate their work into the common sense, and reporters were simply left to convey it.

The availability of generalists who write well or have a good style of presentation is also important for ensuring that the news product is in accordance with the audience's common sense. As stressed by the newspaper executive cited earlier, adherence to a professional discourse such as law is the antithesis of what is required for news discourse. Regardless of any other knowledge or training, the reporter must develop the ability to convert events in the world into the common sense. The attitude, methodology, and form of writing of specialized professionals must be eschewed in favour of the attitude, methodology, and form of writing of journalism. When a member of the public picks up a newspaper or turns on broadcast news, he is not after the genre of the legal case report or law-journal article. He is after the common sense about law that is offered by the genre of news. To the journalist, this is only common sense.

NORMS AND KNOWLEDGEABILITY

If formal training and specialized knowledge are not primary components in learning the craft, we must consider elements in 'the commonsense reality of the organizational members' (Manning, 1982: 124–5), their occupational culture.

The dominant approach in the study of organizations has been to observe members' practices in order to infer the norms or rules that arise among practitioners and seem to direct their work. As Sandy (1979: 529) states regarding the study of organizations generally, 'If, after having completed the ethnography, the observer can communicate the rules for proper and predictable conduct as judged by the people studied, he or she has produced a successful product. The ethnographer is like a linguist who has studied a foreign language so that others can learn the rules for producing intelligible speech in that language.'

The search for members' norms or rules has been the dominant approach in the study of journalists' decisions. Adopting the normative paradigm in sociology, researchers have focused on what they believe to be the 'official and unofficial (but, nonetheless, literal) values, norms, and rules [which] constitute a template against which events sui generis and stories portraying those events are measured for their newsworthy character' (Lester, 1980: 985). This approach is exemplified in the work of Chibnall (1977), whose scrutiny of crime reporters yields a substantial list of the values and norms that are said to be used by journalists to guide their news judgments. Chibnall sees these in a fairly deterministic fashion, referring to them as 'the professional *imperatives* of journalism' (pp. 13, 22ff). Chibnall also uses the rules he derives from observation to explain how journalists report on particular phenomena. For example, 'at least five sets of informal rules of relevancy in the reporting of violence' – '1. Visible and spectacular acts. 2. Sexual and political connotations. 3. Graphic presentation. 4. Individual pathology. 5. Deterrence and repression' – are said to guide journalists' behaviour and are used to explain their behaviour of judging the newsworthiness of violent events. Following the early example of Breed (1955), researchers have also examined how conformity of subordinates and peers is achieved via norms of the occupational culture.

This normative approach is problematic for a number of reasons. The view is created that journalists are automatons who follow the paths laid down in the normative system. A normative determinism prevails which ignores the interpretive, constructive nature of newsmaking, and the ongoing conflicts that characterize relations among journalists. As in other occupations – for example, police work (Ericson, 1981, 1982) or scientific work (Mulkay, 1979; Mulkay and Gilbert, 1983) – there is a significant disjunction between the professional norms professed in the public culture and the degree of commitment to them by members of the working culture. As stressed previously, journalists are very aware of the corporate need to profess values and standards publicly, even if they bear an imperfect and ambiguous relation to what occurs in their everyday judgments.

Academic researchers tend to accept the public-culture values and norms of journalism at face value. Therefore they limit their inquisitiveness to whether journalists are 'following' their normative obligations, and to the nature and direction of their deviations. That is, their focus is upon rules of *obligation* within journalism. What they ignore is occupational-culture rules about *excuses*, which allow journalists to avoid moral criticism or penalty despite taking actions which do not seem to be in conformity with the prevailing norms. As Brandt (1969: 348; see also Edgerton, 1985) observes more generally, 'An anthropologist wishing to give a complete account of the moral code of a society would list not only the prima-facie rules of obligation accepted by most adults in the society, but also the accepted rules about excuses from moral criticism despite breach, in some way or other, of the rules of obligation – just as a description of a system of criminal law would list not only what kinds of behavior are penalized and how much, but also such facts as that insanity is an accepted defense against any criminal charge.' Within journalism, under what circumstances and attendant rules is it possible to act outside the strategic ritual of objectivity? to use deceptive techniques of questioning and deceptive technologies of recording? to use sources other than the authorized knowers of official bureaucracies? etc. Are these exceptions which prove the rules, or do rules bear a different relation to action than the normative approach conveys?

There are serious methodological problems associated with the normative approach. Since the researcher infers the norms of the occupational culture from observation of journalists' behaviour, there is sometimes ambiguity as to whether the norms are those of the journalists used in taking action, or whether they are those of the researcher used analytically. There is also the problem of tautology, in that rules are inferred from observation of journalists making judgments and then used to explain their judgments.

Beyond this, one must consider that there is a level of action which cannot be explained in terms of norms or rule following (cf Harris, 1974). It is commonplace in journalism, as in other occupational cultures, for its practitioners to say that their judgments do not entail following rules. For example, a television producer told us that there are no rules pertaining to newsmaking, that reporters work 'by instinct' and 'from the gut.' A senior newspaper editor told us that news reporting is 'haphazard.' He related a story about teaching a journalism class in which he invited a practising journalist to talk to students about news judgments; this journalist was so tongue-tied when it came to articulating his methodological rules that the teacher had to lead him through the talk with a series of questions.

It is common that actors engaged in a particular activity are unable to articulate the rules about it. Taking an example used by Wittgenstein, children can co-ordinate their activities in playing a game yet be unable to articulate the rules they are following. People can also co-ordinate their activities through the use of a language and yet be unable to articulate the rules of grammar connected with their usage. Our point in the case of journalists is that their own view that news judgments are not rule-governed should be taken seriously as part of an appreciation that it is not just norms or rules which underpin organizational order.

Rules always require interpretation beyond what is specified in the rules themselves, and their meaning is never self-evident in particular applications. Except in the few occupations where the person is required to explicitly rationalize judgment in the normal course of decision-making – such as judges being required to give written judgments – action is usually taken without even explicit reference to rules. Indeed, actors can accomplish a competent performance of their work without even being aware of rules pertaining to it, or disagreeing with one another as to the relevant rules if they are called upon to give an account.

These points about the nature of rules as they relate to action can be appreciated by considering the fact that there are few efforts by news organizations to provide a written manual for journalistic practice. As discussed previously, one news organization did produce a guidebook stating general principles, as well as rules pertaining to specific practices, but this was subject to much criticism because it was seen as impractical in actual decision-making situations and as a means of corporate legitimation in the public culture. One reporter in this newsroom said he also had a style manual that was about a decade old, and other journalists had not even heard of it. A newspaper had its own style manual, but reporters said that it was not consulted regularly in the course of preparing stories. This newsroom had no codified rule book pertaining to news judgments. In general, journalists scoffed at the impracticality of rule books pertaining to the search for information or the style in which it is presented. Learning the craft does not involve consultation of such authoritative texts. It comes from consulting news texts, being scrutinized by editors, talking to more experienced colleagues, and doing the work.

The organizational ethnographer should be most appreciative of this point because of the nature of his own craft. As much as textbooks in qualitative social-science research techniques may be printed and consulted, they do not provide a set of operational rules for bringing off a successful piece of participant-observation research. As Runciman (1983: 243) observes about the participant observer in social science:

> Even if he is satisfied with the adequacy of his underlying theory, he still
> faces the task of establishing criteria of selection and emphasis within the
> group or category to be described. Where and how is he to ground his deci-
> sion as to which of its members is the authentic spokesman for the rest, which
> of the things said and done by different persons within it are to be claimed to

be typical or what degree of self-awareness is to be imputed to those least prone to try, unless prompted, to formulate a description of their own experience to themselves? The technically experienced fieldworker learns, among other things, how to test his own provisional descriptions against the most immediate criticisms to which a failure to surmount these difficulties would expose him. But even after a whole career of participant-observation he will not have arrived at a copybook procedure for doing so.

What is required is knowledge about the knowledgeability that the 'technically experienced' journalist brings to bear on news judgments. 'Actors need considerable background knowledge and experience to communicate successfully, and this knowledge cannot be reduced to rules' (Poole and McPhee, 1983: 207). The same can be said about the ethnographer of news organizations, who must have sustained involvement with journalists to appreciate the background knowledge and experience they use in making news judgments and in communicating successfully in news discourse. *Part* of this is knowledge about how rules do pertain to action: how rules not only regulate action, but enable or constitute action; and, how rules are used to account for action taken to make it legitimate or accountable. But knowledgeability includes many other aspects of the craft that are acquired through collective experience and become established as precedent. Precedent encompasses a much broader range of craft capabilities and competence than rule usage, and it is this which must be understood in order to appreciate both the journalistic craft and how it is learned.

THE VOCABULARY OF PRECEDENTS

When talking about their craft and how skill is acquired, journalists emphasize that it is a matter of learning by experience and precedent on the job. The process is a subtle one, arising in daily transactions among reporters, sources, editors, and news texts. What is learned through experience is 'recognition knowledge' (e.g., how to recognize an event in terms of news frames; how to recognize the type of source who is appropriate for a story of this type); 'procedural knowledge' (e.g., how to go on with developing the story; methods of contacting the appropriate sources; lines of questioning that will work; operating within time and material-resource constraints); and 'accounting knowledge' (how to formulate an item in news discourse; how to justify actions taken if someone questions what has been done). The collective wisdom of the craft is well summarized in the concept of 'the vocabulary of precedents': the ongoing verbal articulation of the current state of recognition, procedural, and accounting knowledge required to accomplish a competent performance of the work.

As articulated by a senior news executive, formal training in journalism school or academic settings is not as important as 'the day-by-day-by-day interplay on the floor between editors and reporters. That's by far the most important part [of training].' He also mentioned the work of the quality editor, who 'always marks up the paper every day and gives it to the editors in the various departments' as a more routinized form of perpetual training. He stressed that the system for learning what is newsworthy and how to produce it in the newspaper genre is embedded in interaction patterns 'on the floor':

A: Well, there's no objective, stated guideline which tells them what's news and what isn't. But there's a daily interaction with editors saying, 'Your lead is here and this is what's important and this is what's new.' And with reporters that are just learning or that are having difficulty with things then you can keep an eye out for what they write, you know, it's a learning process.

Q: So you see the system come through interaction?

A: Yeah, through a long interaction. There's a very great in-built resistance to dealing with stories in a way other than what has been the traditional way of dealing with them. So the paper tends to move very slowly to new usages, new ways of doing things. We still don't use Ms. for instance.

Q: Is that because most training is done by people who are more experienced and who have been trained in the old ways and so on?

A: The news editors tend to be older. The department heads tend to be older, have been around a long time. The assistant department heads tend to have been there for a long time and there is a style to the paper in the sense of what's right and what's wrong and it comes through that long incubation period.

Another person we interviewed had been involved in developing an alternative newspaper representing the interests of a particular social group. His experience was also one of developing journalists on the job.

We had to start out, in a sense acquiring and growing people who could write, could be journalists. And what we found is almost anyone who can write, already knows how to write journalism as it appears in daily newspapers, just by virtue of reading it, they've sorted out what is required of a reporter ... We get people coming here all the time who turn in stories that sound just as if they were written to appear in the *Star* or the *Globe* or the *Sun*. And so, obviously there's a very mass educational process that goes on just from being in contact with the media which a lot of us are ... And so first of all you absorb that way, the idea of what is news and how it's given to people. O.K., well then ... you therefore [can] go through journalism school where all of these practices are in fact drummed into you ... although again there's a contradiction between exactly what you're told in journalism school and what you find when you get into working for a daily paper. And on top of that, of course there's just a pressure of the work place. I mean, how does any employee learn what is approved of and what isn't approved of? Well, you know, you find that your story, certain stories of yours don't get published. O.K., every reporter has that experience, but in picking out which ones aren't getting published, you know. There's also informal control that goes on in any institution. No one issues a set of rules saying you should write negative stories about unions, but you get feedback from your immediate superior and from your co-workers and from readers and so on, you know, so it's a very subtle process. I don't think it's at all conspiratorial in nature. There's something about the feedback ... An important thing I think about journalism which is often over-looked is ... it's one of the few industries in which ... there are no personnel departments, that a given reporter is usually hired directly by the person he or she will be working for ... I always thought that was significant because it means that there's that extra degree of control in weeding out people who you think might not be trustworthy.

For the reporter, the learning process includes a system of rewards and punishments. At stake is job security, promotion, and salary. Beyond this there are the specific recognition rewards of the craft: for the newspaper reporter, getting prominent play and a byline; for the television reporter, making the show and appearing high in the order in which items are broadcast. A reporter described this process as being analogous to the Eskimo carver who eventually learns the standards and taste of the urban marketplace and shapes his products accordingly.

The basis of news judgment is in common occupational experience and the exemplars provided by that experience. What journalists observe is me-diated by the vocabulary of symbolic resources or cultural categories which they develop in their working culture. Hence the 'trained' journalist is one who can readily recognize an event in terms of its significance as news, know how to proceed with selecting and interviewing sources or acquiring docu-ments relevant to the task, and produce an account within news discourse that will be judged competent. The trained journalist sees things differently than the untrained journalist, and it is the task of management to teach initiates their way of seeing.

Crime and police reporting was seen generally as an ideal training ground because it includes the archetypal elements of news stories, routinely available from bureaucratic sources. Reporters begin in this area, and then move to other beats or topic areas where they can employ the basic frames on other issues of deviance and control. The place of crime and police reporting as a training ground, and as a routinized form of newsmaking, means that it is of low status within journalism (Chibnall, 1977). By way of comparing cultural workmen, crime novels are low status in literary circles (Knight, 1980: 138), and criminology is low status in academic social-science circles, albeit for different reasons.

We found that when they were pressed to articulate rules, journalists told stories or anecdotes about particular judgments they made in particular stories (cf Tuchman, 1978: 47, 99; Darnton, 1975). This type of response is not peculiar to journalism, but is common to all social groups (Giddens, 1976), even those occupations, such as police work, which require members to be highly rule conscious and rule oriented. However, these anecdotes, as related among the members of the craft, provide an important part of the vocabulary of precedents: teaching and reminding one another about what seems the right and wrong thing to do in particular circumstances, and what are the likely consequences.

In the process, journalists acquire and carry around with them not a set of internalized norms or precise recipes of how to perfect any given story, but a sense of how to look at an event and consult sources to make a story out of it. The precedents the journalist learns from his own experience and the talk of his experienced colleagues impregnate each judgment, and each judgment in turn is impregnating for future judgments. In this context, the wisdom of Aldous Huxley is apt: 'Experience is not what happens to man. It is what a man does with what happens to him.'

The experience embodied in the vocabulary of precedents is crucial to the journalist's search for truth and the integrity with which the search takes place. Faced with judging what is significant, interpreting the veracity of sources' accounts, and writing in words that convey fairness and truthfulness, the journalist requires both moral integrity and experience in a wide range of organizational spheres and situations with a variety of people. As Bok (1979: 303) observes: '[T]he ethical cannot be detached from reality, and consequently continual progress in learning to appreciate reality is a necessary ingredient in ethical action. In the question with which we are now concerned, action consists of speaking. The real is to be expressed in words. That is what constitutes truthful speech. And this inevitably raises the question of the "how?" of these words. It is a question of knowing the right word on each occasion. Finding this word is a matter of long, earnest and ever more advanced effort on the basis of experience and knowledge of the real.'

Part of learning the discretion (power) one has in decision-making is learning to use discretion (tact) in the process. Since the journalist's products can touch the lives of many, and inflict harm on those directly involved in a story, this is a crucial matter and something which must be worked at constantly. Again discretion is a matter of blending ethical considerations with broad experience in organized life.

At its best, discretion is the intuitive ability to discern what is and is not intrusive and injurious, and to use this discernment in responding to the conflicts everyone experiences as insider and outsider. It is an acquired capacity to navigate in and between the worlds of personal and shared experience, coping with the moral questions about what is fair and unfair, truthful or deceptive, helpful or harmful. Inconceivable without an awareness of the boundaries surrounding people, discretion requires a sense for when to hold back in order not to bruise, and for when to reach out. The word 'tact' conveys the physical sense of touching that these boundaries evoke. (Bok, 1982: 41)

Learning this discretion as well as other aspects of news judgment is derived in part from source individuals and organizations. Particularly if he is on a regular beat, the reporter becomes socialized in terms of source expectations about what is reportable, who are authorized knowers, and how it is to be reported. Reporters acquire knowledge of institutional procedures in the source organization which allows them to know who is in a position to know about a given matter, who are the most reliable spokespersons, and how their statements are to be assessed. They acquire knowledge of where objectivated knowledge is available within the source organization, and of how it is distributed hierarchically, spatially, and temporally. In sum, reporters must also assimilate the local knowledge of the source organizations they report on, and incorporate it into their vocabulary of precedents. The symbolic resources of source occupational cultures must be taken into account, exercising discretion in the formulation of accounts. 'These local structures of knowledge are what reporters must understand, take into account, and manipulate, not only to guide themselves through their beat, but also to interpret what they are exposed to' (Fishman, 1980: 52–3).

The vocabulary of precedents, learned from colleagues, editors, sources, and content, is the stock of knowledge which the journalist has available to take action and provide an account of it. The fact that it is available only through experience and orally, and not formulatable in copybook form, is the key to explaining why journalists perceive their work as not being highly organized or systematic. Among journalists we studied, the belief persisted that judgment was based on having a 'nose for news.' As Schlesinger (1978: 47) found, it is as if news eventuates by 'recurring accident' in the context of 'the belief that news is somehow the product of a *lack* of organization.' This is so in face of the reality of their daily efforts to make their work routine and predictable, and in spite of an historical record which shows journalism has become increasingly collective, hierarchical, and industrialized (Smith, 1980: 203–4).

There was variation in this perspective between media. Newspaper journalists were emphatic that their judgments are based on individual senses rather than on organizational consensus. In contrast, the routine format of television-news items and their technical and time constraints gave television journalists an appreciation of systematic features. Thus a television producer emphasized that all of the essential boundaries are drawn for the image of his show. Reporters are left to give colour and texture within these boundaries. That requires the craft skills of an artist, but the boundaries themselves have little elasticity. In the producer's words, 'The program is paint-by-numbers. The only thing that changes are the parts each day, essentially the structure is the same. Essentially the system of writing scripts and getting scripts into the right order, getting the lineup done, all those things are systems.'

Structures are in place, but decisions are taken situationally in terms of tacit knowledge about the people involved, interests, priorities, resources, and timing. In the process something fairly uniform and predictable in terms of the structure of content is produced. It seems that the news organization's expectations are put into effect despite the fact that they remain implicit and worked out in daily interaction.

An example illustrating this point is derived from our observations in a television newsroom. A reporter was assigned to a story about a continuing matter that he had not worked on before. He proceeded to obtain two news-paper clippings about the story, and a copy of an item done by a newsroom colleague about two and one-half months previously. He then contacted a source and filmed an interview with him, and proceeded to write his script. Upon showing his script to a producer, he was told that another reporter in the newsroom had done an item on the same continuing story three days before, and it was almost identical to what he had done. The reporter obtained the script of this previous item and found that it was indeed the same story.

When asked to account for why two reporters working on the same story produce similar pieces, a television producer attributed it to the fact that they are both trained journalists. In his view, any trained journalist will recognize what is newsworthy about an event and treat it accordingly. He said that in his own work it was quite predictable what items would be high on the lineup and what would be the lead item. He noted that he could not make some trivial matter the lead item. He had a standing bet with the lineup editor regarding what would be the lead item each day on the U.S. network newscasts and claimed a high degree of predictive ability between the two of them.

The question of how uniform and predictable news products are, even though they are produced by procedures that seem equivocal to practitioners, can be addressed by considering the criteria of newsworthiness employed by journalists. The vocabulary of precedents is used to identify the prevailing structure and system, the social and cultural criteria of news organization. Equipped with this knowledge, the journalist can decide what is worthy of consideration as news. A journalist's knowledgeability, and the social and cultural system within which he works, meet in judgments of newsworthiness.

5

Newsworthiness

All of the components of journalism introduced in previous chapters bear upon judgments of newsworthiness. The journalist visualizes newsworthiness on the basis of his knowledge of social organization (material resources, rules, and relationships in his own newsroom and in his sources' organizations) and cultural organization (working and occupational ideologies in his own news-room and in his sources' organizations and the dominant ideology in society). These multi-factor judgments are made situationally and contextually, and can shift repeatedly in the course of choosing a frame, deciding upon sources, interviewing sources, and writing, editing, and slotting a story. The fact that a story involves multiple considerations (e.g., legal, audience, sources, in-stitutional and organizational resources) and has multiple intended functions (e.g., information, entertainment, policing organizational life) means that the criteria of newsworthiness are multiple, intersect, and are not easy to sort out by the research analyst. While the analyst may read a normative ordering into criteria of newsworthiness, they normally enter the journalist's choice-making in an unprogrammatic way. In making a story the journalist draws upon the vocabulary of precedents to program these elements as he sees fit.

General Criteria

A number of general criteria of newsworthiness have been identified in the literature (e.g., Chibnall 1977: chap. 2; Galtung and Ruge, 1981; Hartley, 1982: chap. 5). As we have argued through the notion of the vocabulary of precedents, these are not to be conceived as 'news imperatives of journalism' (Chibnall, 1977: 22ff). Rather, they are elements which help the journalist to recognize significance, proceed with choices among alternatives, and ac-

count for the choices he has made. Along with the elements of social organization, the journalist takes them into consideration in programming the news.

SIMPLIFICATION

The paradigm of newsworthiness available in the vocabulary of precedents
includes the notion of simplification. An event must be recognizable as event-
ful, and yet relatively unambiguous in its meaning. 'In news, the intrinsic
polysemic (ambiguous – capable of generating many meanings) nature of both
events and accounts of them is reduced as much as possible; in literature [and
certain types of social science] it is celebrated and exploited' (Hartley, 1982: 77).
For example, a problematic and complex financial transaction involving many
parties over time is very difficult to deal with in newspaper format, and almost
impossible for television. This may be one reason why the news generally
gives less attention to corporate crime than to street crime. As uneventful as
it may be in terms of impact on a reader's knowledge or personal circumstances, the latest murder in town is at least recognizable in a simple way.

Simplification is also constituted by the cultural proximity of an event.
If something occurs outside Canada, it can be more evidently meaningful if
it takes place in nation-states which are culturally proximate, in particular the
United States, Britain, France, or other countries of Western Europe. Additionally, something done in countries elsewhere but affecting Canada, the
United States, or other culturally proximate countries is of greater salience.
A senior newspaper editor noted the slow and meagre news reaction to the
mass expulsion of immigrants from Nigeria in early 1983. Over the first few
days of trying to give coverage, he complained about the lack of interest in
this event by U.S. journalists, which meant that there were no suitable still
photographs available on the wire. The location of bureaux in foreign countries, and content analyses of foreign news, also indicate that most items
come from or through places with the greatest cultural affinity.

The same point can be made about domestic coverage. In the Toronto
media there are more items from Toronto than from other parts of Ontario,
and more items from other parts of Ontario than from the rest of Canada.
Moreover, what is deemed a prominent concern in the dominant culture will
take precedence over the concerns of a particular minority. This is not to say
that the concerns of a particular minority will not be addressed, but the terms
of address are those of the dominant culture. Moreover, there will be differential attention depending on the relative political significance and power of
the particular minority interest. For example, in contemporary Canadian society the political purpose of, say, crime victims or women is much more
significant than that, say, of accused persons or homosexuals (Rock, 1986),
and their significance as news is elevated accordingly.

DRAMATIZATION

Newsworthiness also depends on recognizing how an event can be visualized as important or as indicating a dramatic development. There is a news threshold below which something will not be reported. Obviously, this threshold varies enormously according to what else is available, cultural proximity, who is involved, and a host of other elements.

A television newsroom we studied regularly reported murders in the city, and even sent crews occasionally to towns more than one hundred miles from the city to cover ordinary domestic murders. However, in the context of a fire in a highrise hotel/apartment complex – which included many dramatic visuals, a death, and the potential for 'endless' questions about safety – murders were no longer significant. On the day of the fire, a murder was ignored as virtually everyone in the newsroom was covering aspects of the fire incident. Even four days after the fire, with only four general reporters available, assignments were made to cover fire follow-ups rather than to report on murders on the weekend.

With cathected scenarios of flames leaping from the eighteenth story, people screaming, emergency-services personnel coming to the rescue, and news-media–contracted helicopters hovering to obtain an overview, the drama seems self-evident. However, in more routine events both sources and journalists must work at conveying their dramatic qualities. We observed examples where the same television newsroom did not use fire-story items because the visuals were deemed not to be dramatic enough. For example, an editor asked in one case whether there was 'a shot of the guy coming out in flames' or a death involved, and when there was a negative reply to both points he gave the 'thumbs down' sign, meaning the story was 'out.' However, a crew who happened to be passing a car which caught on fire, and obtained visuals of the driver trying to put the fire out with a blanket, had their item at the top of the station's local night newscast.

PERSONALIZATION

Dramatization is often bound up with another aspect of newsworthiness, personalization. Events are portrayed in terms of key individuals involved, and the effects on individuals of what has transpired. Key sources who are cast in this role become 'public figures' and in turn actively stage performances that will be played in the news media. While the news is about organizational life, the organizations are personified by the significant players involved. 'In the mass mediated version of reality, organizations, bureaucracies, movements – in fact all larger and enduring social formations – are reduced to personifications' (Gitlin, 1980: 146).

The involvement of personalities extends also to the reporter in some cases. Television news relies on the anchorperson as the focal point of the show, but regular reporters representing 'the people' are also a vehicle of personalization and dramatization. The newspaper equivalent is the daily columnist, who offers personal opinions and the equivalent of signed editorials and often has a head-shot photograph of himself appear alongside his column headline.

The fact that a public figure is involved can be a deciding factor in deeming something newsworthy. For example, in the coverage of crime, those incidents involving a prominent figure are more likely to be reported. This fact extends into coverage on the court beat, where the reporter checked the court list not in terms of serious crimes as much as in terms of prominent people who were offenders or victims. The media personality as 'public figure' was included here, as evidenced by a case of tax evasion on the part of an information-show host being deemed newsworthy. In court, the fact that a prominent member of the local bar was a defence lawyer in a case not only sensitized the reporter to the possibility that it might be an interesting or significant case, but led him to consider covering it through the angle of the personality of the defence lawyer alone.

In the context of serious crime and disaster incidents, it was common to personalize through the 'fear and loathing' of victims or their friends, neighbours, and relatives in grief. This approach was an effort to provide tertiary understanding of what it was like to be involved in, or close to someone involved in, the calamitous event. In our observations, this approach was frequently used on a continuing-story basis regarding ongoing problems or issues: for example, interviewing the mothers of babies who died on the cardiac ward of a hospital where murder was suspected; and, interviewing the family and friends of murder victims, as well as individual women and representatives of women's groups, regarding their fear of attacks on women (see Voumvakis and Ericson, 1984). In this latter case, a reporter from a 'popular' news outlet told us of explicit assignments from editors to obtain accounts from women expressing fear; any competing accounts would simply be ignored. Major items appeared in some outlets which were exclusively devoted to women's expressions of fear (e.g., ibid: 54).

Personalization is not an end in itself, but a key technique used in conjunction with other techniques to communicate with certain ends in mind. For example, 'quality' news outlets engaging in a continuing story with the goal of forcing accountability in the organizations concerned personalized as part of the process. They identified key persons who should be held accountable and drew moral-character portraits of them. Indeed, it is arguable that personalization or individualization is a necessary part of the imputation of moral fault (cf Brandt, 1969), and news organizations interested in finding fault and forcing accountability are therefore bound to personalize.

Another aspect of personalization in fourth-estate stories was the identification of the victims of the problem, and dramatization of their plight, as
a way of generating public sympathy and pressure that something should be
done. During a period in which trust companies in Ontario were being in-
vestigated for questionable or illicit practices, they were closed to depositors
for a short time and then reopened. A news outlet which had a team working
on this matter to actively force government action and regulation sent a reporter
to cover the reopening of the trust-company banking branches. The angle
taken, with front-page coverage, was to find people queuing outside who had
substantial sums on deposit and who could ill afford to lose their money. For
example, a retired person with 'life' savings deposited was quoted regarding
the consequences for her of losing the money. Asked about this coverage, a
senior editor agreed that the strategy was to reinforce the potential victimization involved as part of keeping the wider continuing story 'alive' and
forcing government action. He articulated also the fact that even 'quality'
outlets need to convey complex matters through simple folk. Speaking generally, he pointed out that personalization also simplifies:

> [Q]uite often it helps to understand what's happening if you take a personal
> case and say, look, the impact of this whole thing can be seen in the case of
> Mrs Jones. Here's what it can do. You're reading about all these immense
> financial dealings involving hundreds of millions of dollars and high-priced
> lawyers and government departments and all kinds of things going on and very
> complicated manoeuvres and international financial transactions and Saudi
> Arabians and numbered companies and all this sort of stuff. The outcome of
> that can be seen in the case of Mrs Jones. Here's what it means to her. Her
> husband is dead. She sold her house. She put her money into a guaranteed
> investment certificate and her life savings are locked up in a company that
> looks as if it's going down the drain and here is this eighty-three–year–old
> woman and this is the impact it's having on her. Now there's a need for that
> kind of a story. To take the story into the microcosm, into ... the very per-
> sonal situation of an elderly lady. But you can't do it in isolation, you have
> to do it against the full background of explaining several levels of what's
> going on.

THEMES AND CONTINUITY

For the news media, the full background of what's going on consists of
establishing and using recognizable frames for understanding the particular
item being reported. Newsworthiness involves establishing the flow of news
items in terms of frames for visualizing them. The lack of a basis for visualizing an event in a recognizable news frame will lead to a lack of interest
in it by journalists.

The particular event is more newsworthy if it is continuous with previous events, in the sense that the reporter is able to place it within a salient frame. The newsworthy is not that which is new, but that which fits into a familiar frame or into the existing knowledge of news discourse. Except where the matter seems self-evident, as in the cathected scenarios of the highrise fire described earlier, imaginative effort is required on the part of the journalist. He must de-construct what is going on in the event, and re-make it into an instance of the news theme.

> This procedure requires that an incident be stripped of the actual context of its occurrence so that it may be relocated in a new, symbolic context: the news theme. Because newsworthiness is based on themes, the attention devoted to an event may exceed its importance, relevance, or timeliness were these qualities determined with reference to some theory of society. In place of any such theoretical understanding of the phenomena they report, newsworkers make incidents meaningful only as *instances of themes* – themes which are generated within the news production process. Thus, something becomes a 'serious type of crime' on the basis of what is going on inside newsrooms, not outside them. (Fishman, 1978: 536)

A television reporter was sent to cover a panel discussion entitled, 'The Rule of Law – Terrorism' at a conference of the Canadian Bar Association. The panel consisted of Dr Maurice Tugwell, Department of Conflict Studies, University of New Brunswick; The Honourable Jerome Choquette, QC, former Minister of Justice for the Province of Quebec; and John Starnes, former Director of the RCMP Security and Intelligence Service. Each participant gave a paper, followed by discussion, as is the custom at professional meetings.

As is the custom with television news, there was a need to reduce a lengthy professional session into a brief lay story. At least in this instance the reporter was given five minutes for his item, plus a brief period to chat about the topic with the anchorperson after the item was shown. He made the item familiar by reference to an act of 'terrorism' which had occurred in the previous week, and acts of 'terrorism' in Quebec twelve years before, to suggest that Canada was becoming a part of the international problem of 'terrorism.' It was brought home to the audience that there was now 'no safe place,' including Canada, and that the solution was to be in the form of a 'law-and-order' crackdown including a new security policing system. The conference session was simplified through the familiar international-terrorism theme, and then dramatized through representative statements of the panelists and the reporter's own emotive and evaluative language and selection of visuals. This is evident in comparing the words from the script and a description of the visuals:

TITLE: NO SAFE PLACE

Anchorperson: The lawlessness of worldwide terrorism strikes in Canada. We look at what can be done ...

Reporter: Terrorism ... the unlawful acts usually involving violence that has grown like a cancerous disease in the past twenty years.
[Visuals of a bombed car in Germany. Zoom into a part inside the car until a human foot with toes can be discerned. A shot of blood on the car floor and the wreckage]

Canadians have generally remained observers of such incidents in scattered parts of the globe.
[More visuals of the bombed car]

This summer we've watched IRA terrorists explode bombs in the heart of London.
[Scene of a man in uniform/green trees/wide shot of scene of IRA attack]

Killing British soldiers and strewing the streets with wounded and dying horses.
[Shots of horses on the ground, dead or wounded]

Shocking as it was, Canadians still viewed it from a distance.
[Close-up of horses]

Along with the acts of Italian terrorists in kidnapping an American General.
[Italian police searching for General Dozier]

That ended in bloodshed.
[Dozier sitting in car]

But the assassination last Friday in Ottawa of a Turkish diplomat brought the message home dramatically that Canada is no longer an island secure from such acts, this time by Armenian terrorists.
[Shot of police with car on tree-lined street/focus on victim with head slumped back on car seat/police wrapping body in plastic]

That made today's panel at the Bar Association particularly grabbing.
[Wide shot of CBA meeting with CBA emblem/close in on panel]

Dr Maurice Tugwell of the University of New Brunswick was asked if terrorism has been a successful weapon for a cause.
[Close-up of Tugwell/another shot of the panel]

Tugwell: If the political purpose makes sense, then terrorism is often a very effective agent in bringing it about. The same situation applied to the Armenians.

[Twice during clip, conference audience shots were used to cover a pan from Tugwell to the moderator and back]

Reporter: In recent memory we have our home-brewed terrorists in Canada – the FLQ.
[Stock footage from a network special on the 1970 Quebec October Crisis: shot of FLQ manifesto/man reading the manifesto while standing on a podium]

Their acts of kidnapping and murder have formed one of the most unsettling chapters in Canadian history in the past quarter century.
[Funeral of former Quebec minister Pierre Laporte/soldiers marching]

While anti-terrorist authorities advocate today lengthy prison terms for terrorists.
[Close-up of man being handcuffed/exit of kidnappers accompanied by police escort]

Many Canadians remain critics of how lenient this country was in allowing the FLQ terrorists back into Canada and into our society after a few years' exile.
[Shot of convicted Paul Rose through wire fence]

Quebec's former Justice Minister Jerome Choquette today defended his actions in the FLQ case.

Choquette: I cannot go along with an absolute solution. I was in favour of lenient sentence, because the incident happened ten or twelve years ago.
[Choquette talking head]

Reporter: The RCMP, our main security against terrorists in Canada, has been under fire for its role in the FLQ affair and other activities uncovered in royal commissions. The former security head of the RCMP, John Starnes, was critical of our complacency and urged a new proposed security force be given the legal means to use methods which in the past brought the force into disrepute.
[Again network stocks of the October Crisis/RCMP/found body in car]

Starnes: I believe it is for the legislators and the legal profession to provide the means by which the continuing threat of international terrorists can be effectively controlled. The MacDonald Commission recommended ways in which all the methods I have outlined can be employed while protecting the civil rights and liberties of Canadians.
[Starnes talking head]

Reporter: Starnes was quick to point out that legalizing covert actions by a new force would have to be done with the full and open knowledge of senior ministers in Ottawa. Those ministers in the past have claimed they didn't know the details of the force's activities.

[Shots of Starnes talking/wide shot of meeting/audience/side shot of panel/side shot of Starnes]

Starnes: I do not agree with the theory which has been expounded that a security service should be at arm's length from the minister. I don't think it's possible and I don't think it's right.
[Talking head of Starnes]

Framing a particular event in the terms of a theme involves choices in emphasis and attendant speculations on trends. In this instance – given that there was one 'terrorist' act in Canada the previous week, and before that one had to go back twelve years to the October Crisis – it would have been just as reasonable to observe that Canada had been a remarkably safe place, with only two serious acts labelled as 'terrorism' occurring, more than a decade apart. Instead the October Crisis was placed in the context of 'recent memory,' and it was suggested that the 'trend' in Canada was as bad as elsewhere and there was 'no safe place' anymore.

If the reporter decides to establish the continuity of the present event by marking it with past events or trends, he requires some material on the trends in order to establish the newsworthiness. The lack of the marking material means that the present event lacks significance as news and will be dropped. A reporter was assigned a story involving a man who robbed a taxi driver. When the suspect was approached by two police officers he fired two shots at them out of a loaded revolver, but the cartridges were blanks. A senior editor thought that there were two other recent instances in which the police were shot at and he wanted the story framed in terms of whether there was an increase in gun use in the city. The reporter called various units of the police force, including Public Relations, Homicide, and the Emergency Task Force, to obtain figures on gun use in the course of committing crimes. While placing these calls, he mentioned to the researcher that if there was *no increase* in gun use in the commission of crimes there would be no story. He was unable to obtain the figures he wanted, and eventually did drop the story.

CONSONANCE

The need for a frame which expresses continuity is related to another element in newsworthiness, that of consonance. Often the significance of an event is prejudged to the point where the reporter will visualize what is going to happen and then produce a report which makes that outcome apparent regardless of what else has transpired. For example, impending demonstrations are expected to be violent and reporters focus on whatever scuffles are on offer rather than on the issues involved (Halloran et al, 1970; Gitlin, 1980).

In this type of coverage an enormous stock of stereotyped knowledge builds up to virtually guarantee the 'eternal recurrence' (Rock, 1973a) of the same elements as each 'new' event transpires. For example, in a television newsroom we studied there was a computerized keyword-search system for stock visuals. This system allowed the reporter to obtain old visuals on a particular theme to use in consonance with his present story. There were over 2,000 items filed under the word 'demonstration.' On an occasion we observed, a television reporter and two crews were sent to cover the annual Remembrance Day demonstration at a plant involved in the construction of nuclear missiles. He was in constant radio contact with his assignment editor, who told him repeatedly to 'get the violence' and 'get the arrests' but said nothing about obtaining an account of the issue involved.

It is inevitable that journalists develop preformed story lines to make an event seem less equivocal, to circumscribe their choices, and ultimately to manage the flow of news. Journalists have their own hermeneutic circle, since all understanding requires some pre-understanding whereby further understanding is possible. In the process, their degrees of freedom in story choice become limited, if not foreclosed.

Continuity and consonance are often established by the regular timing or scheduling of events by sources. In the Toronto news media it is an annual ritual to share with the police and other authorities in the pre-Christmas and New Year 'public drama' of 'cracking down' on drinking and driving (cf Gusfield, 1981). Police news conferences on the matter are faithfully attended, statements by the Attorney General dutifully recorded, visuals taken of police spot-checks, and figures given at regular intervals of how many stops have been made and charges laid compared to previous years. During this period the 'drunk crack-down' items are used as 'fillers' if something else doesn't make the show, or held over until another day if there is insufficient space on a given day. As one assignment editor noted, these items are 'timeless' during the one-month period of the campaign. They represent the classic crime filler rather than the classic crime thriller.

THE UNEXPECTED

While the consonant and continuous is always visualized, a sense of the unexpected can make something newsworthy. There can be a major development that has political, legal, ethical, and moral implications, for example, during our research, the issues surrounding surrogate motherhood for a fee were given considerable attention in news items and features. There can be upsets in normal expectations about the order of things; for example, consideration was given to covering what was described in the newsroom as a 'soap opera' involving children suing a stepmother over her alleged squandering of the family estate. Ordinary coverage of deviance and control also provides tales of the unexpected, albeit framed with consonance and continuity so that they appear as the expected unexpected.

The unexpected is something that is newsworthy because it affects people, whether individuals, organizations, institutions, or the public interest. One senior news executive was asked what is newsworthy.

A: Well generally, that it hasn't already happened before, so it's new. That it's going to have an impact on the way people act or think or perceive their situation. I guess that's about as succinct as I can make it.

Q: What would make something cease to be newsworthy? Let's say you're doing a continuing story on something?

A: That it no longer has any of those characteristics. It's not new. It has no impact on the way you perceive things or the way you're affected by it. I mean the first day the milkman comes may be a newsworthy event but after two years it's so routine, so built into your routine.

Q: ... newspapers have this regular menu of crime incidents in which, you know, names change but nothing else. Yet somehow that is considered to be news. Or you could say the same about sections like sports.

A: Well, sports is as much entertainment as anything else. I mean you could say ... with movies, why do they keep doing reviews of movies? Sports is much like that. It's your leisure activity watching sports ... You'll knock 'em all to hell and, I suppose you can use crime in much the same way. That it's a spectacle. It's entertainment ...

The unexpected can be good or bad. After a while the milkman's good work in delivering milk is no longer newsworthy, but contaminated milk is, or the rape of a householder by the milkman. Unexpected events with negative aspects seem to enhance newsworthiness. Bad news is good for news discourse. Indeed the unexpected and negative criteria, and the consequences for the people, generally accommodate the other criteria we have considered. By visualizing the deviance in an event newsworthiness seems assured, and the choices for producing a story brought under control.

Deviance and Control as Prime Criteria

News workers we studied were well aware of their focus on unexpected events. This is the essence of what makes a story interesting, and it is incumbent upon the journalist to bring this essence out. A person with two decades of experience as a reporter, editor, producer, and public-relations consultant articulated what seems interesting from a journalistic viewpoint:

A: So interest has to be the first thing. Then it breaks down into your standard categories of negativism, antagonism, and human interest. And if a thing is not interesting on the surface, then you see what's wrong with it, what's wrong with the situation. Or you see what, who hates it, who's against it. Or does it have any human-interest element? And after you've gone through those four factors and the answer is no, it doesn't, then it usually doesn't get reported.

Q: O.K., why [are being] negative and ... antagonizing important elements of a story in terms of making it interesting?

A: For a couple of reasons. Now I notice in [identifies a college journalism course] ... they're giving out assignments that have one-line scenarios, and they are asking the journalism students to pick out the scenario that would be covered that day, to pick the most interesting news stories. And the teacher is saying no, you would pick this one over that one because this one is more sensational. Well, that's one of the reasons that antagonism or negativism is highlighted in the media, because kids are taught that way in the first place. But on a more general level, traditionally the media doesn't report the planes that land, it only reports the planes that crash. The old cliche. So naturally every reporter has a natural inclination to look for the negative in any story. And part of that is of course that they all think that they're investigative re- porters, most of them think that they're out to save the world, most of them think that there's something wrong with everything. So they will go and look for that angle. The underriding theme of that is that if you get a negative story you'll end up on page one or you will end up with a byline or you will end up in the first couple of minutes of the newscast, simply because you have a neg- ative story and that is more inherently interesting than a positive story ... So you've got two things. One, it's easy, that's what they're trained to look for, and number two, that's what gets them the kudos. And it works.

I think also that you can't deny that negative stories are the most rare sto- ries. You know, you could look at it positively and you could say most of what happens in our normal lives is very positive ... Every day we get through the day with nothing dreadful happening. Perhaps something happens once a year, or twice a year ... So that the negative to all of us is extremely rare. And the more rare things are the more interesting they are or the more news- worthy they are. So it's natural in that way. Then, since it is natural, that's acceptable for the media to cover that. Where it goes overboard is where they go looking for negative stories simply because they want negative stories. And that happens often.

An editor for the letters-to-the-editor section of a newspaper, in noting that his section typified news judgments in all sections of the newspaper, said he also tended to publish more negative letters than positive ones. This applied even to letters that were critical of the newspaper. In accepting a letter from an organization that criticized the coverage given to topics in its own area of concern, the editor noted that it would have been a much less likely candidate for publication if it praised coverage. Here negativism is encouraged in the interest of correction and improvement. Showing itself to be both open and progressive the news organization can contribute to its legitimacy.

Even camera crews commented on the bad-news formula as the kernel of their work. A cameraman observed that his newsroom was becoming increasingly fixated on crime, fires, violence, victims of tragedy, and disasters of all kinds. He attributed this to the 'ratings game' with a competing television news show that had used this formula successfully. 'They will put on whatever improves their ratings. If it is forty-five minutes of sports then that is what they will put on.' He noted that the move in this direction included the gradual acquisition of equipment such as two-way radios, emergency-service scanner radios for cameramen who 'cruise,' and paying a cameraman an additional fee of $260 a week to monitor emergency-service radios twenty-four hours a day (he in turn paid someone else for eight hours a day). He gave as an example a highrise-fire story for which the newsroom paid $450 to hire a helicopter to send him up for pictures. They did not check the feasibility of doing this in advance, and wasted the money because, for safety reasons, the helicopter was not allowed within three miles of the building. He gave another example of a murder-suicide in a home in a wealthy suburb the previous weekend. The newsroom sent three crews there; two other news organizations hired airplanes at $200 each to obtain aerial shots of the scene.

There were other signs of deviance and crime being prime criteria of newsworthiness. An advertisement of a television station promoting their evening news programme featured the 'breaking' of a story in which a man was shot by the police after a car chase. A particular reporter was highlighted as being on the spot first to bring the folks the story. Inside the newsroom, an indication that deviant, evil, and wrongful elements predominated was the use of the term 'brightener' for the exceptional stories that constituted good news.

On some days virtually the entire television news lineup was constructed by connecting a series of deviance and control stories. Our findings are in direct contradiction to Black's (1982: 142) view that television devotes little time to deviance and crime reporting, that the crime waves it reports are 'notoriously short lived,' and that it focuses on trial and judgment. Stories on crime waves of robbery and attacks on women were sustained for months, and significant attention was given to incidents, informal reactions, and investigative processes as well as to trials and judgments.

Two successive days in one television newsroom were indicative. On the first day the entire show was packaged in terms of crime and disorder: in the home, on local streets, and in foreign terrorism. After an item on the Israeli-PLO conflict slated late at the top of the show, there were three items on domestic violence. The first concerned an incident involving a man being shot by police after a 'domestic.' The second was on the local police domestic-response teams; the assignment schedule indicated that this item 'will probably show they're under-staffed and under-equipped.' The third item in the sequence focused on a provincial legislative committee on family violence. An international news segment then included items on 'IRA' bombings in London, 'Armenian' bombings in Paris, the easing of martial law in Poland, the collapse of a construction crane in New York which killed one person, and the 'mysterious' death of actor John Belushi. Back home the continuing moral panic about crime in the streets against women victims was sustained. Coverage included the launch of a campaign by a women's group to protect women against violent assault. This item was followed by a story on 'beat cops,' with reference to a police consultant's report advising that 'old-fashioned' foot patrol should be reintroduced. Next was an item from the United States dealing with the issue of gun control. While this lineup paid respect to the newsworthiness criterion of 'composition' (Galtung and Ruge, 1981) in the sense of blending local and international items, the entire show was composed of 'lawandorder' problems and various efforts by a citizen's group, a legislature, and police, at remedy. Crime at home, crime on the streets, crime abroad, and what is to be done about 'lawandorder' were not coverage by exception: they constituted the entire show.

The following day the assignment schedule indicated that the attacks-on-women panic would be sustained by covering a park 'patrol' by women's groups wishing to symbolize their plight. Environmental danger was also highlighted, with coverage of two Americans in Toronto to discuss a report on the Love Canal situation, and another item concerning a panel of lawyers meeting to discuss environmental law. Additional items included a hostage situation that developed in the city during the day, and a bomb threat in the city. A forthcoming conference of Rastafarians was covered with reference to their allegation that the local police had issued a memorandum to immigration authorities to scrutinize members coming from abroad for possible weapon-and drug-related violations. Another assignment concerned a missing fourteen-year-old boy, who reportedly fell off a raft in a gravel pit. The recommendations of an inquest into a death at a nursing home was covered, as was a court case involving a municipal politician who allegedly breached the trust of political office by using the position to speculate on land deals. A reporter was sent to cover developments in a story where a manufacturer was planning to reduce the salary of its executives, and the executives threatened to intitiate a law suit against the company if it did not reconsider its plans. Again deviance, danger, disaster, and legal controls permeated judgments of newsworthiness.

Such dramatic packaging is a vehicle for engaging the audience by entertaining them. That is what is intended. However, from the journalists' viewpoint entertainment is not necessarily an end in itself. News as theatre, involving titillation, dramatization, and light entertainment, can educate the masses as much as live theatre has done from Elizabethan times onward. In particular, specific information can be deposited with the reader or audience in the course of providing entertainment. Often, this is information that audiences would not receive if they were not enticed by headline, lead, and sustaining elements of risk and remedy.

In journalism, conventional wisdom has persisted 'that the only two things people read in a story are the first and last sentences. Give them blood in the eye on the first one' (Swope, 1958). Well before the days of television, catching illustrations were seen as a means of drawing attention to other material and uniting with it in educating the reader (Fox, 1978: 239). In television the use of visuals and catchy leads (referred to by journalists as 'teases') were seen in this way. The same function was seen in newspaper headlines and leads. Journalists in quality newspapers accepted this as standard practice, hoping to direct attention to their pieces in order to communicate other information and messages; for example, reporters stressed how they visualized 'light leads' to entice the reader into the story. In contrast, popular-newspaper journalists were more likely to lead with heavy stress on violence, disaster, or possible disastrous consequences. In sum, entertaining elements of stories were seen as 'educational bait' in all news media.

In a television newsroom, the producers repeatedly stressed – through their everyday discussions with journalists working on stories and in memoranda commenting retrospectively on previous efforts – that there was a need for a proper composition of 'pleasure and information.' In interview, a producer emphasized that the role of the news media is to 'inform the public ... the public's got to know so that it can make decisions which are intelligent decisions about all the structures that are in the society, including the political structures, and about the quality of life in general in a society. So, we have to be able to give them information on issues and events which will help them make decisions on how to improve society in general.' At the same time he emphasized that entertainment programming before and after the show had a dramatic effect on ratings, and that entertainment was needed throughout the news show itself to keep it alive for the audience. He used the example of 'fire chasing' to explain: it provides the combination of visual appeal, danger, and drama, and in that sense is interesting and entertaining, but in addition it provides the opportunity to interrogate the authorities on public-safety implications.

This point is well illustrated by this producer's approach to municipal-election coverage. As the newsroom moved closer to election-night coverage, he circulated an internal memorandum to his reporters emphasizing that the folks best appreciate the facts if they are visualized more dramatically, as in the mode of sports news.

> In past municipal elections some on air people failed, some simply froze or stuttered or 'um'd' between every other word. But most people who failed did so for another reason. They did not tell you the significance of the results. They simply reported numbers and names. Whatever 'depth' they had were memorized facts from the election book or from the newspaper. So what if ———, the oldest mayor of ——— is leading 35 year old Senior Controller ——— by 1000 votes. The significance may be that [the senior controller's] platform wasn't believed, i.e. how can you talk restraint while voting for UTDC [Urban Transit Development Corporation] cars instead of the cheaper LRVs [Light Rail Vehicles]. Or maybe the significance is that NDP [New Democratic Party] backed [mayor] was a greater supporter of social services than [the senior controller] and the public wants that. Get the picture – give me reasons; make me care.
>
> Sports and elections are the same. Both are games won or lost because of the play or absence of skill. So far only sports coverage gives you a sense of drama and tension and significance. Very early in this campaign I said you will only report effectively if you go to the meetings. You'll report from knowledge not memory. I hope you've done this. There's little time left if you haven't started.
>
> You're all part of the best team in town now. Never mind the numbers; it is my professional judgment your coverage of news is more detailed, more innovative and ahead of the competition's. You do it at 6 and 11. You enhanced our reputations at the conventions. Now we're putting our title on the line. When we win, we'll maintain momentum.

Reporters interpreted this memo as a directive to focus on deviance and control in election campaigns as a means of engaging their audience to inform them about the elections. A week following the circulation of this memorandum, a reporter proceeded to cover the aldermanic campaign in one of the boroughs of Toronto, as part of her four-minute feature on candidates there. She said she chose a particular ward in the borough because the incumbent had been in office a long time, had been charged with municipal corruption two years previously, and it was a 'hotly contested race.' As she talked to the incumbent on the telephone to arrange an interview and visuals of him campaigning door to door, he told her that one of the candidates was running a 'smear campaign' against him. This campaign made reference to the municipal-corruption charge (misappropriation of funds), which he said he had been cleared of as the Crown dropped the charges at the preliminary-hearing stage. Once off the telephone, the reporter picked up on this information as the angle for the story.

Another opportunity for visualizing deviance came the day after the elections when various stories were being worked on to communicate the results. A reporter was assigned to cover the results of the election of school trustees, hardly an exciting topic for television news in anyone's mind. However, in this instance the reporter was given two newspaper clippings by the assignment editor reporting that in a particular ward a woman candidate for school trustee and another candidate had been involved in a tavern 'punch-up.' The woman blamed the man for splitting the right-wing vote, thus allowing a left-wing person to be elected as the second trustee. The man was quoted in a newspaper article saying that he intended to lay a charge of common assault against the woman.

Prior to coming across these newspaper items and hearing about the event on the radio, the assignment editor had told the reporter that the newsroom was not planning to cover the school-trustee results. However, the tavern punch-up report changed his mind, and he wanted this element built into the story reporting the election results. The assignment editor told the reporter that this was to be first and foremost a story about the school-trustee election results, but the 'assault angle' could be 'worked in.'

The reporter proceeded to interview the chairman of the board of school trustees, an elected 'parent activist' who was outspoken about a provincial education bill, and the victorious woman trustee involved in the 'punch-up.' The reporter commented that it would also be good to have a shot of the victim's bruised face, but he was unavailable. The chairman was asked what the election meant for the board, about a particular education bill, and about the future of education. Off-camera the reporter also obtained figures on the political-party composition of the board, which she used in her story without attribution. She made no mention of the 'punch-up,' nor did the chairman mention it. The interview with the 'parent activist' was also conducted without reference to the 'punch-up.'

The next interview was with the trustee who had not only won the election but the 'punch-up.' The cameraman told the researcher that he was instructed that it would be largely a bogus interview, ostensibly on the implications of the results but actually a means of obtaining a visual that could be used along with a voice-over regarding the assault. However, the reporter told the source prior to the interview that she would have to ask about the assault or her superiors would question why she did not cover it. Moreover, the first and main question was about the incident. The source, apparently inexperienced with reporters, said she had known the other candidate in the assault incident for a long time and had warned him about the vote-splitting consequence if he entered the race. She elaborated details of the incident, alleging that he lunged at her and tore her dress and that she defended herself. She added that it was over in a couple of minutes and she couldn't believe what had happened.

Back in the newsroom the reporter asked a producer if he still wanted the assault angle and he said yes. He advised the reporter to drop any discussion of the provincial education bill because it was too complicated for the audience to follow. He suggested emphasis on the left-wing victory. When told there were eleven NDP and three left-progressive victors out of twenty-four members, the producer retorted 'Lump them all together, they're all NDPers, at least there are no commies.' The producer gave the reporter a lead, as indicated in her initial draft script.

> The deck is stacked at the Toronto School Board – stacked with NDP trustees. The voters have elected 11 NDP and 3 left-leaning candidates, ending a bitter fight for control at the board.
>   Chairman Bob Spencer predicts they're on a winning streak, and that future elections will see the same change at other metro boards. [Clip]

> NDP trustees say last night's win means a brighter future for Toronto's children: higher-quality education, smaller class sizes, more parent involvement ... [Clip]

> But the right wing says the voters have chosen the big spenders in a time of hardship. The strongest push to crush the NDP came from trustee ———. She was elected last night, along with an NDP trustee in her ward. ——— was so upset she got into an argument with another candidate last night. Today she's famous for the fight that followed. [Clip]

> We can expect fights of a slightly milder nature at the board these next three years. Fights between a dominant left-wing and a frustrated right. But we can also expect some fresh opinions: from people like ———, the parent activist who was overwhelmingly elected to the board yesterday.

The use of deviance and control elements to bring colour to political-campaign stories was not exclusive to television. During the time of municipal election campaigns in Ontario, the city desk of a quality newspaper in Toronto had a mandate to produce stories on campaigns in regional municipalities outside Toronto. This was not a straightforward task, since the personalities and issues in small-town Ontario politics were not evidently newsworthy to the cosmopolitan readership of this quality newspaper.

The task was eased when editors discovered that in a small town 140 kilometres from Toronto, the encumbent mayor was planning to seek re-election even though he had been criminally charged with possession of a dangerous weapon, pointing a firearm, and being unlawfully in a dwelling with the intent of committing an indictable offence. They immediately visualized a range of issues in deviance and control that might bring small-town political campaigns 'home' to their cosmopolitan readership. The editors thought the Ontario Municipal Act might prohibit anyone with a criminal record from holding political office. This raised a series of questions: Can a person facing criminal charges run for election to municipal office? If convicted, would the person be removed from office? If the mayor knew he would be prevented from running for office if convicted, would he attempt to delay the trial until after the election to keep open his options? If the mayor was prevented from holding office under the Municipal Act, would he be inclined to invoke a challenge to the Act under the Canadian Charter of Rights and Freedoms? This thought was inspired by a news report of a case in Kingston, Ontario, in which a federal penitentiary inmate was invoking the charter in an effort to run for mayor of Kingston. It was also salient to the interests of senior editors, who were encouraging any stories that pertained to possible legal developments under the charter, which at the time had been in effect for only six months.

A reporter was assigned to cover this election campaign and the mayor's case, and he eventually published three stories on it. In the course of preparing his stories he developed a wide range of questions of deviance and control, including the mayor's moral character and criminality, another candidate's moral character and criminality, the propriety of relations among local police and politicians, deviance in relation to political office, police deviance in processing a suspect and accused person, the fairness of judicial discretion in sentencing, the legal regulation of election candidates and those who hold political office, and how many of these considerations might bear upon Canadian constitutional law under the Charter of Rights and Freedoms.

Our point is that this particular small-town election campaign was chosen among hundreds of others only because of the criminal charges against the mayor and how that fact could ramify to other questions of deviance and control. It was an 'obvious' case for making an otherwise routine small-town election into something interesting, entertaining, and instructive about political and legal institutions. Offering such a colourful variety of issues in deviance and control, it was the most newsworthy small-town election campaign for the urban newspaper.

Policing Organizational Life

This small-town election story also indicates that another component of newsworthiness is procedural propriety within and between organizations and institutions. Something is newsworthy if there is a suggestion of impropriety, mismanagement, or wrongdoing by officials or responsible authorities. Alternatively, if nothing is evidently wrong but there is suspicion that there might be more than meets the eye, problems can be visualized and literally created through the actions of the journalists concerned. Newsworthiness is

judged in terms of journalistic involvement in the policing of organizational
life.

INSTITUTIONAL REPORTING

Journalists we observed continually reiterated and practised what they referred
to as institutional journalism. A reporter defined this in terms of a focus on
corruption, mismanagement, human rights, and legal precedent. Other journalists in the same newspaper emphasized that their organization did not focus
on 'crime' news but rather on 'justice,' broadly conceived in terms of human
justice. A reporter who reviewed his newspaper-clipping 'research' files, and
the newsworthy follow-up stories they suggested, gave examples which addressed the questions, Is it a scam? Is it a legal precedent? Are civil rights
being violated? Is it in the public interest to reveal organizational procedures
or practices?

This view was shared by the newspaper's management. A senior executive, who said that advocacy becomes a part of informing the public, articulated his views on the institutional vision of his newspaper:

A: We support a party up until the polls close on election day, and then figure
    our principle in dealing with the government is to be very analytical and to be
    very critical ... We may have supported you yesterday when you were running
    for office, but you drop a clanger on Tuesday and we'll drop you with a thud.
    I think that's what our role is. We don't think of our role as being like the
    role of government or of an opposition, our business is constantly observing
    government and asking questions, particularly if they're embarrassing
    questions.

Q: You mentioned before that you see your function very much as keeping your
    eye on government, you don't have a similar view about keeping your eye on
    business in terms of business practices?

A: It's not as easy to do. The business of government is of interest to everybody.
    The number of business situations that are of interest, that have large-scale
    interest, are more limited ... It's not as easy to categorize as politics.

    [T]hat word 'arbitrary' keeps coming back, we're after anybody who is lay-
    ing it on people, whether he's corporate, or whether he's government, or
    whether he is an academic, a social worker. Some of the most arbitrary people
    I've ever met in my life are social workers. Is that really the only exact
    science?

    If you have regular police reporters and there are three holdups in Becker's
    [convenience] shops in the course of an evening, a reporter goes to each of
    those Becker's holdups and you'll get three stories probably combined into one
    on what's happened at Becker's stores. How do you more usefully employ

your reporter, doing that or by having someone ... doing a long series on what
is the state of drug crime in Canada, which we just recently ran? Both reporters are working on crime. What do you figure is the most important thing you
can do? To my mind doing that kind of story is more important than doing
what I call occurrences. At the same time ... I think you have to be very careful that you don't ignore or minimize certain kinds of crime. The several murders we've had lately of single women ... where there seems to be a kind of
pattern to it. That's an important story, I don't care whether it's happening
here, or in Alberta, or in British Columbia. I don't suppose there's another
newspaper in Canada that has paid as much attention to the freeing and second
trial of the Micmac Indian who was sent away thirteen years ago for stabbing
a boy to death. That to us is not just a crime story, it's a story of justice and
how you get it in this country, and what it takes to turn the wheels of justice.

A senior editor on the newspaper indicated that his basic concern was
with the mechanisms of social control involved in constituting social order
and effecting social change. It is incumbent upon the newspaper to participate
in ensuring that social-control mechanisms are just, and otherwise in proper
working order, and to communicate 'the rules of the game' publicly. Coverage
of deviance and social control is important in this respect. It is a sign of order
organizationally, institutionally, and socially, as well as an indicator of how
organizational, institutional, and societal rules may be changing.

Q: How does crime reporting fit within your definition of the news media?
A: Crime has always been important to societies. In order for any society to function, there has to be law and order. Crime is the antithesis. So it's important
   for a society to cope with social aberration.
Q: And you see legal reporting in much the same way?
A: Well, our definition of legal reporting ... our justice beat, it covers not just
   criminal cases, but anything affecting the administration of the courts and
   justice ...
Q: O.K. Why do you see this as being important?...
A: Because it bears very immediately on the social structure, legal affairs. It's,
   you're talking about the body of law under which people have to live and operate and when you're changing the rules of the game or decisions are coming
   down that affect the rules of the game, it affects not only how individual people live, but it brings into focus your whole philosophy of what society should
   be.
Q: How important is the fourth-estate function, the, if you like, the policing function of the media?
A: Well, that's like saying how important is religion? When you come down to
   the question of faith, if you believe that democracy is important, if you believe it's essential, then by definition you say that the press is essential be-

cause under any definition of democracy the prerequisite is an informed, rational public that is able to judge and make decisions. In order for that to happen, that public has to have information and data on which to make those assessments and decisions.

Q: ... Why don't you have a police beat?

A: If you have a police beat what you're expecting is a whole bunch of stories every day on local crime and you're going to get muggings and accidents and rapes and beatings and thieves and I don't know what that does to your sum total of knowledge of your particular society. Day after day after day to be reading about identical cases, I don't think we need that. I think you can achieve the same end as far as an overall view of your particular society is concerned by dealing with it on a selective basis.

Q: You're saying you don't want this steady diet of police stories, but on the other hand you have steady diets of court stories, of the court people. Why the steady diet of court stories?

A: Well, because there's ... a much greater range of things happening. The court stories are not just crime stories ... In the courts, you're there because the rules of the game are being either changed or confirmed. And it's important for the people to know what's happening to the rules of the game and it's a decision-making body. And you come back to any kind of theory of democracy, the courts are extremely important in that context. So you have, otherwise you're not telling people what's happening to the biggest game in town, which is how the society is changing ... Police beat will give you the routine basis. Police beat is not going to get you the kinds of cases ... where you have the police in some kind of confrontation themselves with the existing social order.

Q: But is the court beat going to get you anything but a routine feed of cases and a ready supply?

A: Well, there is a ready supply out there, but what I expect out of the guy who's covering the courts is that he's going to exercise judgment and say, 'Look, these are the cases that are important. These are the cases that are going to change, that are going to deal with the rules of the game. That are going to change them, that are going to expand on them.'

A senior television-news executive also took the view that crime and legal coverage are important because 'society falls apart without law and order.' He justified particular decisions in these terms, for example, giving extensive attention to the Guardian Angels citizens' patrol group on each successive visit of their leaders to Toronto because their presence signified 'forces that work to break society apart and the forces that work to keep it together.' He also emphasized the need to scrutinize the authorities to ensure not only that justice was being done but was being visualized to be done.

The decisions that the courts reach affect the way the law will be in the future and affect the way society will be as a result of it. Policing is the same. I mean, the element that the police is policing, if you like, is the element that affects the structures of society, it's trying to cause society to mutate to a point that is not what the majority of people that live in the society want. There are certain elements in the police beat which I gotta say are voyeuristic, and foremost among those would be a fire. I mean, you know, the thing burns down and the fire department responds to a fire at Wilson Heights and Sheppard, we'll go. But later, if you're a proper organization you take one step back and you say, 'Hey, you know, we had a series of fires, what the hell does it all amount to?' You know, what's right about it? Are the firemen in good shape? Is their equipment adequate? Is response time fast enough? You suddenly ask many more important questions. Someone might say that there is a voyeuristic element in attending to a hostage-taking of some sort. You know, afterwards you ask questions which will influence the way policing is done. So you say: Did the guy really have to shoot the guy? Why didn't they talk more? Why didn't they wait it out three or four days until the guy didn't want any more? Why didn't they bring the kid's mother to the scene to talk to the kid? So, even though we're just there to show the pictures of the actual incident on any given day, after that, if the organization is worth its money, then it starts asking important questions, because of that.

As indicated by this news executive's statements, the policing of organizational life as a criterion of newsworthiness is bound up with the news organization enacting its environment. Policing of organizational life is considered as a criterion of newsworthiness in the context of efforts to influence public opinion, bring influential public opinion to bear upon problems identified, and ultimately to effect change in the organizational and institutional spheres concerned. The overriding concerns are social control, public security, order, and change, although in a given instance these are articulated in terms of a narrower range of goals and interests. We now turn to a consideration of the aims of this policing, the targets it is aimed at, and the means by which such aim is taken.

INFORMATION POLICING

Most generally, the policing of organizational life entails 'information policing' in which the journalist is after the disclosure of information that fosters public accountability. An effort is made through whatever devices or strategies the journalist can visualize to force the authorities concerned to reveal instances of problems, talk about developments, and state the control efforts being made and remedies sought. This effort often entails going to a variety of sources who might possibly have information, or who themselves might be a source of pressure on the authorities to be more forthcoming.

Apart from the immediate goal of accountability – identifying who or what is responsible for the problem – there is the attendant goal of social control, demanding that enforcement action be taken to bring order to the situation. A senior editor described his newspaper's work on a continuing story about questionable land transactions and the involvement of trust companies in unnecessarily risking the capital of depositors and investors. He stated explicity that the goal of various stories on this matter over time was first to expose problems, and then to force the various organizations and institutions involved to take action. Ultimately, this included legislation and enforcement at the provincial-government level. Discussing the establishment of an investigative team of four persons to look into the matter, this senior editor indicated the nature of the judgments involved.

> [A]t that stage all we had was the fact that there had been a sale of ... proper-
> ties and we thought Saudi Arabians had bought it and tenants were upset be-
> cause they didn't know what was going to happen to their rents. And the
> analysis at that stage, of the guys who'd been working on it was, look, what's
> going to happen to the tenants is not the major issue. What's going to happen
> to the depositors in the trust companies is, because we think something fishy
> has been going on with the trust companies. And I must say at that stage I
> thought well, you know, maybe some of them, but that's going to be one hell
> of a hard thing to prove. So I ended up saying, 'O.K., you go ahead, let's
> chase that angle.' Lo and behold, that is exactly what it turned out to be. I
> didn't think at that stage that a company the size and substance of ———
> Trust with a billion and a half in assets, a company that had ... been in exist-
> ence since the turn of the century, didn't think that it could end up in the
> degree of trouble in which it obviously is ... [I]f you want to look at it in
> terms of crime, a crime is an injustice and it's an injustice because it does two
> things: it eats away at the stability of the state and it causes harm to individu-
> als. It's a twofold thing. What you could see through the mists as this thing
> began taking shape was exactly the same thing except on an immense scale.
> Instead of having a break-and-enter where somebody loses a camera, a one-
> on-one crime – I don't know whether any crime has been committed in the
> Trust affair yet ... I'm using the word 'crime' loosely ... – but I'm equating it
> in the sense of 'social threats,' instead of having a one-on-one you had a one-
> on-tens-of-thousands-of-people. We knew what had happened in [previous]
> cases where people who had saved, put their life savings into the trust compa-
> nies lost them. We knew what kind of anxieties and despair and everything
> else that it caused a lot of people, especially older people. Well, with ———,

I mean if ——— was going that way, the social repercussions for depositors were immense. The repercussions for the whole financial community were immense. You know, not too long ago to say repercussions for the whole goddamn country were immense ... if you shake the confidence in the financial sector. We've already had a bank chairman resign in this affair, the ——— Bank. We haven't heard the last of that. We had the Governor of the Bank of Canada, for God's sake, phone up [this newspaper] and say, 'I would like you to publish me saying that people should not panic, that the banking structure is still sound and the ——— Bank is still sound.' So you had a story which, when off to bat, our people were saying, 'Look ... we don't have very much to go on at all. We've got suspicions, we've got fears. You're going to have to invest a lot of time and a lot of money and you're going to have to gamble, because what we're going to do is we're going to have to go out and we're going to have to do a lot of leg work.' And we did. Searching records, we searched all the property records, we searched all the OSC [Ontario Securities Commission] files, we searched everything in sight. And it took about three weeks before pieces started fitting together and we started coming out with, you know, the heavy stories. Then the government ... brought in its bill on trust companies, then ... they seized [names several trust companies] and the federal government acted on [names two mortgage companies].

In an informal, untaped discussion with a researcher at a different time, this senior editor indicated that the newspaper's barrage of stories had forced the government's hand in these matters. He offered the example of efforts by two companies to merge. The newspaper's journalists went to the Ontario Securities Commission (OSC) and told them that 1 per cent of the shareholders of a trust company did not receive any information about the proposed merger. The person who controlled 99 per cent of the company shares did not inform the remaining 1 per cent shareholders of his actions. This was in apparent violation of OSC rules which state that shareholders must be informed about all large transactions. The OSC was not going to do anything about this situation until the newspaper ran a story on it, and on the same day the OSC stopped the merger.

The senior editor said these dealings entailed the possibility of OSC violations and/or criminal law violations and/or the involvement of organized crime. He mentioned a situation in which a twenty-year-old person was going to purchase a trust company. The age of this person alone indicated how 'ridiculous' the situation was, but in addition this person had a cousin whose name turned up repeatedly in investigations into organized crime. Furthermore, this person's father had allegedly been involved in several bankruptcy frauds that the police were unable to prove. The senior editor commented that trust companies were a 'great' vehicle for laundering money for organized crime. The newspaper ran a story about the twenty-year-old's intended purchase deal. On the same day the government stopped all such deals, and made it retroactive to that morning to stop the twenty-year-old's deal.

This is a clear example where journalists visualized deviance, made searching efforts to 'see through the mist,' and eventually took control actions themselves which they believed had a direct impact upon regulation and enforcement in the organizations concerned. As information police, their goal was exposure of improper, possibly illegal procedures, enforcement of procedures, and advocacy of better procedures 'in the public interest.'

EFFICIENCY POLICING

The policing of organizational life is more routinely focused on questions of efficiency (cost effectiveness). Stories were undertaken regularly on the efficiency of governmental operations. A reporter attending a corrections conference decided a story on employment of prisoners in federal penitentiaries, including the problem of unemployed prisoners, was newsworthy. After interviewing a corrections civil servant on the topic, he picked up on the issue of the correctional service trying to be efficient by employing inmates to manufacture products that could be sold for profitable income to make institutions partially self-sufficient. The reporter deemed this newsworthy because, in the context of the poor economy at the time, the prisons were the subject of complaint from the private sector for taking away sources of employment and profit. In effect they had to be somewhat inefficient, and maintain a certain percentage of unemployment among inmates, in order to avoid hostilities with private-sector companies. The reporter believed this was a particularly significant angle for his newspaper because the paper had an institutional orientation to the business community.

A reporter was assigned to cover a provincial-government all-party committee hearing on the problem of family violence. Apart from the fact that this item itself was an attempt to designate a form of deviance and consider the range of possible control mechanisms, the reporter used her powers of visualization to initiate another story. She observed that members of provincial parliament on the committee, especially those from the political party in power, were frequently absent from the meetings. She began to document the attendance of members, scrutinize their expense claims, and talk to sources on the political beat about the committee structure and expectations about attendance and participation. This efficiency angle, regarding the use of the people's money by the people's representatives, was newsworthy in the context of a more general 'oppositional' stance to the government.

POLICING POLITICS

The targets of journalistic policing included those individuals and their organizations involved in 'public life' on a continuous basis. The news media
helped to give life to the public culture, and played a significant role in
constituting it, by reporting on people in official positions who were apparently
not doing what was expected of them, or by making imputations about others
who appeared as procedural strays. Politicians were a favoured target, either
individually or as members of the government, political parties, or factions.

Any context where something might arise to suggest political impropriety
may be deemed worthy of coverage, in addition to, or in place of, what was
otherwise transpiring in that context. A reporter was assigned to cover the
provincial-government hearing of a civil servant fired for breaking his oath
of secrecy by releasing to a member of provincial parliament information
about a dispute he was having with a superior. The civil servant alleged that
he was ordered to dishonestly report tree estimates to enable a company to
obtain a licence to cut trees. While covering the hearing, the reporter said
the ultimate hope was to obtain testimony indicating more general improper
favouritism shown to particular companies by the government.

Political-beat coverage generally, as well as coverage of the courts, included attending to anything that might reveal deviance in politics or by
politicians. A reporter was instructed to cover the sentencing of an accused
who stole a bracelet worth $40,000 to $50,000, solely because the accused
was the holder of the mortgage of a provincial cabinet minister and there was
potential for discovering political impropriety.

A newsroom sometimes identified a particular person as a target and
pursued coverage of events that could reveal problems with that person's
exercise of the authority of his office. In one newsroom we studied journalists
repeatedly discussed the ongoing 'friction' and 'hostility' between a prominent
politician and the news organization. A range of events covered on the political
beat, in court, and at public meetings, included as part of the criteria of
newsworthiness the fact that they might reveal something deviant about this
politician's use of the authority of his office. There was a sustained consciousness about the newsroom's relation to this politician and how it might
be brought into a range of stories the newsroom would otherwise cover or,
in some instances, not cover. 'Hidden agendas' of this type bore directly on
news judgments, and were clearly visualized by journalists in deciding
newsworthiness.

Arbitrariness in the exercise of any public office is an important criterion
of newsworthiness. Civil servants in public bureaucracies, especially those
involved in more direct delivery of services to citizens, are scrutinized regularly. The obvious example of this is 'policing the police,' but other areas

of public service were regularly scrutinized, for example, through the 'welfare' beat and a health or medical specialist reporter.

Taking an example from the welfare area, a journalist was assigned to a continuing story of a case of child abuse in which the child died and the mother was incarcerated. The occasion for the 'latest' series of stories was the release of the report of a provincial-government inquiry into the case, which included a focus on the lack of intervention by the Children's Aid Society. In addition to a story on the report, the journalist pursued other dimensions, including the 'career' of the mother in the correctional system and the arrangements for her release into the community. The reporter attributed the sustained coverage and prominent play to the her superior's continuing efforts to police child-welfare services in the province. In keeping with an executive's view that 'some of the most arbitrary people I've ever met in my life are social workers' this story was newsworthy for this news organization because of what it revealed about the procedures of child-welfare agencies. Another reporter in the newsroom noted that child-welfare agencies are perpetual fodder because they are criticized, from a civil-liberties viewpoint, for too much interference in family life, but when something goes wrong, as in this case, they are criticized for not enough intervention. This reporter said that he himself had done a series on the Children's Aid Society interfering too much.

This news organization had a similar approach to stories involving the emergency services and police. Covering a highrise-building fire with several reporters assigned, a division of labour was established among the reporters to create different angles. One reporter commented that 'all their energies' would be directed at finding 'malfeasance' by the fire marshall or some other official who could be made to look responsible. This newsroom seemed to pride itself on not having a police reporter – to many, a perjorative term signifying a 'hack' journalist who blended with his sources – and yet gave extensive coverage to the police. This coverage focused again on procedural matters, such as the reluctance of police forces to release occurence reports to the citizens who are the subjects of the report, and the propriety of search-warrant procedures used in specific instances of entry, search, and seizure. In general, this news organization exemplified what Habermas (1975) has identified as a central feature of contemporary culture, the emphasis on procedural form. This emphasis provides a vision of the administered society as the ideal society, reducing arbitrariness by the perpetual elaboration of procedural technicalities.

Television newsrooms that adopt an institutional approach have the added advantage of technical equipment which can show officials actually engaged in exercises of authority. Through film or video, justice can actually be seen to be done, although not as yet in Canadian courts of law. For example, television coverage of public-order policing focuses on the actions of the police in directly dealing with citizens. Thus, while covering an anti–nuclear-weapon demonstration, a television journalist had his crews focus on any signs of physical contact between the police and demonstrators. This coverage included not only arrests but scenes of demonstrators, who sat down across a road to block traffic, being 'dragged' by police to the curb, and police horses being used to patrol for the containment of crowds. After several 'rounds' of 'dragging,' the reporter told his crews, 'It's all the same, don't shoot this, there's only so much of this you can shoot, but we've got to be careful we don't miss something, if somebody gets violent.' He directed camera shots of a police bus carrying 'reinforcements' and spent considerable time obtaining figures on police personnel to use with his visuals of their presence. The reporter agreed to have the newsroom buy a freelancer's film because he had some shots of police horses edging against demonstrators to move them to the curbside, which was about as 'violent' as the 'confrontation' would become.

The thinking involved in this kind of visualization was revealed further in the editing room. The clips selected from interviews with demonstrators focused on their reactions to the policing rather than on details of the issues involved. The reporter instructed his editor to look for 'more severe dragging,' and then scanned for shots of police horses in action. He selected a shot with horses edging against demonstrators on the curb, and one with a horse moving quickly towards a crowd, in relation to which he remarked jokingly, 'That's a good shot, it looks like Poland. The charge of the White Brigade.' Having reminded themselves aloud that this was a peaceful demonstration, the journalist and editor later eliminated a shot of the police dragging the demonstrators through substantial amounts of horse manure. The reporter looked for a long shot of the demonstration scene to use with a script statement 'For the most part police used as little violence as possible,' but even this left the implication that for the other part the police had been violent. Typically, this was not a story about issues in nuclear armament, but about citizens versus political authority in which the police represented the authorities. Police actions were used to visualize dramatically and directly whether the authorities were behaving arbitrarily or in accordance with procedural form.

THE CITIZEN AGAINST BUREAUCRACY

The newsworthy aspect of policing of organizational life also entailed consideration of 'the little guy versus the bureaucracy.' The cause of the aggrieved citizen was taken up, and if it was deemed important enough, reporting was sustained to the point of remedy. In some news organizations this coverage was institutionalized in the form of 'Probe' or 'Citizen Advocate' journalists who reported regularly on cases.

This approach was also a part of general reporting, as revealed in a reporter's work on a series of stories involving a citizen who claimed a police officer perjured himself during the man's divorce hearing, and who was subsequently charged with public mischief after he refused to withdraw the complaint. The man had tried to obtain the police occurrence report pertaining to the incident the police officer had testified about at his divorce hearing, but without success. A week before a Supreme Court of Ontario hearing on the matter, the reporter called a number of police officials in the jurisdictions concerned, and the provincial office of the solicitor general, to ascertain policy about the release of reports and obtain an explanation for not releasing reports. In the process of undertaking these calls over a day, the reporter received a call from the citizen concerned who said the police had decided to release the report to him. The reporter confirmed this with the citizen's lawyer, who thanked the reporter for doing what lawyers had been unable to do over the previous sixteen months. When the reporter informed his editor about these developments, the reporter was advised to frame his story in terms of how a newspaper 'investigation' led to the release of the report. As the reporter was writing what he termed a 'press moves mountains' story, an official from the solicitor general's office called to say they had been working on the release of the report to the citizen for some time and that it was a coincidence that their decision to release it coincided with the reporter's inquiries. The reporter included in his story the fact that this person 'denied there was a sudden change of mind,' in a manner which left doubt as to whether it was coincidence.

PRIVILEGES

The news media also focus on professional groups or officials who seek privileges for themselves which are not accorded to others. During our research observation period the government had a wage-restraint program stipulating that in the first year wage increases were to be kept within a maximum of 6 per cent and in the second year the maximum increase was to be 5 per cent. This '6 and 5' criterion became a standard against which journalists judged whether wage claims or settlements were deviant. For example, while attending meetings of the Canadian Bar Association, (CBA) a reporter learned of a resolution to increase the pensions of federal judges in excess of the '6 and 5' guidelines. The reporter decided this would be her main story for the day. Her decision was augmented by an additional fact of deviance: the Canadian Bar Association was pressing for parliamentary reform in the form of having more committees to deal with issues, but in this case of judges' pensions the CBA urged the minister of justice to deal with the matter immediately and directly without setting up a committee.

PROFITEERING

Professional self-interest for profit from morally questionable enterprises was another target of journalistic policing. A lawyer who profited from arranging, and doing the legal work on, surrogate-motherhood cases was the subject of articles framed in terms of distaste for his practice. Feature articles with revealing headlines – 'Lawyer lists 300 surrogates: Catalogue shopping for mothers,' and 'Baby Broker Arranging Surrogate Motherhood "lot of fun" ' – were written in a tone of critical distaste for his personal profiteering in this area. This was not simply a frame visualized by the journalist, but was directed from above as part of a contemporary debate on the issue of surrogate motherhood. Editorial strategy went to the extent of in-setting in the bottom left corner of one of these features an advertisement from the 'Cash for Life' Ontario Charities Lottery Group which included the winning numbers of the previous draw and the offer: 'This month, play Double or Nothing. Double your instant prize or WIN TWO FREE TICKETS!'

ORGANIZED CRIME

Another target in journalistic policing of organizational life was 'organized crime.' This focus was again related to the 'rules of the game' or procedural emphasis in institutional news reporting: while respecting the power of organizations, that power must be acquired and exercised by legitimate means. Organizations which conspired to gain and use power illegitimately were viewed as an an enormous threat, and efforts were made to identify such dangerous organizations and to undercut their power. In one newsroom we studied, which had a major commitment to reporting on business organizations, and whose reporters identified their news outlet as representing business interests, there was a constant focus on anything signifying 'organized crime.' Court cases involving persons associated with organized crime were covered regardless of other criteria such as the seriousness or the importance of the particular charge or case. Efforts were made to draw links between these persons and legitimate business and political organizations. Often newsworthiness of the activities of a particular person associated with organized crime was bound up with, and inseparable from, the newsworthiness of a political figure whose exercises of authority the newsroom was also especially interested in. Reporters were sometimes assigned for extended periods to undertake investigative pieces on criminal organization, ranging from the loose organization of prostitutes and their pimps, through systematic organizing for the distribution of illicit drugs, to links between the Mafia and legitimate businesses. The coverage of these targets made visible the general tendency of all news media to visualize deviance and push for appropriate control response in all spheres of organized life.

What is visible as a serious crime in terms of legal categories, for example 'murder,' will be more or less newsworthy depending upon other features, including the organizational connections to the murder. The murder of a transient in a rooming house may be 'briefed' in newspapers and on radio, and ignored altogether on television news. The killing of a spouse in the family organization receives little more attention. However, a murder with implications for ongoing disputes between persons in rival organizations, or which represent a threat to legitimate organizations, receives major play. Perhaps the clearest example of this is the murder of a policeman, which typically receives extensive play, including extended television visuals and a full page of newspaper photographs of the funeral, with accompanying text quoting prominent political and legal authorities on the threat this represents to established order. The visuals include shots of hundreds of policemen from the officer's force as well as many other 'brothers' from forces across the continent, suggesting solidarity in the face of such threats to their established authority (cf Manning, 1977: chap. 1).

In interviewing a television producer, a researcher pointed to a large poster on his office wall which stated, 'Only the best murder cases make the six o'clock news,' and asked him what are the best murder cases. He replied with reference to the shooting of two persons in a courthouse (Osgoode Hall), an incident that had a relation to ongoing disputes between rival organizations in an ethnic community: '[E]ssentially all murder cases should be treated equally by television and print and all the rest of it, but you ask yourself why does the Osgoode Hall shooting take up a front page when a transient who's been stabbed to death is metro news in brief on page six. It's because the size of the crime, the nature of the crime, the audacity of the crime, the vitality of the crime, is in one case greater by any kind of measure that you can bring to it.'

As a paradigm case of 'the rules of the game,' sports organization provides a focal arena for visualizing deviance, regulation, and enforcement (cf. Gruneau, 1983). A great deal of sports coverage focuses on deviance in play (e.g., hockey violence), deviance among sports personalities (e.g., player drug abuse), deviance in industrial relations (e.g., contract talk), and deviance among spectators (e.g., fan rowdiness or violence). The potential for such elements to arise in a particular sporting context can itself be a grounds for attending to it. Thus, at an afternoon news conference of editors, the sports editor said that a reporter should be sent to cover a Junior 'A' hockey game between the Toronto team and a team from another town. This level of hockey was not usually covered by having a reporter in attendance, but on this occasion the editor's justification was that 'the game could get ugly.' As in other organized spheres of life, newsworthiness was not visualized simply in terms of goals, but in terms of deviant procedures used in efforts at scoring them. Indeed, focus on 'ugly' procedures can become an end in itself for participants as well as spectators, including the news media.

DIRECT ACTION

Journalists are usually more than spectators. They become 'speculators' who sense that something is out of order, and proceed to visualize what appears to be the case. In the process they become part of the phenomenon they are reporting on, and make active efforts to enact the organizational environment to the point where a remedy is accomplished to their satisfaction. These efforts entail indirect techniques of questioning, helping to organize particular people involved, and more active techniques of literally making news.

A sustained effort was made by several news organizations to organize the families of babies who had died mysteriously, probably by murder, on a hospital ward. In effect the journalists organized these people to function as reporters and informants on a continuing basis. For example, a few reporters befriended and established a trusting relationship with several families. They encouraged each family to get in contact with other families in the same situation to bring collective pressure to bear. They called the families in advance of upcoming events and informed them of what was likely to happen. In some instances, reporters informed a family that their child was included among those suspected of victimization even before the authorities did. Reporters instructed these families to call particular authorities in the hospital and police to demand information. When the authorities were not forthcoming, one or both parents were interviewed, and cited in the news about the lack of information and uncooperativeness of officialdom. This apparently led the authorities to meet privately with a group of organized parents, making disclosures to them in the hope of keeping sensitive information out of news coverage.

On many occasions during our observations journalists were even more direct in their approach, 'testing' the authorities through direct action or even creating the deviance they visualized. Mild forms of enactment included the 'testing' of the post office on the first anniversary of its being a Crown corporation by mailing letters to see if promises of speed in delivery were matched by performance. More dramatically, after a major incident in which a political group bombed a factory involved in the production of nuclear weapons, a television reporter showed how easy it was to purchase dynamite, while a colleague at a rival station went to the extent of blowing up his dynamite purchase for an added visual effect. A newspaper reporter managed to ferret through the garbage of a printing firm to find government budget documents in advance of their release in the House, thereby signalling problems with government security in this area.

Least subtle of all was the effort of one television newsroom to turn fancy into fact by breaking security at a conference of the International Monetary Fund. A week prior to the conference a Turkish diplomat had been murdered in his car in Ottawa, and it came to the reporter's mind that the issue of security for diplomats could be sustained by trying to show that security was lax for delegates at the conference. Accompanied by a cameraman, the reporter proceeded to evade RCMP security and to make his way to the hotel room door of the Turkish delegation. The cameraman took visuals of the door. The story was the 'fact' that security was lax. The fact that the police authorities were very upset, demanding the film and that the story not appear, only made the reporter and his superiors more gleeful that they had uncovered deviance in control mechanisms that would lead to more stringent control. A supervisor recounted the incident in interview.

> We managed to get onto the floor where the Turkish delegation was at the International Monetary Fund Conference – heavily guarded by the RCMP, who I'm sure carried some artillery. We managed to get up there, as a matter of fact we managed to film the exact room, the number, the whole bit; suddenly, somebody realized that there was a breach of security and our crew got hussled off. Got a phone call from the head of security for the whole conference who threatened me, who said, 'Run that and you'll be cut off, you know, essentially you'll be cut off from all information; it's a two-way street, I've got a long memory and there'll be more times, Mr ——— ' ... And I said, 'Listen, here's what I'll do, I won't show, won't say, what floor it's on, won't show the numbers, but I'm going to run the story because the security was breached.' He didn't want to run that because that was an embarrassment to him. All right? It happened to be topical because a Turkish delegate got knocked off the week before. All right? We ran the story anyways.

Official statements of broadcast-news organizations emphasize that journalists are there to communicate reality, not to manufacture it directly. For example, 'It is important to remember journalism is only the communicator of reality; it is not the originator of that reality. We do not invent the problems we report, however discomforting those events may be' (CBC, 1978: 402). This example shows quite clearly that journalists could be quite inventive, from the point of imagining that a problem exists to the point of showing it as a matter of fact.

Of course, as illustrated throughout this chapter, all considerations of newsworthiness are inventive and creative. The journalist approaches each event, process, or state of affairs with a vision of what is relevant, or what can be made relevant, by mobilizing sources, questioning, and more direct action. Having narrowed his vision in relation to standard (although not standardized) criteria of newsworthiness, and attendant news frames, he can position the accounts of sources to get them to say what he sees. Thus visualized, the newsworthy can be communicated to news users, made visible to the mind if not to the eye.

The Unnewsworthy

As a way of summarizing criteria of newsworthiness analyzed in this chapter, and introducing elements of the news-production process analysed in part III, it is instructive to consider a story that did not make the news. Understanding why a story does not make the news helps us to know what does make it.

A television assignment editor handed a reporter a newspaper clipping and told her to do a story from it. The newspaper clipping was headlined, 'Metro boaters hit by harbour crime wave,' and the three lead sentences of the major story were, 'Metro boat owners are suffering from a rash of water-front crimes. Police say there are 10 to 15 cases a month – almost one every two days – among the 5000 people who live on boats in Toronto during the summer. Most cases are never solved.' The story goes on to include the fear and loathing of two victims, and states: 'The situation has forced local clubs to beef up security, including watch towers and guard dogs.'

The reporter decided to call the police department to obtain the names of victims other than those cited in the available newspaper story. The police denied that there was a 'rash' of thefts, and asserted that there certainly was not a 'crime wave.' The police said there simply was no problem, and they refused to give the reporter a list of victims' names and addresses.

The reporter then called one of the victims cited in the newspaper story. He said that he had been victimized two weeks earlier, but he refused an interview on camera. He was asked to give the name of another victim, but he replied that it was not a common problem. After this telephone conversation, the journalist complained about the 'exaggerated' newspaper story. She talked to a fellow reporter who lived on a boat, and he said there was no crime wave.

Rather than terminating the story at this point, the reporter remained determined to obtain some indication that there was a problem with boat thefts. She went out with a cameraman to a boat club, and there spotted a man putting some things in the trunk of his car. He said he did not know of anyone who had been victimized, and suggested that the reporter talk to the commodore. The commodore could not be found, and the reporter then asked another man close by if he had knowledge of boat thefts. He said he knew of two incidents during the year, and that in his fifteen years of experience at the club there was usually one or two every year, but it was not a problem.

After this interview the researcher asked the reporter why this story had been assigned, and was told, 'Probably there's nothing else.'

The reporter tried another yacht club nearby, and chatted with a man who had just emerged from the office. This man believed that there were fewer thefts than in the previous year, which amounted to one incident in the present year and two incidents in the previous year. He attributed the decrease to a night guard and a new security fence. He said there was no problem, and concluded that 'it's bad for your story but good for us.' He suggested another club that might be more vulnerable to victimization.

The reporter proceeded to the club suggested, still hoping to do a story that would confirm boats were being hit with a wave of crime. The reporter had no apparent intention, or even conception, that a story could be done refuting the newspaper story. At the club she approached a man who was scrubbing a boat and asked him if there had been any recent boat thefts. He said that two or three weeks previously there was an incident in which seven boats were broken into, and that one of the two youths responsible had been apprehended. He said he did not know of any other incidents. He refused to be interviewed on camera because as an employee he did not think the club would appreciate it if he nominated himself as a spokesperson for the club. He offered to take the reporter to see the general manager, but he was un-available. The receptionist asked if the reporter would like to talk to someone else. The reporter said she would talk to anyone, but the receptionist then said the only person who would be available was not going to be at the office until later in the day. The reporter took this person's name and number, and then returned to the car, sharing the opinion of the cameraman that the newspaper story was inaccurate.

At the next boat club the cameraman approached two youths about thefts, then returned to say that they were 'just kids' and did not know anything about it. The reporter then shouted at a man in a boat close to shore, and as he moved his boat closer she asked him if there had been many thefts and break-ins during the year. This was the first time her questioning was posed in terms of *whether* there was a crime wave. The man replied that this was their 'best' summer, and that the number of incidents were 'down.' The man suggested a visit to another club, and he also gave the reporter a list of all clubs in the city.

At this juncture the reporter called the assignment editor to inform him of developments. She told him that only one club seemed to have experienced *a* major incident, but it was an isolated one, and that this type of crime was down, not up. The assignment editor told the reporter to try two more boat clubs.

Later the reporter commented about the fact that it was Monday, a slow news day because it follows the weekend when there is 'no news' and assignment editors have to 'live off the newspaper.' At a later date this reporter made a similar comment about this particular story to another researcher, adding that she had great difficulty trying to convince the assignment editor that there were only waves of water, not of crime, hitting boats in the city. 'Around here, as I'm sure you've learned, newspapers are everything – they think if it is in print it must be accurate.'

At the yacht club suggested by the previous source, the reporter spoke to three people in a boat who collectively agreed that there was no theft from boats at the club. However, upon entering an office at the club, the reporter finally found an informant who asserted that there was indeed a problem relative to the previous year. There was a major incident four months previously, resulting in a $5,000 loss. The reporter then showed this man the newspaper story and asked him if he could substantiate it. The man said he could, and then began talking about the harbour police visiting boat clubs over the past two years to encourage members to label equipment for security reasons. The man agreed to talk on camera, but the reporter simply took his card after signifying it was lunch time. The reporter apparently had no intention of pursuing the story, taking the card only in case the assignment editor persisted with his wish that someone be interviewed to say there was a problem, because he needed the item to fill the show.

To fulfil the request of the assignment editor to visit two more clubs, the reporter went to one last marina and talked to a man in a booth labelled 'Dockmaster/Information.' He said he knew nothing about a possible increase in boat thefts. The reporter proceeded to lunch before returning to the newsroom to inform the assignment editor that he would need an alternative item for the lineup.

This case is instructive about newsworthiness. A story for broadcasting was only considered possible if it could be visualized that boat thefts were increasing, and that therefore a serious problem existed requiring more intensive control remedies such as 'watch towers and guard dogs.' Normal crime (cf Sudnow, 1965) is not news, only abnormal crime. Ordinary control is not news, only extraordinary control. If there is no deviance, there is no story.

There is an important qualification to this generalization. Certain kinds of deviance and control in particular organizational contexts are focused on as newsworthy, while other kinds are ruled out. Note that there was deviance perceived by the reporter, and a social-control effort possible in relation to it: this was the deviance of the reporter and news organization that did the original story, the fact that their account was considered fiction. An effort might have been made to do a story to point out this deviance, and to use this as a vehicle to effect control over fellow journalists. However, the reporter never considered the option of producing a story that would contradict the visualization of a boat-theft wave, and thereby point out the deviance of the newspaper reporter and organization responsible for the apparently erroneous nature of that visualization. This bears further consideration.

The reporter perceived two options in the face of her initial inability to find anyone suitable to say there was a boat-theft wave. She could keep looking until she found someone to visualize a boat-theft wave and reinforce what she quickly appreciated to be a fictitious newspaper account. Alternatively, she could drop the matter after persuading her editor that there was no boat-theft problem. Given that it was a 'slow' day and that her item was needed to fill the show, she was especially persistent in pursuing the first option. It was only after many interviews with a variety of sources that the organizational demands receded in favour of not producing a story. It was not an option to take one or two sources and have them say there was no particular problem of boat thefts. Within the normal canons of journalistic methodology this would have been easy since both authoritative sources (the police and boat-club officials), as well as boat-theft victims themselves, stated that the original newspaper story was conveying the wrong impression.

From this we learn that at the level of routine reporting the news media exclude their own kind in policing organizational life. While there are often stories in which different news outlets are critical of one another at the *institutional* level, at the *everyday, practical* level they do not directly address specific faults in one another's accounts. This disinclination to do information policing in relation to one another was reflected upon by a news executive we interviewed.

Q: [Let's say a competitor] does a story that there's an increase in a particular kind of theft ... shoplifting, let's say ...

A: And we checked and found that there wasn't an increase?

Q: Right.

A: No, we wouldn't run a story.

Q: Why?

A: I mean if we had to go around every day correcting [names competing news outlet] we'd be doing that for profit.

Q: But I mean ... that's also information ... it's relevant information on a phenomenon and somebody's reporting there's an increase. First of all there's the element of correcting, possibly, but there's also the element of saying ... we have discovered different data which inform this issue. Our data suggest that this is not a problem, at least there hasn't been an increase in the problem.

A: ... I mean that happens so frequently that it's something we're not going to get into, unless it becomes a major concern. It did on the issue of rape last summer ... at that time I insisted that we check and find out what the increase was and so on and we did do stories saying that there has not been an increase in the incidence of rape. But that was because it had become a major concern in the community, not as an attempt to correct another newspaper. So, instances like that, yes, but in that case you're responding not to a mistake made by another newspaper but to a palpable concern in the community itself [on the rape issue referred to, see Voumvakis and Ericson, 1984].

We found in general that when it came to scooping story ideas, sources, and angles, or merely being the first to publish an information update, journalists were intensely competitive in spirit, intention, and action. However, the quest to 'beat' the competition did have limits. Apparently out of a desire to keep it as a sparring match rather than an all-out war, the competition was not subject to direct published criticism, correction, or contradiction. Accounts found wanting were either ignored, or a story with improved information was published without specific reference to the faulty account in the other outlet. This is also usual practice in science, where 'publication in a journal in no way establishes that a claim has been accepted by the scientific community ... [C]laims which are found wanting are seldom publicly refuted. They are usually ignored instead' (Mulkay, 1979: 57). This is one way in which news is partial knowledge.

This story indicates additional ways in which news-as-knowledge is limited. As we elaborate in the next chapter, reporters' knowledge about the matters they report on comes in large part from *within* news discourse itself. The initial idea for this story came from another news outlet. This is typical: the news itself suggests what is newsworthy. As the reporter observed, assignment editors 'live off the newspaper.' The most the reporter was looking for was a different source to visualize the boat-theft wave and attendant control strategies, perhaps providing a 'second-day lead' rather than a simple 'matcher.' Moreover, there was a persistent belief in the newsroom that the original newspaper story was correct. As the reporter observed: 'Newspapers are everything – they think if it is in print it must be accurate.'

Normally, previous news accounts are verified by simply asking the same sources, or the same types of sources, to say it is so. The reporter started with *the* official source about crime, the police. When the police failed to say there was a boat-theft problem, she sought others who might be in a position so say it was so. What she was looking for was a source who would visualize deviance: making it visible to the mind. She did not seek to make it visible to the eye, through analysis of documents, behaviours, or other objects that pertained to the subject. That is, the reporter did not contemplate other ways of knowing about whether there was a problem. She did not consider a systematic survey of police documents or insurance-company documents to obtain an official overview of trends. She did not undertake a victimization survey, even with a modest sample of fifteen, which was the number of persons she contacted using her own journalistic methodology. She did not begin with any knowledge of what the 'real' conditions were. She simply wanted someone in the know to say it was so.

We now move to an in-depth examination of news process. By considering in turn assigning, reporting, and editing, we make evident that news-making is a fluid and equivocal process, yet highly structured and severely circumscribed by organization, knowledge, and capacity to communicate. This allows us to finally understand how and why news is partial knowledge: not the truth, but truth reduced to the genre capacities of news discourse.

PART III

The News Process

6

Assigning

The assignment desk is the hub of newsroom operations. The assignment editor is an experienced journalist who communicates daily with all reporters working from the desk and with more senior editors and management, and is thus the key articulator of the vocabulary of precedents in the newsroom. In this chapter we consider the assigning task as practised by assignment editors we observed and interviewed. Included is a systematic study of a newspaper assignment editor in relation to 93 stories considered, and a comparable study of a television-news assignment editor in relation to 161 stories considered. We examine how story ideas came to their attention. We then consider judgments about these story ideas in terms of whether and why they were newsworthy, and the omnipresent attention to time and space requirements. The assignment editor's choice of reporters for particular assignments is analyzed, as is his ongoing exchanges with reporters and more senior editors. We also give consideration to the assignment editor's influence over the entire process of news production.

Origins of Story Ideas

ASSIGNMENT-EDITOR ACCOUNTS

In table 6.1 we enumerate a newspaper assignment editor's accounts of the primary origin of story ideas for each of 93 stories he assigned over a five-day period. In table 6.2 we enumerate a television-news assignment editor's accounts of the primary origin of story ideas for each of the 161 stories he assigned over a twelve-day period. While any given story can obviously have multiple origins, the assignment editors we observed had little difficulty choosing a primary origin.

TABLE 6.1

The primary origins of story ideas: newspaper assignment editor

Origins of story ideas	N	%
INTERNAL		
Regular beat reporter	24	25.7
Specialist beat reporter	14	15.1
General reporter	5	5.4
Desk editor staff	3	3.2
Non-city desk reporters	2	2.2
Copy editor	1	1.1
Subtotal	49	52.7
FOLO		
Subtotal	19	20.4
OTHER MEDIA		
Newspapers	8	8.6
CP Wire	4	4.3
Subtotal	12	12.9
SOURCES		
Press releases	7	7.4
Organization caller	2	2.2
Individual caller	2	2.2
Subtotal	11	11.8
UNSPECIFIED		
Subtotal	2	2.2
Total	93	100.0

Approximately one-half of newspaper stories and one-third of television stories were said to originate from people working for the newsroom. In the newspaper, almost 90 per cent of story ideas said to originate internally were attributed to reporters. This fact is consistent with the view of journalists in this newsroom, as well as journalists working for other news organizations locally, that this was a 'reporter's newspaper' rather than an 'editor's newspaper.' In contrast, almost one-half of the stories said to originate from television-newsroom personnel were attributed to supervising editors or producers. This is consistent with our observations that in the television newsroom concerned, the executive producer, producer, lineup editor, and assignment editor were much more actively involved in all stages of the process than in the newspaper newsroom.

Only 12 per cent of story ideas were attributed to sources by the newspaper assignment editor, while the television assignment editor said the idea came

TABLE 6.2

The primary origins of story ideas: television assignment editor

Origins of story ideas	N	%
INTERNAL		
Beat reporter	15	9.3
Other reporter	14	8.7
Executive producer	9	5.6
Assignment editor	8	5.0
Affiliate editor	4	2.5
Producer	1	0.6
Researcher	1	0.6
Vice-president	1	0.6
Subtotal	53	32.9
SOURCES		
Press releases	25	15.5
Organization caller	9	5.6
Individual caller	8	5.0
Subtotal	42	26.1
OTHER MEDIA		
Scanner	9	5.6
Radio	8	5.0
Newspaper	6	3.7
Wire	2	1.2
Unspecified	2	1.2
Subtotal	27	16.7
FOLO		
Subtotal	22	13.7
UNSPECIFIED		
Subtotal	17	10.6
Total	161	100.0

from a source in 26 per cent of all stories he assigned. Television assignment editors were especially likely to work from official releases of source organizations, a fact well documented in the research literature (e.g., Epstein, 1974; Schlesinger, 1978). There is a likelihood of overlap between this category and attributions stating that a story idea originated with a reporter. Especially with beat and specialist reporters, the assignment editor might have attributed the origin of the story idea to the reporter without considering that the reporter in turn obtained information from a source that intitiated the story.

The tables indicate that the television assignment editor was marginally more likely to say that a story idea originated from other media than was his newspaper counterpart. However, this difference is extinguished if one removes the 'scanner' category from table 6.2. The scanner is a multiband receiver which sat on or by the assignment editor's desk so that he could monitor police and other emergency-service radios for possible events to cover. While a scanner was also available to the newspaper assignment editor, he did not use it much and no story in the newspaper sample was assigned on this basis. The television assignment editor also attributed the origin of story ideas to radio newscasts in 5 per cent of all assignments, and 30 per cent of assignments attributed to other media, but no story ideas were attributed to the radio by the newspaper assignment editor.

The attributions to other media are almost certainly an underestimation of the actual influence of other media. It is likely that in many instances where the story idea was attributed to editors or producers, they in turn obtained the idea from another news outlet. Other news media were a dominant intelligence source for assignment editors, especially in broadcast newsrooms.

The 'folo' category was an assignment term for continuing stories that were being followed up through further assignments. The newspaper assignment editor made 20 per cent of all story-idea attributions according to the fact that the story had originated some time before and there were further developments being pursued. The television assignment editor used the 'folo' attribution in 14 per cent of story assignments discussed.

These data provide a general overview of the origins of story ideas as seen by assignment editors in the act of assignment. In addition to observing assignment editors systematically in these terms, we had the opportunity to observe other dimensions of how story ideas originated. We now turn to these further observations to understand more fully how matters are deemed worthy of assignment.

INTERNAL ORIGINS

Reporters were expected to be a constant source of story ideas and to take them to the assignment editor for consideration. The reporter was supposed to derive intelligent ideas from other news outlets. We frequently observed reporters scrutinizing newspapers and clipping out stories as suggestions to the assignment editor. Occasionally reporters would also report to the assignment editor something they had seen or heard on a newscast.

There was a particular onus on beat reporters to generate story ideas in the organizational context in which they were immersed. They were very much assignment editors for their beat terrain, maintaining newspaper-clipping files, scheduled-event files, and a depository of any official paper their sources gave them. They were also expected to cultivate contacts with sources, who would it was hoped, provide story ideas that were original, at least for the few hours before competing news organizations caught up with them.

In addition to the expectation that reporters would feed the assignment editor from these regularized sources, there was the hope that they would exercise their imagination to visualize other possibilities. This often meant reliance upon friends and family, or other personal interests or circumstances. For example, a reporter married to a lawyer informed the assignment editor that he had received a general practice memorandum from the provincial law society indicating that price-cutting on fees for real estate transactions was not appropriate, and indicating that sanctions were available against lawyers who engaged in price-cutting. The assignment editor accepted that the story had significant ramifications for both the profession and the public, and he assigned another reporter to develop the story.

A reporter would be assigned to a story which pertained to a story, feature, or investigation being developed by another reporter. For example, a political-beat reporter was asked to cover a particular hearing because it bore relevance to another reporter's story; a court-beat reporter was asked to cover a particular court case because it was of potential significance to a series of stories by another reporter. Often the reporter asked to do the work in these circum-stances had little idea of what his colleague or assignment editor had in mind. He was asked to do the work because he was conveniently placed to obtain what was required.

Reporters also came across things by chance. Returning to the newsroom from covering a court case, a television reporter noticed a marquee and a large group of people on a lot. He discovered it was a sod-turning ceremony for a new building, involving the provincial premier, city mayor, and other dignitaries. The reporter radioed the assignment editor about it, and in turn was instructed to take visuals. Television stations also had crews in cars, equipped with scanners, and with dispatch radios to the assignment desk. These crews were ready to be reactively mobilized to an event, or simply patrolled in the hope that something would be seen and visualized proactively. This was a means for cameramen to have a direct input into story creation independent of a reporter, although a reporter might later be used to provide a voice-over for the film. This aspect of story creation was not covered in table 6.2. However, this practice provided at least a little substance to the advertising poster of one television station which showed a cameraman leaning out of a car window shooting visuals with the word 'everywhere' blazoned across the poster.

Editors and producers derived story ideas on the same basis as reporters: scrutinizing other organizations' news; maintaining relations with persons in various outside organizations and institutions who might provide ideas and act as sources; and exercising their imagination, or that of friends and relatives.

A focus on trends in society – as depicted by trends in news reporting – was often seen by an editor as a basis for a feature. In a newspaper we studied, the managing editor, in consultation with other senior editors, developed ideas which pertained to contemporary issues. For example, during a moral panic about attacks on women (cf Voumvakis and Ericson, 1984), editors arranged for the assignment of a city-desk reporter to do features on the topic of rape, including epidemiological aspects as well as the women's issues involved. Similarly, the decision to undertake features on the issue of surrogate motherhood was developed by senior editors as architects, engineered through the assignment desk, and accomplished by assigning a reporter believed to have the technical competence to get the job done.

Editors and producers not only derived ideas from the visualization of trends or other observations on what was in the news, but also personal circumstances. A reporter was assigned a story about a university's system for entrance scholarships, in which it only considered for scholarships those students who listed that university as their first or second choice on the standard admission form for all universities in the province. The reporter said that this instance of procedural deviance in an organization was of no interest to him, and that the only reason he was working on it was 'orders' to do so in face of the fact that a senior editor's child had the qualifications for a scholarship at this university but was denied one because she had listed the university as her third choice on the application form. In another instance, an assignment editor was victimized by the theft of a plant, worth $50.00, from the porch of his home. He said the police told him that he should put bars on the basement windows of his home, and that there was an increase in the number of break-ins in his area. He decided to assign a reporter to do a story on trends in residential break-ins, including material on crime-prevention measures available to residents. Both in assigning the crew and upon questioning by researchers, the assignment editor stated his own victimization had led him to visualize this story.

Newsrooms affiliated with other newsrooms, for example through broadcast-network arrangements, were also able to rely upon affiliate members for ideas. The assignment editor in one newsroom we studied had a regular practice of calling the assignment editors of local affiliates to canvass their ideas and offer sugestions in reciprocity. Affiliate editors also called with specific tips for things to cover. They themselves gained if they could make use of interview clips or other elements of stories prepared by the newsroom concerned as a result of the tip.

SOURCE ORIGINS

The assignment editor was not simply a passive receptacle, but actively maintained relations with well-placed sources in all organizations that the newsroom had dealings with. In addition he maintained regular contact with bureaucracies that had a steady menu of items to choose from, such as the police, both through daily checks on releases and calls to public relations officers. The flow of information to the assignment editor's desk was also encouraged proactively in some news organizations by the announcement of 'hot-tip lines' in the newspaper or during broadcasts. These urged citizens to call the newsroom 'if you see news happening,' as if news was littering the streets waiting to be scooped up. Occasionally rewards were offered for this form of citizenship.

Reactively, the assignment editor received a barrage of official reports, company magazines and newspapers, announcements of scheduled events, and news releases. Some were placed in a date file to be reconsidered on the relevant date. Others provided the basis for immediate assignment, or were passed on to another journalist in the newsroom who might be interested. A lot were discarded. This flow of official paper – usually already made news-worthy to the best of the ability of the source – was crucial to the assignment editor's task of keeping informed. In the case of news releases the information was used to decide whether a particular news conference or meeting should be covered, whether a follow-up interview with a named source should be conducted, or whether it should simply be copied or rewritten as news. In the case of official reports or company magazines and newspapers, scrutiny revealed reportable items. Sometimes the source organization made evident what was reportable by the play it gave to particular items; for example, a university newspaper highlighted a professor's important discovery, and a police annual report underscored that while crime was rising they had every-thing under control. Sometimes the inferential leaps were based more on the imagination of the journalist. For example, in scrutinizing the prosecution statistics in the annual report of the city food inspectorate, a journalist dis-covered that something must be amiss in the fact that fourteen cases were not brought forward for prosecution because of missing information.

Assignment editors also received calls directly from sources who rec-ommended coverage of particular events or issues they were involved in. These included anonymous tips from persons inside an organization, who tended to be disgruntled with the organization and pointed out a deviant practice of the organization. Thus a bank executive called to inform the assignment editor that his bank and others were converting money from dormant accounts for bank gain without adequate notice to customers and in possible violation of regulations. Sources called to inform the assignment editor of an upcoming event; or, to remind him of it, having previously sent a written announcement. This was a practice preferred by sources who did not have a regular beat reporter covering their organization, for example, citizens' pressure groups who wanted their meeting or demonstration covered and thereby have the news media participate in their cause. The assignment

editor was contacted directly (instead of going to specialist reporters or reporters who were acquaintances) because of his presumed influence in assignment and play.

The fact that the assignment editor actively encouraged and pursued
source contacts, and the flow of official paper, means that the distinction
between being proactive and reactive is not very useful analytically. Just as
a police department actively encourages citizens to report occurrences and
supply hot tips as a means of generating the very phenomena they act on
(Ericson, 1981, 1982), so the news organization encourages people to visualize what the organization requires and to provide a steady flow of possibilities
from which it can choose. The process also works in reverse, as source
organizations provide a steady supply of official paper, calls, and opportunities
for meeting to news organizations.

OTHER MEDIA ORIGINS

A great deal of the knowledge journalists use to obtain story ideas and make
news judgments is derived from the output of other news outlets. Journalism,
like scientific practice, is 'self-referential' (Knorr-Cetina, 1983: 159). The
accounts of assignment editors enumerated in tables 6.1 and 6.2 underestimate
the pervasiveness of this origin, as many things said to be the idea of other
journalists were derived in turn from journalists' monitoring of other news
outlets.

Keeping up with other news media gives the assignment editor a sense
of what is new and therefore what is news, since the news is concerned with
the present, 'the vivid fringe of memory tinged with anticipation' (A.N.
Whitehead, quoted by Giddens, 1979: 55). Since the news only treats the
past and future 'as a special case of the present' (cf Kermode, 1966: 58–9),
the sense of the new – of timeliness in terms of recency, immediacy, and
currency – is defined primarily in terms of whether other news outlets have
published on the matter, as well as the 'freshness' of their information and
the frame in which it is interpreted. The wise assignment editor is one who
keeps on top of fresh developments, and thereby maintains a sense of news
relevance.

Assignment editors were selective about what other news they scrutinized
for story ideas. Newspaper assignment editors paid very minor attention to
radio news for story ideas, and monitored television rarely. The comments
of a television executive indicate that it is exceptional for newspapers to pick
up something from television: 'The greatest source of pride is that newspapers
follow us with a story. It shows that our editorial thinking is sound and it
proves to us that if we had the manpower, then the people that are here would
be just as capable of "doing" a *Globe and Mail* as the people that do the

Globe and Mail.' In one newspaper the assignment editor used another news-paper extensively for story ideas, but a third newspaper was generally ignored because it was viewed as unimportant, 'not a real newspaper.'

Research shows that broadcast-news outlets are especially dependent on newspapers for story ideas. Indeed this is an established tradition in broadcast news. The original broadcast-news bulletins in Britain were not produced by British Broadcasting Corporation (BBC) staff but reproduced from news-agency material and formally attributed to them. British broadcasting therefore 'began by incorporating wholesale press definitions of news value' (Schlesinger, 1978: 15) and still includes a formal segment of reporting the main items in the national newspapers. In Canadian broadcasting a 'rip-and-read' approach – taking a newspaper clipping and reading from it, or a slightly reworded version of it – is still prevalent. Clarke (1981: 40–1) describes the practices at an independent television station in Southern Ontario, and quotes a news editor: 'Basically, newspapers tend to be *developing* material, where we don't develop anything. We react. All we're doing all the time is reacting: to what the newspapers are doing, to what the radio stations are doing, and to whatever hard news stories are out there happening all by themselves. We're reacting all the time, we're not originating anything at all.'

The Royal Commission on Newspapers (RCN) also discovered that broad-cast-news assignment editors are heavily dependent upon newspapers. In their final report they conclude that 'print remains the agenda setter. The first item of the day's business in every radio and T.V. newsroom is the reading of newspapers, usually the *Globe and Mail* followed by the main regional news-paper, and the scanning of reports from CP [Canadian Press], largely drawn from newspapers' (RCN, 1981: 143). In their research monograph, *Canadian News Sources*, they report their finding that 'newsmen assume (and there is little to challenge the assumption) that newspapers dominate the system by which news is generated and processed and disseminated, even though, par-adoxically, they no longer seem to be the news medium with the highest public impact. These factors operate both in the formal wire service system and in the information processes by which newsmen hear about news and make selections on what to follow up' (RCN, 1981c: 2).

This reliance on newspaper stories is part of the more general fact that broadcast journalism is fundamentally shaped by the assumptions and ap-proaches of newspapers (Golding, 1981). Through to the point of structuring the television news lineup for broadcast, newspaper terms are employed to make the audience believe they are within the news world of newspapers. A television newsroom we studied inserted into the anchorperson's script at the point of breaking for the first commercial, 'And that's our front page for tonite ... our top stories.' They also divided their news into newspaper 'sec-tions,' for example, sports, national, international, and so on. Occasionally graphics were done in black and white to convey the solidity of newspaper news. In terms of the overall lineup, the inverted pyramid, from the most important to the least important, was used. As an executive of this television station explained with regard to some of these practices:

> I think that society in general is television oriented as well now and that's why it has such an impact. But the view of news is still newspaper, and yes it is a conscious effort on my part to say, 'And that's our front page tonight,' because I think people can relate to that. And besides, the front page has become a cliché which means that, hey, those are the most important stories ... [I]t's a conscious effort on my part every once in awhile in the background presentation or graphic presentation, to use black and white plates, because black and white is still, says news to me ... it gives you the sense that it's news, you know, and that's because we were weaned on newspapers.

Television assignment editors we studied began their search for news with their noses a few inches away from the latest editions of local newspapers. Other researchers (e.g., Epstein, 1974: 37–8; Schlesinger, 1978: 92) have observed that television assignment editors exhibit a preference for quality newspapers because of their reputation for reliability, their authority, and their agenda-setting role. We observed no such preference, as assignment editors scrutinized all three Toronto newspapers. Perhaps the difference is in the fact that we studied local television newsrooms, whereas these other studies focused on national news.

A television assignment editor said he actually began his work day upon arising from bed, listening to radio news while washing, breakfasting, and going to the office. A similar routine was followed by the executive producer, who met with the assignment editor early in the day to discuss their mutual judgments about what the news suggested was newsworthy. In interview he confirmed our observations: just as every competent academic is to be on top of the scholarly literature in his field, so every professional journalist is to have his nose in the news.

> [I]t is a profession in that sense that you have to be totally aware of what's going on. Sometimes on the weekend I find it a chore to read the daily, but I read the dailies from cover to cover, I mean I read every word, I read every section because your knowledge has to be rounded. You have to know about the developments ... because when Monday comes along and you go out there on the beat and somebody says 'blankity-blank,' you have to know whether blankity-blank is new or not. How else are you going to gauge whether that's new or not? So, you've got to read the newspapers, you've got to listen to radio news, you've got to read books, you've got to read magazines and, above all else, because you've chosen television as a profession, you have to

observe what other television outlets are doing. You have to understand the techniques that they're using, you have to understand the methods of obtaining information, in order for you to be par with the state of the art. Professional means that.

Assignment editors and reporters appreciated their dependence on news for the generation of more news. On an occasion when a story was not initiated by another news story, the reporter involved remarked that it was 'refreshing' not to be working from a newspaper 'tear-out.' While editing, a technician and reporter discussed with each other how television news has always followed the lead of newspapers, with most story ideas being summarized initially in a 'tear-out' newspaper article. The technician said it was that way twenty years ago, recalling that at the beginning of an International Typographical Union strike against three Toronto newspapers there was grave concern in television newsrooms because there might be a curtailment, or drying up temporarily, of their primary source of stories. They also joked about a reporter who had obtained a newspaper from the assignment editor on the previous day, and complained loudly when he discovered that half of it was missing because the assignment editor had torn out items for assignment.

In contrast to his regular reliance on newspaper sources, the television assignment editor was more selective about the radio stations to which he stayed attuned. He listened mainly to three stations, which he identified as the best source of police stories. He also maintained contact with an affiliate radio station. In contrast to what the Glasgow University Media Group (GUMG) reports (1976: 64), radio was clearly a secondary source.

As part of their judgment, assignment editors considered the play given to the matter by the other news outlets. Assignment editors frequently referred to play in the selection of items, noting the need to keep up with the competition or at least cover the possibility that the competition would have something 'important' which they did not. We also inferred the significance of play from our observations. The *Globe and Mail* had a story about statistics released by the Canadian Centre for Justice Statistics. The television assignment editor bypassed this story on that day. The next day the *Star* used aspects of these statistics for a front-page story and major headline. On this second day the television assignment editor decided to assign a reporter to this story.

A reporter was initially puzzled to be assigned to cover a double murder in a small village more than 150 kilometres from Toronto. She learned that the assignment editor had heard a report on it via a Toronto radio station. On the way to the village she instructed the crew to turn on the car radio to hear the hourly newscast of this station. The newscast had this murder as the lead item. Commenting that the assignment editor sometimes did not assign domestic murders in Toronto, let alone those 150 kilometres away, the reporter inferred that this story was deemed important by the assignment editor because it was the lead item on this 'authoritative' radio newscast.

Wire stories pertaining to local situations were also a source of story ideas for newspaper and television assignment editors. These were usually passed to the assignment editors by wire editors. The newspaper we observed in greatest depth primarily relied upon the Canadian Press (CP) for city-desk purposes, supplemented by other sources on occasion. The television news-room attended to Broadcast News, VisNews (Canadian and American net-works), United Press International (UPI) and Reuters for international stories (not usually the direct concern of the assignment editor), a sports wire, and a 'work wire' (used by large corporations to convey items about company activities). Wire stories did not seem to play a major role for story ideas, although they were often incorporated into reporters' accounts at later stages. When they were used by the assignment editor to initiate a story it was typically a development on a story that was continuing (e.g., a suspect in a major case had been arrested; a product suspected of containing a dangerous substance was ordered removed from store shelves).

The point that wire material was often used as background or additional material in stories the assignment editor had already assigned on another basis pertains also to newspaper clippings. A 'tear-out' handed to the reporter by the assignment editor in making the assignment was not necessarily the origin of the story idea. Rather, it was sometimes a supplementary source of back-ground information, an indication of who were possible sources, and a means to consider what had been done in order to visualize what might be done. For example, a reporter who had already learned about a forthcoming hearing or public inquiry would still be given newspaper clippings on it by the as-signment editor. A reporter who had worked on a continuing story would receive clippings relevant to the story from the assignment editor. The fact that newspaper clippings were used in this way is another indication that they were more pervasive in the work of assignment editors and reporters than is indicated in tables 6.1 and 6.2.

Using newspaper clippings in this way was the major component of what journalists termed 'research' for their stories. Assignment editors and other journalists in both print and broadcast news outlets defined 'research' as searching for previous news items relating to the same matter. Some journalists kept a 'research' file on a topic, which usually consisted of old newspaper clippings, press releases, and other official public documents. When jour-nalists were directed to be familiar with events on an ongoing basis, it was again in terms of reading newspapers and magazines, listening to radio news, and watching television news and current-affairs programmes. A television producer sent a memo to his staff at the beginning of the new season, and included a statement that if one wants to be a good journalist one must pay continuous attention to the news media. He added that there is nothing more embarrassing in assigning a story than to have a journalist say, 'What's that all about?', and emphasized that the journalist who does not know the issues will not recognize new things even if he sees them.

The use of other news for ideas and judgments about assigning news was so pervasive that good work was not defined in terms of independent sources of knowledge, but in terms of adding something a competitor did not include. This was stated clearly by a television producer who said that 'matchers' were to be discouraged and 'second-day leads' encouraged. He also communicated this to his assignment editor and reporters in the form of regular memoranda and critiques. On one occasion this form of communication was full of praise, exclaiming 'Happily we are well past newspaper matchers.' This memo also focused on a particular reporter whose visualization of 'second-day leads' was exemplary: 'I think stories that ——— did this week all were Panasonic (slightly ahead of our time) ... ——— was the guy who asked the President [of a company] the question that led to the response that everyone was quoting.' Good work was defined in terms of other news outlets following what one's own newsroom had done in response to what they had done earlier.

Other than through direct source contacts, the only hope for 'being there first' and obtaining the initial story on an event was through items picked up on the scanner. The scanner was the source of many story ideas both in our systematic observation of the assignment editor (table 6.2) and over the extended period of observation in the newsroom. Among the things that came to the assignment editor's attention, and crew dispatch, as a result of scanner monitoring were major fires, a bombing of a building, murders, robberies, kidnappings, rapes, serious assaults, police 'gun calls,' accidents, and a woman trapped in a subway train. Routine police releases were also picked up on the scanner, for example, announcements about the arrest of suspects, the capture of an escaped convict, and a reward offered for information leading to the arrest of a suspect. The scanner was seen as a primary vehicle by which the television station could 'beat the competition' by 'being there first' for 'on the spot' clips from sources and dramatic visuals. It was as if audiences in turn scanned their output in comparison with the competition and made judgments on the basis of the same criteria. However, in our observations the scanner was not of much help in 'beating' the competition because they too had this equipment and therefore they were also on the scene quickly to join the 'pack' in visualizing deviance.

THE ABSENCE OF READERSHIP/AUDIENCE ORIGINS

These findings underscore the fact that ideas about what is newsworthy derive from *within* the news media. A substantial proportion of story ideas originate with journalists inside the newsroom. Another large proportion of stories are follow-ups to stories published or broadcast previously by the journalist's own newsroom or by another news organization. A significant proportion of story ideas come from sources; since most sources have ongoing relations with journalists and serve in effect as 'reporters,' they are also *within* the news-media institution.

Missing from the assignment editors' accounts of the ideas is the readership or audience. This is consistent with previous research that has found that news judgments are not based on specific knowledge of the general public's interests and tastes, but rather knowledge derived from regular sources, fellow journalists, and existing news accounts (e.g., GUMG, 1976, 1980; Phillips, 1977; Schlesinger, 1978; Burns, 1979; Clarke, 1981). '[T]here is no organizational emphasis on knowing the audience, only on *having* one' (Tracey, 1978: 129). Assignment editors make 'plausible assumptions' (Schlesinger, 1978: 120–1) about what their 'imaginary audience' (Pool and Shulman, 1959) might want.

When asked separately about how they know that a story will be of interest to their audience or readership, assignment editors and reporters gave four types of response. One type of response was to indicate that he intuitively 'knows' the public is interested. When an assignment editor was probed for evidence that the public is scared about dangerous objects being placed in candy or fruit for children at Hallowe'en, which was his frame for a story he had assigned, his response was simply, 'I *know* a lot of people are scared.' Another type of response was for the journalist to say that he had chatted with his friends about the matter, and since they found it interesting he assumed the general public would also find it interesting. A third type of response was for the journalist to say that he took his cues from the many sources in different organizations he had regular dealings with; somehow he saw this as typical of public concerns and interests. Finally, reference was made to feedback from the public in response to published or broadcast items: telephone calls and letters from citizens received in the newsroom, or received by regular sources and in turn communicated to the newsroom. No reference was made to more scientific or systematic evidence of a survey nature, a fact consistent with what has been reported by other researchers (e.g., Clarke, 1981: 46).

The apparent lack of systematic effort by journalists to *know* their public rather than just *have* one appears as somewhat of a contradiction in face of official statements and their own statements that they are agents of the public. For example, a Canadian Broadcasting Corporation (CBC) (1978) document emphasizes 'that in selecting what is to be reported it is essential that national events which are of concern to all Canadians be reflected, as well as news from across the country, taking into account, of course, the interest of the audience' (p. 374). The same document also asserts: 'It is critical for us to maintain a dialogue with the public for whom journalistic organizations are "agents" in gathering and communicating information' (p. 414). An editor made a statement in direct concurrence with the official view: '[E]ssentially what we're here to do is like that famous saying ... "Gentlemen, we have a government to bring down" ... We're there to ask questions that the public wants asked of these guys. We're there as their agents.'

The claim by journalists that they are agents of the interests of their audience, and the fact that they lack systematic knowledge of what the audience is interested in, may be less of a contradiction than it appears initially. While assignment editors may not keep up with audience ratings or readership surveys on a daily basis, these are factors at the management level that arguably filter down to the floor level of the newsroom. Some newspapers have a more narrowly defined target readership, and a given story is assigned on the assumption that only a fraction of the readership will read it. The assignment editor knows that the story is not for the general public but for a particular segment of the particular readership of the newspaper. In contrast, audience surveys may be an influential factor in television news, because television stories are produced for a mass audience on the assumption that they'll please everyone. In relation to television, Seaton (1980: 101–2) criticizes researchers who have stressed that journalistic criteria are derived internally from peers rather than from audiences: 'Producers may ignore the audience; programme planners who arrange the sequence and balance of viewing clearly do not. These authors have overestimated the power and autonomy of those who work in the studio, when many of the decisions made there are already limited by other organizational factors.'

As Tuchman (1978: 105n) notes, television executives initially did not treat the news as a profitable component of their operation, but this gradually changed by the 1970s with the aid of the great barometer of entertainment programming, the ratings. Certainly in the television operations we examined, the news ratings were constantly on the minds of the producers and communicated to assignment editors and reporters in the form of memos posted on the bulletin board. These memos sometimes included interpretations of changes or influences on ratings, as well as encouragement for the newsroom 'team' to persist in their efforts to improve ratings.

An argument against organizing and reporting on the basis of ratings or consumer surveys is that it yields content aimed at the lowest common denominator (Monaco, 1981: 360). Survey research has led newspapers to follow public taste, for example, by giving increased space to entertainment and lifestyles sections (Hirsch, 1977; Murdock and Golding, 1978). The Royal Commission on Newspapers (1981: 172–3) notes this trend, and uses the pejorative term 'disco journalism' to depict extreme versions of it. They cite a former newspaper editor's distaste for market-survey research journalism, whose product he terms 'Pablum Canada.'

In television news it is difficult to provide any other type of nourishment because the content is directed to the mass audience that will in turn provide more advertising revenues as its numbers rise. Television news thus gravitates to commonly available meanings that reduce the possibility of multiple decodings by the audience which would lead some of them to turn off. It thus leads to simplification so that 'everyone' will find it understandable. Epstein (1974: 241–2) quotes a CBS producer as saying, 'We have to act on the assumption that the audience has zero knowledge about a subject' (see also Gitlin, 1980: 231; Schlesinger, 1978: 106, 125). Journalists we studied made frequent reference to the low level at which they had to 'pitch' their items. As one said, there could be nothing that was not understandable or that would shock the family as they digested their news along with their food during the 6:00–7:00 p.m. dinner hour. A similar recipe of lifestyle, simplification, and entertainment is also evident in tabloid newspapers (RCN, 1981). Part of this popular formula is crime, deviance, and other bad news. As Schlesinger (1978: 118) found, decisions to broadcast *fait divers* are justified by statements that it is, after all, what the audience wants. Survey evidence supports this, as consumers 'either show no difference in preference for ''good'' or ''bad'' news'' or ... they actually prefer unpleasant news' (Heath et al, 1981, citing Hartung and Stone, 1980; Clyde, 1968).

Another reason why the apparent lack of effort by journalists to *know* their public may not be a contradiction of the mandate to represent audience interests is the fact that they take an élitist view of their role as knowledge producers. Ultimately it is the journalist who must decide what is the correct consciousness to convey to the public. This is legislated in the Broadcasting Act and other broadcasting regulations, stated in policy manuals, and demanded by supervisors. In the words of the CBC president, in his preface to the CBC journalist's codebook, 'Programming cannot be limited to what the largest audience wants to know; it must include what the public is entitled and needs to know. This implies no disregard for expressed taste but a recognition of the requirement for a source of comprehensive information' (CBC, 1981: iv). The standard here is to be decided by journalists themselves, the professional solution. 'If the media are to do their work of reflecting and revealing reality properly, there will at times be tensions between the media and different elements of society. This should not inhibit the CBC, as long as the corporation in its information programming is carrying out this essential task of informing the public in accordance with its established journalistic standards' (ibid). The professional solution is not exclusive to the CBC, but was the standard response of assignment editors and other journalists we studied.

TABLE 6.3

The primary reasons for coverage: newspaper assignment editor

Reasons for coverage	N	%
Important topic	40	43.0
Continuing news story	20	21.4
Continuing news theme	8	8.6
Human interest/brightener	5	5.4
Prominent politician involved	4	4.3
Prominent citizen involved	3	3.2
Routine spot	2	2.2
Defer to reporter's judgment	2	2.2
Meeting competition's coverage	1	1.1
Unspecified	8	8.6
TOTAL	93	100.0

TABLE 6.4

The primary reasons for coverage: television assignment editor

Reasons for coverage	N	%
Continuing news story	52	32.3
Continuing news theme	32	19.9
Important topic	24	14.9
Human interest/brightener	18	11.2
Routine spot	8	5.0
Developing story	7	4.3
Regular beat coverage	6	3.7
Good visuals	3	1.9
Internal	3	1.9
Opportunity for access to source	2	1.2
Unspecified	6	3.7
TOTAL	161	100.0

Considering Story Coverage

ASSIGNMENT-EDITOR ACCOUNTS

Assignment editors were asked to give the primary reason for assigning each story. The accounts given by the newspaper assignment editor are enumerated in table 6.3, and the accounts given by the television assignment editor are enumerated in table 6.4.

The responses were not given in terms of the various criteria of newsworthiness we considered in chapter 5, except for the newspaper editor's reference to politicians or other prominent citizens being involved. Assignment editors tended to respond in terms of standard news categories related to the timing of story origins and whether a story was being followed up (spot, developing, continuing); or, to indicate that it was intended as a human-interest story or 'brightener' among the dominant inclusion of bad news; or, to state that it was obviously or evidently newsworthy as an 'important story.' When pressed about why it was important, assignment editors found it difficult to articulate reasons. They made reference to the 'fact' that a topic was 'obviously' or 'inherently' newsworthy, or said they were doing it now because they had done it before and it was necessary to follow it up or complete the record on it. They also made very little reference to timing, space, or material considerations which are, as we have shown elsewhere, crucial components of assignment editors' judgments. The television assignment editor did mention good visuals as the primary reason for coverage in relation to three stories, but the importance of this element in television coverage seems by other accounts to be far greater than this (Epstein, 1974; Schlesinger, 1978).

What did seem most influential in the accounts of assignment editors was how a particular item related to other items. Did it fit with a salient news theme? Was it a 'folo' of a story done previously? Was it related to other items on the assignment schedule? Would this item provide a good basis for developing additional items over subsequent days? Apart from what was 'intrinsically' important, assignment editors tended to emphasize that the present item was part of a continuing story or theme. Events fell into place for the assignment editor in terms of a series of items that were visualized as part of a theme in the news. The assignment editor discovered a theme among the story ideas that were developed on the day. He then made assignments, and contributed to the layout or lineup, in these terms.

It is the job of assignment editors to make everything fall into place. It is desk editors, layout or lineup personnel, managing editors, and producers who have to worry later in the day about things falling apart (see chapter 8). As assignment editors were in a position to type up the day's assignment 'outlook' sheet, they often made reference to the fact that 'everything is falling into place nicely,' or similar phrasing. This usually meant, especially in television, that a theme had been discovered to 'order' the items and connect them in a 'flow.' The term for linked stories was a 'wrap'; for example, doing a 'murder wrap' was to *package* the present murder item reported to connected items and murders with similar *modus operandi* in the past. Another term meaning the same thing was simply 'pack' (package). Potential items were often judged in terms of how they would fit into a 'pack' or 'wrap.' An assignment editor wanted to do a story on an exhibition of 'ugly art' (art work rejected by major galleries), but was vetoed by the producer on the grounds that 'it doesn't go with anything' else in the outlook. An item on research into developing a cigarette that would extinguish on its own was considered for packaging with a report on an inquest into the death of a person in a fire, believed to have been started by 'careless smoking.'

The police scheduled a news conference in which the star of 'Barney Miller,' a television detective show, was to promote a 'cops are regular guys' theme. On the same day the police released the results of their investigation into an incident that had been controversial (involving the police shooting a suspect after he had been stopped by police in his vehicle). In order to package this item with the 'Barney Miller' pro-police news conference, it was suggested that a story could be added about the psychological trauma police officers suffer after shooting a suspect. A suggestion was made to locate a psychiatrist who had dealt with policemen regarding this problem, possibly arranging an in-studio interview. This suggestion, as an effort to sustain the pro-police imagery set by the news conference, was quite distant from other occasions when newsroom journalists professed and practised a fourth-estate orientation to incidents of policemen shooting suspects in questionable circumstances. It would have been incongruous to do a critical piece on the police after the staged event with 'Barney Miller.' In this case it seemed that the need to sustain consistency in the lineup package predominated. It is conceivable that the police in turn visualized this in releasing the results of their investigation into the controversial shooting and staging the 'Barney Miller' news conference on the same day.

ASSIGNMENT OUTLOOKS

Another sign of what assignment editors regarded as newsworthy was the assignment-outlook sheet which they prepared within two or three hours of beginning their day. This sheet was an internal communication to reporters and editors of what the assignment editor had decided was reportable for the day, along with a hint as to why he thought it was reportable. These reasons were scripted in a shorthand which could be decoded by others who were concerned to know what possible news angles or themes were available, how they might be linked into 'wraps,' what seemed important for layout and lineup, and so on. They indicated the 'working leads,' what seemed intitially significant in a story, although everyone was aware that these could be changed or dropped along the way. They also provided the assignment editor's justification for assignment. Absent was anything about what came to the assignment editor's mind but was deemed unworthy of being listed.

The nature of these assignment-outlook sheets, and the type of things which justify an assignment as newsworthy, are revealed in two examples chosen at random. The names of journalists and television crew members assigned have been removed.

Television

Assignment Outlook [date]

1 –*Consumer's Strike* started today with pickets stopping traffic. looking out for vandalism like had in last strike. also including update of strike situation in Ontario.
2 –*Hi-Rise 3.* day 3 of hearings – head of superintendents assoc. expected to testify.
3 –*Extinguishable Cigarettes.* research being done to find if have this – to avoid fires.
4 –*Council Apartments.* city council expected to debate some part of growing problem of cadillac-fairview apartments being sold to greymac.
5 –*Child Abuse.* this to be V/O, CLIP or REPORT, depending on if have time. this interim report on problem – 1 in 4 girls sexually abused in metro before 18.
6 –*Metro Warning.* gas rebel selling gallons has been given warning by feds to stop or else.
7 –*Chrysler-*UAW. apparently statement coming after 2 p.m.
8 –*Argosy Charged.* abt. 20 execs. of argosy appeared at OPP HQ this morning to answer charges of fraud. court appearance 2 p.m. – old city hall #23. apparently bigger than remor scam.
9 –*Flashback Nov. 3.*
10 –*Cop hit 'n' run.*

Newspaper

CITY DESK [Desk and name of assignment editor]

City schedule for [date].

– Closing arguments in Marafioti ticket-fixing trial.
– Ministers of Education conspire to press for increased financing for bilingual education.
– Owner of Bomb-wrecked Arrow disco surrenders in Miami.
– NDP ask for emergency debate over leaking memo to Drea.
– Debate on controls plan continues.
– Saturday's lottery draw the biggest in North American history but chances of winning it are 14 million to one.
– Police investigating gangland-style slaying of Scarborough man.
– Nursing homes brief.
– Checking CBC staff cuts.
– Court rules natural father's consent not needed in changing baby's name.
– Timbrell, Whelan meet at plowing match near Lucan.
– Ford-Canada – UAW talks near midnight deadline: settlement expected.

- Obits on Allan Findlay, Rev. Dr. Hugh Davidson.
- NIGHT: Broadview-Greenwood all candidates' meeting, 8 – pix. (Pic of main-streeting MacGuigan, O'Connor for use in bulldog).
- FEATURES AVAILABLE: Police not sure why they find one out of three rape cases unfounded.
- High property taxes the big issue in borough of York this election.
- Police lying through their teeth, judge says in dismissing drug charge against lawyer.
- Judge says he doesn't want Toronto to get Montreal's bank robbery problem, sends Brinks robber away for 12 years.
- Editor of Polish-Canadian newspaper fired for editorial criticizing Canadian academic
   avis meets OMA Thursday to plead for restraint.
- Snow says UTDC yacht-club deal cheaper than building a cafeteria
- It took $400 to fly clerk up to see Aird's signature on York South by-election

The assignments were stated factually, as if the facts spoke for themselves in justifying coverage. Knowledgeable newspaper editors and reporters were supposed to know what the 'controls plan' was, the background to the case of the 'leaking memo,' what was entailed in the 'nursing homes brief,' and so on. This newspaper schedule also indicates that the assignment editor was generally more non-directive regarding angles in the process of assignment, and therefore stated 'what is happening' or 'what is scheduled to happen' without including a newsworthy angle. In contrast the television assignment editor sometimes indicated more directly the newsworthiness by stating angles under consideration ('looking out for vandalism' in a strike situation); adding facts signifying newsworthiness ('1 in 4 girls sexually abused in metro before 18'); or providing his visualization of how a story was linked to previous stories ('apparently bigger than remor scam').

The assignment schedule, as an initial enumeration of what other editors should look out for, was no more than a guide to the possible. It was a mechanism which the assignment editor had to show others that things had come together, and to reassure copy, layout, desk, and supervising editors that the day would not fall apart. It was something upon which the members of the newsroom could fix their minds even if it did not fix rigidly what was done about the particular stories subsequently.

Reporters and other editors observed that their work varied according to who was the role-incumbent at the assignment desk. In the newspaper three different people were assignment editors at the city desk over the period of our research observations. According to their own description of their style, confirmed by reporters who worked with them, two emphasized 'spot' and 'hard' news, especially as these related to what competing newspapers were

doing in terms of event coverage and updates. The other assignment editor was more interested in having reporters address the question of 'why?' rather than 'what?' alone, and was described as being 'featurish' in that he wanted issues addressed even in regular news items. He was also seen as giving the reporters considerable latitude in developing a story and an appropriate angle, while the other two editors were seen as more directive about angle and length, and supervised more closely.

TIME AND SPACE

Regardless of who was the role-incumbent, the assignment editor had to look out for the constraints of time and space. For the newspaper assignment editor there was concern over the time available to obtain a story, the ability to penetrate the source organization to obtain sufficient information to tell the story, and the amount of column-inch space available for the particular story in the context of others being filed on the desk. For the television assignment editor there was a similar concern about timing to meet deadlines and the ability to obtain information from sources, as well as the time available in the broadcast lineup to tell each story. The assignment editor must consider simultaneously aspects of news timing, news space, source timing, and source space in deliberations over whether or not to assign a story.

News timing involved consideration of how much time was available to obtain sufficient information to do the story, and how much time it would take to prepare the story. This in turn entailed a consideration of the staff available to do the story, for the ability to initiate source contacts and compose a story quickly was not evenly distributed in the newsroom. If the crew available for coverage of a television item was working with film then the time required for film processing had to be taken into account. If time was likely to be very limited and a choice was available between film and video crews, the video crew was assigned because time for processing was eliminated.

News space was a matter of how much total space (newspaper column inches and television air time) was available to the assignment editor's desk on the day, and how it could be divided among the stories being considered. Obviously the lack of space – resulting, for instance, from the lack of newspaper advertising revenue – could decrease the likelihood of covering some stories at all, because there was no room to publish them. Television newsrooms in particular employed minimal staff and when a reporter and crew were assigned there was a strong expectation, related to a strong need, that they would return with 'the goods' to help fill the show. In this respect, the television assignment editor seemed less concerned about the specific outcome of an assignment than the fact that at least something came out of it, thus confirming his original judgment that the allocation of scarce resources to the story would contribute to filling the space.

In the television newsroom there was a prevailing expectation that a story would be 75 to 90 seconds in length. This was a general guideline to the assignment editor regarding the number of stories required vis-à-vis the number of reporters and film or video crews available. Reporters were repeatedly reminded of this norm through memos, and sometimes reprimanded when they completed an assignment which deviated substantially and affected a colleague's play or the lineup editor's and producer's structuring of the show.

In the newspaper the assignment editor had more direct input into play decisions, including recommendations regarding what was suitable for front-page coverage and who deserved a byline on their stories. Their directions regarding length varied according to space available as well as the person who was serving as assignment editor. When space was more restricted during a period when advertising revenues were down, reporters were assigned to fewer stories and/or told not to file multiple stories from their beats, and explicit instructions were given to keep particular stories to a few column inches. Unless a story was prejudged as an important one requiring significant play, one assignment editor regularly told a reporter to file a story of ten column inches. However, other assignment editors would give no advance instruction on the length required, even if a story was likely to be 'briefed' into a couple of inches. We observed instances in which a reporter was working close to deadline on two or three stories, and even at this stage could not obtain information on the news space available for them which would allow him to write at the appropriate length. Reporters attributed this situation to the editors' desire to have a 'full' story before them so that the editors themselves could decide what was most salient to report, and the play it deserved, in the context of other filed stories and overall space available.

Source timing pertained to aspects of time that were controlled by the source individual or organization and which the assignment editor had to take into account in giving consideration to coverage. If the source provided an official news release, consideration had to be to given to when the information was released vis-à-vis what could be done with it (e.g., a rewrite? interviews with this source and others? checks on the information?). Often the source released information to news outlets but placed a restriction on the timing of the actual publication or broadcast of the information. One news organization was well known for not honouring such restrictions, in the context of a policy that any official release crossing the assignment desk was subject to immediate coverage.

If coverage was planned that involved telephone or personal interviews with officials, then respect had to be given to the official hours they kept. Normally contact could only be made in business hours, therefore the main shift for reporting coincided with the main period for bureaucratic business, roughly from 9:00 a.m. to 5:00 p.m. This was so regardless of whether the news outlet published or broadcast in the evening, morning, or at more frequent intervals. Indeed problems arose for assignment editors when official sources, for example, at the legislature or courts, closed for public holidays or summer recess. They were forced to look elsewhere for images of deviance and control, and relied even more heavily on police and crime stories in these periods.

If the source organization schedules a news conference, the timing of it is also salient. Source organizations sophisticated about the local news-media culture often time news conferences to obtain intitial coverage in particular outlets over others. The assignment editor has to decide the place of his own organization in this timing, and whether it is worth attending at all in the context of what can be done.

Public hearings – government legislature and committee sessions, courts, inquests, official inquiries, etc. – also transpire during 'business hours.' These are predictable events in terms of both timing and public access, beginning at a designated time and having a predictable duration on the given day. Experienced assignment editors knew what part of these sessions required attention and when the important aspect was likely to occur. Hence it was rare to assign coverage of the day's session from beginning to end. A newspaper assignment editor did not begin work until 10:00 a.m., and on occasion would not get around to assigning a reporter to a public hearing he wanted covered until another hour or so had passed, even though the session was well under way. He apparently believed that the competent reporter could glean all that was necessary by selective attendance and attention, and made assignments accordingly.

Source activities can be timed without particular regard to news timing, and the assignment editor must be sensitive to the ramifications of this fact. In the course of working on a major continuing story it was learned that the police were about to lay charges against suspects. Once charges were laid there would be legal restrictions on what the newspaper could report on the matter. Therefore, the assignment editor had a summary article prepared on the matter, hoping to publish it before the police action of charging accused persons curtailed news reports.

The source organization's space – its geographical location, physical space, and attendant question of access – was another consideration for the assignment editor vis-à-vis the other dimensions of time and space we have outlined. The distance to the organization's setting was a factor related to both news timing and material resources. Was there time to get there, obtain sufficient information, get back, and prepare the story? Who had shown in the past that they were capable of doing this? Was it worth the risk of committing a reporter and/or crew and the cost of getting there? Connected with this was the particular assignment desk's responsibility for maintaining some notion of geographic or regional balance in their stories. Toronto news outlets extended their coverage to regional municipalities around Toronto, and sometimes beyond to other communities in Southern Ontario. A story which offered the potential for a sense of regional balance might be covered in the context of considering the questions noted above about distance to the field setting.

The primary considerations related to source space were of access and what type of information could be obtained readily. The assignment editor had to work to reduce equivocality in this respect, and did so largely by ensuring that stories he assigned were scheduled events where some type of access was guaranteed. This issue was directly related to questions of timing. Assignment editors developed a day file of upcoming events which they examined on the date concerned, or on the day before, to ensure a supply of pre-scheduled events. These events included not only upcoming public hearings, but also news conferences and the activities of citizens' groups, such as public demonstrations and strikes. The concern to have a stock of these events on file was particularly evident with the television assignment editor. Schlesinger (1978) observes, 'It is estimated that 95 percent of these advanced diary arrangements are embodied in the following day's diary, and that some 70 percent on average are finally used, in some way or other, in the production of bulletins' (p. 68; see also Epstein, 1974: esp. 103). In television this concern is understandable because of the limited personnel and other resources available, and the fact that an assignment involves committing film or video crews as well as a reporter.

The significance of scheduled events, or other forms of structured and predictable access, is clear in examining stories that did not get assigned because accessibility and availability were in doubt. A researcher sat in on an assignment meeting between the television assignment editor and producer, on a day when few reporters were available as a result of holiday leave being taken. Assignments were made largely to scheduled events, for example, preparations for the opening of the Canadian National Exhibition; following a person raising funds for the city's Santa Claus Parade; a court case; a professional conference on criminal corrections at a local hotel; and a news conference by a person planning to swim Lake Ontario underwater. Other assignments were considered but dropped because of the standard justification of involving 'too much leg work.' There had been an outbreak of salmonella poisoning and one or more deaths attributed to it. The producer and assignment editor initially had difficulty visualizing a new angle on this item. The producer then suggested the possibility of examining hospital procedures in connection with the salmonella problem, and added that a 'state of the art' piece could be done including a call to the Centre for Disease Control in Atlanta, Georgia. Having stated this, he quickly added that he was in 'dreamland,' given the shortage of staff, and the idea was dropped. The assignment editor suggested

TABLE 6.5

The primary reasons for choosing a particular reporter: newspaper assignment editor

Reasons for choosing a particular reporter	N	%
REASONS		
Beat reporter	33	35.4
Specialist reporter	24	25.8
Availability of reporter	10	10.7
Developed by reporter independently	6	6.5
Reporter continuing previous work on matter	6	6.5
Reporter's contacts with source	3	3.2
Reporter's special abilities	2	2.2
Unspecified	2	2.2
Subtotal	86	92.5
WIRE COPY ONLY		
Subtotal	5	5.3
LEFT FOR NIGHT DESK		
Subtotal	2	2.2
Total	93	100.0

a story on how school buildings were being, or might be, used after being left empty with declining student enrolments. The producer interjected that again the story would require too much 'leg work' and the story did not make the assignment-outlook sheet.

Assignment Editors and Reporters

ASSIGNMENT EDITORS' REASONS FOR CHOOSING A PARTICULAR REPORTER

In the systematic study of story assignments, assignment editors were asked to give the primary reason for choosing the particular reporter for each story. The accounts of the newspaper assignment editor are enumerated in table 6.5, and those of the television assignment editor in table 6.6.

The newspaper assignment editor's responses indicate the extent to which he saw the choice of a reporter as almost 'automatic,' in the sense of entailing little effort on his part. In most instances the reporter was 'pegged' for the assignment by established organizational arrangements, rather than chosen by the assignment editor from among other reporters available for the task. In one-third of the story assignments, the reason for choosing the reporter was the fact he was the beat reporter and hence the 'obvious' choice. In

TABLE 6.6

The primary reasons for choosing a particular reporter: television assignment editor

Reasons for choosing a particular reporter	N	%
REASONS		
Availability of reporter	40	24.8
Beat reporter	32	19.9
Specialist reporter	13	8.1
Area reporter	9	5.6
Reporter continuing previous work on matter	5	3.1
Reporter's contacts with source	2	1.2
Unspecified	4	2.5
Subtotal	105	65.2
CAMERA CREW ONLY		
Subtotal	19	11.8
NO FOLLOW-THROUGH ON STORY		
Subtotal	17	10.6
NO INFORMATION		
Subtotal	20	12.4
Total	161	100.0

another one-quarter of assignments the reporter who worked on the story was equally 'obvious' because he was a specialist on the topic concerned. Hence, 60 per cent of the stories were assigned to reporters in terms of their pre-established role as topic specialists or source-organization-beat regulars. Furthermore, most of the remaining stories were taken care of by the reporter's own initiative (6.5 per cent) or by the fact that the reporter had previously worked on the matter and was continuing to do so (6.5 per cent). In a few cases the reporter was selected because he was known to have the best contacts with the sources concerned, or special abilities or recipe knowledge regarding the topic. Only 11 per cent of all assignments were made in circumstances where the choice was not obvious in terms of the reporter's abilities and previous work, or established specializations and beats. In this small minority of stories the assignment editor ended up selecting from among those who happened to be available for general assignment.

The circumstances for the television editor were substantially different, as indicated by the data in table 6.6. The most frequently cited reason for assigning a reporter was simply the availability of the reporter, accounting for 25 per cent (40/161) of all assignments considered, and 38 per cent (40/105) of those assignments which included a reporter actually being assigned.

These data signify that the television newsroom was organized much more in terms of having reporters available as generalists, ready to work on whatever the assignment editor, in consultation with the producer, chose for them. About one-third of the television stories considered for assignment were accounted for in terms of beat, topic, or area specializations. (The area specialization refers to a reporter who covered particular regional municipalities outside of Toronto.) However, even in these cases there was more involvement by the television assignment editor than was evident at the newspaper. The television assignment editor would frequently suggest story ideas to these reporters. The assignment editor and producers regularly had direct contact with reporters because most of them began their day in the office, and all had to return to the newsroom to complete the editing and production of their items. Moreover, the fact that few generalist reporters were available to the assignment editor meant that specialist reporters were assigned to stories outside their specializations if the need arose because of staff shortages or major event coverage.

The television assignment editor had the option of sending a camera crew without a reporter, leaving the decision until a later juncture as to whether the visuals were good enough to include in the newscast, and whether a statement by the anchorperson or a reporter's voice-over should be used along with the visuals. In 12 per cent of all assignments considered the assignment was to a camera crew only. In another 11 per cent of stories initially listed on the assignment outlook there was no follow through in assigning a reporter or crew. This was largely a result of a change of priorities; for example, more important events came to the assignment editor's attention after the assignment outlook had been prepared and were considered in the context of the limited personnel resources and the limited time for news items in the show. In the initial sample of 161 stories considered for assignment, for 20, or 12 per cent we have no information on the reasons for choosing a particular reporter because the question was not addressed by the researcher.

In our observations, supported by these data, the television assignment editor had much more direct input than the newspaper assignment editor as to who was going to work on what story. While the television assignment editor needed to organize to reduce equivocality and ensure fruitful assignments, he was less able than his newspaper counterpart to do so through established beats and topic specializations. It was up to him, in consultation with producers, to generate story ideas, and to choose among the few reporters available to get the job done. An additional factor in television that necessitated this approach was the need to produce connected items in segments of the lineup with an eye to dramatic structure. The assignment editor and producer visualized this factor from the outset as they met to consider story ideas. This was an overview which was not usually within the vision of the individual reporter as he worked on his particular item.

The choice of who to assign to a beat, specialization, or individual story was a matter of editors' recipe knowledge of what type of reporter was best matched with what type of assignment. A senior editor in a newspaper emphasized the importance of this matching process in an interview.

> [D]ifferent people have different skills. We have some who can dig out information remarkably well, without the use of special contacts. We have some who rely on contacts, who have built up a good system of contacts. Now there are some who can deal around with records and you give them a problem and they'll go and find the people who are essential to completing a story and interview them and collect all the information that's necessary ... We've got some who are good writers, beautiful writers and there are certain kinds of stories in which you need somebody who can write well, you need the colour and the flow, the feel and the pathos and so on, the joy or the exhilaration, whatever, and you need them. There are some who live and breathe politics. Love it. Who like the daily rubbing belly to belly with politicians and on the subject of politics and you need them. They come in all different shapes, sizes, whatever ... Joy is getting the right person in the right job.

'Getting the right person in the right job' includes knowing what reporters have recipe knowledge regarding what topics. Assignments were often made on the basis of the fact that a particular reporter had acquired knowledge about the topic through activities beyond his role as a journalist. A reporter whose hobby was flying aircraft was assigned stories involving aviation, including stories about missing aircraft and airplane crashes. A reporter who was involved in buying houses and renovating them for sale, or for rental income, was assigned to a story involving the possible illicit sale of apartment buildings. In these instances the reporters' recipe knowledge extended to knowledge about sources who could provide pertinent information.

Some reporters specialized in stories conveying empathetic or tertiary understanding. The reporters who had the 'stomach' to invade the private lives of people who had just suffered criminal victimization or disaster, and the ability to convey their fear and loathing sensitively, were assigned regularly to stories of this type. Efforts by assignment editors to recruit other reporters into this type of story were resisted strongly by the reporters concerned because they objected to this type of reporting and the methods required.

In other instances, assignments were made in terms of the reporter's apparent sympathy, rather than empathy, for the cause of those involved. For example, an assignment editor had the choice of assigning a sympathetic reporter or an unsympathetic reporter to a story about the Guardian Angels citizens' street patrol group beginning their patrols in Toronto. He chose the sympathetic reporter, apparently because he also believed that this organization should be given the opportunity to account for itself and find its degree of acceptance among local citizens. Sympathy was also judged in terms of a particular affinity between the reporter and the organization involved in the story. For example, a story involving an ethnic minority was sometimes assigned to a reporter who was a member of that minority. In one newsroom this basis of assignment was structured more generally in terms of having 'community relations' (e.g., ethnic minority groups) specialists who themselves belonged to particular visible ethnic minorities.

Similar to the specialist in empathy or sympathy was the reporter who was able to relate 'what it is like' for the participants in an interesting and humorous way. The reporter who could be counted on to do a 'brightener' was assigned to stories the assignment editor believed had the potential for that approach. A television newsroom had a reporter whose full-time task was the production of a daily 'brightener' item.

Preference in assignment was given to reporters designated by management as 'rising stars.' This preference included giving stories earmarked for prominent play to these reporters even though the story topics were not within their specialization. A general-assignment reporter pointed out that a general-assignment story on an ascent of Mount Everest, which received front-page coverage, had been given to a reporter on the social-service beat and a reporter on the agriculture beat. He attributed these assignments to a more general policy of favouring these two reporters as part of promoting them to star status.

Assignment editors had a propensity to assign a reporter to a story which involved an element the reporter had worked on previously and completed with competence. However, this was often not possible, given reporters' availability for assignment and personnel shortages, the latter being a fact which also pervaded efforts to match reporters to stories based on other criteria. Pragmatism often superseded the matching of ideal types. The availability of a reporter because his previous story had fallen apart, the availability of a beat reporter to obtain an interview clip about a story located elsewhere, and the availability of a television crew to obtain visuals of something on the way to or from something else often provided the basis for the assignment of personnel rather than idealized notions about who was best for the job.

ASSIGNMENT EDITORS' RELATIONS WITH REPORTERS

The assignment editor was a supervisor and controller as well as consultant and adviser. He controlled both positive and negative sanctions, including having some say in who would be assigned the better (more interesting and important) stories. The assignment editor also had input into play decisions; for example, in the newspaper he made recommendations for front-page coverage, for column-inch allotments, and whether or not a reporter would have his byline on his story. In his everyday choices and use of sanctions the assignment editor was judging reporters continuously.

As with any organizational setting in which someone sits in judgment over others, there was ongoing disagreement, tension, and conflict between assignment editors and reporters in the newsrooms we studied. While many assignments were made and accepted in a straightforward manner, and most disagreements were negotiated amicably, we found that newsrooms were not characterized by a consensus in norms and values which everyone had internalized and made use of in their everyday judgments. This finding is very different from the view in the research literature that newsrooms are characterized by consensus, compromise, and preset formulas so that 'overt confrontations hardly ever occur' (Hirsch, 1977: 24). This later view was put forward by Breed (1955) in an early and influential article. He explained the degree of consensus he observed in terms of reporters' deference to the authority of editors; the desire for friendly relations; the desire for rewards such as advancement; time pressures; and, the lack of intense feelings about the topics available for reporting. This view has been conveyed by successive observers of newsrooms (e.g., Sigal, 1973; Chibnall, 1977; Tuchman, 1978; Schlesinger, 1978) to the point where the image is sustained that journalists are a cohesive lot who adhere closely to professional norms and values and thus experience great occupational solidarity. Accepting the dominant normative paradigm in sociology – that action takes place in conformity with the rules laid down in the normative system – researchers have thereby limited their capacity to know the socio-cultural reality of the newsroom: that there is considerable ideological cleavage, personal self-interest, and attendant conflict.

Of course many assignments were made with direct orders from the assignment editor and no overt challenge from the reporter assigned, indicating a degree of mutual assumptions and social consensus. There were occasions when the assignment editor felt he had to say little or nothing about the angle because any competent reporter would know what was newsworthy and develop the obvious angle. Thus, on one occasion an assignment editor informed a researcher that he had no discussions with a reporter assigned, adding 'straight news writes itself.' On another occasion, a reporter was handed a newspaper clipping about a woman who had been reported missing. This was 'obviously' related to a series of stories in which women had been reported missing, and sometimes found dead, and also to an attacks-on-women moral panic. When the reporter asked the assignment editor what he was supposed to do with the clipping, he was told simply and finally that he ought to know, that there is always an angle, and that he could do a stand-up in front of the home of the missing woman.

When an assignment was connected to an ongoing theme, the newsworthiness usually seemed obvious to both the editor and reporter. Thus during the moral panic about attacks on women (cf Voumvakis and Ericson, 1984), sustained over a period of several months, a television assignment editor assigned a reporter to cover two founders of the Guardian Angels citizens' patrol organization each time they came to Toronto. Coverage was so complete that he even assigned crews twice on the same day to the same self-defence demonstration by the two founders, one in the city hall square and one at a park where a rape incident connected to the moral panic had occurred. These assignments were routinely accepted by a number of different reporters in the newsroom. They concurred with the assignment editor's visualization that there was 'a fear out there' among citizens. They also accepted that although, taken individually, both stories on the Guardian Angels looked the same, each story had a different meaning in the context of the other stories related to the fear theme on the day on which it was broadcast.

We observed many occasions on which an assignment was simply not negotiable. A television reporter was assigned to cover impropriety on the picket line in a strike which started on the day of assignment. She complained about the assignment, saying she should have been assigned another industrial-news story because she had worked on it the day before and had developed background material and recipe knowledge. Her superior was not amused, and exclaimed, 'Why don't you let us run this place?' The reporter argued that there should be some continuity in reporting, and her supervisor retorted, 'We're not the ———,' naming the newspaper this reporter had worked for previously.

The negotiability of an assignment varied considerably, depending on the assignment editor and reporter involved; the availability of other possible stories in the context of arguments about relative importance and newsworthiness; criteria of time and space; and a number of other situational elements that could be invoked by the editor or reporter in favour of his respective arguments.

The perceived freedom of a reporter was related to his overall assigned role in the newsroom. In the newspaper one reporter was given considerable freedom on an ongoing basis to undertake investigative and adversarial reporting tasks. Another reporter described this reporter as having 'earned his freedom' through years of quality work, suggesting that the opportunity for more independence and self-initiative comes to those who work hard. Beat and specialist reporters were generally regarded as having more autonomy in assignments, although they were required to inform assignment editors of what they were working on and often offered the assignment editor the choice of what should be focused on among several possible stories being considered.

Autonomy was also licensed to reporters who were working on a major continuing story insofar as they were given the freedon to keep producing new angles to keep the story alive. While they had an imperative to produce something, what that something consisted of was for them to choose. An assignment editor discussed folos on the bombing of a factory involved in the production of nuclear missiles:

Well, we're running through a number of angles, and ideas on the story ...
We haven't really got a focus on it yet ... He went out there to try to develop
one of the angles, let's see how he's going to do on it ... It could be a first
[priority], it could be a third, could be no story. This is one of those stories
you come up with every time where it's an important story, as a result of it's
a continuing story. And especially in the week of these stories, you make it a
continuing story, and you give the reporter the autonomy to go out and get it.
It depends on the reporter, of course, but he's one of the reporters who could
do that.

In contrast other reporters were typed as 'followers' because they typically
obliged their superiors and were otherwise dependent on them for advice.
This same assignment editor mentioned some reporters who were of this type,
including one who was known as the 'Young Tory' because he did everything
he was told but lacked initiative or innovative approaches. This assignment
editor said another reporter panicked when he did not know what to do, and
in these circumstances called him to beg for direction. He described this
person as a good reporter 'if you set him on the right track.' Our observations
of this reporter indicated that this was indeed the case. For example, while
working on a routine story which initially entailed calls to several sources,
he constantly asked the assignment editor and other superiors whom he should
call, reported back what particular sources had said, sought advice on further
leads and possible sources, and sought assistance with writing.

While much could be left on an implicit basis, and reporters were often
eager for advice, assignment editors also appreciated that some assignments
were unpopular and accepted the need to 'sell' a story to a reporter. Some
assignment editors took the soft or gentle approach of talking about a story
idea to the point where the reporter became interested, if not eager. One
assignment editor who had just finished talking a reporter into covering something which would take her away from what she was working on stated to
the researcher that he used this approach with success because he made
reporters think they would be missing a good story if they refused.

In turn reporters negotiated their working space with reference to their
knowledge of what assignment editors regarded as newsworthy. Reporters
who were assigned stories which appeared uninteresting, based either on initial
impressions or after preliminary inquiries, invoked other story ideas which
were made to appear more important. Reporters complained frequently about
spot assignments which interfered with investigative or feature pieces they
were working on, and typically made reference to professional imagery, and
to previous declarations of superiors that 'real' journalism is thorough and
investigative, in the hope that they could fend off the need to contribute to
daily production.

Reporters also invoked the prevailing sense of newsworthiness to argue that a story had been done previously, or another folo story was unnecessary because the matter was exhausted. However, this strategy sometimes resulted in leaving the matter open to the assignment editor to decide what should be covered, who should be contacted, and what angle was appropriate. A television reporter who was trying to work on a feature was first assigned to cover a press conference scheduled by the husband of a missing woman. He complained that the husband had already given an exclusive interview to another reporter in the newsroom two days previously, and he was unlikely to add anything new. The assignment editor conveyed this to the producer, and returned to the reporter saying 'they still want the story.' He stressed that the reporter was to ask 'pertinent questions.' When the producer emerged from his office, the reporter put his case directly to him, emphasizing his important feature against the news conference where 'he's going to say the same thing.' The producer responded that the same questions would not be asked, and went on to offer suggestions for questioning, for example, Does he think the police are doing a good job helping him look for his wife? What about the 'weirdo' reported to have been working in the same building as the one where his wife dropped off their child for day care? The reporter eventually obliged the producer.

Experienced reporters told us that it was sometimes easier, and more conducive to good relations and rewards, to accept an assignment but then formulate subsequent developments so as to discourage the assignment editor's interest. A television reporter, in discussing the general imperative to return with a story once assigned, said that he used to go along with everything his superiors directed, but after several years in the newsroom he had changed somewhat. If he thought there was no story he still went through the motions of following the supervisor's directions but later returned to 'show' or argue that there was no story. He gave an example of being assigned to do a story on whether the Toronto emergency services were prepared to handle an airplane crash of the type that a particular airline had just been involved in at a U.S. city. The reporter thought this 'What if?' approach was absurd, and was put off the story further when he found that it had even less realism because the airline concerned did not use the Toronto airport. The supervisor told us independently that he too was 'put off' – by the reporter's lack of initiative on this story. We observed many instances in which a reporter attempted to control the level and pace of his work by keeping information from the assignment editor, or by formulating matters to the assignment editor in such a way that it would lead the assignment editor to tell the reporter that no story was required since 'nothing was happening.'

Reporters also tried to negotiate with assignment editors in terms of time and space dimensions. After a fire that destroyed a boat, a television reporter was assigned to call various authorities concerned with questions about boat safety and the adequacy of emergency services, including response time. The reporter said he could not do an adequate story, covering a range of sources, before the deadline and asked for two days to work on the story. He was told that something was needed by the deadline because it was a 'down' day and the assignment editor needed everything he could get to 'fill out the list.' A newspaper assignment editor asked a reporter to 'look into' a situation in which a contractor was threatening to sue a government ministry because the ministry had given him misleading data pertinent to his contract bid, and the job turned out to be far more expensive than the contractor said it would be in his successful bid. The reporter said that he called the lawyer for the contractor, who indicated that a civil suit was likely. The reporter told the assignment editor it would take 'days and days' of investigation to write a proper story and the assignment editor agreed to let the story 'die.'

Resource availability was always at the forefront of the assignment editor's considerations, not only in choosing what stories to cover but in how they should be covered. On a day in a television newsroom when resources were so short that the lineup editor was helping with assignments, and the assignment editor was helping reporters with calls to sources, a story was assigned concerning high levels of pollution in the city and consequent health risks. After arranging for a cameraman, the reporter was told by the lineup editor to obtain shots of a generating station contributing to the pollution, and to 'hang around' hospitals to obtain shots of old people suffering the effects of pollution. The assignment editor in particular was astounded by this suggestion, given the lack of resources, and raised his voice in argument against this suggestion. The lineup editor in turn said he was only trying to help out, but this served to escalate the communication to the level of shouting. The lineup editor, having previously made reference to the fact that competing stations were covering this story, insisted that an 'important story' might be missed. They exchanged heated comments, threatening the filing of a grievance against a fellow guild member. Eventually the hospital-admissions angle was covered by having the assignment editor and assistant call five hospitals each to discover if they had been receiving admissions as a result of the pollution problem.

The resource limitations in the television newsroom caused considerable tension, conflict, and morale problems. Supervisors worried about filling the show. Reporters worried about restrictions on their autonomy to do a feature which might require several days' work, or to not produce a story on a given day because the event covered was deemed not to be newsworthy. One very experienced and senior reporter had a running conflict with his supervisors over several months as a result of his choice on many days not to file a story. Attending a court case, inquest, or other public hearings, he often decided that there was no significant development on a given day or that a particular aspect covered in the hearing would be brought out more fully or better by other witnesses at a later date. Sometimes he produced part or all of a story, but then 'killed' it at the last minute so that it would not be used in the show. This was a source of great concern to his supervisors, who were placed in a position of not being able to depend on him to file a story and leave the judgment to them as to whether it was suitable for broadcast. His actions were also against the assignment editor's view that a good reporter can make any event newsworthy enough to be reported. He repeatedly referred to this reporter as 'getting away' with doing this, but arguments, meetings, and reprimands from higher levels of authority in the newsroom seemed to have no effect. The reporter insisted that it was within his sphere of organizational autonomy and professional judgment and integrity to decide whether something was worthy of reporting. In a newsroom where at the best of times fewer than a dozen reporters were available on any given day, this exercise of autonomy was taken as defiant of the collective, and a significant element in introducing equivocality and unpredictability into the task of constructing the show lineup.

In contrast, for a period of several months a newspaper newsroom had an excess of personnel on the city desk. This situation arose as a result of factors external to the newsroom, and provides an example of how external structural factors can affect assignment. The economy in Canada at the time was recessionary, one sign of which was a substantial decrease in advertising revenues for the newspaper concerned. Since advertising determined the amount of news space, this meant that the news hole was shrinking while the journalist staff complement remained the same. The consequence of this for reporters was a decreased likelihood of having a filed story actually published, and a decreased amount of play given to a story even if it was published. One reporter on a regular beat said that he cut back from filing three or four stories a day to filing one or two because he knew that more would not be published. Reporters thus faced a minimization of their efforts as a result of space restrictions. For example, a reporter worked all day calling a large number of sources on a major story she had broken the previous day. At the end of the very long day an editor told her to keep her story length to six column inches. He justified this decision by saying that the city desk had very limited space for the edition: only one front-page story plus seven columns on an inside page. He added that he was holding back stories 'left and right.' The reporter pleaded that she had 'all kinds of stuff,' and appeared very deflated. A few minutes later a more senior editor approached the reporter, apparently with the intention of cooling her out. He urged her to pursue her investigations of the matter the next day, and talked to her about general matters. Having filed a detailed account of eighteen column inches, the reporter was asked to sit down with a copy editor to effect the necessary reductions.

The reduction in space also affected reporting in other areas of operation. A city-desk reporter who specialized in a particular topic, including the writing of major features on the topic, said that in the circumstances he no longer wrote long and detailed feature articles because there was no space for them. An editor of a special-features section which appeared from time to time said that the lack of advertising for the products this section featured meant that the frequency of publication, size, and quality of this section suffered. Fears that some reporters might lose their jobs – and the fact that a number of editors and clerks were terminated – also meant that expensive trips to cover stories were curtailed, and reporters who occasionally managed to obtain permission for such trips were criticized by colleagues who felt that the money could be better spent. In sum, factors external to the newsroom can create periods of too many resources (as in the newspaper newsroom) or too few resources (as in the television newsroom). Conditions of too many or too few resources can produce tension, morale problems, and overt conflict among journalists in the newsroom.

Clashes between assignment editors and reporters also occurred on ideological grounds. A reporter approached his assignment editor and a more senior editor and said that he would like to do a story on conditions for prisoners in the holding cells of the local jail. The conditions for inmates in the jail had received some publicity in other media and the reporter wanted to pursue the story. The senior editor said, 'Who cares?', and after the reporter 'mumbled' a response the senior editor added, 'These people are criminals anyway.' He said he wanted the reporter to do a story on police reorganization to provide for more foot patrols, a story he and the assignment editor were lining up with a number of other items to cohere as a segment on control actions being taken in relation to the prevailing moral panic about attacks on women. The reporter persisted in expressing his desire to do the story on the jail, and the assignment editor then told him he could do it on the following day. The reporter replied that something else would come up the following day to prevent him from doing the jail story then, and the senior editor interjected, 'I hope something else *will* come up tomorrow,' indicating his objection to coverage of a cause to which he was blatantly unsympathetic.

On another occasion a reporter approached a television assignment editor and asked for a crew in connection with his story on the forthcoming holiday period of a religious minority group. The assignment editor said he could not give him one. The reporter expressed annoyance, saying that if he did not shoot the story now he would not be able to do it at all. The assignment editor became increasingly upset as well, arguing that 'the way things are now' he knew it would not get into the lineup. He said he was just being 'realistic,' pointing to the fact that this reporter had done a 'hell of a good story' the day before but it did not make the main show. The assignment editor initially formulated his argument in terms of the producers' running a 'tight show' with 'thousands' of feet of film being wasted every day. When the reporter argued that the newsroom was getting out of touch with the community, the assignment editor altered his account, saying the reporter knew it was not up to him to make the play decisions. It was revealed that other editing- and producer-level staff did not like the kind of story the reporter was producing, and were taking it upon themselves to exclude the reporter's items from the lineup. The assignment editor argued that he could not commit resources to stories he knew would not make the lineup, even though he himself had an affinity for what the reporter was doing. The reporter argued that the assignment editor should 'stick together' with him in a planned protest against these lineup decisions. He then showed the assignment editor a newspaper article about a man, married to a Canadian and a resident in Canada for five years, who had been ordered to leave the country because immigration officials thought it was a marriage of convenience. The reporter asserted that this was the type of story he should be doing, and the assignment editor agreed even while recognizing that it was not possible 'the way things are now.'

In spite of the professed emphasis on policing organizational life by challenging the authorities, when it came to choosing topics and targets it depended upon the dominant ideology of the authorities in the newsroom. An instance close to home arose out of a confrontation with the police. A reporter and crew happened upon a police raid on a house party where some gambling was discovered. They started filming the incident, impressed by the fact that the police Emergency Task Force was called to the scene, and by police officers pushing the crowd back with their shotguns. They were even more impressed when a police officer tried to stop the filming by pushing the camera against the camerman's head; when another police officer broke a camera light with his billy club; and, when threats were made to lay charges of obstructing the police against them. The two newsroom members involved, as well as the assignment editor, wanted a major story on this incident to be broadcast as an item on the main show, and perhaps sustained as a continuing story. This coverage would include the fact that a formal complaint had been laid with the police department and a police investigation was underway. However, following meetings between the police, senior newsroom personnel, and the newsmen involved it was decided not to do a story. The reporter and cameraman involved came out of the meeting very disappointed, saying it was as if the incident was their fault. The assignment editor noted to a researcher that his superiors would have done a story if it involved another television station.

Differences in assignment also arose in the context of reporters having views discrepant from editors' views as to the evidence required to sustain an angle or story line. In the course of an assignment meeting involving the assignment editor and two producers, the assignment editor said that a listed story called 'Hallowe'en Scare' – involving the possibility that children would be given poisoned candy or apples containing razor blades at Hallowe'en – might have the effect of encouraging 'crazies' to do so. A producer replied that he thought the 'crazies' who would do such a thing would do it regardless, and the story would not make a difference. The other producer asked if an 'educational' story was wanted, and the producer said they should find a housewife who had decided to have a children's party instead of having children go door to door. He added that a police spokesperson might be able to give a special warning to children to throw away suspect apples or candy, and referred to 'razor blade' stock footage from eight to twelve years previous which might be 'trotted out' to use in conjunction with the story. The reporter assigned was not keen to do the story, and became even less keen after talking to a parent and police. The reporter told the assignment editor the parent who was having a children's party, in lieu of having children go door to door, did not have strong feelings about the issue. Moreover, she did not attribute her decision to have the party to the safety factor. The reporter also informed the assignment editor that she had talked to a police spokesperson. She reported that the police spokesperson thought they would be doing the public a dis-service if they did this story. The police spokesperson said the Toronto police had never charged anyone with putting razor blades in apples, although they had charged some people with public mischief after they had falsely reported finding razor blades in Hallowe'en treats. The reporter later related the same accounts to the two producers, but she was nevertheless instructed to do the story and eventually complied.

While the assignments and ideas of supervisors often prevailed, there were many examples of outright refusals to accept assignments. For example, a reporter objected to covering personal fear-and-loathing stories of persons who had suffered through personal tragedy. On one occasion she refused an assignment of this type, and on another occasion she booked off sick to avoid such an assignment.

A particular reporter repeatedly asserted the independence of his judgments, and general autonomy, by persistently refusing assignments, questioning them vigorously, and not filing stories even though they were needed to fill the story quota. He refused assignments in favour of his own story ideas and argued with the assignment editor and more senior personnel that he was experienced and therefore did not need to be told what to do. We witnessed many of these exchanges. Many more were the subject of gossip in the newsroom as journalists marvelled at how he 'got away with' refusing stories and 'killing' stories after assignment. In one instance we observed, a senior supervisor approached this reporter as he sat at his desk at mid-shift reading a newspaper. The supervisor asked him if he was going to cover his assignment of a police news release about alleged police brutality in raiding a house party. The reporter replied there were better things to do, and mentioned an inquest. The supervisor asked if he was going to cover the inquest and the reporter replied, 'Probably not.' The supervisor departed, exclaiming 'Get off your ass and do some work!'

In one newsroom there was substantial staff turnover, with 'bouts' of firings and resignations at both the reporter and supervisor levels. More regularly and routinely, it was in conflicts among senior editors or producers, assignment editors, and reporters, that the vocabulary of precedents about autonomy, newsworthiness, resource use, and methodologies was articulated. The fact that the norms and values were not rigidly set or predictable, but worked out on the occasions of their use, explains why the occupational culture was characterized by disagreement and conflict. It is hard to imagine that other researchers have visualized it as being otherwise. It seems that they have been prisoners of the dominant normative paradigm in ethnographic studies of news work.

These considerations remain salient throughout the news process. Assigning, reporting, and editing are entwined in practice, and the influence of the assignment editor does not cease with the initial negotiations over assignment. This is evident as we examine how reporters manage the stories they have been assigned.

7

Reporting

In this chapter we consider how the reporter visualizes what a story should be about, who and what are appropriate sources of information, and what he should do with the information. We show that the reporter imagines typical demands on organizations and their key actors on a particular occasion. He then proceeds through questioning or listening to choose interview quotations and to construct factuality. The story is told in terms of his sense of what the actors represent in the roles in which they have been cast socially, as interpreted by him. That is, the reporter seems to follow the ancient tradition of Thucydides, as enunciated in *Peloponnesian War*: 'It was in all cases difficult to carry [speeches] word for word in one's memory, so my habit has been to make the speakers say what was in my opinion demanded of them by the various occasions: of course adhering as closely as possible to the general sense of what they said.'

We analyse reporters' use of documentary, direct-observation, survey, and interview methodologies. We examine also the sharing of information among reporters. Consideration is given to the special demands on the television reporter related to the acquisition of visuals. We relate this methodological detail to story construction: what is known but left unsaid; criteria for establishing factuality; and citation and quotation practices. Finally we consider how contingencies are dealt with, including, at the one extreme, dropping a story, and at the other, exercising the imagination to make something that will fit.

Managing Angles, Space, and Time

STORY SCENARIOS

In chapter 6 we stressed that often little is left to the reporter's imagination. The assignment includes an angle, who to contact, and what information to pursue, because editors or producers have already visualized what is demanded of sources in the events that are to be reported on. Furthermore, the angle desired is often bound up with the reporter assigned, because that reporter specializes in angles of the type the editors or producers want for the story. However, even when the reporter receives direct orders for a particular angle, or implicit direction in the fact that he has been assigned to do his 'usual,' there is still some autonomous space for him to construe the matter in terms of his own views and attendant mobilization of resources and information.

In this section we consider how the reporter imagines a suitable frame initially. This stage is an essential part of his job, for a good imagination at the outset reduces the time and effort required to bring the matter into focus, obtain information, and establish factuality. Of course, the angle visualized initially can be altered or dropped as contingencies are faced in the field; however, a sharp focus at the outset reduces the experience of equivocality and the accompanying anxiety that the story may 'fall apart.'

Even if he is working on a continuing story, such as successive days of a court case, the reporter requires a new angle each day. The sense of what is new is derived from existing news content, what the reporter and his newsroom colleagues have already done, and what competing news outlets have done. While 'matchers' are sometimes done for the record or as a matter of expediency, they are generally frowned upon and are not a source of satisfaction or reward for reporters. The reporter who cannot come up with the 'second-day lead' risks disapproval, or having his story 'killed' altogether. Thus, a reporter assigned to an inquest into the death of a baby was concerned that the most important testimony pertained to the role of an insecticide spray in the baby's death, but since two competing outlets had used this as their lead in the previous day's coverage he would have to come up with something else. He considered the possibility of an angle related to the parents' refusing help from doctors and a public-health nurse. He stressed repeatedly to the researcher that the role of the spray was the important element, while noting that the imperative for a new lead often forces journalists to report something that is not as significant or is even far-fetched, such as alleged parental negligence in this case.

Like assignment editors and producers, reporters need a sense of how their story scenario might fit into acts which are beyond it, and yet are linked to it. Much of the visualization of possible angles takes place in these terms.

Often links are clear and bring the matter into focus immediately, such as when a well-known figure is involved, or when the story is continuous with well-publicized past events. When links are clear the scenario – scene distribution, angle, and imagined sequence of future events – unfolds in sharp focus.

When possible links seem more distant and hazy, the reporter must exercise his imagination and make more substantial inferential leaps. Thus, a reporter initially defined as 'uninteresting' a police incident report on a man arrested for mailing obscene material to five women, including newspaper 'pinup girls' and a cheerleader. However, he exercised his imagination and decided he could make this event newsworthy by linking it to an unsolved murder that had occurred almost a year previously, and involved a victim who had been a 'pinup girl' and cheerleader. Even though police had informed the reporter that there was probably no link, and the reporter had written a side-note to this effect on the script for the anchorperson, the story script was put forward with the link drawn in these terms: 'It may be coincidence that Argo Sunshine girl Jenny Isford, whose picture also appeared in the *Sun*, was raped and murdered last spring. Nevertheless, ——— will be questioned in connection with the sex-slaying.'

A reporter was handed a front-page newspaper story in which it was reported that a secret government handbook on ethnic groups in Canada was used by RCMP Security Service, immigration, and citizenship personnel as an intelligence source to assist in their decision-making. The reporter entered into a fishing expedition directed at discovering the reaction of various ethnic minority groups to the existence of this handbook. After calling fourteen different sources, the reporter settled on three: a representative of the black community to express his 'shock'; a doctor who said his in-laws were denied citizenship for twenty-one years because they belonged to a particular Polish group, that his sister-in-law was watched by the RCMP and denied a job because her parents belonged to this Polish group, and that many of his patients were South American refugees who complained to him repeatedly about RCMP harassment; and a representative of the Polish community. The reporter began to visualize the angle in terms of 'fear' and 'shock' caused by the revelation that this 'ethnic list' existed, and statements to the effect that such lists were characteristic of communist totalitarian regimes but not of democracy. Since the Polish Solidarity movement was very much in the news at the time, the focus on the Polish community was an obvious way to provide the totalitarian/ democratic contrast. The reporter framed the story in terms of the anchor lead: 'News of a secret federal handbook on ethnic groups compiled by the RCMP has sent waves of anger and tremors of fear through some of Metro's ethnic communities.' The link was drawn with policing in Eastern European communist regimes: 'Those thoughts bring back a rush of bitter memories for many immigrants, particularly the people who were forced to flee the totalitarian regimes of Eastern Europe where a secret police society was accepted. They don't understand how this could happen here in a democracy.' This statement was followed by a clip of a Polish-community spokesperson asking rhetorically how someone could defend against allegations contained in intelligence information of this type, and the reporter's statement that 'Solicitor General Robert Kaplan admits the government handbook has been used by the RCMP in immigration cases.' The reporter's statements before and after the clip of the Polish spokesperson included visuals of a Toronto street well known for being the hub of the local Polish community, including shots of Polish shops displaying Solidarity emblems and souvenirs. These visuals were used to enhance the visualization of repressive policing of a minority group in Eastern Europe, and the shock that minority groups were also police targets in Canadian democracy.

The interpretive latitude available to reporters is made especially evident when reporters from different news organizations report on the same matter. Reporters from two different news organizations were reporting developments in the police search for a missing nine-year-old girl. One reporter mentioned to the researcher that he suspected 'trouble' since the girl had been missing for forty-eight hours and did not turn up in school after the weekend. However, he said he would not include in the story his suspicions that she had been the victim of a sex slaying until it was discovered to be so. His filed story focused exclusively on the search, with his lead being the addition of a police helicopter to the search resources.

An OPP helicopter was called in this morning to aid in the search for a missing Toronto youngster ...

About 60 Metro Police officers are searching a 10 block radius of the Bathurst-Dupont area – going over this [illegible word] for a second time in the hopes of finding 9-year-old Sharon Morningstar Keenan.

The child disappeared about 3 o'clock Sunday afternoon from nearby Jean Sibelius Park. A mobile command post has been set up here in the parking lot of a Brewers' Retail store on Dupont west of Bathurst – just across the street from the house of Sharon's parents. Police Staff Sgt. Richard Collett told me here at the scene that a decision will be made later today on whether or not to enlarge the search area. He says a helicopter from the OPP was in the air this morning, backing up the ground searchers!

Many volunteers, including truck drivers, have picked up photographs of the girl to search as they made deliveries and rounds!!

Police officers continue going door to door with photographs, which have also been handed out to commuters at subway and TTC surface stops!! But still – no sign of Sharon Keenan.

Sharon's mother Linda Keenan has publicly thanked the citizens and Metro police, including many off-duty officers, who have stopped by to comfort her at the end of their shifts.

The second reporter also suspected the likelihood of foul play, but he proceded to frame his entire story in these terms complete with repeated reference to a case from *three years* before in which a little girl had been found strangled. The first reporter, in emphasizing that he himself would not draw the link, attributed the difference between his approach and that of the second reporter to 'personal taste' rather than to diverging expectations between the two newsrooms. While the first reporter's account gave due testimony to policing efforts, the second reporter visualized the worst in spite of these efforts:

> There are almost as many police in the hunt today as there were yesterday, in what is the biggest search since Lizzie Tomlinson vanished on a May Sunday afternoon in 1980 only to be found strangled ... a victim of a sex pervert. Her death is still listed as unsolved, since an uncle who's charged with the slaying was freed at a preliminary hearing. Police say they are going all over the same ground today working out of a trailer in a parking lot in the Bathurst-Dupont district where Sharon vanished Sunday afternoon. Staff Supt. Frank Barbetta says there is fear that a sex pervert may have abducted Sharon. That's what happened to Lizzie Tomlinson ... the OPP helicopter was used this morning, and police are going door to door just like yesterday hoping that they might find a clue missed yesterday. They gave out a thousand pictures of the attractive Irish-born girl with dimples, who was wearing an Irish Tartan skirt when she left to play in a neighborhood park. Seasoned police officials fear the worst while still hoping for the best.

On a continuing story such as this one, or even updates on investigations into more ordinary crimes, the reporter's search was often limited to a snippet of information or a new source person not used previously by competing news outlets. As they visualized story scenarios, reporters frequently sought an interview with a relevant party which would constitute a 'first' or 'exclusive,' or pictures of the principals not previously published or broadcast, or any updates on information or new information which others did not have. Radio reporters were especially reliant on updates. They frantically pursued snippets of information such as whether a suspect was known or apprehended, or the revised figure for the amount lost in a robbery, so that each hourly newscast seemed new. Indeed, radio news leads were often constituted by the latest police lead in a criminal case. A radio reporter we observed over several shifts would rewrite the same story (e.g., about the latest bank robbery in the city) several times during a shift, using a different lead each time, thereby making it appear that both he and the police were doing their jobs.

Reporters were more creative in adding secondary (explanatory) and tertiary (contextual, human-interest) understanding. A reporter attending court was 'tipped' by a colleague at another newspaper that a judgment in a child-abuse case was about to be given. Upon calling his assignment editor about this case, he was told to keep it brief because there was no space available except for a statement of the judgment and sentence. After listening to the judge's statement, the reporter commented to the researcher, 'I think I'll have to jazz this one up to make sure it gets the play it deserves.' He proceeded to do this by developing a frame of 'good girl turns sour,' contrasting the judge's condemnation of the accused as violent and a liar with statements that her mother, 'weeping,' had testified she was a model child. Since the reporter was not present for the testimony, he was left to imaginatively construct the scenario from the judge's statement, and from a retrospective interview with the Crown attorney in which he asked more details about the accused's 'model child' background. With the intention of competing for space in the newspaper, he constructed the story in the dramatic detail of a person gone wrong in spite of good opportunities, of a weeping mother, of a helpless victim, and of moral and legal authority completely discrediting the offender in preparation for condemning her. The reporter was successful in having published a story of twelve column inches, with his lead intact. The lead paragraphs read:

> A 22 year old woman whose young child was found with several fractured bones, multiple bruises and burns to a hand and foot lied outrageously in attempting to exonerate herself, a County Court judge has ruled.
>
> In convicting ——— yesterday of failing to provide the necessities of life to her 4-year old child, Judge James Trotter said the woman was cool, remorseless and callous, while her testimony was 'utterly incredible'.
>
> The findings were in sharp contrast to her mother's testimony that she had been a model child and precocious enough that at 13 she taught music to adults at a music conservatory.

CONSIDERING INFORMATION SOURCES

While the reporter requires one eye for imagining story scenarios, he must also have an eye for sources of information. Such binocular vision is required to bring the story to life. The reporter must consider what people represent the best sources of information. He must determine if those people can be cited in representation of the information. He must consider also if there are relevant documentary sources of information; these are usually controlled by other people, but the documents rather than the people may be required for sustaining the story scenario being established. Another possibility is that people can offer relevant information verbally even if they cannot be cited to represent that information.

The most basic approach is to set the story up in a point/counterpoint format and to choose representatives of each side. This approach was especially typical when the item was a one-shot matter and balance was looked for in the item rather than over several items. Often the visualization of opposing positions in a controversy and who were appropriate spokespersons seemed evident: go to the head of each organization concerned and have that person make a representation of his organization's position. Occasionally more effort was required to come up with suitable sources to represent the positions established, as revealed in the following example.

An assignment editor listed a story on his assignment-outlook sheet as 'Prison policies – what's happening and what is considered reasonable in our fed. prisons – is lax policy working?' This story was listed shortly after guards had been killed in a penitentiary riot, although the assignment editor was aroused to this story by a newspaper article of the same morning: 'Officials O.K. Sex Shows 'Because Inmates Want Them'/Prison Life: Porn, booze and dope.' Further, an inmate of a medium-security penitentiary had written a long letter to the newsroom about the freedoms prisoners enjoy (including 'booze' and other drugs, and sex), and the high quality of food and facilities. In turn he used these conditions to argue that prison does not punish and hence does not 'work.' He also offered his services as an interviewee upon his release the following month.

The assignment editor wanted the reporter assigned to confront the warden of the penitentiary in which this inmate was being held to put these statements to him. The reporter observed that the inmate would be identified to the prison administration in the process, and perhaps suffer negative consequences. However, he did not see anything wrong with what the inmate described since this was not a maximum-security institution. This exchange became heated, as the assignment editor expressed his shock at the letter and his shock that the reporter was not shocked. He asserted that the authorities should put an end to such activities in prison, and expressed further shock when the reporter countered by saying that inmates would get around such restrictions and in any case these things help relieve tensions created by being locked up for so long. The argument continued, with a cameraman joining in on the side of the reporter. The assignment editor concluded that there was obviously a difference of opinion between him and the reporter, and conceded that a psychologist or sociologist could be used to discuss what are reasonable penal policies.

The reporter proceeded to consider who could serve as an expert, and thought of a psychologist he had interviewed two weeks earlier who was committed to the rehabilitative ideal. When the reporter mentioned this psychologist's view that cutbacks in prison rehabilitative services caused problems, the debate ensued again. The assignment editor became intense, at one point raising his voice and asking rhetorically why these people are in jail in the first place (meaning that they are criminals and deserve restrictions). When things quieted down, the assignment editor suggested the John Howard Society as a source, while a cameraman pressed for a trip to Kingston to visit the penitentiary of the inmate who had written the letter. The reporter observed that all institutions were closed for a half day in mourning for guards killed in the riot, and that prison officials had already told him that going into a prison at this time was like 'waving a red flag in front of a bull.' With tension persisting between him and the assignment editor, the reporter announced that he was going to do it 'his way' first and returned to his desk. There the argument was renewed, this time between the reporter, backed up by another reporter, and a third reporter who was opposed to 'privileged' inmates.

The reporter who had been assigned the story eventually called some correctional-services officials and a representative of the John Howard Society. When the researcher asked him if he had a story after these calls, the reporter said, 'I'll know by six [i.e., broadcast time] what the story is.' Four hours after the original assignment, the reporter talked to a colleague and asked who he should 'get' as sources for a story on prison policies setting 'hardliners' off against 'liberals,' that is, duplicating the type of debate that had occurred in the newsroom. This reporter suggested the chief of police, or any police spokesperson. The reporter rejected this idea, adding that he had called the prison guards' union in an effort to have one of their members serve as a spokesperson, but they had not yet returned his call.

In consultation with a producer, the reporter arranged to do the story in the form of an in-studio interview. After this consultation the reporter told the researcher he would rely on the psychologist he had used two weeks before to represent the liberal position, adding that he wanted him to shred the 'hardliner' to 'bits' with his research evidence. As this source had experience on television he was able to converse for television. Shortly afterwards, the reporter asked the researcher for the name and number of the director of the Centre of Criminology, University of Toronto, in order to obtain in turn the name of someone who could represent the 'hardliner' position. The director was apparently not available, and the reporter waited another hour, until 3:00 p.m., for return calls from prospective sources who could lead him to a 'hardliner.'

At this time a producer emerged from his office and the reporter asked him what he should do about his situation of not having a 'hardliner,' given that time was short to the deadline. The producer suggested a man whose daughter's fiancé had been murdered and who had since started a citizen's 'lawandorder' campaign of his own. He had frequent media contact and would be able to handle the format. He told the reporter to ask a newsroom researcher for this person's name, and another reporter and editor joined in the search. The reporter finally found this person's name in another reporter's files and called him immediately. He was successful in having his 'hardliner' and 'liberal' meet in the newsroom at 4:15. A spokesman for the guards' union subsequently called to volunteer for interview, but was told he was too late. With his 'liberal' versus 'hardliner' binary opposition, the reporter said his strategy would be to stay out of the debate and let the two 'get at each other.'

This story indicates a number of features of considering information sources. There was concern to find sources who would make representations in terms of established cultural categories: 'hardliners' versus 'liberals.' They were not in any sense taken to be *representative* of citizens in the respective categories, but to make *representations* of their positions. They were required to be, as far as possible, at opposite ends of the spectrum. They needed to be articulate and television-wise, a key consideration in selecting sources, especially for in-studio television debates (Elliott, 1974: 86). The hope was that they would articulate things that reflected the ideological cleavages of those in the newsroom, surrogates who could encapsulate in four minutes and thirty-seven seconds the essence of the positions argued in the newsroom over several hours. The reporter relied on his prior contacts with the psychologist, trusting that he would represent well his 'liberal' position. The lack of prior contacts with someone who was a 'hardliner' sent the reporter on a snowball sampling search for a representative of this position. Typical of this approach in our observations was the rather indiscriminate consideration of a wide range of organizations typified as being likely to suggest or provide a suitable spokesperson: the prison guards' union, a citizens' 'lawnandorder' group, the police, the director of the Centre of Criminology, University of Toronto, and correctional-services officials. Moreover, editors, producers, and fellow reporters were canvassed for ideas, opinions, and direct assistance in the search for a suitable source.

This story certainly does not exhaust the range of possibilities in the search process. Most regularly reporters began by simply expropriating sources cited in newspaper articles they or their assignment editors had expropriated, a practice described in previous chapters. They also relied upon official directories supplied by source organizations, or a general directory such as the trade publication *Sources*. Reliance on directories was sometimes taken as a negative sign because it indicated the reporter did not 'know' his sources, in the sense of having the recipe knowledge to pinpoint the best possible source and get on with the job.

The lack of recipe knowledge about the source organization was manifested in different ways and affected the reporter's work. We observed several instances in which reporters ran into difficulties because they were not court-beat regulars and had little or no previous experience with courts. One reporter assigned to report on a continuing court case repeatedly asked the researcher about the organization of the court, role identity of case participants, and the history of the case. He expressed frustration at not knowing what to do, and eventually filed material that proved to be legally restricted. Lack of knowledge was also a cause of wasted time and resources, as when a television reporter and crew went to cover two court cases only to discover that the cases were in assignment court and there would be no reportable hearings on this date. Experienced court reporters would likely have known that these cases were scheduled only for assignment because of the court involved, or at least have checked before committing resources.

Faced with ignorance or a lack of ability to penetrate the organizational space of the source bureaucracy, the reporter sometimes mobilizes members of the source organization to do the work for him. This procedure is formalized in source organizations which have their own public-relations unit and/or research staff to generate information for the media. Otherwise the journalist uses established informal relations or friendly persuasion to convince the source that time should be spent developing information sources for him. This situation obviously creates some dependency on sources.

The reporter often finds himself searching in the dark, going through a maze of bureaucrats in the hope that he will eventually discover some information sources that can at least be subject to consideration. He may also find himself stranded at a dead end. A reporter investigating possibly illegal financial transactions called the director of public relations at Corporate Affairs in Ottawa to obtain information about a mortgage company that had changed hands recently. He said he knew that the mortgage company was sold but expected that the board of directors had been retained, and asked if there was a reporting requirement if companies changed hands. He was routed to another number, and the person there in turn re-routed him to the Department of Insurance on the belief that there might be a requirement for sales to be reported to that department. The Department of Insurance person in turn re-routed the reporter's call to the chief of Registration and Analysis, but he was said to be unavailable and the reporter left his number to be called back. The reporter commented to the researcher that in doing work of this type it helps to have read Kafka.

When bureaucrats cannot be mobilized to assist in the search for information sources to be considered, another alternative is to undertake the search directly. Source bureauracies may allow access to some of their organizational papers. If the matter is deemed serious enough the reporter may take the initiative, or be directed, to go to greater lengths. One technique we were told about in relation to one matter, and that was publicly revealed in relation to another, was to surreptitiously collect and search the garbage outside the building of an organization connected to the story in order to see if there was any organizational paper that might provide investigative leads or reportable information. In the reported incident, reporters had salvaged part of the provincial-government budget statement from the garbage of the company that printed it, prior to its official release. Apart from publishing this information in advance of the official release and having government officials scream that this method reeked of foul play, reporters were also able to visualize and enact subsequent stories about security arrangements for important government documents.

The reporting task entails putting competitive considerations at the forefront in choosing what to write about and who should be mobilized as relevant actors and sources of information. The reporter scrutinizes the related stories of competing news outlets to learn what they have not done in order to decide what might be done. The actual process of obtaining information is also conducted in competitive terms. For example, reporters tried to have sources reveal information in advance of scheduled press releases or news conferences in order to beat the competition.

Reporters who learned that another news outlet was about to do what they were planning to do sometimes accelerated their actions in order to beat the competition to it and thereby maintain their feelings of exclusivity, at least for a few hours. A newspaper reporter writing a feature on surrogate motherhood decided she would go to Detroit earlier than planned to interview a key source there because she anticipated that a television network would be interviewing the same person and she wanted to beat them to it. In a newspaper which prided itself on its reputation for leading rather than following both print and broadcast media, and which was giving substantial play to the surrogate-motherhood issue, this competitive thrust was arguably located at the organizational rather than personal level. As we shall see in the next section, stories of less value in the newsroom were not subject to the same sensitivity to competition or to the same sense of urgency.

Sources who were useful in providing information leads even if they did not wish to be cited were encouraged not to co-operate with the competition. In a major continuing story, reporters from one newsroom had a secret source who, in the words of one reporter, was enabling them to more or less conduct their own public inquiry. The reporter said it was annoying that some things this source said could not be corroborated, and therefore could not be published because the source was unwilling to have them attributed to his name. Nevertheless, the reporter said that he did not want the source to 'go public' until the newsroom had all the information they could get from him because it was a great advantage in beating the competition to have exclusivity with this source.

Such resources were not routinely available in the more typical context of covering spot-news items. Even if the reporter initially imagined that his angle and choice of information sources were unique, he usually discovered that, quite to the contrary, the story was no secret. The vocabularies of precedent and the values of preference in a given newsroom turn out to be similar and even coalesce with other newsrooms. The 'pack' converges on the same source, who quickly learns to repeat the same responses to his series of visitors.

Assigned to do a story on high levels of pollution in the city, a television reporter obtained the name of a meteorologist at the Ministry of the Environment from a wire-service story. He called this source, who advised the reporter to call another source who could likely provide better visuals. However, this second source was unavailable, and the meteorologist agreed to an interview and to show the computer room and pollution-index room for visuals. Just as the reporter finished the interview, a crew from another local television station arrived. The reporter from this station told the source that he would do the interview from the same spot. The cameraman from the newsroom we were observing left his lights up for the other station's crew to use, commenting to the researcher, 'the guys out in the field have to co-operate, it's the producers that compete.' The researcher observed that this second interview was visually and orally similar to the first. After this crew had finished, the crews from both stations were escorted to another building to see the air-monitoring operations. On the way they came across a reporter and crew from a third local television station who were on their way to interview the same meteorologist source. It is little wonder that many sources have a preference for news releases and news conferences.

As illustrated in earlier examples, reporters have considerable interpretive latitude, and certainly have more autonomy to be imaginative and creative than they have been given credit for by academic analysts (e.g., Breed, 1955; Chibnall, 1977; Tuchman, 1978; Schlesinger, 1978; Fishman, 1980). Nevertheless, this last example illustrates that convergence occurs in the routine story. 'Pack journalism' or 'group think' can be accounted for by a number of factors, introduced in previous chapters. The similar socialization of journalists in different news organizations means their nose for news picks up some scents and not others. The fact that the most respected body of knowledge for their purposes is accounts from other news outlets limits them further. The aperture is circumscribed even more by the fact that – as we saw in the boat-theft–wave story (chapter 5) – they do not publicly call into question one another's frames and accounts: great effort is expended to seek confirmation when there are competing accounts, and disconfirmation of an existing frame is not reportable in a routine story. Weick's (1979: 156) observations on 'group think' explain the process:

Having become true believers of a specific schema, group members direct their attention toward an environment and sample it in such a way that the true belief becomes self-validating and the group becomes even more fervent in its attachment to the schema. What is underestimated is the degree to which the direction and sampling are becoming increasingly narrow under the influence of growing consensus and enthusiasm for the restricted set of beliefs. As Janis [1972] demonstrates, this spiral is frequently associated with serious misjudgements of situations ... [A]ny idea that restricts exploration and sampling will come to be seen as increasingly plausible by the very nature of that restriction. If a person has an idea and looks for 'relevant' data, there's enough complexity and ambiguity in the world that relevance is usually found and the idea is usually judged more plausible. One of the prominent characteristics of schemata is that they are refractory of disproof ... It is our contention that most 'objects' in organizations consist of communications, meanings, images, myths, and interpretations, all of which offer considerable latitude for definition and self-validation ... It's certainly obvious that saying is subject to numerous interpretations, which means it can appear to support quite divergent schemata. This seeming universal support does not arise from stupidity or malevolence on the part of the actor but rather from the combination of an intact, reinforced schema and an equivocal object. Actors with bounded rationality presumably are more interested in confirming their schemata than in actively trying to disprove them.

PACING THE DAY'S WORK

The concept of pacing expresses the need of reporters to manage simultaneously angles, time, and space. The reporter must consider what angles are feasible given capacities to penetrate the space of sources for information, the space available in the news outlet for his item, and time to deadline. The managing of these aspects over the course of a shift often gives a sense of immediacy to the reporter's actions, and as the deadline approaches, a sense of urgency. Especially in news organizations where resources are limited – which seemes endemic, for example, to local television news – there is a prevailing expectation that one will produce something each day, pull one's weight in contributing to the daily output. In the television newsroom there was little time or social space for the general reporter to do anything major or elaborate. The managers of this newsroom could simply not afford to risk giving a reporter freedom over days to develop something which might or might not prove worthwhile, and in any event they did not have substantial air time available to give extensive play to more elaborate pieces.

General-assignment reporters respected the need to 'come up with the goods' once assigned. By their own admission they were sometimes 'stretching it' in order to meet this requirement. Thus, a reporter assigned to cover a 'patrol' and 'vigil' by a small group at a park site where a woman had been raped expressed her distaste for the 'types' involved. She rejected one source who gave responses that did not fit her frame – that women are or should be fearful of attacks in public – and was bolstered in this decision by a camera-man's observation that this source was wearing a 'Mao' button. Having rejected a second, male, person as a source, she settled on a woman who also initially expressed the group's view that women should not be fearful and should not stay indoors. The reporter talked to her for a half an hour in order to glean what could be used for her 'fear' frame. She finally managed an on-camera interview in which this source addressed a personal rape-vic-timization experience (from seventeen years previously, in New York); a statement that their symbolic patrol would have looked silly a year ago but not in the context of the recent spate of attacks on women in Toronto; and a statement that if control actions were not taken immediately there would be real trouble. As the crew took background shots, the reporter told the re-searcher she did not like the story, adding 'But I can't say that to [the producer].' She typed the sources as 'professional protesters': she made ref-erence to their statements that they had recently participated in a disarmament peace march; and she pointed to their 'protest shirts' on disarmament, and to one that stated 'Don't Let Acid Reign.' The reporter asserted repeatedly that this was a 'non-group,' that they had nothing better to do, and that they did not deserve media attention.

The reporter managed to reject some individual sources to whom she was ideologically opposed and who did not fit the 'fear' frame. She also juxtaposed statements in her script with activities from the source and used them to sustain the 'fear' frame: for example, a script statement that the group 'say Toronto women are being swallowed up by a fear that tells them it's unsafe anywhere' (which was the opposite of the group's position) was followed by an actuality of the source talking about her personal victimization (seventeen years ago, in New York, in a private rather than a public space). Faced with having to cover a group which she would have preferred to ignore completely, the reporter did manage to sustain her own angle. The reporter's item was in turn led with an anchor script statement about the latest rape in the city which had occurred overnight. The reporter had helped the show to be filled and to flow.

In addition to dealing with the immediacy of construing sources of in-formation to fit the angle and make the show, the reporter must handle the technical aspects of meeting the deadline. While reporters began the day in contemplation, and eased into making source contacts, as the deadline ap-proached there was intensity and tension. In the newspaper newsroom re-porters were concerned over access to video-display terminals to enter their stories in time. In the television newsroom access to editing technicians and their facilities was constantly in mind. As mentioned before, there was a general preference for using video crews because of the ease video provided for editing compared to film and the fact that video does not require processing time. However, since technical editing was usually left well into the afternoon and right up to broadcast time, problems arose frequently. Producers sometimes had to choose which items had priority, moving the others down the lineup or excluding them because of the pressure of demand for technical facilities. These choices in turn were a source of friction between the reporters concerned. For example a reporter's item did not make the show because the available video technicians were involved in another story which had been given priority. The reporter whose story was dropped was angered by this situation, blaming not only the scheduling of editing facilities but also the other reporter who allegedly had had two days to produce his story and could have scheduled the editing earlier in order to avoid the problem.

While things seemed hectic when the deadline approached, not all items were considered immediate. In terms of newsworthiness, immediacy was ascribed according to when something was first made known publicly through the media, regardless of how long it had been going on or had been known about privately. A reporter working on something he predicted would not be made public by other news outlets, or whose coverage, including his angle, was likely to be substantially different from that of competitors, was not always in a rush to complete the story. Especially in the newspaper, reporters kept a reservoir of stories to work on when there was nothing more pressing.

A reporter read a story in a computer trade magazine about a Canadian company that used elaborate means to ship computer equipment destined for Eastern-bloc countries. Such export was apparently in violation of regulations restricting Canadian companies from selling computers or computer technology to those countries. The equipment had been seized in Switzerland pending further investigation. The reporter told the researcher that it was unclear which of a number of laws may have been violated, but even if it turned out not to involve illegality, the story was still significant in terms of the moral and political ramifications. He said he was not going to work on it for another week because he had other commitments, such as completing an item for a weekly advertising supplement on shopping. We can add that he probably felt safe about being scooped by other journalists since he assumed that the computer trade magazine was not part of their popular media consumption for story ideas.

In working on stories in reserve reporters also took more time to contact a range of sources and to prepare preliminary outlines or drafts of the story. Sometimes drafts were written in anticipation of what events were likely to transpire, or what sources were likely to say. In these instances the reporter took the opportunity of the eased pace to visualize more precisely the scenario and its component parts, and wrote his piece with blanks left to be filled as and when things occurred. For example, a reporter preparing to go on holiday for two weeks had received a tip from a source pertaining to two possible murder suspects. He said he passed the information on to police with the understanding that he would have the 'scoop' if a suspect was charged. He prepared a draft story which would be the basis of the first story to be published if one of the suspects was charged. He seemed disappointed when the police eventually called to say these suspects had been questioned and were no longer suspects.

A very common reason for slowing down the pace was the need to connect with sources who were not immediately accessible. Once reporters decided who to call, they placed calls in the hope of making contact. If they did not make contact, they left messages and/or called again at regular intervals. Even if contact was made it often resulted in a determination that other people, not previously thought of, should also be contacted. The lack of contact could eventually result in a story being dropped. If contact was made with some people but not others, those contacted could be the basis for a story on the day concerned, and the others followed up on a subsequent day and used as the basis for another story advancing the first one. The ability to connect with sources was a major source of uncertainty and equivocality in pacing the day's work. The newspaper reporter with more than one thing to work on could 'plant' calls on various stories and eventually file a story on the one in which contacts were most abundant, leaving the others for another day. The television reporter facing a specific story assignment at 10:00 a.m. and the imperative to fill a slot at 6:00 p.m. was less advantaged in this respect.

Pace also varied by aspects of the calender as well as special occasions. Weekends and public holidays were characterized by a more relaxed atmosphere, although if too few reporters were available those that were present were sometimes expected to do extra stories and/or were given considerably more space for their stories. Special coverage – for example, of a major disaster or an election – entailed considerable work at a hectic pace and overtime, but was often followed by a day of 'let down,' in which some did not show up for work and those at work had little energy or inclination to recharge to their usual level of intensity.

On an individual level, reporters also created personal space in pacing their work. Reporters did manage to avoid assignments, not file on an assignment, or to turn an assignment into something more personally agreeable according to their own ideological preferences. On days when reporters wished to do less, they could do the minimum required to file a basic spot story or not file at all. We observed reporters who did not file in preference for shopping, attending a Miss Canada luncheon, and playing pool. However, not filing was much more typically a result of deciding there was no story either because they tried hard but could not generate information, or because they did not like the assignment and tried hard to avoid it.

The elements of resources, space, and time were not only very real material constraints on reporters in getting the job done, but culturally shared and agreeable justifications and excuses for not getting the job done, or for doing it in a way that did not meet the original expectations of supervisors. The inability to connect with sources; the lack of time to talk to a range of sources; the unavailability of a crew or technicians to complete the visual requirements; the lack of space available for the item; the need to cover for personnel shortages on the day: these and a large number of other material elements not only influenced what got done, but provided the range of legitimate accounts of what was not done but might have been done under more favourable conditions. Reporters routinely invoked these elements to account for what they had discovered and what had been left out. Resources, time, and space were incorporated into reporters' account ability to satisfy their accountability to editors and producers. We return to this subject at the end of the chapter.

Reporting Methodologies

INTERVIEWS

The interview is the primary method used by reporters. In this section we examine the strategies and tactics of reporters in producing interview material. In the final sections of this chapter we examine how this interview material is used by reporters to establish factuality in their stories.

In approaching an interview with a source, the reporter is looking for informative statements that are consistent with his emerging frame and angle. Regardless of what medium he is working with, the reporter is after 'the good clip': a source statement that fits the frame. The process may require a long discussion that is discursive or expatiating, but the goal is to telescope this into a short quotation that is fitting. The source who is able to give a fitting comment almost immediately is particularly valued. In various contexts reporters repeatedly referred to 'the good source' as the one who was non-discursive, non-expatiating, and came to the point with a quotable quote. The good source rephrases the question into his answer so that it is clear to all what he was required to say. Especially in television – where, according to a producer's memo, the ideal 'actuality' with a source is a twelve-second clip – the ability to proceed at a good clip by incorporating questions into answers was *the* sign of the ideal source.

Journalists do face considerable obstacles with sources beyond the perpetual annoyance with those who are inarticulate, discursive, and expatiating. Sources often put up obstructions so that obtaining a suitable clip was something that reporters had to constantly work at, using a range of strategies and tactics. In the words of one newsroom manager:

> [T]he most important fight that we have as newsmen ... [is efforts to] shut us out, to not tell us. It is a government ... that deals in secrecy, and it is, to bring it back to the area you are studying, a police force that deals in secrecy, they only allow us to know what they want us to know as an official organization. They'll only tell us what they think is safe for us to know when it gets down to a one-on-one between an individual policeman and the guy that's covering the beat. And often it will come down to sources telling the police reporter information which is off the record, or which cannot be attributed. But all in all, all those factors conspire for us not to know completely what is going on within the police force. It's a closed organization ...
>
> [W]e're very aware of, not to go to people with axes to grind because there's a ready-made statement there which is going to jive with the theory that a reporter has about where the hell all this is going, and we have to be very careful of that ... [Y]ou know Pollution Probe has expertise in that area, but you don't want to go running off to Pollution Probe to always act as the mouthpiece for environmentalists who aren't happy with a table being laid under Fort Erie, you know what I mean? So that you have to be very aware of that so that you can gauge what the hell those people are saying in order to give it the proper perspective. And that's the role of a journalist and that's also the role of the editors and producers who end up getting those scripts and getting the ideas along with the journalists.

Source-organization authorities choose whether to speak, who will be the spokesperson, and whether the statement will be in the form of a written release document, verbal, or both. Reporters have to appreciate the nature of source 'feelers' through releases, news conferences, or public statements. As one reporter noted about the news release from an organization whose news conference he was on the way to attend, it did not reveal what would be revealed at the news conference. Its purpose was to lure reporters there, and to avoid the possibility of having someone report in advance and outside the control offered to the source by the news-conference format.

Reporters also face fellow journalists who make their living as public-relations spokespersons for a given source organization, or as consultants. While these persons do the work of mobilizing material from the source organization to turn it into news discourse, reporters know that first and foremost such material is constructed to construe the truth in a way that favours the source organization. In their everyday dealings with sources, reporters experience the sense that people within organizations, and across organizations related to the same institution, conspire to make only their partial truths known.

A reporter trying to establish police policy on the release of police occurrence reports to citizens in relation to a specific case placed calls to senior police officials and the provincial Ministry of the Solicitor General (which was responsible for police in the province). He was unable to contact relevant sources in either organization after successive calls, being told repeatedly that he would be called back. Repeatedly through this process the reporter remarked that the two organizations were probably delaying in order to provide a uniform and consistent account between them. He recognized that of course this attempt at corroboration was strategic on their part, since he himself was looking for inconsistency to further his own goal of policing the police.

Sources sometimes released information in advance to one reporter representing a single news organization in the hope of receiving sympathetic coverage that would be given substantial play and would frame the approach of other news outlets. Sources wishing to have the agenda set in terms of primary factual discourse often fed the wire services first, so that at least the initial accounts of all news outlets would focus on 'the facts' as construed by the source and conveyed relatively statically by the wire services.

Sources *staged* scenes in the hope that reporters' scripts would be coincident. Usually, if the reporter wants a story at all, he must accept this staging. He must report what goes on in court, not the dealings among police, lawyers, judges, and Crown attorneys that occur backstage. He must film or describe the protest group's demonstration in terms of their staging efforts – whether it be spray-painting slogans on walls or burning an antagonist in effigy – as a dramatic visualization of the cause. Often he must print or restate the bureaucrat's news-conference statements almost verbatim, even while expressing doubts about them privately.

There is always the desire, and occasionally the option, of circumventing the regular official channels and writing something derived from other sources. Nevertheless, the reporter still must be attuned to the possibility that in doing so he may be acting as a conduit pipe for somebody else's preferences. Even circumventing the official source, he can end up circumscribing the account in the terms preferred by the source.

> In the circumstances of competition, the reporter is constantly looking for material from outside the regular channels that form the central route for information, but his desire to obtain exclusive information also increases his vulnerability; he can as easily become a carrier of information outside the normal channels for the same officials. One man's scoop is frequently another's carefully camouflaged handout.
>
> In the circumstances of the newspaper as an organized management system,

news choices and content emerge far more as a result of the structure of relationships than as the result of a conscious working professional ideology.
(Smith, 1980: 188)

Reporters were frequently cut off from relevant sources because they or
their colleagues had said or done something offensive which put the source
organization on the defensive. This situation occurred frequently in continuing
stories aimed at policing organizational life. For example, reporters were cut
off by trust companies and their lawyers as the news organization pushed for
government regulations and enforcement against specific trust-company activities. Individuals looking out for their interests also wisely refused; for
example, the owner of a tavern which used a satellite dish to bring television
transmissions to his customers refused a television interview concerning the
legality and regulation of satellite dishes. The resort to citing a source saying
'no comment,' leaving the implication that he had something to hide, was
only useful on rare occasions. It is not usually newsworthy to cite a source
saying 'no comment,' and frequent use of 'no comment' was itself a sign
that the reporter was not capable of doing his job of quoting knowledgeable
informants.

These findings are quite discrepant from the view in the research literature
that journalists manage a predictable supply of sources who turn over their
information with little questioning on either side. Certainly there are a number
of regular outlets with standardized releases or verbal accounts, but many
reporting needs are not met by routine access. Reporters faced continual
constructions and obstructions from sources which made their work difficult.
Reporters devised a range of strategies and tactics in efforts to overcome
these problems, including expressions of affinity and acts of reciprocity;
inducements; special pleading related to occupational considerations; deception; threats; and maintaining control over the text.

Expressions of affinity and reciprocity ranged from subtle signs of support
to outright bargaining over the commodity of information and its control.
During interviews reporters would make comments aimed at reinforcing their
affinity with the source's views: for example, using pejorative names for
suspects in talking with police about them. The reinforcement was often
perpetual; some reporters on some beats genuinely take on the perspective of
their sources and share their frustrations and concerns (Chibnall, 1977; Fishman, 1980; Ericson et al, forthcoming a). On beats reporters developed friend-
ships involving minor acts of reciprocity, such as giving a source a personal
copy of a photograph taken for publication. There were also more formal and
institutionalized exchanges, such as police-beat reporters organizing and publicizing a policeman-of-the-month award; arranging large-scale parties in hotel
facilities where journalists and their sources could meet informally; or inviting
sources for chats at the local press club.

Much effort was devoted to cultivating relationships with key authorized knowers. If a person was in a prominent position, or deemed a rising star who would be in a prominent position shortly, then effort was devoted to engaging him in conversation as well as eliciting material needed for 'the twelve-second clip.' Friendship and reciprocity were also established with individuals who were in the news on a continuing basis because they were 'fighting the system.' They were given advice, direct assistance, particular kinds of publicity, etc., in exchange for preferred or exclusive coverage by a single reporter or news outlet. Much of this exchange went on at a *sub rosa* level, and the specifics were not always known to the reporters' newsroom colleagues or reporting associates on a beat.

In public meetings or gatherings there was a certain deportment required of journalists which was aimed at expressing the formal distance they are supposed to have from those whose events they are reporting. For example, at a panel session of the Canadian Bar Association meetings involving prominent politicians and experts, each speaker received applause for his words from everyone in the audience but the reporters. Reporters do not publicly express their enthusiasm for what people have to say at the time of saying it, however much they endorse these people enthusiastically in less visible settings.

Buying news with money was forbidden and we did not learn of any occasions on which this was even contemplated, let alone practised. However, there was much dealing in the commodity of greatest value to sources and journalists in the contexts which brought them together, namely information. Sources were often offered the inducement of some coverage, and sometimes the additional hint that it would be favourable, in exchange for co-operation. One reporter said he had an ongoing relationship with a citzens' pressure group concerned with police misconduct. He expected tips from this group concerning instances of alleged police misconduct in exchange for coverage that was sympathetic to their cause in the process of being critical of police. Deals were also struck in the particular instance. A lawyer whose client was scheduled for a hearing in connection with alleged misconduct in the course of his occupation did not want advance publicity or publicity focusing on his client. He made a deal that in exchange for meeting his wishes he would not ask for a private hearing, thereby enabling the reporter to attend and report what transpired at the hearing with suitable retrospective commentary by the lawyer as a source.

In addition to specific inducements offered in these reciprocal exchanges, reporters offered various general inducements. The most pervasive and persuasive general inducement was the argument that the reporter was simply offering a 'fair hearing' to the source to get his viewpoint included in the story. This offer pertained not only to situations in which the source was the focus of attention (e.g., subject to allegations of deviance), but also where persons who had relevant information could say something about the people or issue involved which might be helpful to them in their cause (e.g., associates of the criminal offender constructing the positive side of his moral character). Here the journalists appealed to the source's sense of news values – fairness, objectivity, and balance – to argue why it was important for the source to offer an account.

Occasionally the inducement was more grandiose. A reporter would suggest to a reluctant source that news coverage would help his cause. The relatives of a woman who was believed to have been abducted were very reluctant to talk to journalists. As a television crew arrived at the victim's house, where several of the relatives were gathered, one man told the reporter to talk to the police because the relatives did not want to say anything. As the reporter turned back towards his crew car, the man put his coat over his face and ran towards the car and cameraman. The reporter intervened and tried to cool out the man by saying he was only publicizing the event in the hope it would lead to the discovery of the woman's whereabouts. The reporter repeated this formulation at several points during the day.

One form of inducement that was especially attractive to some sources was the offer of not identifying them in any published or broadcast stories on the matter. The person would be left 'off the record' in exchange for providing the information. Information on these terms came from 'insiders' within a source organization (e.g., a person with his job in jeopardy, supplying information relevant to a reporter's investigations into the firm's financial dealings); relatives of 'insiders' (e.g., a policeman's wife, about a senior officer's affairs entailing a possible conflict of interest); ex-'insiders' (e.g., a former hospital employee about developments in the hospital related to a series of deaths under suspicious circumstances); a citizens' pressure group itself seeking to generate information inside another bureaucracy (e.g., a group concerned with police misconduct); relatives of persons victimized in crime or by a bureaucracy; and friends, or friends of friends, of the reporter. Most of the individual citizens who wished to remain off the record were motivated to supply information because they had been aggrieved by the organization being reported on and to stay off the record because they did not wish to be aggrieved further. As one reporter expressed it, 'the best sources are those who have been injured.'

In source bureaucracies there were also persons who felt that they could co-operate legitimately off the record to provide background information or leads which would enable the reporter to produce a more intelligent story. However, they did not wish to 'go public' because they were prevented by their own organization from doing so, or they deemed it otherwise impolitic to do so. Sources from various bodies – unions, police, courts – mentioned 'internal' matters that had to be left off the record because of specific rules prohibiting them from making such information public or even indicating that they had talked to a reporter. Sometimes reporters approached a particular series of interviews with the prior knowledge that the sources could not be cited on certain matters but in the hope of obtaining general knowledge about developments. Thus, journalists from one newspaper surveyed some riding presidents of a political party contemplating a leadership review. As revealed in an editors' conference discussion of this survey, some presidents made off-the-record comments about the poor prospects for the leader, indicating that a formal leadership review was forthcoming.

Reporters who valued being generally informed along with sustaining reciprocity with sources devoted considerable time and effort to 'off-the-record' discussions. Some reporters had what was termed an 'off-the-record' day, in which they took the time to chat with various sources on a range of matters, with the understanding it was to be without subsequent citation or quotation.

With some regular sources there was no need to negotiate over having their comments kept off the record. Their relations with reporters were so routinized and established that they could say things that were tacitly understood to be off the record. This was particularly the case on news beats. For example, court-beat reporters emphasized that lawyers, and especially Crown attorneys, had a tacit understanding of what was to be reported and of what was to be left off the record. Basic 'facts' of the case are on the record: the identity of the parties, the accused's record after conviction, and details of the incident(s) and charge(s). However, when lawyers or Crown attorneys talked about backstage dealings or opinions, which they often did and enjoyed doing, it was off the record. That went without saying if the audience comprised reporters who were court regulars. In one case we observed, a lawyer told the reporter details of what he would not state at the hearing for his client, because it would harm his client. The lawyer also talked of his future strategies in the case – all of this with an understanding that it would not be reported. In another case a Crown attorney made very damaging statements to a reporter about the parents of a child whose death was the subject of an inquest, knowing that the reporter would know enough not to ruin his career by citing him.

Of course, there was always the possibility that the understanding had not been perfected and the source would be cited and 'burned.' Reporters articulated the 'strict rules' for off-the-record comments as being that the source had to state it was off the record *before* making the statement, and had to specify what was to be left out: the source's name; particular information; whether particular information could be used if it was confirmed through another source. However, the interpretations of this rule varied. There were instances in which sources objected that they had imposed an off-the-record condition that was not adhered to. There were also instances where reporters agreed to keep something off the record, and kept that fact from their editors, even though the source had made the request after giving the information rather than before. Moreover, while news executives admonished that reporters were to 'be straight' with their sources, they also admitted that there were instances important enough to bend the rules and 'play hard ball,' taking straight aim regardless of how the information was obtained.

Often the request for something to be left off the record had a temporal dimension. The source's concern was to have the reporter understand developments at some specific time, and therefore revealed information that he did not want made public until later. This was the case when reporters were working on an organization's development of a new policy, and the organization was anxious to keep the reporter informed but not have the unformulated suggestions revealed until the policy was crystallized into a rational public statement. It was also typical in court cases where the reporter was asked or expected to hold the information in reserve until it came out in the public forum of the court proceedings.

Another means of seeking co-operation for an interview was to make special pleas in the context of the time, space, and other resource constraints of the news media. As we emphasized earlier, those elements of an occupation which constrain are also useful as enabling justifications to take a certain course of action. In requesting an interview, that sources call back immediately, that sources change their appointments in order to facilitate the news interview, etc., reporters would often refer to their sense of urgency: in terms of deadlines; editors' pressure; the need in television to schedule crew time so as not to tie up resources; the fact that space had been allotted for the source's side of the story; and so on. Time, space, and material constraints were constantly evident in reporters' communications to sources about what interviews were needed when and under what conditions.

Special pleas were also made with regard to considerations of hierarchy or influence in source organizations. If a reporter was having difficulty obtaining information at one level of an organization, appeals would be made at higher levels to enforce co-operation. When a reporter was having difficulty obtaining even basic information to update stories on two criminal cases, he mentioned this to his editor who in turn wrote a formal letter of complaint to the chief of police. Sometimes persons in superordinate positions in the source organization were used to convince a reluctant subordinate to co-operate. For example, the president of an organization that ran halfway houses for prisoners was used to convince the local representative of the organization that he should co-operate in a story about resistance to establishing a halfway house in a particular local community. If inmates or clients of penal or welfare institutions were being sought for interview, it was managed through the authorities in charge of them. Similarly, lawyers for accused persons were sometimes used to talk their clients into doing an interview in their own interests.

In turn reporters had to respect the organizational position and rules of sources from whom they sought co-operation. Some sources were prevented by organizational policy from talking to reporters without explicit permission. For example, a police force had a policy that no officer under the rank of inspector was to speak to the news media without permission. Indeed, this rule was backed up further by the Ontario Police Act which had a section prohibiting police officers from talking to non-police personnel about the specifics of their work.

Sometimes source organizations sought to cover themselves by asking the news organization to authenticate the reporter's credentials. A reporter who wanted to interview an inmate of a psychiatric facility was asked to obtain a letter from her news organization attesting that she was up to the task. The reporter obliged, drafting a letter which her desk editor signed. A reporter who wanted to interview a lawyer in another city about a controversial aspect of his practice was asked to send samples of her writing so the source could assess her ability.

In general all negotiations over conditions for an interview and its use were to be completed prior to the conduct of the interview. It was not a practice to agree to allow a source to see the reporter's filed copy, and requests by a source in this connection were denied. After one such denial the reporter informed the researcher that allowing the source to see the filed copy is prohibited because it is a sign that the reporter does not have the competence to construe the facts and write the story. It would undercut the specific reporter's claims to competence, as well as the professional imagery of journalism, to 'play back' stories to sources in advance of publication. Keeping a draft story from a source was also related to the problem of time, in that it would be virtually impossible to file a story on the same day if sources were given it for advance scrutiny. Moreover, keeping the story from the source is a key aspect of journalistic control over the process (cf Carter, 1958: 140). Given journalists' all-too-familiar knowledge that any text can be subject to multiple interpretations and readings – that knowledge is perspectival – allowing the various sources cited in a story to give their critical interpretations of the reporters' interpretations would create substantial blockage of the process and its temporal, spatial, and material limitations. Just as many other occupations and professions write accounts of the activities of their clientele without giving them the full account – for example, police officers do not give victims copies of police occurrence and investigation reports, and victims are left to decipher the case when and if it is recounted in the public forum of the court – so journalists patrol the facts they have generated through to the point at which they tell the story publicly.

When they lack means of reciprocity, inducement, or special pleading, reporters are left to devise means of deception or threats to get the job done. Certain elements of deception were routine and indeed are probably accepted as standard practice in journalism or any other business. For example, leaving telephone messages for sources required particular techniques. One was generally advised to be as vague and general as possible to prevent the source from being turned off and not calling back, or being too turned on and doing a lot of preparation which would yield an account that was less open and honest. If the person taking the message asked for the topic, it was sometimes better to mention several topics in the hope that the source would be enticed by one and therefore call back and agree to co-operate.

Deception was also commonplace in the context of conducting interviews. Reporters would sometimes lead the source to believe that one agenda was on the table while he was actually trying to visualize the source as a deviant. Thus, a political candidate who was ostensibly being interviewed and filmed for a story about the election campaign in his riding was also being watched in terms of past allegations of corruption in political office. The reporter instructed her cameraman that during her questioning of the candidate about opposition candidates and the issues, she was going to 'drop' the question of corruption and at this point the cameraman was to zoom in on his face in order to visualize his reaction. Reporters and film crews sometimes left their tape recorders or cameras running beyond the recognized limits of the formal interview in the hope that they might pick up some dirt. They could still feel clean in the process because what the source thought was off the record was in fact literally on the record, as no statement was made by the source to the contrary.

Deceptive questioning is often connected with the construction of factuality by the reporter. The reporter calls the investigator into crime or other deviance and asks if there are any new developments. When he is told no he asks if the investigator is considering the possibility that 'X' is the case and is told that 'X' is a possibility, as any open-minded investigator would admit in pursuing the range of possibilities. The reporter then leads his story with the fact that there is a new lead in the investigation, namely 'X.' Similarly, the reporter may ask the source if there is a possibility that a bureaucrat's fault, error, or lack of adherence to procedural propriety is the cause of the problem under investigation. If the source mentions that as a possibility, errors or faulty procedure provide the frame for the reporter's follow-up investigation.

In interaction with the source the reporter very often presented the accounts of other sources representing conflicting views on the matter, in an effort to have the source feel compelled to 'clarify' his position and elaborate more than he had been willing to up to that point. In essence the source was treated as an accused confronted with allegations against him and asked to account for himself. Like the police interrogator, the reporter relied on the human inclination to provide an account in justification and excuse, thereby expanding the reservoir of information from which he could understand the matter and make his case in writing. Of course the other sources' accounts were only given verbally by the reporter, with the full intent of leaving it to the source's imagination to fill in the blanks and actually say much more than had yet been visualized by the reporter.

This aspect of deception was entwined with the threat that the reporter would do the story in any event, so the source might as well try to account for himself. The reporter reminded the source that he had and would obtain publishable accounts from other sources, and was only being 'fair' in giving this source a chance. Often the implied threat of negative coverage was stated directly when the source did not comply initially, and if this did not work negative coverage was actually given in the hope that subsequently the source would decide to be more forthcoming.

One reporter told an illustrative anecdote. He wrote two stories for a newspaper which were critical of a police force. In response to these articles the chief of police threatened to cut off the newspaper from regular channels of information, and shortly after he did so. Subsequently, there was word of a major traffic accident involving several injured people. A reporter from the newspaper called the police department for details, but was refused. The newspaper then published an article with a headline to the effect 'Several People in Serious Accident, We think,' and in the story stated that they did not really know because the police would not tell them anything. The chief of police complained to an editor about this article, and the editor responded that as long as the police refused to provide information the newspaper would run a prominent box daily with the headline, 'No Crime Reported by Police in Last 24 Hours.' The reporter relating this anecdote said this had the immediate effect of reopening the regular channels of police information.

SURVEYS AND TREND DATA

Reporters have the option of sampling a range of opinion from a number of sources, subject to considerations of the time it takes to do the work and the space available to represent the opinions canvassed. Alternatively or in addition, the reporter can rely upon survey or epidemiological data produced by his sources and reproduce it to indicate broader opinions or trends. In this section we consider the ways in which surveys and survey data were understood by journalists and used as a way of knowing.

Typically the survey for the journalist simply entailed contacting more sources than usual to comment. Especially in a context where the reporter anticipated extra space because it was a major event or a feature on an important topic, the list of authorized knowers was expanded and the potential for a greater breadth of information enhanced.

A reporter doing a story on sex offenders was told by a source that there was an increase in cases of mental illness in the prison population and that his colleagues across the country also found this to be the case. This increase was attributed to 1 / an increase in mental-hospital decarceration and the fact that some of these people released into the community end up in prisons; and/ or 2 / an increase in mental illness in the general population mirrored by the prison population; and/or 3 / an increase in social stress to the extent that people are not able to cope and hence resort to deviance. The reporter decided to put these possible explanations to prison and mental-health officials from nine of the ten Canadian provinces. In addition she talked to a researcher about her research into criminal-control–system screening of the mentally ill, and obtained data from Statistics Canada on the epidemiology of mental illness in the general population to compare it with that of the prison population. In essence, this method consisted of getting a number of authorized knowers to talk about their *perceptions* of epidemiology and the reasons for variations between their region and other regions of the country. This approach was the standard one of using authorized knowers to state what appeared to be the case, but it involved mobilizing more of them than usual and introducing more variability and equivocality into a story than is usual with fewer sources.

Another population surveyed is 'the person on the street' who is either indirectly connected to an event reported on or asked for an opinion on a phenomenon in the news. The reporter asks the neighbours of a murder victim what the victim was like and what it is like to have this event occur in the neighbourhood; asks citizens generally whether there has been a change in quality of life (e.g., more fear) as a result of a series of reported crime incidents; talks to citizens participating in a demonstration or industrial strike about their cause and its causes; asks people likely to be affected by a new government policy about its presumed or actual impact; and so on. This 'vox pop' orientation is a technique used especially in popular news outlets (Voum-vakis and Ericson, 1984) and television news (Hartley, 1982). The survey involving popular perceptions and reactions to public problems was typically conducted with a pre-established frame. If the frame could not be sustained, then the story was dropped to avoid producing something opposite to what had been believed initially. Reporters said that a survey often entailed talking to a large number of citizens and using only those statements that could be cited in support of a frame.

In a story about community resistance to the purchase of a home to be used as a halfway house for federal prisoners, the reporter framed the matter in terms of the comments of the head of the organization establishing the house and the head of a community organization opposing it. In addition the reporter decided to interview citizens who happened to be strolling through the park opposite the house. The first citizen said he had just moved to the area and knew nothing about the issue. The second citizen said he had heard of the issue but did not have an opinion one way or the other. The reporter decided to have a film clip of one of these citizens walking his dog through the park and had him retrace his steps for the purpose. There was no further canvassing of popular opinion, but in the anchorperson's tease for this story before a commercial break it was stated: 'A halfway house for [names area]. Half of the residents don't want it, half of them do, and [names reporter] reports from the battlefront when we return.' This was typical of how journalists used the *representation* of a few citizens interviewed to appear as *representative* of the entire community.

The fiction of popular interest, concern, and anxiety was a common one, even though the story was based on a sample of one. A woman telephoned the newsroom to say she was a library employee and was concerned that voters' lists were sold by her borough through the library to anyone who wished to purchase them for $25.00 each. She feared that being identified on the voter's list as a single, female occupant would make her vulnerable to possible commercial exploitation and criminal victimization. In a later brief conversation with the reporter the woman said she had been the victim of a break, enter, and theft twice and was concerned that someone might use the list to identify her as an easy target since she lived alone.

The reporter talked to a borough official who explained that the lists were in any case public documents, that the main purchasers were insurance companies and real estate proprietors, and that in the two years following the previous election only ten to fifteen lists had been sold. He also mentioned that the lists from the present election would not be on sale for another week.

The reporter then talked to the alderman for the ward in which the informant was a constituent. The alderman complained mainly about the commercial uses of information given out for other purposes, but downplayed the potential for use by rationally calculating criminals except to mention that a woman living alone might *feel* more vulnerable.

The reporter called the other five boroughs in the city and asked if their lists were publicly available, whether they were for sale, and if so at what price. Having completed this 'survey' the reporter also called various provincial-government authorities, and talked to the director of the Assessment Office, Ministry of Revenue, who said he had never heard of the sale of voters' lists but if it proved to be a problem he would look into it. He gave the name of the ministry lawyer, and the lawyer told the reporter there appeared to be no legal problem in connection with the sale of voters' lists. The lawyer suggested the reporter call the minister's office, and in doing so the reporter was switched to an assistant. The assistant was apparently unaware of the sale of voters' lists, indicated that he did not have much to say because the matter had been 'sprung' on him, and referred the reporter to the ministry's legal department. The reporter, facing time constraints, dropped the idea of using a ministry source.

The reporter proceeded to prepare his story in terms of three negative consequences of the sale of voters' lists. First, it can increase the annoyance of junk mail (even though the borough official told him that there were few purchasers, that purchasers were companies who did not use the voters' lists as mailing lists, and that the current lists had not yet gone on sale). Second, it can be used for commercial purposes (even though the citizen gives the information without knowledge of this use, which the alderman underscored). Third, it can be used to identify vulnerable people as targets (which the original source was fearful of, but would not be formally interviewed on, and which the alderman had downplayed).

These elements were put into the story, along with an anchorperson's statement that 'abuse' of these lists was a question being raised across the city. This was true only in the sense that the reporter had raised the question himself by calling various officials in borough and provincial-government offices! There was no survey of citizens' opinion about the matter. The reporter took his lead from a sample of one. In the opinion of those he canvassed, except the alderman on some points, it was not a significant problem since the number of purchasers was minimal. Since no one emphasized the problem of junk mail, the reporter had 'fake' visuals taken of mail passing through the letterbox of a colleague who lived near the newsroom, using various pieces of mail collected within the newsroom, and added his own comment about this component. A transcription of the story follows:

Anchorperson: Are enumeration lists used in the recent municipal elections being abused? It's a question being raised in several municipalities across Metro, municipalities where lists of voters containing personal information are being sold across the counter. ———— reports.

Reporter: If you've been receiving even more junk mail than usual, it could be because you've voted in the recent municipal election.* |visuals of mail through house mail slot| The city clerk's office in the boroughs of North York, Etobicoke, York and here in Scarborough are selling the voters lists. |stand-up at clerk's office in Scarborough city hall| It's a practice that's been going on for years, but now it's coming under scrutiny. The issue came to light when a constituent of Scarborough Alderman elect ———— complained that the practice was an invasion of her privacy. |visual of front of voters' list, then to shot of source|

Alderman: If we continue with this, I think we are betraying the voter because we are asking him for information on one basis and subsequently using it for another. |source taking head|

Reporter: [names alderman] says information contained in the list could be put to commercial use, and the municipalities shouldn't get involved. [source at his desk with reporter]

Alderman: You can identify whether the person owns the property because there's an 'o' by the side of the voter if they own it. Insurance, house repairs – all these are definite sales means for potential commercial activities. And then you have spouse, and I don't think most of the voters, nor the ladies in my ward particularly, like the idea of being identified as single people living alone in a home, and frankly I just won't have it. [source points to list, then cut to close up of the list and source points to 'o' for owner and later 's' for spouse']

Reporter: In North York the voter list costs $12 a ward, in Etobicoke they're $5 each, in York they're also $5 each or $40 for a complete set. In Scarborough a complete set goes for $25. East York and the City of Toronto don't sell their voter lists, but the information is available to be copied. [shot of front page of list, fading to 'supers' of prices for lists in each borough]

* Note that in the main borough concerned, the reporter was told that the lists for the recent election would not go on sale for another week!

While there was no evidence of general public concern before the broadcast of this item, a public-opinion survey afterward might have revealed a heightened awareness!

It was in fact exceptional for reporters to go beyond what authorized knowers said was general opinion about a matter to the people who were said to hold the opinion. One instance in which this did occur involved the president of a company victimized by a bombing who said his employees were most upset; the reporter then went to some employees to get them to say that they were upset. This extra effort was deemed exceptional enough by the reporter's superior for him to remark favourably upon it in a general memo to staff assessing their performances.

Reporters rarely conducted more elaborate surveys to test their presuppositions. However, one reporter would have pleased even a professor of social research. He called twelve local taxi companies, and posed as a customer asking for a taxi to be dispatched without a black or Pakistani driver. One taxi dispatcher said he would try but he could not guarantee it; another said they had no black drivers; and the rest refused or added that it was discriminatory and/or illegal. The reporter remarked that he was surprised the story made the show because it was 'good news': he expected that it would only make it if more than half the companies had agreed to send a non-black, non-Pakistani driver.

As in the voters' list story, even when survey questions arose it was often not a viable consideration – and perhaps not even thought of – to conduct a small survey on one's own. The typical response was to either ignore pursuing the question, or to consider whether sources might have relevant data to pass on or cite. At an afternoon newspaper-editors' conference, discussion focused on what angles might be pursued to sustain continuing stories about trust companies in trouble over illegal practices. The question was raised as to whether the trust companies involved were experiencing heavy withdrawals by depositors and whether depositors were now favouring banks. One person responded that it would be very difficult to find out because the trust companies would not divulge that sort of information; he added that he was going to check if there had been a lot of sales in gold. No mention was made of surveying banks, let alone a survey of the public to ascertain from them their banking habits and preferences in light of the trust-company affair. In summary, when the idea of survey or trend data came to mind it was usually only visualized in terms of whether a source would have it available for citation. The most standard example of this was to report the latest homicide or robbery in the city by obtaining police-produced data on how many crimes of the type had been committed in the year and whether this represented an increase over the previous year.

Often the source's visualization of an increase in a deviant phenomenon was relied upon exclusively. Thus, in a story about prison violence the evidence for an increase, and hence the visualization of it as a serious problem, came from one source's account (an ex-offender turned criminologist), as did the explanation that it was attributable to harsh conditions. Similarly, rates of victimization were cited from sources without any effort to understand how the figures were produced, or to verify them by other means. The going rate for 'battered wives' during the research period was one woman in ten. The same one-in-ten figure was regularly cited by a range of sources as the number of rapes reported to the police compared to the number which 'actually' occurred.

The impact of deviant events was also cited in terms of the source's fancy for figures. After a commonly used pharmaceutical product was poisoned by a saboteur in an isolated incident in the United States, the Canadian manufacturer decided to sell the product only from dispensaries. A pharmacist was pressed in interview to state the impact of the 'scare' on sales, and eventually offered a 'wild guess' of sales being down '75 per cent,' which the reporter then cited as fact. Such citations, even if 'wild guesses,' were generally preferred to any more searching inquiries. As long as the source said it, it could be made to stand for the fact of the matter without the bother of developing other ways of knowing or introducing the possibility of interpretive error.

In the halfway-house story outlined earlier, the assignment editor handed the reporter a scholarly monograph on the issue based on research conducted by a professor at a nearby university. This was not part of the normal reading digest for the assignment editor, but he had a copy from a press conference held at the time of the book release two weeks earlier. The reporter did not even bother to take the book from the assignment editor, telling him that it was about mental health rather than criminal halfway houses and that she had heard the methodology was suspect. She preferred to work from her newspaper clippings and her source clips. As the Glasgow University Media Group has commented (GUMG, 1976: 135), there are readily available data from government and university sources pertaining to the range of questions raised by journalists in covering the news 'staples' of crime and industrial matters, but journalists rarely engage or address these materials directly. When they do take them up, it is as interpreted and visualized by official sources rather than by the reporter himself.

In one newsroom two journalists independently stated to two different researchers that one superior on occasion encouraged them to present figures unchecked, or fabricate part of a story, or complete what the reporter deemed to be no story. While they regarded this as wrong, it was unclear how the boundaries were drawn because of the fact of fiction embedded in journalistic modes of story-telling (see also the last section of chapter 8).

An extended case example of a reporter's efforts to survey a social problem is illustrative. A television assignment editor and producer were discussing the lineup for the day in the context of doing continuing stories. They focused on what else could be done to further stories about a spate of attacks on women. They also talked about a story the previous day regarding robbery trends on the occasion of the one-hundredth robbery in the city that year. The assignment editor suggested that a similar story could be done on trends in residential break, enter, and thefts. The producer agreed, and a reporter was assigned. The frame established at the outset was that a problem existed and preventive measures taken by the householder were the solution.

The assignment editor asked the two researchers in the newsroom if they could offer any suggestions for the story. One researcher mentioned a research monograph on burglary in Toronto by Waller and Okihiro (1978). The reporter took the reference but did not follow up on it. While the reporter had graduate training in social science, he had a clear sense of the news-genre requirements for a story of this type.

The reporter proceeded by calling the information officer at police headquarters and obtained data on the number of household break-ins for the year to date compared with the same period the previous year. Those numbers were broken down in terms of apartment break-ins (which were up) and house break-ins (which were down), and also by divisional area for both apartment and house break-ins. Eager to visualize an increase in this form of deviant activity, the reporter decided to photocopy a map of police divisional areas and have a cameraman take a shot of it plain; then a shot of it coloured in for the division with the greatest increase in apartment break-ins; and finally a shot of it coloured in for the division with the greatest increase in house break-ins. The reporter commented to the researcher that the figures were 'really indicators of nothing.' He observed that what was 'really' required was data on population density and apartment-to-home ratios at risk in each division. He added, 'It would be impossible to get these figures.' The reporter recognized the disjunction betweeen his own knowledge of what would constitute a more adequate account with trend data, and the account he was required to produce for news-genre purposes. He proceeded to ignore the complexities he himself had raised.

After obtaining visuals of a locksmith's shop, the crew drove to the divisional area where the rate of increase in apartment break-ins was said to be the highest. The first activity was to drive slowly along a typical middle-class street of detached houses taking film shots. The reporter then rendez-voused at a street corner with the crime-prevention officer from the local divisional station. Before the interview commenced the reporter said he was going to mention that apartment break-ins were up but house break-ins were down. The crime-prevention officer said that the reporter should not mention the decrease in house break-ins in his division or in the context of his interview clips. The reason for this request was that it would undercut his project of having summer students going door to door distributing pamphlets empha-sizing that there *is* a problem and that people should take preventive measures. An introductory letter included with the pamphlets began by stating, 'There has been an increase of breaking and entering into homes in this community, the majority of which take place during the daylight hours when *no one is home*.' One pamphlet was called 'Home Security' and outlined preventative measures to take, and the other one was called 'Operation Identification' and described a program for labelling valuable property. The crime-prevention constable also told the reporter that the distribution of pamphlets was actually a 'make-work' project for students. A government student-employment pro-gram had made the students available to the divisional station, and it was decided to use the students to deliver the pamphlet information packages. These packages were left over from the previous year and were about to be discarded when the students were made available and something had to be found for them to do.

In the interview the crime-prevention officer addressed questions on what people should do to prevent crime in their area; what are the best locking devices; the time at which burglaries are most likely to occur; and a description of the pamphlets being distributed by the students under his supervision. After the interview the crime-prevention officer located some students and had them go along a street near the divisional station, delivering the material door to door so the cameraman could film them. The crew also took shots of a nearby apartment building, focusing on an open garage door and open front door to give emphasis to the visualization of lax security.

While the film was being processed the reporter wrote his script and did his voice-overs. The anchorperson's 'roll-up' included the fact that apartment break-ins were up while house break-ins were down. In the script the actual percentage increase for that year compared to the same time period the previous year was given, but the decrease figure for house break-ins comparing the same periods was not given. In editing the film, the maps were included first, followed by a clip of the crime-prevention officer's description of what householders should do by way of security measures. The preferred–security-devices clip was dropped as irrelevant. The time–of–break-in clip was dropped because the officer had responded they were equally likely to occur at night as during the day. (Note the introductory letter with the pamphlets said 'the majority of which take place during the daylight hours when *no one is home*', but it was not clear whether the reporter had read this.) The officer's description of the pamphlet distribution was included, followed by visuals of the students delivering pamphlets door to door. The reporter told the film technician to include a shot of the delivery of the pamphlets to a citizen who was sitting on his front porch wearing huge bandages around his waist and chest and with his arm in a sling. The technician said this shot was too 'phoney' and edited in a shot with a pamphlet being put through a mailbox. However this shot ran longer than was practical at this point of the item and it did not fit well with the reporter's voice-over. The technician said, 'I guess we'd better go with the phoney shot,' and the reporter obliged without comment.

This story displays the nature of news ideology. It is ideological in the ways that it seeks not to know. It is also ideological in how it construes problems to impinge on public sentiments, and in favouring particular forms of, and greater degrees of, social control. Visualized increases in attacks on women, in theft, in robbery, in burglary, is news; the inability to sustain such visualization is not news. The way to know about these things is official figures, or official accounts of official figures, over brief time periods in recent memory, not sustained systematic analysis involving different data sources over long time periods and indicative of statistical trends. The way to know how to deal with things is also through the reactions of officials, especially the police and other front-line controllers who presume to know from years of experience of 'being there.'

This is not to criticize news discourse for not being more rigidly scientific in its approach. There is little room for scientific method and its attendant discourse in news, just as there is little room for journalistic method and its attendant discourse in science. News seeks to objectify moral sentiment, in the construction and protection of collective values. Science seeks to be objective in sentiment, in the construction and protection of analytic values. In this regard Geertz (1973: 230–1) is the authoritative source:

Science names the structure of situations in such a way that the attitude contained toward them is one of disinterestedness. Its style is restrained, spare, resolutely analytic: by shunning the semantic devices that most effectively formulate moral sentiment, it seeks to maximize intellectual clarity. But ideology names the structure of situations in such a way that the attitude contained toward them is one of commitment. Its style is ornate, vivid, deliberately suggestive: by objectifying moral sentiment through the same devices that science shuns, it seeks to motivate action. Both are concerned with the definition of a problematic situation and are responses to a felt lack of needed information. But the information needed is quite different, even in cases where the situation is the same. An ideologist is no more a poor social scientist than a social scientist is a poor ideologist. The two are – or at least they ought to be – in quite different lines of work, lines so different that little is gained and much obscured by measuring the activities of one against the aims of the other.

Where science is the diagnostic, the critical, dimension of culture, ideology is the justificatory, the apologetic one – it refers 'to that part of culture which is actively concerned with the establishment and defense of patterns of belief and value' [citing Fallers (1961)]. That there is a natural tendency for the two to clash, particularly when they are directed to the interpretation of the same range of situations, is thus clear; but that the clash is inevitable and that the findings of (social) science necessarily will undermine the validity of the beliefs and values that ideology has chosen to defend and propagate seem most dubious assumptions. An attitude at once critical and apologetic toward the same situation is no intrinsic contradiction in terms (however often it may in fact turn out to be an empirical one) but a sign of a certain level of intellectual sophistication.

DIRECT OBSERVATION

Direct observation is a method that reporters employed regularly, but largely in contexts that were highly structured for them by the source organization. They were allowed to observe public hearings, meetings, and news conferences at which they could take quotations from sources regarding an activity that was located in a different social space. In some of these contexts, such as legislative sessions, inquests, and trials, they were allowed to be witnesses to the hearing only and not ask questions themselves in the formal session. In other contexts, such as the scheduled news conference, they were able to ask questions about matters that did not arise in the formal session. In the formal news conference, as well as in the less formal 'scrum' of journalists chasing after a source outside of a formal setting, the journalist's observations were typically a matter of listening to other journalists asking questions and then taking down the source's answer for his own uses.

There are two important features of these contexts for direct observation. First, the general purpose and use of the material from sources was usually the same as that derived from direct interviews with the source. The reporter listened to the account for key information and/or a quotable quote; if it was not forthcoming in the formal session he tried to interview the source separately, framing his question to derive what he expected to hear, given the occasion. Occasionally the reporter added 'colour' in the form of describing the emotions of the participants. For example, in reporting on a sentencing hearing in court the reporter sometimes included a description of the judge's tone as he admonished the offender, and whether the offender showed signs of remorse. This information was aimed at providing a sense of what it was like in the hearing (tertiary understanding) but usually only as a supplement to the main purpose of saying what the judge said about the facts of the case and how they were to be construed in justifying sentence.

Second, direct observation was nearly always limited to what transpired in the formal setting of the hearing. While it is well known to reporters and other informed citizens that the essential transactions in defining deviance and negotiating control remedies are usually conducted in back-region settings – such as plea-negotiation discussions among lawyers, Crown attorneys, police, and occasionally judges, to settle criminal cases (Ericson and Baranek, 1982) – these settings were rarely open to the direct observation of reporters. Reporters were expected to only set their eyes on the forum and decorum of the public setting (e.g., the courtroom), listening to accounts of matters that had already been settled in other places by other means.

In court or legislature coverage what was observed in the session other than conversation was often recorded and reported; however, it tended to be for tertiary understanding and/or for adding a touch of humour. Most of what was recorded was the highly structured and controlled discourse which characterizes what can be said in formal public hearings. Left unsaid was how this discourse had been in turn negotiated in low-visibility conditions, defined and accounted for in advance of the hearing (cf Atkinson, 1979; Gusfield, 1981). In short, the reporter was left to provide an officially structured account of what had transpired elsewhere and what had already been accounted for.

Other than in this very limited context and respect, the eye-witness account is exceptional. As Hall et al (1978: 68) remark, 'what is most striking about crime news is that it very rarely involves a first-hand account of the crime itself, unlike the ''eye-witness'' report from the battlefront of the war correspondent. Crime stories are almost wholly produced from the definitions and perspectives of the institutional primary definers.' It is the occupational and personal experience of those involved that are relied upon to give authority to what appears to be the case. Moreover, even if he witnesses an act of deviance or has evidence believed to be relevant to the investigation of deviance, the reporter is advised to report it to the appropriate policing authority and await their confirmation and designation before reporting it in the news outlet (Roshco, 1975: 41; Fishman, 1980).

There were, however, a few occasions on which reporters made an effort to undertake direct observation to obtain information not available otherwise. This effort was sometimes directed at the discovery of deviance: for example, 'staking out' a bank in the hope a robbery would be committed there, or the outside of buildings believed to be centres for illegal gambling and prostitution. As with police stake-outs for the same purpose, this activity involves a lot of time with a high risk that nothing will happen, as was the case in the few instances we learned about. Another effort at direct observation was made by a reporter who tried to wander about a hospital ward where a series of deaths had occurred under suspicious circumstances, to learn if there had been a transfer of nurses on the ward. The reporter said he was removed from the premises before he had an opportunity to learn from his experiential method. We observed reporters making the case that in order to do a story properly they required at least a brief observation of the organization they were asked to talk about. For example, a reporter doing a story on prison conditions told his editor he had never been inside a prison and wanted a day visit to one prior to completing his story. Similarly, a reporter doing a story on a planned halfway house for prisoners wanted to visit one that was already in operation. Both of these requests were refused by superiors.

DOCUMENTS

Reporters generally shied away from documents, especially if they could obtain all they needed to know from sources' verbal accounts. This reluctance was based partly in the fact that using a document alone to write a story entails interpretive work that can prove troublesome, especially if the reporter does not have specialist or recipe knowledge pertaining to the organizational activity discussed in the document. It is also based on the fact that factuality for the purposes of news discourse is grounded in having a source person say it is so or not so, often regardless of whether documents or other ways of knowing would lead one to believe otherwise.

We witnessed occasions on which a reporter acquired a document, but said he found it too difficult to understand and went to a source to obtain quotations which summed up the matter. Even if the reporter did obtain documents and seemed to understand them, he often checked with sources and quoted them in confirmation of the interpretation. This was done routinely in instances where the interpretation of a particular law was concerned. Even if the reporter bothered to obtain a copy of the relevant act and section, he would call a legally trained official in the government office concerned with its enforcement for an interpretation.

Most often the reporter did not bother to obtain relevant documents, even when they were available without too much effort. For example, at a news conference involving university-based researchers announcing the results of a preliminary study into environmental pollution in a local area, the research report itself was available to the reporters present to consult or photocopy without charge. Of the twenty or so reporters present only one took the trouble to photocopy selected pages of the report, and he did not cite directly from these but rather from interviews with the sources after the formal news conference had terminated.

A reporter attended a news conference called by Rastafarians to complain that there was a secret police document, sent to Canadian Immigration officials, warning them about delegates attempting to enter Canada for an international conference of Rastafarians. The press release for the news conference read in part, 'Because of the distinctive stereotyping of Rastafarians, we fear that efforts will be made to prevent these delegates from entering Canada at their point of entry ... It has come to our attention that [a] certain interdepartmental memo has been circulated to justify our fear. The memo's instructions have a clear attempt to stop the international delegates from entering the country.' The news conference focused on the memo as yet another sign of police harassment of Rastafarians, and there was an allegation that particular suspects were named in the memo, and the contention that the Toronto police, RCMP, and Canadian immigration authorities were conspiring to 'scuttle' the Rastafarian conference. The reporter asked repeatedly for a copy of the memo, but the Rastafarians responded only by insisting that they had seen it and that it had originated in the Toronto Police Intelligence Bureau.

The reporter decided to counterpoint the Rastafarians' account by arranging an interview with the deputy chief of police. On the way to the interview the reporter and cameraman speculated that the deputy chief would say there was no memo. At the deputy chief's office, the reporter initially asked him off camera what 'he has' on the matter. The deputy chief said immediately that the police did have a memo on the conference that asked police and immigration authorities to exercise 'caution' with the Rastafarians, with 'caution' meaning to look out for drugs and weapons. The reporter asked him to repeat that statement on camera, and he did so. Off camera, the reporter asked the deputy chief for the memo. The deputy chief said he would have to call the Intelligence Bureau for it, and he did so in the reporter's presence. On the telephone, he asked for a specific person, then told the reporter that this person was not in and hung up. The deputy chief said the reporter could check back later to obtain the memo. He suggested that the reporter could go and see someone in the Intelligence Bureau about the memo. On camera, the deputy chief said it was not surprising there was a memo on this conference since it is a police practice to circulate memos on international conferences generally. He referred to an International Monetary Fund conference scheduled for Toronto later in the year as an example of another conference for which a memo would exist. Off camera, the reporter asked if the memo named a particular person or persons as suspect, and the deputy chief replied he doubted that it did.

It would not have required much effort by the reporter to return to police headquarters to pick the document up since that building was only a few blocks away from the newsroom. Nevertheless, the reporter did not make any further effort to obtain it, nor did he contact the officer in the Intelligence Bureau as suggested by the deputy chief. As he had with the Rastafarians, he was content to accept the deputy chief's accounts of what appeared to be the case.

This story points to an important feature of news methodology and the nature of evidence deemed necessary to serve journalistic standards of objectivity and truth. Obtaining the memo itself would have allowed the reporter to judge whose account was closer to the actual nature of the memo, and whether the Rastafarians' vision of police deviance or the police version of Rastafarian deviance was indicated therein.

The researcher asked the reporter in retrospect why he did not obtain the memo. Initially he said he was concerned to meet the 6:00 p.m. deadline. One can infer that he was concerned that if he waited over the afternoon for the memo, the police might not produce it in the end, or they might produce it too late for incorporation into his story. The researcher asked the reporter whether he would have obtained the memo if he had been given a longer time to produce the story. He said he would have, and again attributed not bothering to obtain it to the constraint of making the deadline for the show that evening. He then added that another factor in not obtaining the memo was his evaluation that the story was not particularly significant. As Epstein (1974: 265) observes, the lack of time and other resources itself feeds into news doctrines of neutrality, since they prevent reporters from pursuing other ways of knowing the facts of the matter. Resource decisions, made at the corporate level well beyond the newsroom, have the effect on reporters of 'not encouraging them – if only by not making sufficient resources available – to attempt to resolve controversial issues in favor of one side or another by conducting their own investigations' (ibid).

In a retrospective interview the reporter commented that for his own standards of balance, neutrality, and objectivity, it did not matter if he saw the memo. He stressed that what was important was the fact that he had accounts from the two sides involved in the dispute. We might add that he probably did not bother to contact the Intelligence Bureau source suggested by the deputy chief because he represented less authority than the deputy chief. Close to the pinnacle of the police bureaucracy, the deputy chief was the most accountable person available to give an account of the matter.

What the reporter did not say was that obtaining the document would have complicated matters greatly. It would have compelled him to make judgments that might well have led him to violate journalistic standards of balance, neutrality, and objectivity. It may well have forced him to favour one side over the other, thereby loosing his sense of balance. In this sense the story might have fallen apart, since the controversy might have dissipated or even been resolved.

> This model of 'pro and con' reporting is perfectly consistent with the usual notion of objectivity – if objectivity is defined, as it is by most of the correspondents interviewed, as 'telling both sides of a story.' It can, however, seriously conflict with the value that journalists place on investigative reporting, the purpose of which is 'getting to the bottom' of an issue or 'finding the truth,' as correspondents put it. Since a correspondent is required to present contrasting points of view, even if he finds the views of one side to be valid and those of the other side to be false and misleading (in the Fairness Doctrine, it will be recalled, truth is no defense), any attempt to resolve a controversial issue and find 'the truth' can become self-defeating. (ibid: 67–8)

The reporter was assured by both parties in the dispute that a memo existed, although he did not know it otherwise. He was given varying, and on some points discrepant, accounts of what the memo contained, but saw his role as conveying these versions rather than enlightening the viewer with the document itself. This approach in turn allowed for conflicting visualizations of the intentions behind the memo, reinforcing the stereotypes of a 'minority versus authority' binary opposition that had inspired attention to the matter in the first place.

Even if they are required to report on a report or document released by an organization, reporters tend not to read it. They prefer to infer what it is about from source-prepared news-release reports about the official report and/or interviews with sources concerned. A reporter talked to a researcher about a story he had done on an official-inquiry report into a government institution. He said that officials were upset at his story and were contemplating a legal suit. The researcher asked the reporter if he had a copy of the official-inquiry report and the reporter said no, but that he 'knew' what was in the report. A legal suit was eventually launched against the reporter and this organization, and settled out of court in favour of the plaintiff.

An exception indicating the reporter's feelings of trepidation towards documents was occasioned when an official-inquiry report was leaked to one news outlet in advance of its official public release date. A reporter was told by her editor to do a story on the basis of the report document alone. He did not want her to call anyone to clarify issues or obtain reactions because he did not want it known that they had an advance copy of the official inquiry report in case other news-media outlets were tipped off. The reporter expressed the problems in doing this to the researcher, saying she was left to rely on her own files on the matter to interpret the report. In retrospect she felt that her interpretive errors had been minor, although she did receive a call from one of the persons cited in the story who pointed out inaccuracies and complained about word usage.

Some types of documents were sought and used for particular purposes. Reporters did sometimes obtain documents readily available to use as background information or to help them understand a case better, even if they did not use them directly in a story. Especially in stories that were being developed over time, the reporter's file on the matter sometimes contained relevant official documents and reports. For example, a reporter following a case through the courts, involving allegation of conflict of interest against a politician, had a file which contained the following: copies of past stories he had filed on the case; a story clipping from another local newspaper; a copy of the Municipal Conflict of Interest Act; an affidavit by a person who took minutes at two meetings involved in the case; a notice of motion; a report of the municipality residential-development task force (the allegations concerned the politician's misuse of office to gain from real estate speculation); minutes of a special council meeting of the municipality; an affidavit from an applicant in the case; minutes of a general committee-of-council meeting chaired by the politican concerned; and, minutes of one other council meeting.

Even if the reporter did not have his own file of documents on a matter, he could sometimes turn to and rely upon the documents of sources. For example, on the political beats political-party researchers regularly supplied their own research materials or packages knowing that a reporter would be more encouraged to give coverage if he did not have to do the 'digging' himself. Alternatively, sources could discourage a reporter by telling him to read a report or consult other documents, knowing that the time and news-discourse constraints on the reporter would mean that he would simply drop it if he could not get the source to say it in summary for him.

Reporters also turned to documents when they had missed, or did not want to take the time to attend, lengthy public hearings or discussions. Sometimes when a court hearing was missed, the court judgment was cited, often in connection with a conversation with the Crown attorney. In a big court case, transcripts were purchased for purposes of accuracy and background consultation. The task was even easier and less expensive in parliament, where *Hansard* was consulted regarding discussions that had been missed.

Relying upon bureaucratic documents which have settled what a matter is does not pose great interpretative difficulties to the extent they can be treated as factual. In the same way that direct observation of public hearings, or direct public utterances by sources in interview, state official versions orally, official written documents, formulated for public consumption, can be cited and treated as stating the facts of the case.

> Bureaucracies are established and maintained precisely for the purpose of constituting the socially appropriate circumstances under which a variety of public acts can be accomplished successfully ... It is not hard to see, then, why reporters are inclined to believe what they read in performative documents. How could things be other than what these documents say they are? A conditional plea agreement cannot incorrectly describe a plea bargain because it *is* the plea bargain. As long as it is a valid document, what it says is what it has to be. Journalists love performative documents because these are the hardest facts they can get their hands on. (Fishman, 1980: 97–9)

Reporters did occasionally seek documents to substantiate what a source was saying to them. A spokesperson for an organization interested in establishing voluntary citizens' patrols of city streets kept referring to the large number of letters of support the organization had received from citizens. Some reporters asked to see the letters, but they were not forthcoming. A reporter, interviewing union members about their allegations of deviance against the head of their local, asked them for a copy of a cheque they mentioned in relation to a questionable payment. He said, 'Look, I can't write about things I can't prove' as a way of encouraging them to obtain documentary evidence on this and other allegations they were making. Note, however, that these instances involving requests for documents to support allegations of deviance were in relation to unofficial and marginal sources.

In a major 'investigative' piece, documents were also searched in the hope of discovering deviance, as was done in a major way in relation to a continuing story, which we observed in part. Reporters used an array of different techniques regarding a range of different source organizations to obtain documents relevant to their investigation. Their main approach was to employ 'matching' techniques through audits of documents (cf Marx, 1984) in the hope of uncovering irregularities in the sales practices of the organization under scrutiny. For example, relevant documents were obtained from an acquaintance of a reporter in exchange for some information he wanted; from a disaffected employee of the organization under scrutiny; from a fellow reporter who had had dealings with the organization under scrutiny; from a representative of an organization whose constituency was in opposition to the organization under scrutiny; from the research staff of a political party; and, from systematic searches of publicly available legal documents pertaining to the transactions of the organization under scrutiny.

We observed only one occasion on which a reporter wished to undertake a systematic survey of normally confidential official documents in order to establish trends and characteristics of a phenomenon. In this instance, in the context of a moral panic about attacks on women, the reporter asked the police for permission to examine the official occurrence reports on rape incidents. She arranged to meet the chief of police, and upon entering his office handed him a letter of request signed by her editor. She said she was interested in discovering whether rapes were more violent in the current year compared to previous years. The chief said he could not give her access to these files because the victims gave this information in confidence. He mentioned that a university researcher was doing a government-sponsored study on rape and some police officers from the force had been seconded to go through the police files to retrieve 'relevant' information. He suggested the reporter could talk to this researcher, or to members of the Criminal Investigation Bureau, or to a detective who was the liaison officer to the Rape Crisis Centre, or to representatives of the Rape Crisis Centre. The reporter then asked if she could go through past 'major occurrence report' news releases sent by the police force to news outlets. The chief said that was fine with him but he did not think the reporter would be able to judge whether rapes were more violent now on the basis of a scrutiny of these documents. Apparently sensitive to news discourse, the chief advised the reporter to obtain interview accounts from researcher, police, and Rape Crisis Centre spokespersons on their perceptions of changes in the 'quality' of rape occurrences. The reporter eventually interviewed the chief and a policewoman for their perceptions on the matter. She later scrutinized some major occurrence-report news releases, but to no avail. From this exercise the reporter learned that 'performative documents' (Fishman, 1980) made for the purpose of police performance are not the same as those available for the performance of the news media.

OTHER REPORTERS

We have seen already how the generation of story ideas in the assignment process depended on scrutiny of the stories of other news outlets. In the reporting process other reporters were used for ideas, sources, information, and story construction.

Within the same news organization reporters assisted one another whether or not credit would be given for the assistance. Assistance was based on time and space considerations. When a reporter working on a story wanted to include a politician's reponse to the matter, he would sometimes ask a reporter based on the political beat to obtain an appropriate quotation for him to incorporate into his story. Assistance was also based on knowledge of what others were working on, and if something of relevance came up it was passed on to the reporter concerned. A reporter working on the court beat told a general reporter doing a story on a politician that certain charges against the politician had been withdrawn. Reporters working in small teams on an investigation were expected to share, but in addition other reporters in the newsroom who discovered relevant materials, sources, or ideas passed them on to the team. While reporters talked about the professional ideal of being autonomous individuals, they sometimes exhibited signs of co-operative effort and teamwork which recognized the collective predicament of temporal, spatial, and material limits as well as special requests from editors.

Special knowledge and skills held by one reporter were shared with others. A generalist reporter who had a law degree regularly consulted with other reporters who did not, including those reporters on the court and legal beats who were not legally qualified. A reporter was known for his ability to come up with a good lead quickly and he was consulted by colleagues who were having difficulty in formulating a lead. This reporter was referred to as a 'lead doctor,' who could 'write his way to the front' of the newspaper on the basis of his leads and writing style over and above the other merits of the story. In a team of four reporters working on the same continuing story, this reporter did the writing of a story which was nevertheless published with the bylines of all four reporters. He remarked that he was good at writing to deadlines, and the labour was divided willingly with his particular skills in mind.

In television, co-operation was mainly brought to the fore in the coverage of major events. It also arose when one reporter could obtain a clip for another because it was more convenient for him to do so. Film and video crews also co-operated in going out on their own to take visuals that would fit into a reporter's story, when the reporter and his own crew were otherwise engaged. However, television reporters generally acted much more as individualists and often refused to co-operate with colleagues within their own newsroom. Reporters had a conception of a story being their exclusive property because it was their beat, their specialization, or they had worked on it on previous dates. There were continuing property disputes on each of these grounds, often accompanied by hostile verbal exchanges in the newsroom and even formal union grievances against one another. In one instance, when a reporter was assigned a story related to continuing stories a colleague had been working on, the colleague even refused to give him the telephone number of a well-known source who had been cited frequently on previous occasions. A reporter complained that pages had been torn out of his source contact book, and another person in the newsroom had had his contact book stolen. He said this usually happened when someone was leaving the organization, but on this occasion no one was known to be leaving.

There were regular exchanges with reporters from other news organizations. Beat reporters in particular developed exchange relations regarding story ideas, sources, and information needed for a story, especially in circumstances where it would enhance their respective coverage in face of limited resources on the beat. In relations of this type reporters exchanged ideas and information they would not necessarily pass on to certain reporters in their own newsroom. A beat reporter was part of another organization – the culture of his peers on the beat – and what that organization could provide in the way of support and direct assistance forged relations of reciprocity which did not exist between the reporter and his newsroom colleagues. As Tuchman (1978: 74) observes, 'If reporters were merely bureaucratic employees operating according to the rules and needs of their organization, they might be expected to hoard information from reporters working for competing media and share with all reporters from their own company. Instead, exercising their autonomy, they may share with competitors and hoard information from other bureaus within their own organization. Identification of information as either bureau or personal property is determined by the reporter's need to maintain control of his or her work.'

In obtaining some information from a reporter for another news outlet, a newspaper reporter remarked that exchanges are easier the more distant the two news organizations are in competitive terms. The reporter said that, for example, it was much easier to exchange with someone from a wire service than with someone from the local newspaper seen as the closest competitor. Another reporter, working on a beat for the same newspaper, had regular exchanges with the beat reporters from a newspaper that was seen as a lesser competitor; however, there were virtually no exchanges with the beat reporters from the other newspaper that was seen as *the* competition in the local news-media market.

What was requested from reporters in other news organizations included just about everything except a reporter's final copy. Most common were requests for background information or primary facts which the reporter had missed or did not wish to use his time pursuing. This information was usually given because, as one reporter said, it was not material which required a lot of time or effort to obtain, and it was a means of reducing work and of establishing a relationship. We observed reporters turning over all their notes to reporters for other outlets so they could 'catch up' with the story.

Specific requests were often met with a counter offer in reciprocity, especially if the reporters involved did not have an ongoing relationship where meeting a request now would guarantee a favour later. Two reporters for news organizations in different cities were covering government hearings regarding a particular social problem. During a discussion about a key source, one reporter told the second he had a quote from this source which the second had missed while he was out of the room. The second reporter copied this quote down with permission. Later they discussed another source interviewed by the second reporter. At one point the first reporter said, 'O.K., I gave you a quote you owe me one,' and the first reporter reciprocated by reading his notes and saying that he was unable to give an exact quote but would give what he thought were the main points derived from the interview.

Tit-for-tat deals were usually made *sub rosa*, although occasionally the signs of reciprocity were made more visible. A television reporter gave a newspaper a picture of a source who was receiving prominent play in the newspaper, on the understanding that the newspaper would reciprocate in future. A few days later the newspaper did reciprocate, offering a reporter from the television station a document of relevance to one of their stories. In turn the reporter asked a cameraman to obtain an exterior shot of the newspaper building so that he could make visible the source of the document.

The reporter typically entered into an exchange of information to obtain more and better information, in less time, than would be required otherwise. However, there were occasions on which a reporter looked for a benefit that was more organizational than personal and more idealistic than pragmatic. A reporter was working on a continuing story for a considerable time, with an understanding from his superiors that the goal was to pry information from the source organizations concerned, and in turn to force greater public accountability in relation to the matter under investigation by the authorities. While working on a particular story related to this matter, he received a call from a reporter who worked for a newspaper in another city that he himself used to work for. He told the researcher that he and this reporter had traded information before about the matter under investigation, taking each other's leads and checking them further on an independent basis. On this occasion he gave this reporter a possible angle of significance to pursue further, and also the name of a source in his city whom he could interview in relation to this angle. In retrospect, the reporter said to the researcher that he was willing to co-operate in this way because the more newspapers that printed the type of story he was doing the more the situation was being kept alive and therefore the greater the likelihood of a public inquiry. He said the ultimate goal of his own news organization was a public inquiry. In turn this would provide a continuing supply of material to report on, obtainable by more predictable and routine methods than was possible without one.

Information mediated by other reporters was also gleaned from overhearing and overseeing them interview a source. Reporters at news conferences, or who followed 'the pack' of their colleagues into a 'scrum' with a source, simply let their colleagues do all the questioning while they themselves took notes or tape recordings and/or had their crews take visual and sound recordings.

All means of relying upon other journalists contributed to pack journalism and had implications for similarity in coverage. One senior news executive attributed this to beat subcultures – involving both other reporters and sources – and attendant aspects of peer pressure. The pressure was said to come in various forms:

It will be everything from as explicit as [a reporter complaining another should not have reported something], to not sending a Christmas card, to not inviting them to a party, to essentially ostracize them from the group ... That's pack journalism. The worst thing of all is, number one, peer pressure not to publish stories like that, peer pressure to all publish the same story, like, 'What's to-day's big story, Joe?' And you'll notice that sometimes it's very strange that that day's lead by all the radio stations, or that day's lead perhaps by some of the television stations, or that day's lead by the print guys, all happens to be the same. And it's because, ... essentially there's a pack mentality, they all run the same story, they all run together. One guy comes up with an idea, and they all sort of like vultures hover around that guy to find out what the response is. There isn't necessarily a lot of individual and free thinking done by pack reporting. So, there are all sorts of pressures, by other journalists and by sources, to fall into line.

In contrast some reporters adopted a different line. Their concern was for editors sensitivity to what a reporter filed in comparison to the competition. Their sense of accountability to editors was in terms of their ability to account for why they did or did not cover what a competitor's reporter covered regarding angles, sources, and information. It was often believed to be better safe than sorry, thus the reporter followed the pack to the same sources for the same information pertaining to the same story. If a researcher was with a reporter following the pack and asked the reporter why the pack found the matter so newsworthy, a common response was that they all *had* to cover what one another were doing or they would be in trouble with their editors. This perception did seem to vary somewhat within a news organization according to who was the desk editor at the time, since some editors were seen as paying more attention to the competition than others. Nevertheless, 'pressure from the desk' was a common explanation for pack journalism among reporters.

While checking information with one another may have given reporters a sense of validation, it is arguable that it also limited their scope for discovery. And, as in the scientific research literature (Mulkay, 1979), inaccuracies are perpetuated because second-level reproducers of knowledge typically do not bother to check what their respected peers have said appears to be the case.

Reliance upon other reporters, as with reliance upon all other sources of information, could not be taken for granted. The reporter had to work at establishing the reliability of another reporter-as-source in the face of denials of his requests and the use of techniques to keep other information from him. The denials again depended on how the reporter-as-source viewed the importance of the information, what was on offer in exchange, and who was making the request for what purpose.

When in public settings with 'the pack,' reporters were well aware of the pack mentality and frequently took measures to circumvent it. The questions asked at a news conference or in a scrum can be used to provide general information or primary facts, but the reporter's own angle is kept secret by restricting questions pertinent to it to private interviews with the source. This technique is easier to use for a newspaper or radio reporter; the television reporter is more confined by needing to obtain a clip from the source within the trappings of the formal news conference or hearing. Newspaper reporters regularly took a source aside for a one-to-one interview, explicitly for the purpose of not tipping their hand to reporters from competing outlets. As one reporter expressed it, he did not see why his organization should have to 'subsidize' the 'research' of other news organizations by having him obtain answers to pertinent questions with other reporters as an audience.

We observed instances in which both newspaper and television reporters were in the process of conducting a one-to-one interview which they interrupted so as to terminate eavesdropping by lingering reporters from other organizations. Faced with a persistent reporter trying to duplicate the reporter's own efforts in building relations with a source and developing useful information, reporters sometimes went to the source to request exclusivity. Some even went to the point of taking control of a source's problem and literally taking him out of reach of reporters representing competing organizations.

Thus, a reporter decided to interview the husband of a rape victim who claimed that she was turned away from a public hospital where she sought a medical examination. The interview was being conducted at the scene of the alleged rape, when the reporter saw that a television crew from a competing station had arrived to do a stand-up across the road. The reporter completed the interview hastily and packed her source into her own crew car. The other station's reporter came up to the car and asked to speak to the source, but he said 'no comment' and the driver drove off. The reporter told the husband she would take him back to the newsroom to help him make calls to various authorities (Ministry of Health, College of Physicians and Surgeons, member of provincial parliament) to lodge complaints against the hospital. He agreed, but he wanted to use his own car. The reporter then 'invited' herself to accompany him in his car to the newsroom, later commenting to the researcher that this strategy was designed 'to keep him locked up,' that is, away from the reporters of other news outlets. In the newsroom, the source was filmed making calls to the authorities, while the editors and producers expressed excitement about this literal 'scoop.' The following day an editor noted that the station's coverage of the story was different and better than the competitors'; the angle of having the aggrieved man shown to be seeking redress from the authorities fit well with this newsroom's desire to be even more populist than their rival station.

Exclusivity was the operative consideration in deciding upon complete stealth. If a reporter had been the first to publish or broadcast a story that was then being pursued as a continuing matter by reporters from other news organizations, then the reporter was very reluctant to impart information that would allow the others to 'catch up.' We observed several instances in which requests by other reporters were denied in these circumstances. The reporter's view of a story as personal property was indicated when a reporter attending a conference of a professional association managed to obtain a ninety-minute interview session with the past president and incoming president of the association. Later in the day he was annoyed to learn that a news conference had been scheduled by a competing newspaper involving the same two sources. The reporter was annoyed because a reporter from the competing newspaper saw him with the two sources and asked what was happening, and he thought that this had led to the scheduling of the news conference, undercutting his exclusive. He emphasized that he had taken ninety minutes to obtain interview material that now would be repeated in the news conference, and had missed another important session at the conference in the belief that he would have an exclusive with these two sources.

The question of exclusivity always had to be understood and worked out in the circumstances. What one reporter cared about in the context of his own interests, editors' expectations, and organizational requirements, another reporter could care less about. What one reporter thought should be shared might be treated by another as personal property, for reasons that were evident only to the reporter treating it stealthily. In these circumstances the reasons were as unknown to us as researchers as they were to the reporter whose request was denied.

VISUALS FOR TELEVISION

Television reporters have special requirements in obtaining visuals. These constitute both constraining and enabling features of reporting peculiar to television.

Reporter-Cameraman Relations. The cameraman is a highly valued member of the television newsroom. This was symbolized by the fact that while he was formally under the direction of the reporter, he was paid substantially more than the reporter, sometimes double or more. Moreover, the reporter was very dependent on the cameraman to understand what the story was about so it could be visualized appropriately. 'While the presence on the screen of the television reporter gives the story journalistic credibility in the traditional sense, it is heavily reliant on the news judgment of the cameraman' (Schlesinger, 1978: 160–1).

The basis of the reporter-cameraman relationship was tacit understanding of requirements. The cameraman has to become part of the newsroom culture and learn the vocabulary of precedents of reporters, editors, and producers. He must learn the approach of each reporter and the subtle differences in the way each works. Over time a reporter develops a preference to working with a particular cameraman and vice versa. However, since reporter and crew assignments were done on the basis of situational availability rather than keeping a team together, it was not possible to expect a regular matching of those who felt that they worked well together.

Beyond tacit understandings and cues in the field, cameramen often offered specific advice and direct assistance. Advice was given freely on what shots to take, what clips or source quotations to use from shots taken, and what reporter voice-over phrasing might be appropriate for particular visuals. The cameraman also helped to encourage sources to co-operate generally, and to phrase particular notions when they stumbled or seemed unable to articulate in the manner expected.

As would be expected where aesthetic preferences are constantly being worked at rather than already worked out, reporter-cameramen relations were often marked with tension and conflict. Reporters carped about cameramen who took poor shots; packed up too early and therefore missed something of relevance; did not follow directions well; and failed to 'hustle' in the face of time limitations. In turn, cameramen were critical of reporters' judgments about the selection of sources; questioning of sources; overshooting, and otherwise obtaining too much information that risked missing the slot; and making stories where there were none in the opinion of the camerman. Some of these disputes were taken to the level of supervisors. Underlying the reporter's concern was the fact that he was dependent on the cameraman for a good public face, while the cameraman could remain invisible after completing his visualization work.

On Locations. One picture may not be equivalent to a thousand words, at least not in television news. However, television does have the ability to show as well as to tell. It can show the location of an event and can also picture what the people involved look like, thereby providing for the audience readings of their moral character. It provides a form of tertiary understanding not available to print except through still photographs: during our observations, efforts ranged from committing a crew for hours to obtain a visual of a suspect leaving court with a bag over his head, to hiring a helicopter so a crew could obtain an overview of a fire.

Television actuality shots are quite rare. Visuals rarely capture an actual event in the world, only talk of an event. Hence, most often the choice of a location is a matter of finding some place or someone that will stand for what is being talked about. In terms of physical locations, these were termed 'generic spots.' The release of a government report on domestic violence was represented by a reporter stand-up in front of the legislative building. A politician whose election campaign included disputing a highrise-building development was interviewed near the site of the development to represent this point of the campaign. When a place of a type could provide the sign, then the most convenient one would do: for a story about the contamination of a pharmaceutical product sold in drugstores, the handiest local drugstore was chosen for the visuals; for a story about lawyers' fees for real estate transactions, a street near the newsroom was selected for shots of houses with 'for sale' signs.

If official reports or other documents were being talked about, these were sometimes also shown to exist. These visuals focused on title pages or bold headings, as well as taking key words or phrases to print across the screen with the document shown above or in the background. As in showing events and people, this treatment did not provide documentation of the matter being addressed but only a sign that the document being talked about actually existed and appeared in a particular form.

Most television stories were built around interview clips with a few sources, 'the talking head.' While the key aspect of these clips was the person's words rather than the context in which they were said, as shown in the visuals, the context was often deemed by the reporter to be a relevant component of his visualization of how the source was to be represented. An important consideration for the reporter was how to represent the source's authority, in the context of the matter being reported and the other sources involved. The basic choice was whether talking-head visuals should be 'on the street,' or in the physical office which represented the source's official office. One executive producer encouraged 'on the street' accounts from ordinary folk, the vox pop. He circulated memos to reporters to this effect, including one that stressed the need generally of 'going to the street' rather than letting 'institutional mouthpieces get air time with no real people.' However, what was done in this respect depended on the particular story and the contexts in which sources were dealt with.

In stories of the basic point/counterpoint format, involving leading representatives of each of two organizations in dispute, the usual approach was to represent each in the authority of their physical office. An instance of this, in which complications arose, is illustrative. A representative of a citizens' organization trying to establish a halfway house for prisoners was also an executive of a large corporation, but did not want visuals to be taken in his corporate office because the matter did not pertain to that corporation. Similarly, the representative of a citizens' organization in opposition to the establishment of this halfway house did not wish to have his unrelated corporate office used for visuals. The reporter, wishing to represent both as men of significance, found alternative physical space to convey the authority of their offices visually. One person agreed to come to the television station for interview. He was interviewed sitting behind the desk of one of the station's senior executives, appearing as if it was his own. The other interview was done in the lobby of a quality hotel across the street from the source's corporate offices, with permission of the hotel. The lobby furniture was rearranged so that the source could be suitably visualized sitting in a stolid wingback chair, indicating that he too was talking from, and within, an authoritative office.

A reporter was assigned to do a story on the reaction of various ethnic groups to the revelation that RCMP security services had an 'ethnic list' of suspicious persons connected to various ethnic types. The reporter planned to do the story by filming the representatives of different ethnic groups 'on the street' to emphasize the 'voice of the people,' against what was portrayed as a possible sign of totalitarian practice of government. The first represent- ative agreed to a street interview. The reporter then proceeded to interview a doctor who said that in his practice he had many patients who complained of abuse by immigration and RCMP policing authorities. However, upon ar- riving at this doctor's office it was discovered to be in a poor part of town and the doctor himself did not look the part: he was in his late twenties or early thirties, and casually dressed without tie or jacket. The reporter decided that a street interview with this person would undercut his authority as a family physician speaking sympathetically about aggrieved patients. In spite of crew grumblings about having to set up their lights inside, the reporter insisted on representing the source in the authority of his office to add credence to his story. In contrast, the third source, a representative of a Polish group, was wearing a quality business suit. He refused an interview on the street in spite of the reporter's efforts to convince him. Instead he insisted on being shot behind his desk, flanked by flags of Poland, Canada, and Ontario that were placed there by him for the purpose of the interview. In this instance the source's desire to appear authoritative won out, and the reporter ended up, against her initial wish, with two of three sources 'off the street.'

It was a convention to shoot two sources with opposing views from opposite angles. On one occasion a reporter thought that the cameraman tacitly understood this procedure when he asked him to obtain a clip from each of two opposition-party leaders making statements outside the legislature. When he discovered that the cameraman had taken shots of both from the same angle he was most annoyed, stressing that it was simply 'common sense' to shoot from opposite angles.

When sources were not available to be filmed, or a crew was not available to film them, other means were devised. A common practice was to telephone a source and obtain a voice recording that could be used along with a still photograph of the source and/or a shot of the reporter in the newsroom making the call. This was done in particular when a source was some distance from Toronto and the newsroom did not want to go to the expense of obtaining something that they knew could be captured in essence through a voice clip. In this circumstance something had to be shown with the voice clip, and if a still photograph of the source was lacking, that something was usually the reporter shown to be doing his job. While this representation was useless in terms of its relation to the source's statement, it was at least useful in showing the authority of the reporter's office.

Staging. The imperative of television journalists to represent visually people doing things related to the story often poses difficulties. Crews cannot always be on time at the place where the events are occurring, and even if they are they often face technical difficulties in obtaining shots with proper lighting, sound, and focus. When such difficulties arise the solution is to have sources stage their activities, or in the words of the vocabulary of precedents, do a 'fake.' Indeed, the resource limitations and technical requirements of television news are so well known to sources that they usually take elaborate measures to script the event in advance and stage everything so that television crews can obtain their clips expeditiously. In this activity Goffman's dramaturgical model of social life is acted out in considerable detail.

When the requirement is talk about events, and 'talking heads' for television visuals, the news conference is a standard format. Well-prepared and -groomed organizational representatives represent what is organizationally in order. After the basic presentation at a news conference, sources are asked by a television journalist to repeat a part of their performance for the purposes of a television clip. This approach saves film and editing time, since shooting the entire presentation expends a lot of film and requires a lot of sorting out back in the film-editing room.

The two leaders of the Guardian Angels citizen-patrol organization, based in New York City, came to Toronto on several occasions to stage news events that might help them with their cause. They chose significant locations – such as the city-hall square, the main indoor shopping precinct, and a space in a park where a woman had been sexually assaulted – to conduct interviews and give displays of self-defence techniques. On these occasions television journalists co-operated in the staging of each event by helping with locations, props, and suggestions for the enactment of representative action such as self-defence–technique displays.

Similar staging techniques were employed by citizens' groups with other causes. Groups in opposition to nuclear weapons held several marches and demonstrations, engaging in acts guaranteed to result in arrest by police, and equally guaranteed to be visually represented as the dominant frame of television-news items. At one demonstration television reporters from two different outlets discussed the various staging techniques being employed. They were very negative about the sources' representations, but nevertheless felt 'forced' to treat them as a central aspect of how they visualized the deviance. They pointed out that the source organization selected a key location (a plant involved in weapons manufacture); a good day in summer when 'news' was likely to be 'slow' because key source bureaucracies were in recess; and, sent a release, along with promises via telephone calls, that there would be 'violence' of some sort. One television station had three crews on location. The source organization arranged for five people to jump over a fence to throw red paint, signifying blood, on a wall. They were stopped and arrested for trespass or public mischief. Meanwhile two women were able to paint with stencils six green doves on a wall before they were arrested for public mischief. A spokesperson for the organization, wearing a shirt displaying an anti-nuclear statement, was asked by a reporter why these acts were necessary. The source replied that it was a way of educating the public, through the media, about the role of Toronto-based firms in the manufacture of nuclear weapons. The reporter asked what acts of civil disobedience had to do with educating the public and was told that the organization wanted to remind employees of these firms, as well as the general public, that people have strong feelings about disarmament. The source organization had also come equipped with a variety of props – including banners (e.g., 'Ban the Bomb') and a coffin – all of which were focused on by cameramen, along with shots of the paint on the wall and the persons responsible being arrested. The reporters recognized that they were simply following the script of their source, and one remarked while editing that this item was a prime example of creating the news.

Virtually all sources work to create appearances for visuals in some way. Persons are selected who photograph and speak well. Background materials are also attended to, for example, piling papers and documents on the office desk to sustain the dominant cultural impression that good people work hard. If television crews are to be allowed inside private space to visualize what goes on there, it is in the terms of public culture.

Reporters did on occasion object to a source's staging techniques or props and were sometimes able to get rid of them. Ultimately it was for the reporter to decide what was an appropriate sign, and whether it was useful or in good taste. A reporter doing a story on a citizens' group campaigning against anti-Semitism included an interview with a source who had a collection of artifacts that were anti-Jewish, such as bumper-stickers, pamphlets, and a Nazi flag. The source offered to hold the Nazi flag as she was being filmed, but the reporter regarded this as out of place and rejected it.

Reporters sometimes moved into the director's seat and used equally elaborate techniques of perfecting the 'fake.' A reporter doing a story on the introduction of a major foot-patrol–beat system for police arranged through the public-relations office of the police to meet two officers on patrol. The location selected was the 'Yonge Street strip,' a segment of a street widely visualized in the city as a centre of vice and disorderliness. One police officer was wired up with a tape recorder, and two were followed down the street by the reporter, cameraman, and researcher. Shots were taken of the officers going into stores, talking to people on the street, interviewing people in an automobile accident, and writing a traffic ticket.

Efforts to film events occurring 'naturally' sometimes ran into difficulty so that staging was necessary. Television crews waited in the mayor's office for the arrival of two people who represented an organization wanting to meet the mayor's executive assistant about a social problem. When the two people arrived and entered the office of the secretary to the executive assistant, they and the television crews 'broke up' laughing at the effort to appear 'natural' in face of a pack of reporters and cameramen. After everyone had regained composure, one television reporter asked the two people to go out of the office and enter again. A proper representation of the event was made on this 'retake.'

Reporters sometimes set out to recreate what had occurred previously without always stating to the audience that it was a recreation. The RCMP had sent some illegal drugs to an incinerator, but part of the shipment was lost. A reporter decided to visualize the incineration process on film. At the incineration plant, she had visuals taken of the fire itself, a 'pretend' run of a crane picking up the garbage and dropping it into the incinerator, the temperature gauge, and a conveyor belt carrying indestructable materials left behind after the ashes were washed away. These visuals, visualizing the process, were then used by the reporter in juxtaposition with a description of what was believed to have taken place weeks before, when the drugs went missing. The result was a blend of illusion and accounts of reality, as is evident in the following script of the story.

Anchorperson roll-up: The RCMP had it ... but it slipped out of their hands. In the process of destroying the largest-ever cache of drugs seized in Canada ... one million dollars' worth went missing. The mounties had wanted to get rid of the stuff but not in the way it disappeared. It has been recovered ... but police are still trying to figure out how it got lost. [Names reporter] has more.

Reporter: They tried to burn it away ... faced with the problem of disposing 6 tonnes of methagaeline ... a heroin substitute ... [fire burning in furnace]. RCMP took it to the Metro Toronto incinerating plant [Sign: Metro Inc. plant]. On that day in June, an RCMP truck arrived with its precious cargo ... [truck dumping garbage] it came and went 4 times with 200 million dollars worth of drugs, packed in Sunlight detergent boxes ... [Sunlight detergent box].

While 3 RCMP officers supervised ... a crane picked up the drugs with the other garbage and dropped it into the hopper leading to the incinerator. But inside the incinerator ... [a Metro works official] explains, the drug made it too hot [crane and hopper travelling and dropping].
[Metro works official talking head]

Reporter: When the temperature went up to a critical point they shut down the incinerator ... One truck load was turned away and the RCMP were informed the drug clogged the incinerator. Somehow one box was neither burned away nor returned to the RCMP [temperature gauge, followed by shot of truck coming down ramp].

The RCMP didn't even know 1 million dollars' worth of drugs was missing ... that is until Metro Toronto police stopped a car 3 weeks later and found hidden in a suitcase 35 pounds of meth ... 3 people were subsequently charged for possession of drugs and one of them is an employee of the incinerating plant ... [stand-up]

Inspector [name] and his staff were the ones who announced the huge heist of meth ... last October ... [Super: stock film showing RCMP] it was a dramatic seizure of drugs at Collingwood airport ... [still graphic: police firing guns with an airplane in the background].

Even though the missing box went unnoticed for 3 weeks ... [the inspector] says he's sure there isn't any more on the streets ... [box]

RCMP Inspector: I would be very surprised if there's another box missing ... [etc.] [talking head]

Reporter: The RCMP has used this plant three times ... [Sign: Metro Inc. Plant] workers don't have special security clearances ... the RCMP assumes full responsibility [truck going down ramp]

RCMP Inspector: Our procedure ... [etc.] completely recalculated to make sure they get into the fire box. [talking head]

Reporter: The remaining drugs will be neutralized by a chemical process [pick up drug in box].

This story used visuals of the incineration process – including 'fakes' – to represent what happens in talking about what happened. The audience was offered the illusion of watching the actual dumping of the drugs, the detergent box used, etc., at the time. There was no mention that this was a reconstruction of what *may* have happened. Similarly, the artist's graphic of the original seizure of the drugs ten months before was simply his visualization of what happened at that time. Apart from the talking heads, all the visuals were simply visualizations of how events might have appeared, and of how things might have looked in the improbable event a 'live-eye' television crew had been there at the time. Faced with impossibility of being 'everywhere,' television news is left to visualize things as if they are.

Stocks. Time and space considerations influenced decisions about whether to use stocks (old visuals) from previous stories to represent something. A reporter faced with a distant event, an event that had already occurred, an event occurring in a physical space he could not penetrate, and/or an encroaching deadline, often turned to the stocks for something to add vision to his story. A considerable amount of 'research' in the television newsroom consisted of searches for appropriate stocks, and special 'researchers' were employed to assist reporters in this regard.

The choice of stocks also involved 'fake' elements. A reporter doing a story on an Ontario government report concerning domestic violence, including police response to it, had difficulty finding appropriate shots of police attending a domestic call. He and an editor searched for and eventually found stock footage from a story done five months earlier, involving the domestic-response team for the city of Detroit, Michigan. This footage visualized police officers talking with a woman, and was used with a voice-over stating, 'The report says wife battering must be treated as a crime ... that the onus for laying charges in such cases should be with the police.' Of course the reporter's intention was not to lie with these shots of police – not to indicate that Detroit police should be seen to be helping Ontario women – but that the police institution should be doing more of what was represented in these pictures.

The only real concern in using this form of representation was that it not be seen through as an obvious fake. Thus, there was concern that repeated use of the same stock clip, especially to represent aspects of different stories rather than the same continuing story, would look bad. Moreover the stock clips usually had to look as if they appeared to have been taken at the time of the shots actually taken on the day. A reporter was preparing a story about an accused person, released after a preliminary hearing, who had decided to sue various officials for malicious prosecution and negligence. The reporter relied on stocks of the attorney general's office building to use with a voice-over stating this office was named in the suit. This story was in August, but the stock shot of the building showed it to be winter. The reporter had a close-up 'freeze' of the building edited to get rid of the snow in the wider shot. The reporter relied on stocks of police officers on motorbikes to use with a voice-over stating the chief of police and investigating officers were also named in the suit. This stock film had a background of trees with no leaves, indicating that it was not in August, but in this case the reporter did not ask for it to be 'frozen.' The regular memos from the executive producer included critiques about the use of stocks which laid bare the fact that they did not represent the time the story was done. One such memo complained that a particular reporter had all day to shoot new footage, but had relied on stock footage with snow on the ground when it was summer. Even though everyone could see that a particular visual clip was a representation, it was not to appear as a 'fake.'

Visuals and Texts. The research literature emphasizes that television journalism is still dominated by the written text, and most of the conventions of print journalism are therefore applied in television journalism. If anything, the visual requirement serves as a limiting factor on television texts, meaning that they have less depth and range of opinion than is available in the quality press. Nevertheless the construction of a coherent text is paramount in most instances. 'The serious business of agenda setting is too important, as far as we can tell, for the visual imperative to be a major consideration' (GUMG, 1980: 248). The early news broadcasts of BBC television included sound only, and even a decade after its establishment in 1957, the BBC television news bulletin was in essence a radio bulletin read to camera, with a few illustrations. Even in the contemporary period television news has been portrayed as 'visual radio' (Gans, 1980) because the spoken word predominates, linking and ultimately binding the visual images (Williams, 1974).

The traditional interpretive role of the print journalist is sustained through the considerable degree to which the journalist himself appears, or voices-over, other visuals, talking about things that happened elsewhere. While clips with sources are termed 'actualities,' they too involve the source talking about what has gone on, or is going on, in another time at a different place. The need for talk from sources, and for the reporter to connect their talk in the maintenance of a flow, means the text forecloses on the range of visual options. Visuals only rise to the forefront 'when the material is exclusive, exceptionally dramatic and has unusual immediacy' (GUMG, 1976: 121). A shot of a person leaping from a building that is leaping with flames may speak for itself. However, most visual material consists of people speaking for themselves. In this respect television most often pictures the sources who form part of the text, a capability also available to newspapers through still photographs.

The reporter constantly visualizes what visuals can be obtained in relation to the text he imagines to be appropriate and what can fit with what his sources have said. This relation is dialectical, with amendments to both text and visuals being made at every stage of the reporting process. The extent to which one or the other predominates is related to the nature of the matter being reported on. In a story on a public demonstration several video cameramen were sent to obtain copious material; video was selected because it does not require processing and can be edited with much greater speed. The reporter then returned to the newsroom to screen the videotapes and in that process took notes for an accompanying text. Only after the screening was the text prepared, with the reporter indicating explicitly to the researcher how the script was written in accordance with the visuals obtained. In contrast we witnessed scripts being written in advance and then tinkered with as required by source-interview material obtained and stocks available. When the requirement was simply to update a continuing story, then the updated information – augmented by background information, usually from newspaper clippings – was the core of the matter and written much like a newspaper journalist would write it. However, because something had to be put up on the screen, the journalist scrambled to obtain generic visuals, stocks, graphics, or whatever else would fill the bill.

The importance of visuals was revealed when there were problems in obtaining them. If particular visuals could not be obtained, or if obtained were deemed to be lacking in drama, immediacy, or exclusivity, then the entire story was sometimes dropped. Thus a reporter assigned to a story on Monday regarding a murder on the previous weekend initially screened some film a weekend crew had obtained. The film was of poor quality and there were only two things shown: the apartment building where the incident occurred, showing a third-floor balcony, and two detectives looking around for evidence. With no body and no police-car visuals, the reporter said he did not think he could build a story around it and the item was eventually dropped.

When there were inadequate visuals – often in the face of severe time limitations to search for stocks or to dispatch a crew, or in face of the material limitation of no crew available – one option was to do a script for the anchorperson to read. This script was sometimes accompanied by whatever visuals were available, but usually only included a head-on shot of the anchorperson reading what the reporter had written for him. This situation arose also when physical space was difficult or impossible to penetrate for visuals. For example, reporters doing court stories were prevented from filming in the courtroom or courthouse. They usually relied upon a graphic artist's representation of the key actors during the day in court, supplemented if possible by source interviews outside the courtroom and stocks of the original incident or investigation related to the court hearing. A typical court story we observed entailed the use of five graphics with the reporter's voice-over. We also observed instances in which not even an artist's conception was obtained, and the anchorperson was left to say what the reporter had written.

Visuals were used to make statements beyond the scripted text. A reporter was doing a story on fear among women, in the context of a reported series of incidents of attacks on women. She decided to take shots of a 'secluded' area in a park where a woman had been raped while sunbathing in her swimming suit. On location, there were approximately one hundred men, women, and children in the area. The reporter had the cameraman isolate two women in swimming suits sitting on a bench, with no other people in the background. This clip was later used in the story, suggesting that even after the rape there were women foolhardy enough to be in this 'secluded' area of the park and wearing only scanty clothing.

In the ideological use of visuals there was usually textual material to set the stage and give preferred readings of what the reporter was representing. '[S]uch commentary does not tend iconically to describe the shots, but rather forces the viewer to see shots indexically or even symbolically within a framework of understanding thereby established by the professionals' (GUMG, 1980: 332). A reporter covering a well-policed demonstration by persons opposed to nuclear weapons began his item with a series of shots of police dragging demonstrators off a roadway. Instead of his own words, he used a background audio clip of demonstrators elsewhere on the site singing 'Give Peace a Chance.' A shot of a woman being led by a policeman who had hold of her hair was selected to fit with a textual statement, 'For the most part police used as little violence as possible.' Here the reporter was suggesting visually that this was a possible instance of excessive use of force, even while the text standing by itself was less suggestive of police excesses.

In a story on local residents' opposition to the establishment of a halfway house for prisoners, the reporter wanted to visualize a view that people felt threatened and there was potential for danger. In order to do so she not only obtained a talking-head of a spokesperson for the citizens in opposition, but went to the location of the house proposed for this use to obtain suggestive visuals. On location she had the cameraman picture the house alongside the one next door, which had a for-sale sign on it. This was done in the context of a newspaper story which cited the potential centre's next-door neighbour as being concerned about the safety of her two children. 'Are they sex offenders, drug offenders, or what?' The suggestion to be left was that the house was for sale because the neighbour was concerned about 'criminals' moving into the neighbourhood. Shots were also taken of young children walking through the park across the street from the house, suggestive that with the park so accessible to the house, children might be easy prey. Visualizations of deviance of this type were rendered more easily and subtly with the aid of television visuals. In print, reporters would be quite unlikely to say, 'Since this park is directly across the street from the house, criminals are likely to watch for children playing in the park and calculate whom they can victimize.' They might obtain a quotation from a local resident expressing this fear, but even that is arguably less immediate and dramatic than *showing* the physical possibility with visuals.

Visuals were occasionally used to obtain direct statements from sources to supplement what had been acquired in words. Persons at demonstrations carrying banners and placards, or wearing shirts with slogans on them, could be filmed with their written statements clearly in focus, to be read by the viewer even while the reporter was making his own voice-over statement. Reporters attended a meeting of the city police commission at which there was discussion of an incident where police allegedly assaulted a number of persons as they were escorted from an unruly party at a house. Among the visuals taken by several news outlets at this meeting was one of a man who wore a black T-shirt with white letters stating, 'I survived the Moorish Road

Massacre.' It is an open question whether a citizen would have been quoted in this context, describing the incident and police actions as a 'massacre.' In the event the written slogan allowed the television crews to visualize it as a statement in addition to whatever words they wished to include in their scripted texts.

Visuals also allowed reporters to capture a sense of 'what it was like' for the participants involved in an event. While the ability to do this directly (as opposed to retrospectively in accounts from the people involved) was limited, it was occasionally done with effect and valued as an important component of television news. A producer screening visuals of a major fire came across a shot of a fireman on a stretcher receiving oxygen. The producer exclaimed 'beauty!', in appreciation of the fact that he had a rare example of an iconic clip that contributed tertiary understanding to the event.

Another option of the reporter or producer is a graphic artist's representation of what has taken place. The fact that these are entirely fictive representations may be one reason why in certain physical contexts where cameras are banned graphics are also banned, such as in British (although not Canadian) courts of law. The graphic allows imagination to rule, without pretense of actuality, and its ideological signs are laid bare. In a story on a strike at a car-manufacturing company – a company which had been in the news for some time as suffering financially – a graphic was adopted depicting a 'hammer-and-sickle' type hammer smashing the hood ornament on a car, the ornament being the logo of the car company. At the meeting where this graphic was decided upon, it was pointed out that the item would fit nicely with another one in the lineup. This other item concerned one hundred Japanese businessmen on a trade mission to Canada, juxtaposed with a Canadian trade minister's plea to buy Canadian, all contextualized with reference to the sale of Japanese cars and car parts in Canada. Through graphic representation, and wrapping the two stories together, the threat of workers and foreigners to Canadian economic well-being was made evident.

Establishing Factuality

SOURCES AND THE HIERARCHY OF CREDIBILITY

The primary means of establishing factuality is to find sources to make statements that can be quoted as fact. However, not just any source will do. The sources selected must be the best persons available to *represent* the organization involved in the matter, often regardless of whether they are in the best position to know the facts. The key to being the best person is to be credible and convey authority, since source quotations often provide the only factual basis of the story. Social hierarchy and social exclusion are not only determined in terms of specialist knowledge (Böhme, 1984); they also relate to who is authorized to represent the common sense.

Sources are normative witnesses to events in the world, and are selected by normative criteria. Infused with value – in terms of their own position as representatives of their organization, and as making value statements on matters of designating deviance and effecting control – sources must be selected according to criteria valued in the culture. In every story the reporter must size up the prospective candidates who might serve as normative witnesses and ascertain whether they fit the representation the reporter has in mind for them. Reporters we observed constantly made comments about the position and moral-character attributes of those under consideration, indicating the sources' degrees of print – or air – worthiness. These comments were not articulations of rules of thumb, but contributions to the vocabulary of precedents concerning how a given source might be fitted into a given story in terms of the situation and context of the matter under consideration.

The reporter has a ready-made cultural resource for determining the representation a source can make in the way organizations are hierarchically organized. Those at the top, regardless of what they know, carry the authority of office and requirement of accountability to make their comments 'a must.' 'Bureaucratic hierarchies constitute "hierarchies of credibility" (Becker, 1967) for journalists' (Fishman, 1980: 94).

It thus seems 'natural' to journalists 'to go to the top.' If a citizen alleges that the police force is violating his sense of fair play, or a journalist decides that lack of progress on a major investigation violates his sense of efficiency, then the 'obvious' approach is to go to the man at the top. In the words of the boss of one newsroom: 'We have to hold the [police] force accountable for what it does as well as the people who are the bosses of the force, they have to keep the force accountable ... When the structure is set up [in] any organization, there should be one person in that place who knows everything about everything. And if he doesn't, then the structure is wrong. He is the boss. The boss in my opinion is the guy who knows everything that is going on and knows it better than anybody else. So that at least there's one person making quality decisions.'

Reporters generally tried to go to the top when they were 'policing organizational life' and pushing for an authoritative resolution. This happened in a story that focused on banks charging customers for dormant accounts, and closing dormant accounts and keeping the money if small sums were involved, netting them millions of dollars in the aggregate. The reporter sought a response in high places. She went after the nature of legal and political responsibility in the matter, as well as responsibility within the corporate structure of each major bank. Thus, in one day she called more than a dozen different sources in a range of institutions she construed to have a say in the matter. These included the federal minister of Justice; the federal minister of Finance; the Ontario Ministry of Consumer and Corporate Affairs information officer; the Alberta Ministry of the Attorney General (general); the assistant deputy minister in the British Columbia Ministry of the Solicitor General; the legal branch of the federal Ministry of Justice; the legal branch of the federal Ministry of Finance; the Inspector General of Banks for Canada; the Bank of Canada (information office); a member of parliament for an opposition party, who said he had planned to ask a question of the minister of Justice; and, the information officers of four major banks regarding their policy in relation to dormant accounts and the legality of their policy. Her approach was to find key persons in key organizations to state deviant practice, to state existing legal controls for the practice, and to advocate particular control remedies.

Reporters examining the policies of organizations also went to the top to obtain the views of the person with most authority. This practice was exemplified by how routinely the chief of police and a deputy were contacted whenever police malpractice was revealed, but it pertained more generally to any organizational forum when policy and practice were at issue. Thus, a reporter attending the annual meetings of the Canadian Bar Association was developing three stories regarding the association's activities or position: the process of parliamentary reform; pension increases for judges outside of government guidelines for wage increases; and law firms establishing themselves interprovincially and thus within the jurisdiction of more than one professional regulatory body (provincial law society). The reporter interviewed the president-elect of the Canadian Bar Association as *the* authority on all three matters to represent the perspective of his association.

The fact that reporters went in these authoritative directions seems 'obvious' and in many cases it was. However, the situation was not always as straightforward as common sense might suggest. Journalists also had to use their common sense to decide whether persons or organizations were legitimate parties to a matter. For example, the reporter considering the three stories at the Canadian Bar Association meetings eventually dropped the one on parliamentary reform. When the researcher asked why the parliamentary-reform story had been dropped, the reporter said it was boring and she did not see the Canadian Bar Association as having legitimate standing to comment on the matter. She commented that what the Canadian Bar Association had to say was no more important or interesting than what 'you or I' had to say about it, this being a clear indication that the association's members were not authorized knowers and thus would not be given 'jurisdiction' by the reporter.

In deciding upon the value of a source as a purveyor of fact when he was not at the top, much credence was given to the source's experience. A reporter covered a case in which a person was being tried before an administrative body concerning misconduct in the course of his employment. The reporter was anxious to convey the accused's perspective with empathy, and in doing so he was heavily reliant upon the lawyer for the accused. This emphasis was of concern to the reporter since the lawyer had only been practising law for eighteen months, and this meant that he had not established his trustworthiness in terms of his reputation or experience in the profession. With a professionally prominent media regular, such as Edward Greenspan, it would have been a 'natural'; with a relatively inexperienced person, in both professional terms and as a news-media source, caution was called for along with the realization that newsworthiness was diminished.

A person making imputations of deviance or critical statements without an organizational or professional affiliation is usually without standing in news discourse. A reporter covering a provincial-government committee on family violence returned to the newsroom to tell her editor about a person who addressed the committee about the bigotry faced by native women. The reporter said the editor was not enthusiastic about the story because it was only one native woman saying this. However, when the reporter told the editor that the source was director of a native-women's centre in a nearby city, he reconsidered and said it was appropriate to file a story. Her organizational position had rendered her suitable for representing the plight of the social group of which she was a part. It was not the voice of the people, but the person with authority for the people, that counted.

The question of self-interest is part of the valuation of sources. While reporters realize that sources are not going to give objective accounts, they think it is a matter of degree and that some can be more objective than others. A source who did not have a direct stake in the matter was believed to be more objective than the one who did, and was treated accordingly. This meant that a citizens' interest group was usually accorded less status and consideration than an official body overseeing a dispute or problem. Thus several reporters had a negative view of an organization established to assist victims of rape, labelling it as 'anti-men' and 'anti-police.' The police or other officials responsible for handling the troubles of both victims and offenders, were preferred sources.

A story on habitual offenders was initially to be given less prominence because it was based on a report believed to have been prepared by a prisoners' rights organization. However, the story was eventually given prominent play. When a researcher asked an editor why, he replied that it was discovered the report was written by a provincial corrections association and parole board. In his mind, this made it more 'independent' than if a prisoners' rights group had authored it.

Reporters also gave credibility to 'the little guy' in face of an official bureaucracy that appeared unjust. However, this was usually part of a strategy aimed at forcing official accountability regarding citizens' rights, rather than an effort to give a particular citizen an elevated public status in his own right. Moreover, it was often persons in authority who were initially consulted to find an underdog to represent the plight of his similarly situated fellows. Interviews with criminal offenders (e.g., 'rapists') and victims (e.g., 'battered wives') were usually set up on this basis, with the authorities controlling who would appear to give a statement on the conditions under which authority was being exercised.

Of course 'the people' as a social category can also be represented outside of any other organizational designation. We have emphasized previously that reporters were on occasion explicitly encouraged to 'take it to the streets' in preference over using 'institutional mouthpieces.' However, the folks were not mobilized to express institutional positions on what had occurred, why, and what was being or could be done. Moreover, it was not a random survey that was important, but individual assertions held to represent popular opinion. This approach ensured that news-media discourse would continue to convey the consensus as constructed by the powerful and vocal few rather than the silent majority. In short it was not a check on 'pluralistic ignorance' (Dollard, 1937), but another guarantor of it.

QUOTATION AND VERIFICATION PRACTICES

The reporter's main task in producing a text is to find quotations from each source that represent what the source represents in the story. While the reporter frames his questions to elicit answers that represent what he himself imagines to be the facts of the matter, it is the source's words which constitute the facts. The reporter must decide what accounts can be treated as factual; whether factuality can only be constituted by attributing it to a source; and where factuality can be expressed by the reporter himself without attributions to a source because of the source's status, the nature of the facts, or independent means of verification.

The reporter has to be especially careful that he does not accept a source's allegations against another person or organization as fact unless the allegation has been officially authorized as fact. In our observations reporters regularly faced the situation of hearing allegations from sources that they felt they could not report without running the risk of a libel action. This situation typically arose when a source alleged an act of crime or other deviance which had not been reported to the police, or, if reported, was still under investigation without enough evidence to specify the culprit. In this circumstance the reporter told the source to report the matter to the police and the reporter would then be able to report on the official designations. In this respect reporters saw the law of libel as the law of authorized accusations. Accusations can be made in the public culture once the police, or other authorities of the state, have invoked their own means of construing the truth about deviance. The authorities are clearly the primary definers (Hall et al, 1978), and the primary cover and coverage for the journalist is to quote the authorities on their factual determinations.

Nevertheless, the reporter can still achieve partial cover by having the parties subject to imputations of deviance state their case as they see it, and by attributing the facts directly to them. A reporter worked on a story involving a legal suit of breach of contract against a prominent person. The reporter was concerned that he could not report facts relevant to the legal discovery process. His strategy was to interview the plaintiff and then confront the person being sued to have him state the facts which could then be reported. It was not a story if he could not get quotations from the person being sued. This was an instance where it was of no direct benefit to obtain the documents pertaining to the dispute as a source of information because they could not be cited in a matter before the courts. However, the persons themselves could be quoted, a practice circumventing legal restrictions, meeting journalistic requirements of fairness, and requiring little effort.

Once official designations are made the reporter can take them as fact without attribution, even if he has only obtained the facts from an official's verbal accounts. The Crown attorney's statements about the facts of a case before the court were routinely accepted and reported as fact without attribution and without independent checks. These statements included information about the parties involved and charges against them. Also included were the Crown attorney's accounts of testimony or judicial pronouncements which the reporter had missed. The Crown attorney was high enough on the ladder of credibility, and in enough of a strategic position of authorized knowledge, that journalists were able to accept his statements of others' statements or characteristics as fact.

This practice was repeated in other organizational settings where people were deemed to be in a position to know basic facts. In a story about the results of municipal school-trustee elections, a reporter interviewed the chairman of the board of school trustees and learned the composition of the board, number of trustees, and political affiliations of the newly elected members. In the filed story these were cited without attribution. It would seem peculiar to say, 'The chairman stated that the board consists of twenty-four members,' just as it would seem peculiar to say, 'According to the Crown attorney the accused was twenty-four years old and was charged with robbery.' The peculiarity lies in the fact that to name the source as authority in this context is to raise doubt about his authority and thus the validity of the facts. Reporting something in the name of the source might be appropriate if the Crown attorney is saying the accused is a 'known con artist,' or the chairman of school trustees is saying there is an unfavourable left-wing bias on his board, but not in stating facts of the type noted above. Additionally, it looks better if the reporter can convey basic background facts without appearing to be dependent on sources.

Spokespersons for bureaucracies can give statements about what is going on 'inside' that are taken as fact without attribution. A television reporter doing a story connected to a moral panic about attacks on women decided to include as a component an update on the condition of a rape victim. She called a hospital spokesperson and told a researcher that he said the victim was conscious but was unable to speak to anyone but her family, adding that not even the police were able to interview her. The reporter included this fact as part of the stand-up for her piece, without mentioning the hospital spokesperson as source.

A senior newspaper executive was asked whether there was any policy or understanding in the newsroom pertaining to these practices. His responses indicate that it was deemed important to assess the credibility of the source; that attribution to a named source was expected where the facts were in doubt; and, that it was not necessary to independently verify facts if the reporter knew that they could be verified through routinely available sources.

Q: How do you judge the credibility of a source? What kinds of considerations go into that?

A: Well, cross-checking with other sources. You never just take the word of a source. *Ever*. Without cross-checking. That's the major, I mean that's the main, number-one thing to do.

Q: What sorts of cross-checks?

A: Well, with other sources, with other factual material, whether it's documents or people or whatever. Track record. There's a danger in track records. If you've used a source successfully on fifteen occasions and you build up that confidence, you also build up the vulnerability to being used if you come to trust the source too much ...

Q: How does the relationship develop between yourself and a reporter in terms of, a reporter coming to you and saying, 'You know I trust this source, I think we should use this information'?

A: Well, sometimes I insist on knowing who it is, and in fact it will be either a case of me saying 'I want to know,' or, 'You tell your department head who it is,' and I'll ask him if he's satisfied or is she satisfied.

Q: Do you then do independent checks, or ... ?

A: Of?

Q: Of the person, the information the person has provided, and so on?

A: Oh yeah. If it's your first time around with the person, you nose around and find out who they are and what their reputation is and all the rest and then you try and verify the information in a couple of other ways.

Q: Talking generally ... any person who is interviewed, would you regard their accounts as facts? In other words, do you see an account as a fact?

A: No, I see it more as a proposition until we've cross-checked it to the point that we think we can rely on it.

Q: But we've noticed in some circumstances, some things that a source might say might even be reported as factual without making an attribution to the person, whereas other people might say the same thing and it will be said that, 'Mr Jones said such and such.' You know, what is the distinction there? Why in one case and not in the other case?

A: Well, in one case you yourself are absolutely, totally sure that that is the fact and the other case we're attributing it because you're not sure that you can establish yourself independently that it is indeed a fact.

Q: Also it makes better legal cover to make the attribution, or ... ?

A: It's not legal cover so much as the fact that you yourself can't back it up. You can only put in the paper what you yourself can prove, otherwise you attribute it.

Q: But you may have a situation, I'm thinking in court for example, where the Crown attorney will be consulted regarding certain aspects of a case which you would then not bother saying, 'Crown attorney Jones said such and such,' you just say that that's the fact of the case but you have not really done any independent checking on those things, you just talk to the Crown attorney and the Crown attorney said that and you in turn say that. Now is that on the basis of long-standing credibility? ...

A: Well, you're supposed to check the charges on the charge sheet. If he's suing for X amount of dollars or such and such damages, we don't need to attribute that because that's what he's, I mean that's verifiable. You know, so long as you can say that that is what happened then you can go out and say it is as a fact, that happened, but unless you can stand up and say it happened, I've got it in my notes, and I was there, and I know it did, then attribute it.

As with other aspects of newsmaking, there were no rules of thumb for these practices but rather shared understandings, articulated through the vocabulary of precedents, that could be used to visualize what should be done. Ultimately factuality depended on who the source person was within the hierarchy of credibiity, and the nature and extent of verification varied accordingly. 'In science, the problem of facticity is embedded in processes of verification and replication. In news, verification of facts is both a political and a professional accomplishment' (Tuchman, 1978: 83).

If official designations or 'confessions' from the accused could not be relied upon, reporters were left to seek verification by other means. Their degree of effort in this regard was largely a function of the power of the source the facts were about. The only 'rule' which reporters articulated was to go to supervisors if in doubt. It was superiors in turn who would determine the kind of checking required in the particular case and whether legal consultation was necessary. If it was a powerful source facing a powerful allegation, two and sometimes three independent reliable sources were required. Imputations involving occasions and people of less import required one additional independent account. The routine expectation otherwise was that no independent accounts were required, but the reporter should be able to know where to obtain such accounts readily if called upon to do so. Again it must be emphasized there was nothing fixed about this, and it was very much a matter of the reporter deciding in the particular circumstances how to be sure of himself. In the vast majority of instances no effort was made to verify facts because the reporter could rely on construals of fact by the authorities or direct quotations from the person making an imputation and the person subject to it.

Reporters routinely referred and deferred to officialdom. In courtrooms and other official settings where persons were testifying under oath, it was preferred practice to take quotations from the accused, victims, and witnesses while they were testifying rather than interviewing them separately. The second-best alternative was to interview the witnesses, lawyer, or the Crown attorney about what he had said. Even when witnesses or parties to the dispute were interviewed, the material was often used only for background knowledge, or withheld to be understood and used in the context of direct testimony under oath. Again the official ordering of the process reported on framed how the reporter ordered his materials in construing and constructing factuality.

Disputed facts were usually resolved in favour of official sources. A statement by a political group that a bomb used to blow up part of a weapons factory contained five hundred pounds of dynamite was dropped in favour of a police statement that it contained one hundred pounds. It was also evident that not just any official source would do. A senior editor described a case in which a secret informant had passed on information and relevant documents indicating that criminal theft charges had been laid by an official of a company against officers of a management-consultant company that had been appointed by the government to manage their affairs. These charges were laid via a private information before a justice of the peace, not by the police. Checks were made with the justice of the peace concerned to ensure that he had signed the private information. Moreover the decision was taken to name only the management-consultant company concerned but not the accused. The rationale for this was the belief that the standard of proof in a private information is lower, and in lesser conditions of accountability, than that governing the police. As the senior editor stated:

I was questioning why the names weren't in there and the answer that I got back was, well we talked about it and we decided that it wasn't fair because the standard of proof was so low in these circumstances ... it just wouldn't be fair. They wouldn't be acting under the same kinds of constraints that we expect a Crown attorney or a police force to operate under. In other words it could be absolutely and totally frivolous and there is no – unlike the situation with the police – there is no social penalty for being frivolous. I mean the police are frivolous and they get heavily criticized for being frivolous. Individuals, well it's all part of the game, even laying a charge. So there'll be plenty of time to name people as the charge is proceeded with, if it is proceeded with. We said we thought we wouldn't name them and I agreed with them.

The hierarchy of credibility is at the core of practices of quotation and verification. Since the reporter rarely has the time, material resources, or access to penetrate the source's space to independently establish the facts, his version of the facts is what his sources say it is. It is therefore necessary to judge the credibility of who is saying what – to raise questions of organizational position and interests – to decide whose versions of the facts are reportable. These matters were addressed by a television news executive.

Q: But do you see some safety in having a source give you a quotation directly rather than you making the statement?

A: Well, the only measure of safety there is that presuming that the man is one of integrity and honesty. That he is willing to make the statement publicly, for the record, increases my confidence enough to think that the man is, understands the fallout that could occur from an inaccurate statement and that he's not making the statement with malice and that it's not a false statement. I mean it gives the statement a little more credibility in my eyes. However, if again the statement is credible, the final test is to go and ask the opinion of the institute or the individual that's had the statement made about him and report it, to get their side of it. Because there are some statements that are in dispute. A statement that's in dispute is a fact, but you don't know what side of it is a fact.

Q: What techniques would you use to try and establish that it was a fact?

A: Well, we try and go and verify. I mean we go into, we're in a search for evidence at that point. We're going to documents, we're going to other people who might have been there. I mean, it's the same as police work, in order to obtain evidence without any of the powers, and without any of the malice, sometimes ... If we examine facts and attempt to prove facts with any less thoroughness than a Crown or the court does then we're not doing our job.

In practice, investigation usually entailed doing whatever was necessary to determine the credibility of the source. If the source was known by position or regular use, veracity was assumed and factuality existed in what he said.

If the source was not in an authoritative organizational position and was not a regular, then checks were deemed necessary. Other sources were contacted to give an account of the source in question, or document checks were undertaken if the matter was deemed of sufficient importance.

Reporters in one newsroom said they had contacts with police officers who would run Canadian Police Information Centre (CPIC) computerized checks for them regarding a person's criminal record. One reporter discussed this practice in a way indicating that its functions were very similar to how the police themselves use it (see Ericson, 1982: chap. 6). The reporter said that the CPIC information was the basis for assessing moral character of the source. Does the source have a criminal record? If so, does he admit to it when confronted, thereby suggesting that he is not likely to be deceitful or to hide things generally? As in other policing enterprises where moral profiles are drawn and used to judge the veracity and facticity of an account, there is a need to use whatever resources are available inside or outside the organization. Reporters were very resourceful in this respect.

Having taken investigation to the point of establishing the credibility of a source – which is often 'automatic' because the source is in a known authoritative position and/or is a news regular – the journalist rarely goes farther. It is sufficient for the reporter to quote source A making truth claim 'X,' and source B making truth claim 'Y,' rather than independently seeking and establishing his own version of the truth. Indeed, probing efforts that result in discovery of competing facts can soften the hard facts of source quotations, and even lead to a version of the truth of the matter that results in having no story to report (e.g., the Rastafarian story outlined earlier). Reporters are therefore inclined to go no farther than the performative utterances of official sources. In the process they constitute a select group of normative witnesses to uphold the normative order. More often than we think, news discourse consists of what *should be* the facts of the matter.

Factuality without verification also resides in already broadcast or printed news. Reporters expressed the normative sentiment that one should never 'lift' material from another news source without checking it oneself. In practice material was lifted routinely without attribution to the news source. This material included background information as well as quoting the quotations of sources in other news outlets. The fact this is institutionalized in news work is indicated by the BBC's former 'two-agency rule' which 'firmly prescribed that no report should be treated as adequately confirmed if it had not appeared independently on the tape of two news agencies' (Schlesinger, 1978: 90). That is, other news agencies were treated as authorized knowers. Presumably their material was deemed to be factually adequate because their reporters were trusted to produce only source quotations or other information that met the requirements of news as knowledge.

When faced with wanting to verify a fact of the matter, reporters typically used two methods: they asked the source concerned and/or they checked existing news accounts. A reporter was trying to establish whether any government minister or ministry had received a letter which would have affected their decision regarding a senior civil-service appointment. This appointment had been made controversial because of patronage overtones. The reporter's own method for checking on this was to obtain print-outs of related previous stories from her own newspaper to see if it had been reported that a government official had received this letter. She also interviewed a minister and the deputy leader of an opposition party. At the same time a reporter from Canadian Press interviewed the premier and said she asked him directly whether he had read the letter in question. The newspaper reporter in turn took this Canadian Press interview material and told her editor to incorporate it into the story. Three paragraphs in the middle of the story included this interview material with the premier, prefaced with the statement, 'In an interview yesterday with a Canadian Press reporter ...' This approach was used as if the newspaper reporter herself had obtained the material, and with no effort to check independently whether the wire-service reporter's material was reasonably accurate. When it came to credible news outlets, it was the same as credible persons in source bureaucracies: the fact-value of the matter was decided on the basis of face-value.

Quotations from sources were seen as having a performative character beyond primary factuality. In particular, quotations were also used for tertiary understanding conveying a sense of what it was like for persons involved. For example, at an inquest into a death during a fire, reporters all settled on a witness's description of a locked exit as 'a death trap.' Newspaper reporters cited this as stated in court, while broadcast reporters rushed to interview the witness outside the court to have her restate for camera and microphone what it was like in the 'death trap.'

PARTIAL KNOWLEDGE

While reporters worked hard to establish a suitable frame, once a frame was established they were disinclined to consider information or alternative frames that did not seem to fit into the picture. Thus, useful information, with implications for alternative frames, was ignored in favour of the preferred frame. A reporter attended a scheduled public meeting announced through a press release as a task force on public violence against women and children. As the meeting evolved it turned out that the deputations and expressed concern were primarily focused on violence in private space (domestic violence, incest, child abuse, shelter for battered women and children), pornography, and aspects of prevention (including sex education and counselling

services for victims and men). Nevertheless the reporter ignored these deputations over several hours. Instead, while out in the corridor for a smoke,
he saw the chairperson and asked 'What do you do now?' She said a working
group was being established to make specific proposals to police and government to counteract violence on the street. According to the reporter, the
chairperson was not interested in domestic violence. After this interview the
reporter said he had his lead: he would focus on women's fear to be on the
streets and what the chairperson said would be done to make the streets more
safe. He proceeded to do just that, quoting a woman president of a resident's
association saying: 'It's not safe to be alone on the street even in broad
daylight,' and related comments, in conjunction with the chairperson's calls
for more police patrols in subways and parks; a neighbourhood-watch system
specifically for women; and recommendations to the federal government regarding sentencing and parole of sex offenders based on 'strong evidence
from the public that it wants tougher sentences handed out and sexual offenders
kept in jail longer.' There was no mention in the story of domestic violence,
which clearly predominated the concerns expressed at the meeting through
citizens' deputations and discussions.

Sometimes when a reporter learned of something salient he decided that
he already had a story for the day and thus ignored the new information. A
reporter attending provincial-governmet task-force meetings on violence in
the family was approached by a man who apparently had been at the meetings
every day. He told the reporter that he was a 'battered man' and would like
publicity for his case. He said he had applied to the committee to be allowed
to address them but was denied. The reporter listened to him but made no
effort to interview him for a story. Although it was still several hours from
her deadline, the reporter told the researcher that she only did one good story
a day and she already had it. This man's situation fit well with some criteria
of newsworthiness – including an inversion of roles (man as victim instead
of woman) and denial of access by the authorities – but she made no effort
to develop a story on it.

It was often the case that the reporter's own visualization of a story angle
superseded any need he might have felt to produce a story. If his favoured
frame could not be constructed around what was transpiring, he would not
bother to develop an alternative. A reporter attended an inquest into the death
of a transit-system employee hit by a subway train while working at track
level. The reporter had hoped for testimony of a key witness, such as the
train driver, but the day was taken up by medical and police testimony,
showing pictures of the scene, and an extended and repeated consideration
of a request by the employee's union to be given standing at the inquest. The
reporter showed no interest in several possible angles, such as the denial of
standing to the union, and did not bother filing a story even though he had
been there with a cameraman all day.

In each of these examples information was available that would have allowed the reporter to develop an angle that was reportable. In the first example the reporter ignored information that would have complicated what he wanted to report. In the second instance the reporter already had a story and felt no organizational pressure to produce a separate one arising out of the same hearings. In the third instance the reporter simply decided that there was nothing of interest to him even though he recognized possibilities, such as the question of the union being given standing. In all cases, the consequence was partial knowledge: information about some phenomena and not others, and information about only some aspects of phenomena reported. Ideologically a lot of what was presented and ignored was in terms of the reporter's favoured causes: safety in the streets rather than the family; women and children as victims rather than men; official structuring of occupational safety rather than the cause of unions. The favoured causes and causal responsibility were entwined in this process.

As we have shown through previous examples, visualizations of deviance disconfirmed in source accounts were not reported. In chapter 5 we related the story of the television reporter who was given a newspaper story on an increase in boat thefts but could find no one to say it was so; the final decision was not to produce a story rather than to produce a story citing sources saying there was no problem. Similarly information disconfirming other news accounts was simply ignored if the disconfirmation would have to be included as the main frame. Thus, a reporter working on a story updating the medical condition of a lung-transplant patient who was said to be facing imminent death, decided to do a telephone interview with the patient's father in a distant city. During the conversation with the father, he mentioned that contrary to some Toronto news-media reports, he had no intention of suing the hospital with regard to the treatments his son had received. The reporter did not introduce this into her story at all, although she almost certainly would have if he had said that the other news reports were accurate and he was intending to sue.

In the instances cited to this point partial knowledge was produced in face of other information that was available but not used. The reporter also experiences the problem of information not being of sufficient quality even though a source is willing to provide it. Even a regular, notable source who did not 'deliver the goods' in the reporter's terms was not reported on. A prominent local politician, with sustained and close links to the news organization in question, called a news conference to state his views on a continuing investigation into questionable land transactions and the affairs of several trust companies. The reporter missed part of the news conference, and afterward arranged to interview the politician in a private room. Following the interview the reporter described the politician as a 'bullshit artist' who did not know what was going on in this affair. He decided not to file a story on this politician's views even though the conference itself was well attended by other news outlets.

In summary, researchers who have overemphasized the normalization and routinization of news production have also overemphasized the belief that just about everything is reportable and reported. For example, Tuchman (1977: 53) observes, 'Unfortunately, the observer of news routines does not frequently encounter the unreported. The reason is simple: the observer is accompanying a reporter to an assigned event and so sees what the reporter sees. Like the reporter, the observer may be seduced by the news net.' In our observations, even when the reporter went to a scheduled hearing, news conference, or personal interview, the unreported was very evident. We observed reporters struggling through the day to find something, anything, that might be reportable, altering their angle accordingly. There were occasions on which reporters simply gave up, informing their superiors that no newsworthy angles were evident.

Editors are very dependent on the reporter in this regard. They can reduce this dependency by creating a strong expectation that the reporter must file something on a regular basis, and through their system of rewards and punishments which socializes the reporter into visualizing stories in their mould. When stories are filed, the control shifts directly to editors. Editors scrutinize and alter the reporter's product to ensure that what he visualizes fits with what they have in mind. We now turn to an examination of this fit as it emerges in reporter-editor relations.

8

Editing

Editing is not a discrete part of newsmaking because aspects of editing occur throughout the process. Sources edit their releases and verbal statements for journalists' consumption. Assignment editors choose only some matters for coverage, and assign them with a specific angle, so that only limited sources are used, limited questions asked, and limited answers formulated. Reporters themselves edit in the process of visualizing their stories, and choosing sources and appropriate formulations. The television reporter, after obtaining materials in the field and writing a script, remains to edit and produce the visuals and thus has considerable control of the product to the point of broadcasting. Those designated formally as editors are left to do 'readings' of the reporter's filed copy, and whatever else the reporter has to say about his story. The editor can work only from the text he is presented with, a text that has been edited substantially by the sources and journalists involved previously.

The editing that occurs at all stages of the newsmaking process has an invisible quality (Black, 1982: 115). Moves are made to contact sources, ask particular questions, and write stories, in a manner analogous to the game of chess: the editorial expectations regarding the end-game filter down and affect practice even though they are not visibly displayed in the game. While journalists must present their stories within a dramaturgical model of organized life that is highly normative, their own work processes are more attuned to a game model, in which systemic expectations are taken into account in formulating action, even if the expectations are not manifest and are difficult for the participants to articulate. What is articulated is the vocabulary of precedents, what experience shows is the recognizable feature of a story and how it should be edited down into an account worthy of the news genre.

With the reminders that editing occurs at all stages of the newsmaking process, and that the influences on it are often difficult for the observer to detect, we turn to an analysis of editing processes. First, we outline the roles of editors who have a hand in influencing the alteration of the filed copy. We then consider the focus of substantive editing: ensuring that the final product is both ideologically correct and attuned to the common sense. Next we analyse the choices made regarding the degree and nature of play given to an item. Finally we show how fiction is a fact in editing news stories, ensuring that they are presentable for public consumption.

Editing Roles

THE RELATIVE AUTONOMY OF SENIOR EDITORS AND PRODUCERS

Senior editors and producers are in a position to set the tone and continuity of their news product, as well as to direct specific coverage in specific terms. However, they in turn are controlled by higher authorities as well as market conditions. The newspaper owner and publisher can influence what are the 'sacred cows' of the newspaper (Royal Commission on Newspapers [RCN], 1981). Television networks can establish corporate policy as well as resource limitations that circumscribe the degree of freedom of the local station's news producer. Audience ratings – one 'sacred cow' of television productions – are also a key component of the television-news producer's decisions on what to cover and with what emphasis. Television-news producers and newspaper editors are in essence 'middle men' who negotiate with reporters, superiors (publishers or networks), sources, and the public for products that appear to satisfy all (Cantor, 1971; Sigal, 1973).

The Editorial Board. One formal setting in which this product negotiation occurs is the editorial board, which meets to decide what news items are worthy of special comment in the name of the news organization. This aspect of editing is more developed in newspapers than in broadcast-news organizations. The editorial board constitutes an élite group of 'reporters' who are allowed to write explicitly opinionated pieces. In French-Canadian newspapers these editorials are usually signed, and there are often two in disagreement over the same topic published on the same editorial page. In English Canada, editorials are unsigned and express a unitary opinion in the name of the organization.

Taking the example of one newspaper we studied, the editorial board consisted of the editor-in-chief, the assistant editor-in-chief, and four other persons. Each person was a designated specialist in a topic area, although he was also allowed to write on other topics. The topic areas covered by the four other persons were foreign affairs; national, provincial, and municipal affairs; energy and economics; and justice and education. The members were recruited by the editor-in-chief for long terms. He himself had been a member for twenty years, another had been serving longer than that, and a third person had served for seventeen years. According to the editor-in-chief, his desire was 'to keep a balance of ages and interests, you try to get people who are of different political outlooks and attitudes than your own, so that you get a healthy discussion.'

The editorial board met at 1:00 p.m., Monday through Friday. The editor-in-chief said he expected one filed editorial per person per day, and that 80 to 85 per cent of them were used. Use was at his discretion. An effort was made to obtain topic balance: 'something foreign, something national, something perhaps cultural, and not always but as often as we can, something of humour or whimsy.' Reporters were sometimes invited to attend or participate for short periods, including foreign correspondents who informed the board about their postings abroad. Otherwise reporters were simply consulted or asked to run checks on things an editorial writer wished to address in his item. The editorial board was seen as exclusive by reporters in the newsroom, and by the editor-in-chief himself.

The following description by an editor-in-chief of the board meetings indicates his expectation that members were well versed in the knowledge of the news of the day, and that their main task was to advance this knowledge. While they were the elite, they were essentially reporters whose job it was to write second-day leads on the news of the day by scrutinizing other news products and calling other authorized knowers. While their editorials were intended to be leading, they were led by the knowledge of news discourse.

> The members of the board are expected to have read [our newspaper] pretty thoroughly before that [daily] meeting. They also read a number of journals and read material that relates to their areas of expertise, and a variety of sources, they listen to radio broadcasts, they look at other newspapers that cross their desk, and I'm doing the same. I usually prepare a list of subjects that I think are worth discussing on that given day, that should be addressed editorially. I will go through the list that I have and other members of the board will make suggestions as we go along, even about subjects I have raised, or they will introduce other subjects. In the course of a day we may discuss ten different things, and probably write on four or five of them. We sometimes quite deliberately discuss something to keep ourselves abreast of the subject – we're not really ready, it's not really our purpose, yet, to write about it. We're making ourselves aware of what's going on, and that will spark our interest in going out and finding more information. I have a belief that unless you're writing a very short editorial which is usually a bit of humour, or a bit of whimsy, or just a bright remark, that an editorial should include material that our readers haven't had before. It shouldn't just be our

opinion on a story that's already appeared. We try to add some new material,
we try to organize material that may have appeared in several different parts of
the paper on several different occasions, bring it together to give it some
body, some direction. We may spend more time on exposition than we do on
comment. In fact there are some editorials that are best described as informative editorials, you don't really have something to stand on a platform and
shout about it, you simply say this is the situation we're following today, this
is how it has deteriorated, this is the reason it has deteriorated, we're giving a
piece of analysis more than a piece of opinion. That is often the case with
foreign editorials, where you will indicate where you are aghast with what's
going on or whether you are pleased with what's going on, but you don't always have solutions.

The role of those on the editorial board was defined by the editor-in-chief
as contributing to the overall goals of the newspaper in the same way as
reporters. The difference in his eyes was the latitude given to board members
to be advocates regarding what they visualized to be public problems and
their most appropriate remedy. He argued that regular reporters must not be
seen to be advocates, for fear of undercutting their professional ideology of
neutrality, and therefore the plurality of their access to sources. Editorial-
board members, on the other hand, were above it all. They could use the
name of the newspaper to speak with authoritative certainty on the designation
of deviance and appropriate control remedies.

Q: What do you see as being the purpose of the editorial as distinct from, say,
features or news story? Can you compare those three?

A: I think the purpose is really basically the same, is to inform, primarily, to tell
people what's happening. We add to that in the editorial, we add something in
the way of writing to make some complex issues at least a little clearer than
they might be otherwise. And ... advocacy becomes a part of it too ...
   I insist that there be balance in what we do in the newsroom, when I wear
my other hat. I'm not interested in the opinions of reporters. I'm interested if
they want to give me their opinions, I'm not interested in printing them. We
allow them some latitude in a feature piece, say on page seven [op-ed], to be
highly interpretive, but basically a news story should be without advocacy of
any kind. You can't be totally pure, just the selection of quotes and views
whatever you, I suppose, betray a viewpoint, but I get very upset if I find a
story in our paper can be classified as advocacy. And yet I think that's essential on the editorial page. And I don't think it's essential on an editorial page
if we run an article against the national energy policy, you then have to run an
editorial talking about the virtues ... We may acknowledge that so and so
claims that the national energy policy is doing this and doing that to help Canada, and then say thus and thus, but that is properly the job of an editorial

page. That is not properly the job of a news reporter. So if [names reporter who is a labour specialist] writes a piece for page seven about the Canadian Labour Congress, he's allowed to write with considerable latitude, but he shouldn't at the end say that CLC is a lousy organization or that it's a great organization. We will buy the work of outsiders who'll say one thing or the other about the CLC, but it's understood if you buy an article by Cliff Pilkey, that you're going to get Cliff Pilkey's opinion and that doesn't properly belong on our editorial page, it belongs on the op-ed page. And we commission people to write about what's wrong with the press. We don't agree with them, always. We'll have them write about a host of subjects ...

Q: Would you have a different approach to your own reporter writing on page seven to an outsider?

A: Yes. Our reporter is allowed, as I say, a high degree of interpretation, but not advocacy. Our Cliff Pilkey or whoever it may be, including a fair number of academics ... we put no limits on you other than good taste and the federal Libel Act, but our own reporters know that they're not allowed to because they have to go out and be reporters the next day and they shouldn't be showing that they have a bias. Columnists, that's another matter. Columnists have every bit as much freedom as the editorial page, in fact more, because they're not bound by – they have one rule around here, one rule on the editorial board. That is, if you change your position in any major way on a given subject, you must say why you changed your position. This produces a fair consistency. Now, you have to watch out then that you don't become so circumscribed by what you said in the past that you can't innovate and alter your policy in the future ...

Q: Do you ask people, if they've changed their minds, to actually present you with evidence that they've come across that would lead them to change their mind? Just to say hypothetically, someone changed their mind about the marijuana issue and decided they would like to have it kept under the existing legislation, would you ask them to provide you with some evidence as to why they changed their mind?

A: Yeah, and they do and they have, and that is, you hit on one where we had someone on the board who changed after we'd been involved in advocacy for quite some time, and the evidence was duly presented and we all mulled it over and chewed it over and decided, yeah, that's very interesting, we're glad you feel that way but we don't. And it's perfect democracy, I have more votes than all the others.

Q: What do you mean by that, you can always veto?

A: Yes, even if I have the board collectively disagreeing with me, I can say, well that's not the attitude we're going to take. I have to feel in those instances that I don't just speak for myself, I speak for the publisher, and the chairman, and then I have to take a position on my own. It doesn't happen very often. Usually if we come to something like that we take a breather, we'll not write on it for several days, then talk it over again. We'll finally decide, it's almost never me against the rest of them. We do split. It's the mark of a professional approach in the members of the board that even if they disagree with the stand we're going to take and it's in their area, they would rather write it than have someone else write it. They say at least then they can temper it.

Editorials are a primary means by which the reporter learns what are the 'sacred cows' of his newspaper. While he is not thereby directed to choose stories, sources, and formulations that are consistent, there is a tendency to do so. This tendency is difficult to document directly, but the scenario can be visualized. Assignment editors and reporters perceive through editorials what their superiors deem to be the most significant problems, and approaches to their resolution. The urge to follow, and add further to, the information in an editorial in a 'third-day lead' seems inevitable.

Other editors in the newspaper were very sensitive to this tendency. One senior editor responsible for news operations stressed that: 'We have a division between the editorial functions and the news functions,' and therefore the editor-in-chief 'has to be very circumspect to make sure that he's not leaning on news to enforce an opinion of the editorial board. I mean he is very circumspect.' The editor-in-chief also saw the influence of editorials on reporting as subtle and inevitable, although not always in the direction of supporting the authoritative position of the board.

> I'm sure a good many of the people in the newsroom read them and don't agree with them, and don't agree with our main arguments. I sometimes am convinced that reporters will think it is essential that if we've made a point, they'll try to make the opposite. And that rather requires some nifty work because they're not allowed to write a piece of advocacy, they have to try to produce facts I guess to tear down the case we made. But I don't think we have any people in the office who feel, ah ha, this is the editorial position of the [newspaper] on a subject, therefore I will write stories that will enhance that position, and goodie goodie I'll get ahead, because that becomes immediately obvious, you stop that right away ... I filter down on news policy but I certainly don't filter anything down on what attitudes I expect from other people. Occasionally I will ask that we look into something, principally because I don't know anything about it; I'll say, you know, there's something strange going on at the Widget Company, we carved two or three little bits, but they don't make sense to me, I think we should get a real thorough piece done on widgets, the Widget Company. But I don't give any directions on where I want to go. If I've heard any gossip I'll pass it on, because it might be useful to a reporter. The same with politics for that matter. But no, I don't want our people to bear in mind what our editorial concerns are ... [O]ur reporters were

generally aware that as a newspaper we were very much interested in the constitution, the changes, and therefore wrote a good deal about it. Now I think
that they got that direction from the managing editor, who thought it was a big
story and an important story. So they weren't always writing material that was
useful to the arguments we were making about the constitution. I think the
constitution is probably one issue in which the majority of the news staff probably didn't agree with us. They're wrong! ... You develop a kind of instinct
for news. I forget exactly, we carried an item in the Briefs about two weeks
ago, half-way down, that said three people had died in Chicago of adulterated
Tylenol. I came into the office that morning and saw the item, I clipped it out
and I wrote a *dirty* note to the managing editor and I said, 'That's your idea of
a brief! That's a big story that's going to be on the front pages.' It was, and it
is. You know, you didn't subsequently write a little piece about Tylenol that
didn't have anything to do with how we were displaying the story, it was just
that I could see it, all my instincts are going, there's a story that's going to be
all over the place. Because Tylenol, probably the next to aspirin, is as common a drug as you'll find, and everybody identifies with it. So I do that kind
of thing.

There was no similar editorial function or direction in the television
newsroom. One anchorperson was given some time to comment on items in
the news, and also a five-minute feature segment in which he and the reporter
involved would comment and make recommendations for solving the problem
covered. However, unlike other parts of the newscast which borrowed newspaper terms such as 'the front page,' the term 'editorial' was not used. One
reporter told us that the television organization did not even like the use of
the term 'commentary' for the anchorperson's comment segment, and settled
on 'analysis' as the preferred term. Obviously television provided no opportunity for anonymous editorials in the name of the organization as a whole,
as was the practice with newspapers. The anchorperson's analysis pieces were
in effect the equivalent of newspaper-column opinion pieces by a regular
contributor. There was no indication that what he had to say in these analysis
pieces had a bearing on reporters' work, since reporters did not regularly
watch newscasts to even learn what he had to say.

Senior Editors. Another élite corps of the newsroom consisted of editors who
participated in the daily news conferences. Just as the newspaper editorial
board sat in judgment over what deserved further attention and thrust, the
news-conference group of desk editors, managing editors, and news editor
gathered once a day to consider what required emphasis. News-conference
meetings were formally designated as the context to make major play decisions, especially what items from each desk were appropriate for front-page

coverage. This primary function of making play decisions was signified by the fact that the news editor sat at the front of the table at the meeting, with the desk editors giving him input of significance.

Beyond the issue of play decisions, these occasions were used to consider what angles might be used to further continuing stories. Usually angles being pursued at the time were discussed, then further questions which could be addressed were raised. The desk editors concerned used this process as a means of learning what to do next, and in turn communicated to reporters the directions to take in their assignments and story construction. The meeting was also characterized by discussion about possibilities for assignment, with an editor mentioning something he had heard about and was putting on the table to obtain a reaction from others.

These meetings also provided the opportunity for feedback on operational matters. We observed the managing editor and the asitant managing editor commenting on filed copy being late and urging editors to get the material in on time. Errors were discussed, including the need to reprint things that were grossly wrong. An editor who had urged that a story appear on page one was most upset to discover that it had been given less prominent play than that given by a competing newspaper. This anomaly was pointed out to other senior editors as a confirmation of his previous judgment, and the faulty judgment of his colleagues.

In summary, the news conference was *the* formal setting for the daily articulation of the vocabulary of precedents among editors. The result was rarely a direct order to cover things or formulate accounts in particular ways. Rather it was a process of reminding one another about what was expected, including the expectation that reminders would in turn be communicated to reporting staff.

Similar articulations were developed in the television newsroom, albeit on a less formal basis. The executive producer, producer, lineup editor, assignment editor, and anchorperson met regularly, although not formally, to discuss possible new directions and formats, as well as specific story ideas, angles, and themes. Again these were communicated to reporters in memoranda and/or in specific assignments and the preparation of stories. The senior personnel clearly controlled and gave direction on overall format and themes, and were also much more directly involved in day-to-day story production than was the case with senior newspaper personnel.

EDITORS' SUPERVISION AND CONTROL OF REPORTING

Television producers and editors often had a direct hand in the reporting process. The executive producer took over script preparation and film editing in major disaster stories involving several reporter-and-cameraman units. He also took over film editing on occasions when reporters were having difficulty close to the deadline, and when several reporters required access to the editing technicians quickly in order to make the show. On a regular basis the executive producer consulted with reporters on the preparation of their stories and writing of scripts. Compared with previous role-incumbents, he was seen as the most directly involved in the reporting process. Some reporters saw him as 'too involved,' especially since the producer, lineup editor, and assignment editor also urged, hectored, cajoled, and advised reporters on what to do. There were complaints of 'too many chiefs,' creating conflict and confusion in what was expected and who most required pleasing. There was also a depiction of the editing process as 'writing by committee' as two or three persons (executive producer, producer, lineup editor) asserted control over the script and production.

Reporters were required to have their scripts reviewed at the producer or executive-producer levels. This review was often perfunctory, but at times there were requests for further information and even major rewriting. For example, a reporter was assigned an update on an investigation into deaths at a children's hospital. It had been announced that the Centre for Disease Control in Atlanta, Georgia, had been contracted to do some research on the problem, and the reporter called an official there for a voice-tape interview. She decided to do a stand-up, along with stock pictures of dead babies and of digoxin bottles (digoxin being the drug believed to be the cause of death through overdose) to use as visuals along with the audio-tape of the interview. A producer then told the reporter that he did not want her to use stock film. He said 'You don't want to start with history,' and asserted that he wanted a 'today's story.' He told the reporter to write a script and he would then help her.

The reporter drafted the following script:

Anchorperson Roll-up: Medical experts at the Centre for Disease Control in Atlanta say foul play may not have caused mysterious baby deaths at the [names hospital]. While experts there haven't ruled out foul play – they say they are looking at other reasons for the deaths ... like medical errors and faulty drugs.

Reporter: The speculation continues ... but so do the studies. How did 28 babies die at the [names hospital]. We contacted experts at the Centre for Disease Control in Atlanta, Georgia – by phone. They are doing a statistical study to see if they can say how these suspicious deaths occurred. We talked to Dr Clark Heath.

Source: The focus, of course, has been on foul play – but other possibilities exist, like systematic errors, procedures that go on in the hospital, the use of medication, the clinical condition of the patients, afterall, all these patients are very ill.

Reporter: Do you have any evidence that these deaths were *not* due to foul play, but due to other possibilities?

Source: I can't say.

Reporter: The Centre is doing the study for the Ontario Ministry of Health at the request of [names hospital]. It should have its results ready by the end of January. Dr Heath warned people not to jump to conclusions ... about the baby deaths. It's still an unresolved issue ... he said – a complicated matter. Maybe the Centre of [*sic*] Disease Control will reach some answers ...

Upon completion of this script the reporter said to the researcher that she was prepared for a fight with the producer. She wanted the facts of the baby deaths 'up top,' saying the audience does not listen to dull introductions.

The producer proceeded to rewrite the script. As he made changes he said he was doing so because 'I'm the boss.' The reporter complained that it now sounded like a radio story. The producer wanted a freeze with the words 'Atlanta study,' and then vistas outlining the things they were investigating (systematic errors, clinical conditions, etc.). The producer suggested the second half of the script could be done as a stand-up, but the reporter countered that was too dull and boring. The reporter mentioned to the producer that she had called a spokesperson for a judicial inquiry into the deaths. The producer then suggested that the reporter mention that there were now three studies regarding this matter, using visuals of a baby nursery. He also suggested that a close-up of a baby in an incubator could be used for a 'freeze.'

After talking to the producer, and watching him rewrite her script, the reporter also complained to the researcher that the producer had transformed it into a 'radio story.' She said she liked to have things well written, and hated to begin a story with 'I contacted ...' as the producer had written in. She complained about the producer's lack of 'style,' and said the story was boring. Nevertheless, as all the changes to the final script were done by the producer, the reporter obliged. She also obtained visuals and had vistas made to make it appear a 'today's story.' The revised script follows:

Anchorperson Roll-up: A new probe into the mysterious deaths at [names hospital] says there may not have been foul play. But foul play hasn't been ruled out.

Reporter: I contacted experts at the Centre for Disease Control in Atlanta, Georgia ... by phone. They are doing a statistical study to see if they can say how those suspicious baby deaths occurred. We talked to Dr Clark Heath.
[visuals of reporter using telephone, then babies in incubator one to another, then freeze]

Source: The focus, of course, has been foul play but other possibilities exist like systematic errors, procedures that go on in the hospital, the use of medication, the clinical condition of the patients, after all, all these patients are very ill.
[vistas on other possibilities under exploration]

Reporter: Do you have any evidence that these deaths were *not* due to foul play, but due to other possibilities?

[fake shot of reporter on telephone asking the question]

Source: I can't say.

[fake shot of reporter listening to answer]

Reporter: This is the third study on such trends.

[outside shot of hospital]

There's the continuing police investigation

[woman nurse, hand in incubator]

The Dubin inquiry – which will wind up its probe of practices at the hospital next month ...

[Pan from shot of Donald Duck picture to hospital ward]

And finally this latest study being done for the Ministry of Health. The results should be ready in about a month.

[Nurses at incubator]

[stand-up in front of hospital]

Later in the afternoon another senior supervisor in the newsroom told the reporter that he liked her version of the story better than that of the producer. The reporter then asked the producer in a joking manner if she should sign-off with his name, the other supervisor's name, and her name, all included. She later commented to the researcher that 'writing by committee' was now common in the newsroom.

Television reporters have been depicted as lacking in autonomy. Observing the situation at a Southern Ontario independent television station, Clarke (1981: 26) depicts the reporters as being in an 'already alienated and dispirited position as non-autonomous, de-skilled television journalists, who, in the words of one news editor, "have been reduced to clerical workers." ' Similarly Schlesinger (1978: 59) notes that both television and radio newsrooms he observed in Britain were characterized by close supervision of editing. These findings of close supervision are consistent with what we observed, although not as extreme and uniform as that suggested by the wording of Clarke. Supervision varied greatly according to the producer's own predilection, how preoccupied he was with other business, and his regard for the experience and competence of the reporter involved.

One explanation for the closer supervision in television compared to newspapers was the producer's need to give coherence to items in a segment. The individual reporter usually did not know how his piece would fit with others, and it was the responsibility of producers to make alterations as they saw fit in terms of themes and segment continuity. Moreover, in television-news production reporters were more involved to the point of publication than were newspaper reporters. The newspaper reporter most often filed his copy and then learned what had been done with it when he opened the newspaper after publication. He had no say in the headline, nor did he know what was added from wire copy or other reporters, by the editors' own phrasing, or what was deleted. In contrast, in most instances the television reporter stayed with the production of the item to the end and thus had capability to at least negotiate final outcomes. The television reporter's control over the product to the end was a good reason for the supervising editors and producers to at least 'stay on top' of what was being done at each point along the way, and especially at the point of script and visual editing.

While reporters were generally monitored quite closely, they in turn kept an eye on their editors and developed their practices accordingly. Part of the vocabulary of precedents among reporters was a typing of editors according to their expectations and approaches. Some reporters said the most important influence on their work was the expectations of editors they had to take into account in producing a story, and they spent considerable time and energy articulating who liked what and what should be done accordingly.

Desk editors were especially important to newspaper reporters because they controlled most assignments, play decisions, and the granting of bylines and other rewards and punishments. We witnessed a turnover of editors on one newspaper desk that led reporters working from the desk to test over time the likes and dislikes of the new incumbent. For example, a beat reporter who had been filing only one or two stories a day because he knew there was insufficient space for publication of more, started to file three on some days. He said he was doing so to 'test' what the new editor would select. Over time this editor, in comparison to his predecessor, was typed as giving preference to hard-news stories over 'featurish' or interpretive pieces. He was also viewed as being in favour of traditional deviance stories, such as sex and violence spot news, which his predecessor seemed to disfavour. We witnessed a reporter filing material of this type, stating in justification that this editor seemed to favour it whereas his predecessor had not.

Reporters also wrote particular aspects of a story in accordance with the preferences of their desk editor. The new editor mentioned above was believed to like tertiary understanding and attendant dramatization of a story, and a reporter writing to obtain more play for his story from this editor said he was 'jazzing it up' accordingly. Some reporters were explicit in stating that they were developing angles to please their editor, emphasizing that the primary reference for their work was 'the audience of one' at the news desk.

Similar typing occurred in relation to the slot and copy editors who were responsible for preparing filed copy for publication. Again those new to the role were tested and talked about by reporters trying to make them predictable and their own work less equivocal. Reporters were particularly sensitive to editors who did substantial editing or 'rewrites.' In the words of one reporter, some slot editors approached their work by asking 'How would I have written this story?' instead of respecting what the reporter had put into it. Where possible, reporters developed filing strategies to maximize the possibility that their story would be handled by a slot editor who respected their approach. For example, a reporter talked about a slot editor who hated 'colour' and would always edit it out. Since this editor was always at work early and thus had his quota established early, the strategy was to file a story with 'colour' late so that another slot editor would be given it.

Reporters could also play on time and space limitations faced by editors to obtain the play they thought they deserved. It was generally regarded as being an advantage to file a newspaper story early, because there was less chance of it being cut in the context of the desk's allotment of column-inch space. Moreover making the deadline of the earliest edition was seen as an advantage. That edition's layout established the layout for subsequent editions, and one therefore received more consideration throughout successive editions if one's item was given a place in the first edition. Beat reporters who did not have access to a computer terminal in their beat office saw themselves at a disadvantage in this respect. They were often in the situation of having to wait for information to unfold at an official meeting or hearing on their beat, and then to rush back to the main office to file their material before deadline. General-assignment reporters working from the main office had usually managed by then to have filed their material, and to have established priority in the editing process.

The less overall space available to a desk the greater the control of editors in terms of the volume of material to choose from, and what from each item seems choicest. When space contracts the reporter wanting play is forced to be more pleasing to editors in angle, formulations, and format. This circumstance arose in one newspaper as a result of a decline in advertising. The same number of reporters were competing for less space. Reporters on the city desk were in agreement that this occasioned less autonomy for them because editors had more than enough material to choose from. In this context reporters talked about filing stories in terms of days of the week when space was believed to be more plentiful. For example, in spite of the extra pages in a Saturday edition it was seen to be 'tight' because the extra space was largely given over to features and special sections. On the other hand the Monday edition was 'light' because fewer reporters worked over the weekend and source bureaucracies were closed.

While editors of all types influence story production at all stages, the influence is often indirect and a matter of perception as articulated in the vocabulary of precedents. The reporter does maintain substantial control over the information he obtains from sources. Indeed, in the Canadian television newsroom observed by Clarke (1981: 28), reporters were called 'general news editors.' As Clarke observes, this is 'a telling admission ... that their work consists more of editing copy prepared elsewhere than of reporting either self-initiated or assigned stories' (ibid). In this arrangement the reporter's loss of autonomy is in relation to sources much more than editors, who suffer along with reporters in being 'nth-level' reproducers of copy prepared by sources. What autonomy exists lies in the particular ability of reporters to organize contacts for information and to imaginatively construe the information according to the genre capacities of their particular news outlet and medium. 'Whereas a newspaper would formerly publish *documents* and the official and nonofficial *records* of events, now it more often exploits its reporters' contacts and their ability to interpret events, to perform a kind of brokerage between the makers of the events and the surrounding society. The power of brokerage has thus passed from news editor to correspondent and specialist reporter, and as a result the editor cannot wield the same kind of authority he did in previous generations' (Smith, 1980: 186).

The editor is in a situation similar to the social scientist who does content analyses of the news. He is left to do readings of content, with little *direct* knowledge about the processes by which the content was produced. However, there are some major differences between the editor and the content analyst. In the rare major story the editor becomes involved because of its importance or his personal interest. The editor frequently questions the reporter about his product, while the content analyst rarely engages in such questioning. Also, the editor does his readings of *filed* stories, and of course has more than an academic interest in how they are turned out.

What the editor picks up on as important or praiseworthy may be quite different from what the reporter had in mind at the time of producing it. To offer a simple illustration, a television producer included in his regular memo to staff a commendation of a reporter for using a new location for her stand-up on a continuing story. So many items had been produced over time on this particular story that the producer believed the location chosen showed a degree of initiative and careful thought on the part of the reporter. He did not know that at the time the reporter and film crew had only chosen this location because it provided some shelter from the snow and cold.

The routine exchanges between reporters and copy editors during the course of editing also indicated that copy editors were mainly there to ensure a proper reading stylistically rather than to police directly the process of information brokerage and formulation by the reporter. In our observations of copy editors' requests to reporters, the information requested was usually a matter of primary facts (more facts, corrected facts); background information on the event and persons involved, including that which would contextualize it (e.g., relation to a theme; if crime incident, how many of the type compared to previous year; etc.); and, the meaning of words or phrases. Often a copy editor wanted clarification of something and the reporter was in a position to supply it.

Queries over texts often focused on what the copy editor thought was a formulation acceptable to news discourse. In a story on the reaction of prominent government ministers to the establishment of abortion clinics in the province, the copy editor had trouble with the sentence, 'He [a minister] refused to say what evidence persuaded him to oppose abortion clinics and whether this evidence was scientific or political.' The copy editor changed 'this evidence' to 'these considerations' because she thought the term 'evidence' was legalistic and did not apply in this context. She also thought the phrase 'He refused to say' was a little 'heavy handed' until the reporter explained that the minister had virtually slammed a door in his face. She questioned the reporter on his use of 'scientific and political' since her understanding of the minister's position from previous stories was that he saw it exclusively as a legal matter. The reporter said there were two questions. First, would the minister apply the law? The answer was yes. Second, why? Was it for political reasons? Was it for scientific reasons? The copy editor then decided to put in the phrase 'to support present laws' in place of 'to oppose abortion clinics' and the reporter agreed. The line was thus rewritten as, 'He refused to say what evidence persuaded him to support current laws regarding abortion clinics and whether these considerations were scientific or political.'

These efforts to grasp meaning in the formulation of fact were an everyday component of reporter-editor discussions. These discussions were usually not in the spirit of antagonism or disagreement, but co-operatively working out how best to give meaning to the reporter's story. Copy editing was one part of substantive editing of the filed copy, a matter which was ultimately in the hands of all journalists in the newsroom from reporters to more senior editors.

Substantive Editing

POLICING COMMON SENSE

Copy editors act on behalf of more senior editors to ensure that filed stories achieve a degree of uniformity. They police for accuracy, clarity, and consistency in news items. They enforce company policy regarding preferred readings and style. They ensure that the translation of an event, process, or state of affairs into news discourse fits with what is believed to be common knowledge, including knowledge about previous related matters in the news. In sum, they are to ensure that the working cultures of the newsroom (articulated in the vocabulary of precedents as a body of knowledge) and the dominant cultures of society (articulated in the common stock of knowledge, including news itself) coalesce in the final product. Their task is policing common sense.

The policing of common sense is worked out by daily negotiation and directives. The goal is to make the news texts understandable to a broad audience, and a primary means is the use of simple words and phrases. Reporters were constantly reminded that they are not purveyors of specialist knowledge, but translators of specialist knowledge into the common sense. These reminders were given most subtly when the reporter read the published copy and learned the preferred writing given by the copy editor without consultation. Reminders were also given directly when the editor discussed the reporter's filed copy with him to discern meanings and to clarify, as in the example above. More senior editors also articulated what was expected through their comments on the matter, as indicated in the following memo to reporters from a television news producer:

> It is with great pleasure that I declare September and October WRITING MONTHS. Sound month was so successful ([names reporter] was by far the class of the field) that we've moved on to another problem area. Our sentences run on and on and on ... many have a nasty habit of using link words to make one long sentence out of what should be two sentences. So *long* is out, *short* is in. (Pay especially close attention to 'ing' words ... They tend to make sentences run on and on ...) Flair is in. Use some imagination in writing your leads. You use the lead to sell the story. If it's humdrum why should anyone stay tuned in. Conversational, simple style is in: no more '-tion' words. We are not professors scientists doctors; we do not need to use words to impress people. We want to get a message across in a simple and easy to understand way.
>
> And grammar counts. Little slips here and there add up (almost was going to use a link word to run on and on). We have a reputation to maintain.

So a large component of maintaining a reputation is simply a matter of grammar, style, and interpretive flair. Each news organization develops its reputation through the use of words as 'trademarks' of its distinctive discourse. Through a limited stock of words used repetitively (Glasgow University Media Group [GUMG], 1976, 1980), each news organization draws upon the common sense, and in the process contributes to it and reproduces it.

Reproducing the common sense does not imply that everything must be reproduced for *the* lowest common denominator. While journalists often expressed a low view of their audience, there was also concern not to insult them with worn phrases or empty clichés. A television reporter handed a producer his story script. In the presence of the researcher, the producer berated the reporter for using a concluding statement, 'Only time will tell.' The producer later said to the researcher that this was a 'meaningless' conclusion, especially since their audience was above 'the lowest common denominator' and were turned off by such 'mindless statements.' He emphasized that the audience wanted to learn something from each item, and if they repeatedly felt they were not learning they were likely to stop watching. On another occasion this same producer was looking through scripts and muttering about the poor quality of writing. He said that his role was to act as 'grammar police.' Again this policing was seen as crucial to authority. Shortly after a producer's memo was circulated to reporters which included a heading 'Grammer [*sic*]' and stated, 'There isn't a night that goes by without a mistake. Please be careful. This more than anything else erodes our credibility.'

In the art of choosing words the writer and editor also choose preferred meanings. As we have emphasized throughout, and as asserted in the producer's memo cited above, reporters were actively encouraged to 'Use some imagination in writing your leads' and in sustaining the narrative which flows from the preferred leads. Giving imaginative interpretation is in turn a matter of choosing an ideology, and the editor scrutinizes in this respect also. The ideological labour of editing ranges from leads and story construction in general to the use of a single word or phrase.

A senior editor in one newsroom we studied experienced recurring disagreements with some reporters over the coverage of industrial conflicts and their resolutions. He was essentially pro-management in orientation, not sympathetic to unions and especially negative about strikes. On one occasion there were two items on strikes available for the day, and he urged a third general piece on strikes in the context of the depressed economy at the time. In his words to another editing colleague, this would focus on 'why people are so stupid now that they would go on strike.' On another occasion he was critical of a story that highlighted the 'victory' of a union over a major car manufacturer. In his general memo to staff concerning the show of the previous day, he listed this story as his lead example of 'bad news': 'Bit disappointed with the angle of the story, my understanding was that we were to see where Chrysler had won or lost by doing some arithmetic to find out how long it would take for them to make up lost money given their new contract and we were to explore lost mortgages, lost cars, etc. ... I had seen enough stories already with people claiming that this was a victory for the *Canadian* UAW [United Automobile Workers of America].'

The effort to encourage a particular reading occurred in the ongoing exchanges among editors and reporters. Reminders came from above in the form of memos such as the one just cited. They were evident also in the angles negotiated between reporters and editors and written onto the assignment schedules. Taking an example from schedules submitted to a newspaper editors' afternoon conference, stories listed included: '[named] Church trying to muscle in on Foster Children Plan' and 'our boys teach the Government a lesson about democracy as they try to get Crown Trust order made public.'

If the story turned in failed to meet editorial conceptions of preferred readings, editors made amendments. There was much more direct control of this type by senior editors in television newsrooms, because it was usually one of the producers who checked the reporter's script. In newspapers it was the copy editors who were charged with the task of making amendments as they saw fit, although desk editors and more senior editors also occasionally scrutinized material.

Reporter-editor ideological disagreements over phrasings were commonplace. For example, a newspaper reporter wrote an article about a woman who had physically abused her child over time and who was ultimately convicted of killing the child. The story arose in the context of a report on the Children's Aid Society's handling of the case, and at a time when the woman had been released from prison. The story went through three drafts, and was scrutinized by a senior editor whom the reporter believed was against publishing the story because he thought the woman should be left alone. In the eyes of the reporter as well as a colleague, the changes in the filed story took away the colour and made the phrasing sound more factual. For example, the reporter wrote the phrase 'the child bride from Jamaica' but an editor changed this to 'the young mother.' The reporter said a senior editor did not want any reference made to the woman's racial background, but the reporter thought it was relevant. Rather than argue directly with the senior editor, the reporter accepted the revised phrasing but then included a statement at the end of the story that at one stage there had been an attempt to have the woman deported to Jamaica.

Newspaper reporters often had no opportunity for negotiation when editing changes based on ideological considerations were made without consultation. A reporter filed a story on conditions at a local jail, which he said was altered by an editor to make the conditions seem worse. What the reporter wrote in as more positive aspects of the jail was taken out, and phrasings were altered to give a more negative connotation. For example, he had written that the jail was so crowded that some inmates had to sleep on mattresses on the floor, and the editor took out the words 'on mattresses' so that a person reading the story would visualize them actually sleeping on the floor. The reporter said he was annoyed that when he went for a tour of the jail on the day this story was published, the official who was supposed to be his host kept him waiting and then spent only ten minutes with him. It was another four hours before he was given a view of sections of the prison. He attributed this cool reception to the story that was ultimately not of his own making.

Reporters subject to editing they themselves did not approve of could seek remedy after the fact. However, just as news sources do not see much hope for effective remedy (Ericson et al, forthcoming a), reporters were reluctant to complain because they knew that editors had the last word on content as well as the structure of rewards and punishments within the newsroom. A novice reporter was observed while working on the reporting of an inquest into the death of a baby in which an insecticide spraying of the family apartment was cited as a key factor. He said he was asked by a copy editor to rewrite his story, moving some material more towards the beginning and setting up controversy by inserting a new paragraph. The focus of controversy was that doctors involved in examining and treating the baby did not give uniform accounts: some did not know about the spraying at the time, others thought it irrelevant, and still others thought it was the likely cause of death. The reporter told the researcher that he thought the editors' controversial lead, along with their headline, 'MDS disagree over cause of infant's liver damage,' was rather misleading because all the doctors had said in testimony that the fact of spraying would not have altered their course of examination and treatment. He said that the effect was to set up a conflict that was not really there. However, he did nothing to remedy this.

In contrast, an experienced reporter was most upset about editing changes that he was not consulted on, and complained to his desk editor. The story originally focused on a judge's decision to acquit three persons from a non-profit publishing company that distributed a newspaper for homosexuals. These persons had been charged with distributing an indecent article through the mails. The reporter said that his filed story simply reported on the judge's decision and what he said in court to justify it. The filed story follows:

TEXT:

For the second time in three years, a Toronto homosexual newspaper has been acquitted of distributing an indecent article through the mails.

An article on pedophilia printed in the December, 1976 issue of the Body Politic did advocate the practice but was nevertheless not indecent or immoral, Provincial Court Judge Thomas Mercer ruled yesterday.

Charges against three officers of Pink Triangle Press, which publishes the newspaper, were abruptly dismissed by Judge Mercer last week at the end of the trial.

In his brief written judgement yesterday, the judge said no proof had been produced to show that the men had been involved in the mailing of the issue in question.

He said the 'acts' described in the article, 'when tested by the Canadian community standard of tolerance, are indecent and immoral.'

While the newspaper does, in fact, advocate pedophilia, 'the issue I must determine is whether the element of advocacy renders indecent or immoral an article which without the existence of that element of advocacy is not indecent or immoral,' he wrote.

The article, entitled 'Men Loving Boys Loving Men', did not meet the criteria for indecency, he concluded.

Judge Mercer's decision yesterday was the same as that arrived at by another Provincial Court judge in 1979. The Crown successfully appealed that decision, winning the retrial.

During the four-day trial, defense counsel Clayton Ruby called mainly witnesses who work in the media to discuss whether they thought the article advocated pedophilia and whether it had any merit.

Several editors and producers said they found the article reasonably balanced and would print it or produce it themselves in their own medium.

Crown attorney Peter Griffiths said in an interview that no decision has been reached on whether the Crown will appeal the decision.

Mr. Griffiths based his case solely on the article and did not call any witnesses. In the interview, he said he had no regrets about not making a case for what he felt community standards were. 'He made no reference to the defense experts at all. They said it (the article) didn't advocate pedophilia but the judge said it did ... It appears he made up his own mind.'

After filing the story the reporter said he called the defence lawyer in the case. Another reporter was assigned by a night editor to interview a spokesperson from the newspaper for homosexuals and a spokesman for an anti-gay fundamentalist group. Completely outside of the reporter's control, these spokespersons were quoted in the published story. The reporter said he was especially annoyed that the fundamentalist leader had been quoted and expressed concern that his 'whole reason' for the story, the judgment, had been removed in favour of giving space to the opinion of interest-group representatives. The published story follows:

May sue McMurtry

Body Politic cleared in 2nd obscenity trial
For the second time in three years, a Toronto newspaper for homosexuals has been acquitted of distributing an indecent article through the mails.

And the next step may be a malicious-prosecution suit against Attorney-General Roy McMurtry, defence counsel Clayton Ruby said in an interview.

'We know who made the decision (to prosecute) in this case.'

An article in the December, 1976, issue of The Body Politic advocated pedophilia – defined as sexual desire of an adult for a child – but nevertheless was not indecent or immoral, Provincial Court Judge Thomas Mercer ruled yesterday.

Charges against three officers of Pink Triangle Press, the non-profit company that publishes the newspaper, were dismissed by Judge Mercer last week at the end of a four-day trial.

Mr. Ruby said a suit to recover documents seized in police raids on Pink Triangle Press is also contemplated.

He said freedom of the press took a giant stride with the decision.

'It means to advocate or discuss unpopular ideas is permitted. A free flow of ideas is essential to a democratic society.'

In this judgment yesterday, Judge Mercer said there was no proof that the three officers of Pink Triangle Press – Kenneth Popert, president, Edward Jackson, secretary, and Gerald Campbell Hannon, treasurer – had been involved in mailing the issue in question.

Judge Mercer's decision was the same as that of another Provincial Court judge in 1979. The Crown appealed that decision to win the retrial.

Rick Bedout, a spokesman for The Body Politic, said the decision was 'a vindication of our right to publish what we publish.'

He said: 'It's not our intention to be intentionally provocative ... (But) you can hardly talk about anything sexual without running a risk. It didn't matter how we talked about pedophilia. It was something they did not want us to discuss.'

Meanwhile, the president of a fundamentalist Milton, Ont., group promoting anti-abortion, pro-family values suspects the Ontario Government wanted merely to harass The Body Politic.

Rev. Ken Campbell, president of the Renaissance group, complained that the Crown did not seriously attempt to have The Body Politic publishers convicted. He said the Government pursued the case to pretend it was defending family values.

Mr. Campbell also lashed out at the Government for pursuing its prosecution twice.

'I couldn't be more opposed philosophically to everything that the publishers of The Body Politic represent,' he said. 'But at the same time, here is a case where fellow citizens are left paying the bill after being twice acquitted of the same charge.'

The Ontario Attorney-General's office should 'pay the shot' when defendants are acquitted, Mr. Campbell said.

The Body Politic says it paid $80,000 in legal fees.

Mr. Popert said: 'There is a determination on the part of somebody in the Ontario Attorney-General's office to make it increasingly difficult for us to operate.'

The aim of the Attorney-General's office was more to 'drain the resources' of the newspaper than to obtain a conviction, he said.

Nine members of the Pink Triangle Press face another charge – obscenity – in November.

The reporter initially called to complain about this published story to the assistant desk editor. When he returned to the newsroom later in the day his strong feelings about the editing had not subsided, and he wrote a memo to the desk editor as follows:

re my story on the Body Politic acquittal. The quotes and paraphrases from the judge's decision – which was after all what the story was about – were cut out after I left last night, apparently in order to make room for the comments of one Ken Campbell of Renaissance International. The well-known gay-haters organization. What is his relevance to the story. Did we need the rantings of a gay-hating bunch to 'neutralize' or 'balance' the comments of the defendants in the case? Is this a precedent? Do we now have to phone John Cacy or Clifford Olson for comment to balance stories on murder acquittals?

Several other people have mentioned precisely this to me today, remarking on the lack of judicial comment and the bizarre appearance of Campbell in the story. The only saving grace is my byline was not on the story. So the question is (and I have been careful not to find out whose decision this was lest that affect this memo) – who is making these kind of decisions at night and where did they learn their journalism?

Reporter-editor ideological conflicts over use of additional sources and information, and particular meanings and interpretations, were frequent. This is another indication that the newsrooms we studied were not the normative machines of consensus visualized in previous academic research. Rather, they were characterized by conflicting ideological claims and competing normative expectations. These were reformulated continuously in the vocabulary of precedents, and under negotiation constantly.

The articulation of working ideologies and dominant cultures through choice words and phrases was one central component of substantive editing. Beyond this, editors had other organizational considerations to take into account in policing the final product. One key consideration was the law pertaining to the limits of news discourse.

LEGAL CONSIDERATIONS

The law was highly salient in the newsrooms we observed, in sharp contrast to what Gans (1972) has observed in the U.S. context. As enumerated in chapter 1, there is a substantial range of types of law pertaining to Canadian news-media operations (RCN, 1981: 41–2). However, in terms of everyday concern in the newsroom, few types of law were taken into consideration. Most salient were the laws of defamation, libel, and contempt of court, which restrict what can be published or broadcast (cf Robertson, 1981). As is true of the way law enters into judgments generally (cf Bittner, 1970; Ericson, 1981a), much of it was 'invisible' to us as observers except when the journalist was required to given an explicit account of his legal considerations to others.

Editors felt vulnerable legally to the judgments of reporters. They had to accept reporters' versions of the facts because it would undercut reporters' sense of professionalism for an editor to undertake independent checks routinely, and because editors did not have the resources to do so. In a television newsroom a memorandum was circulated to reporters, in light of several recent legal suits, that while editors could alter reporters' material, reporters were not to alter what the producer had finally decided was legal reporting. Advice was added that, if in doubt, the reporter should have the item 'lawyered – it's free.' Two lawyers were available for consultation, and were consulted regularly by reporters, editors, and producers. The ultimate decision to use questionable material rested with the executive producer, although he had the option of going to his station superiors for a final judgment. The executive producer was interviewed on this topic.

Q: How salient are legal considerations to you on a day-to-day basis?

A: Extremely. I mean we're not here to break a law. We're not here to get sued ... There'll not be a week that'll go by without me being in touch with [our lawyers] one way or the other. The world has become especially suit crazy lately. Life after Vogal and Munro [two major legal cases] has been a real nightmare for newsrooms. Everybody suddenly thinks that they can sue and make a small fortune. I have three or four suits pending and they're basically all after Vogal and after Munro.

Q: What do they involve? What particular stories are they?

A: Just penny-ante stuff ... But, I mean, I expect those things now. In the beginning, if I got a suit, I got totally worked up, became nervous and anxious about it, but now I realize that if we've made a mistake we issue a correction, apology, pay the damage if we have to.

Q: You're probably quite dependent on your reporters in this respect?

A: Totally. If the reporters come back and say X, Y, Z, if it's into a legal area I'll question them closely and say, 'Well, did you get a statement from here? Did you find this out, did you find that out?' I question them closely, but the version of the facts that they come back with, I have to believe what they tell me. There's that trust. I've never been in a position where I've had to independently go to a source to verify what they've come back with. If I get to a situation like that, then the whole organization is in jeopardy because there is just not the time to do that ... [A]nd the whole notion of reporter professionalism at that point, goes out the window. I mean, we're in real trouble. And that is a spectre that sometimes haunts me, that I could end up with a rookie reporter some day who ends up, like for instance, the story about ... I assumed that the reporter had checked all that stuff, that it was not contentious. That it was just a series of facts. You have to assume that the reporter knew that. Well after that I never trusted the reporter again, that was it. The reporter is since gone ... [W]e have two lawyers in Toronto, and we have the capacity to get in touch with even finer minds ... So if a script is controversial, it gets zipped up right away ... to the lawyers. The lawyers come back and then we may engage in a session, a long session, where we discuss the pros and cons of what's said. The risks, they assess the risks of each area and decide whether or not to gamble. Ultimately that's my decision, although if it really gets into a controversial area, then you start bringing in the bigger guys and let them make the decision.

The law was also at the forefront of consideration for senior editors in newspapers. There was sometimes consultation with lawyers in advance, especially if substantial resources were about to be invested in a major task which might not pay off because of legal restrictions. The examination of copy by desk editors, and the evening news conference where the pages were scrutinized, provided a regularized opportunity for judgments about possible legal complications. In some instances a reporter was forewarned of possible problems as well as having his copy checked in detail. These aspects were discussed by a senior editor:

Q: How much are legal considerations in terms of possible suits, contempt charges, and so on, a part of your everyday existence? How often do these things come up?

A: Many times a day.

Q: Can you give me some recent example of things?

A: You're constantly looking at what people are saying with the libel laws in mind. Every time you've got a court case going [to report on] you're looking at libel, at contempt. There's not a day goes by that there isn't, there are several occasions in one day. Yesterday I was, we had a very tough one, we had the story on ... I was on the phone to our lawyers and ... personally on the phone to our correspondent out there and we wrestled with it and wrestled with it and suddenly finally came up with it. I guess that took the best part of, well forty-five, fifty minutes of my time to sort through that. I guess throughout the entire day, I suppose I spend the best part of an hour. There are some that are more difficult and there are a lot that are not really as difficult.

Q: Do most things come up in advance ... of the reporter filing a story ...?

A: ... If you're lucky you have it, and it's rare, you know that there's something coming and you can brief the reporter beforehand on how to approach it. Like with ... One of the troubles in that case is that he was saying that people that testified against me lied ... that they were forced by the police to lie, well, I mean that's about as big a libel that you can commit against the police ... When we know that's coming up, we can tell a reporter beforehand, 'Hey, you're going to have to tread very carefully in areas,' as we did in that case. But even so ... that was a really tough one. We had to get the lawyer over here and go through the copy. That took us a couple of hours. But sometimes you can deal with them in a matter of ten minutes or five minutes.

Q: Would you have many suits, actual suits?

A: Oh, I suppose fifteen, something like that.

Q: ... Most of these presumably would be settled out of court?

A: Oh, most of them are just dropped.

Since it was deemed to be the responsibility of editors on behalf of management to ensure legal safety, reporters who sensed legal complications sometimes filed the story, with the comment that they would leave it up to their superiors to decide. More often, they consulted with their editors along the way, or at least drew the possible legal complication to the editors' attention upon filing the story. This was a sign that in spite of editors' responsibility for these judgments, reporters, too, felt vulnerable. The reporter was the one most visible, the person in the public eye, when there were problems. Moreover, since the final decision was taken by editors, the reporter was affected by that decision regardless of whether he agreed with it or had input into it.

In a television newsroom, concern was expressed about the way in which items for the six o'clock show were edited by the night producer without consultation for the eleven o'clock show. Reporters said that the cutting of material – including qualifiers, or clips or comments from particular sources – made them more vulnerable to lawsuits than if their items were left intact. Newspaper reporters also felt legally vulnerable to what editors made of their stories. It was for this reason that they kept a copy of the filed story. It served as a means of covering themselves in relation to what editors did to their stories.

While reporters generally complained about management being too cautious with respect to the law (see also Minority Press Group, 1980a: 24), there were instances where the reporter was more cautious than his superior because he had better knowledge of the relevant law. A reporter attending a trial obtained what she regarded as newsworthy material during a *voir-dire* hearing before a judge, with jury excluded. The reporter's superior wanted the material reported, but the reporter insisted it was not permissible legally. After a heated exchange the editor told the reporter to call the newsroom's lawyer, who supported the reporter's position and no story was published. The next day the reporter covered the same trial and again obtained the 'best' material from the *voir dire*. The editor again decided that unless this material was included, the reporter's story would not be used because it was of less significance than other stories available for the newscast. The reporter argued the legal restriction on reporting this, and the editor told her to consult with a lawyer. She reported that the lawyer confirmed her view, and the editor stopped her in the course of giving a full explanation of the legal position. The filed story was not published.

According to reporters concerned, the caution of editors sometimes even extended to omitting material that had been scrutinized and approved by lawyers. Such caution was based in part on the pragmatic consideration that future space would have to be given to the source to correct or retract a story. We overheard a news executive's telephone conversation with a lawyer in which he negotiated giving play to an aggrieved source in exchange for dropping a libel action. The offer was for two paragraphs in a particular section of the newspaper, and the executive emphasized that it was not to be major play. We learned of several other instances in which similar deals were made, and this news executive himself stated in interview that negotiation was the most common means of handling threatened or actual legal suits.

Questions of law were entwined with questions of fairness and balance. In the area of reporting on political elections, television outlets were legally obliged to maintain balance. During our observations a television newsroom was served two writs for lawsuits because the station did not give two candidates in a riding equal time to that given the other main candidates. Two weeks later a 'fun' story on a woman political candidate who was portrayed as an 'Annie Hall' character, awkward and lacking in seriousness, was rejected. In justifying this decision, the producer referred to a suit against another television network for unfair coverage of a political candidate.

TASTE

Another consideration for editors is 'taste.' As with many other aspects of news judgment, 'taste' was difficult to define or articulate precisely except by reminders deposited in the vocabulary of precedents when instances of lack of taste were perceived. Here the reference group for editing decisions was the imagined audience, and what aspects of reality their values were presumed to tolerate.

To offer a flavour of the official view, the policy handbook of a television newsroom offers the following insights on 'good taste':

> The audience for broadcast information is composed of differing groups, and notions of good taste vary substantially between them. The broadcaster therefore cannot expect to enjoy the same complete freedom of expression of vocabulary or of visual presentation as is enjoyed by the book publisher, in live theatre or in the movie, whose readers and viewers by and large make conscious choices about what they read and see. Where matters of taste are concerned, therefore, care must be taken not to cause gratuitous offence to the audience.
>
> However, there will be occasions when in reflecting reality it would be inappropriate to excuse certain uses of language or depictions of violence or sexuality which normally would be avoided. To do so would be to deny ...

audiences access to certain events which may contribute materially to an understanding of the world in which we live. The following sections are intended to illustrate when and how such occasions might occur.

The policy book proceeds to illustrate how editors and reporters can use their common sense to ascertain what is the public's common sense of taste. Aspects of language, sex and nudity, violence, and grief and suffering are addressed. Also offered are an outline of applicable law and broadcasting regulations and advice on giving the audience a caution before broadcasting possibly distasteful material. Again the emphasis is on avoiding sensational or exploitive effects, and including the material only in the interests of reality. For example, 'Private grief may sometimes have a legitimate program purpose but must not be exploited for sensational effect and personal privacy must be respected.' Similarly, 'Violence must not be exploited on radio and television ... [The Corporation] as a matter of general policy does not portray violence, except where its depiction is an essential fact of the reality being portrayed. The presentation of violent scenes or events must be an accurate reflection of reality and appropriate to the context of the program.'

At a seminar for journalists of this television newsroom, discussion focused on whether the common sense in this regard should be a matter of reporter or editor judgment. The observation was made that there was a need to separate two decisions: the gathering of information and the use of the information. Using a case example, a news executive said he would be very angry if a reporter did not 'chase after' the information. His opinion was that it was up to the reporter's superiors to decide whether the method and material was in good taste and to edit it accordingly.

In our observations of this television newsroom, the question of taste arose often, and always with reference to the human body. In a story on protests by tavern strippers against municipal regulations, what visual angles were appropriate for showing the strippers on the job? In a story on police control of an anti–nuclear-weapon demonstration, was it appropriate to show policemen dragging protesters through the manure deposited by police horses? In stories about death, what could be shown or said that did not offend the dignity or undercut the tragedy of the victims and bereaved?

Taking the example of stories about death, producers made decisions pertaining to the appropriateness of visual approaches to victims. A producer viewed film of a victim of a fire, and expressed annoyance that such a close shot was taken of the dead man. Stating 'there's a matter of taste here,' he decided to use a side-shot instead. On another occasion he wrote a memo to reporters comparing the station's coverage of the suicide of a prominent person to a competitor's coverage: 'From the first day we have given strong pictures and script in a tasteful way. Originally we were quite angry at not getting a shot of the body coming out. ([A freelancer and competitor's crew] were on the scene for this. Despite having their own shot, [the competitor] bought out [the freelancer] to stop us from getting it.) In seeing the shot on the air I'm glad we didn't get it and I would like to believe that had we got it one screening would have convinced us not to use it.'

There were also recurring debates in the newsroom about whether and how to cover funerals. The common taste in this coverage was addressed in terms of whether it was appropriate to invade the privacy of the bereaved rather than in terms of the dignity of the deceased. A woman had been charged with the murder of four babies on the ward of a hospital where she was employed as a nurse. Her case was the subject of enormous news-media attention in the city, even after the charges against her were dismissed owing to a lack of evidence at the preliminary-hearing stage. When her father died, a reporter was assigned to cover his funeral but refused the assignment by booking off sick. Another reporter and crew accepted the assignment, and managed to obtain visuals in spite of being 'booed' and 'hassled' by the local people in the process. Her material was edited for taste and was broadcast. Several other reporters stated in retrospect that it was not appropriate to send a reporter to a funeral in this circumstance, and wondered whether this was a precedent meaning that more coverage would be given to the funerals of parents of infamous people. Over a month later, the reporter involved attended a staff seminar which addressed the question of taste, and she and an editor said they had to defend themselves regarding the coverage of this funeral. Colleagues were critical of the fact of coverage at all, as well as of the short distance of cameras from the people at the funeral. The reporter said sarcastically that the way the newsroom chose to cover funerals was to have other reporters refuse to do it and then dump it on her, referring to the other reporter who refused the assignment and booked off sick.

Obviously the matter of taste in this regard is judged situationally. When the funeral is of a noble figure – such as of a statesman or a man who serves the state as a police officer – the private grief of the bereaved family becomes insignificant compared to the symbolic satisfaction in the public culture of seeing large displays of loyalty and support from state officials. When the funeral was used vicariously to have yet another peak at someone whom many reporters believed was wrongly accused by the state and wrongly stigmatized by the news media, it became a different matter. There was distaste for using a private trouble to compound previous wrongful treatment of this person by the news media. In this instance most reporters' sense of common taste was quite discrepant from that of their editors.

Beyond the policing of common sense, editors must give order to the news by deciding relative merits of items, their links, and how they should be displayed in particular layouts and sequences. Their substantive-editing decisions in relation to particular items are considered in the context of what else is available. Editors apply their criteria of value to all that is before them to tailor each individual item, and to suit their need for a finished product that is more than the sum of the individual parts.

ORDERING THE NEWS

The decision of what play to give to an item in relation to other items involved many of the organizational considerations delineated in previous chapters. In this section we give emphasis to the fact that play decisions were not a matter of rules from senior editors which could be applied directly, but situated decisions in terms of time, space, material contraints, internal cultural criteria of value, external cultural criteria of value, and the need to give order and coherence to the overall product.

In table 8.1 we present the publication outcome for the stories originally assigned by the newspaper assignment editor in our systematic study of his work (see chapter 6). Similar data are not available for the television assignment editor. Table 8.1 enumerates that only 10 per cent of the stories were not published in some form. Moreover, among the nine stories in this category, three were left pending further choices rather than being eliminated completely. Another quarter of the stories were 'briefed,' that is, they were designated for only two or three column inches to state primary facts for the record, instead of being published as a regular story or feature, characterized by source quotations and the appearance of secondary and/or tertiary understanding as well as primary facts. Two-thirds of the 93 stories appeared as a regular story or feature. Most of these (40 out of 62) were published as initially expected by the assignment editor, while a small proportion (10 out of 62) were 'front-paged' and an equal proportion were reduced or added to by editors of filed stories.

While this table indicates that in the assignment editors' eyes, the majority of stories were published routinely and as expected, reporters sustained the view that it was difficult to predict the play they would receive. They appreciated that the editors had knowledge about other items and priorities that would come into play in shaping their own individual items. In this context, they generally wrote in the time-honoured pyramid style, putting their less important material farther down the story so that it could be routinely chopped by the editor conscious of space availability. However, this was not always a routine accomplishment since the editor's criteria of value could differ from the reporter's. Some stories were cut 'all over,' removing in particular less important sources, source quotations deemed to be embellishments, and what was termed 'light' material.

Leads and angles were also altered within the text at the time of first

TABLE 8.1

Publication outcome: newspaper assignment editor

Publication outcome	N	%
REGULAR STORY OR FEATURE PUBLISHED		
Routine	40	42.9
Front page	10	10.7
Reduced – space limitations	5	5.4
Other stories incorporated	3	3.2
Reduced – uninteresting	1	1.1
Reduced – later editions	1	1.1
Omitted – later editions	1	1.1
Sent to another desk	1	1.1
Subtotal	62	66.6
BRIEFED		
Planned or predicted as brief	16	17.2
Space limitations	5	5.4
Later editions	1	1.1
Subtotal	22	23.7
NOT PUBLISHED		
Reporter decides no story	3	3.2
Feature less important than others available	2	2.2
Reporter requires more time	1	1.1
Unspecified	3	3.2
Subtotal	9	9.7
Total	93	100.0

editing or even subsequently. A reporter told a story about his copy being changed the previous week. He said he was asked by his desk editor to obtain the reactions of a municipal politician to revelations about a possible major offence by a large corporation. This politician alleged that attributions about foreign interests being involved was a provincial government 'smokescreen,' and that it was a matter involving primarily Canadian money and prominent politicians from the party in power at the Ontario-government level. The reporter said he used this as the lead for the story and it appeared that way in the first edition. However, a more senior editor read the published story and said he did not want this lead because the municipal politician was always seeing a conspiracy by the provincial-government party in power. The senior editor rearranged the story so that the municipal politician's statements were placed at the bottom, and this revised version appeared in the subsequent edition. The reporter raised the question of what politicians and readers would think when they saw the two different versions, and provided the answer that they would conclude it was an 'in-group' newspaper of the party in power. Stories of this type were circulated among reporters as a reminder that play was difficult to predict because the reporter's hierarchy of value in the pyramid did not necessarily accord with his editor's and/or his editor's with that of senior editors.

In interview, more senior editors stressed that while they had the final word, and that this word had educational value for reporters, there was nothing fixed or rigid about it. Rules were sometimes made, but they did not last. A senior editor told a story about a former colleague at his level who ruled that crime stories were to be played down, literally.

> [Y]ou are concerned about overplaying stories as much as you are about un-
> derplaying stories. One of my predecessors made a rule because he thought the
> news department was getting a little excessive in its handling of crime stories,
> he made a rule that no crime story could appear above the fold on the first
> page. I was managing editor at the time, and we got a story that we put in the
> flare, top of the page, nine columns, it was crime, and he didn't object. The
> rule went down the drain. The story was the theft of a Rembrandt from the
> Art Gallery of Ontario. It was held up for a long while as [our newspaper's]
> ideal crime story, but no, we don't have rules like that ...

What does rule for the editor is time and space. Schlesinger (1978: 21) cites the BBC *Review of the Year 1930* in recording that 'when there was not sufficient news worthy of being broadcast, no attempt was made to fill the gap, and the announcer simply said, there is no news tonight.' Today, jour-nalism is defined as 'an ability to meet the challenge of filling the space' (West, 1956). There are to be no gaps in the nightly allotment of television-news time, and one's fill of news in the newspaper is simply determined by what the volume of advertising leaves over.

The newspaper editors' concern was that a sufficient number of stories are filed from which a choice can be made. Extra material in an item can be pared down, or the item can be 'briefed' or omitted. Reporters overwrite and write in a hierarchy of importance for the editor. Features and other 'timeless' items can be held on reserve to call upon when a day's supply is slightly under the demand. If things are light 'at the wire,' the wire services provide an endless supply of fillers. Therefore, the newspaper system from the editors' perspective does not convey a sense of falling apart.

In contrast television line-up editors and producers seemed much more actively concerned about time and space and the possibility of falling apart. This concern is mainly attributable to the fact that the broadcast-news show only comes together as it is being produced. New items are introduced, and existing items re-ordered or dropped, right up to and into air time. There is a live performance in the show through the on-camera work of the anchorpersons and the backstage efforts of the producer in the studio. There is a sense that the performance might not be brought off, and sometimes it isn't.

The producers do everything possible to remind reporters to set the stage for them in various ways. Reporters were constantly being told to schedule crews and technicians so that their items would be ready on time. They were also told to limit the time of their items to a predictable length that would make them manageable for producers. One memo about this issue urged reporters to operate with a length of one minute and fifteen seconds. It played on their spirit of colleagueship by reminding them that if they exceeded this time limit they were forcing editors to make 'either-or' choices which meant some items would be excluded. Reporters were also told to write in the margins of their scripts the time taken for each segment of their item, and the failure of reporters to do this consistently was a great source of annoyance to the in-studio producer.

As with newspapers, the television newsroom had a stock of 'timeless' items that enhanced flexibility. These items included those that did not require immediacy for their newsworthiness (e.g., the annual police campaign against impaired driving at Christmas time), as well as regular features that could be taken out if more important items required their time (e.g., a 'flashback' item recalling historic events in the city; items from a reporter who specialized in amusing 'brighteners'). The sports segment of the show was always placed last, and the length expanded if other parts were 'light' or contracted if other parts were 'heavy.' Also in keeping with newspaper practice, the wire services provided ample fillers if the programme was light 'at the wire.' Another option was to take the latest edition of the most readily available local newspaper and do a rewrite of one of the more prominent stories not otherwise included in the lineup, reporting only as much material as was required to fill the time.

Again flexibility was the order of the day. The one and one-half hours before the six o'clock broadcast on one day is illustrative. Between 4:30 and 5:00 a producer watched video feeds and scrutinized and wrote scripts, making several changes. He decided to drop a story that failed to be what was originally expected. He initially told a reporter to write the script for her story, but shortly after she was told to write only a copy story because a wire story on the same matter was available and would be used. The producer was particularly anxious about receiving the feed on another, major wire story, which had yet to come in. At 5:13 the director announced that they were 'five light.' The producer went to check progress on film and video editing of his reporters' items, and returned to tell the lineup editor that only one item might be late. At 5:30 the lineup editor announced that they were still light and suggested that they search for wire stories. The producer quickly found one story, and watched another one which he rejected. At 5:38 they were '2:45 light,' and the producer said he would give an extra two minutes for sports and make the rest of the time up with updates. At 5:44 the feed on the major wire story the producer had been waiting for finally came through. It was three minutes and ten seconds in length, and they were now three minutes and fifty seconds too heavy. The producer then informed the sportscaster that he might not be given the extra two minutes after all. At 5:47 the lineup editor suggested dropping the wire story found by the producer at 5:30. The producer decided instead to drop another story, and put in its place yet another new wire story with suitable timing. At 5:55 the producer went to the video room, and saw his major wire story get in one minute before air time.

For all news editors, the management of time and space is also a material and technical matter. A breakdown in video equipment meant that a scheduled item simply did not make the show. More common was the situation where the desired sequence of items in the lineup, combined with problems in production and/or insufficient editing resources to meet the heavy demand close to deadline, meant re-ordering the lineup and altering the items concerned. Reporter A was assigned a story out of the city regarding a woman reported missing by her husband, while reporter B was sent to a different location out of town to cover another case of a woman reported missing by her husband. The plan was to run these two items together in a prominent position, before the 'national' segment of the news. The factor of travelling time, plus the fact that reporter B managed to obtain an exclusive interview with the husband concerned in her case, meant late returns to the newsroom for editing. Reporter A was using film, and with processing and editing delays his item was not ready until 5:55. A copy clerk had to literally run it over to the studio, and did not make it on time. Reporter B's material was not ready until into the show. Hence, the scheduled slot was lost. The in-studio producer decided that the two items should be kept together. He moved them to the least prominent and only slot available, the 'recap' at the end of the show.

Play decisions were also understood in terms of criteria of value internal to the newsroom. As outlined in the previous sections of this chapter, editors and producers expressed and effected their own ideological preferences for coverage, and it was generally acknowledged among reporters and editors that these preferences were inserted into play choices. In one newsroom there was ongoing major conflict regarding the ideological preferences of one senior editor. Two reporters in particular repeatedly faced this person's alteration of their stories, allotting them more limited play than was reasonable, and frequently dropping their items entirely. Their beliefs about this person's ideological bias were shared among a much larger group of reporters, and also concurred with on numerous occasions by another editor. One reporter who repeatedly had his stories dropped was eventually dismissed. Even after the dismissal, he and others still in the newsroom attributed the problem to the ideological differences between him and the senior editor. Just before, and continuing after, this dismissal, other journalists took up the cause, retaliating against the senior editor in various ways. For example, they listed the reporter's rejected story from the previous Friday on Monday's assignment schedule; they produced stories of extra length and complexity than expected in order to disrupt the senior editor's efforts to give order to the final product; they 'sabotaged' his office; and they complained to higher authorities. Shortly afterward the senior editor himself was dismissed.

Editors' internal criteria of value are reflected in whether a story is given substantial play; in newspapers, they are also reflected in whether the reporter is given a byline. The higher in the television lineup, the greater the reward for the reporter because high placement is taken as a sign of the relative significance the producer gives to the reporter's work. This view was sustained in spite of an appreciation by reporters, editors, and producers that order in the lineup was not just a matter of 'intrinsic' importance of the story or the quality of the reporter's work, but contingent aspects of temporal, spatial, and material resources as documented above. Similarly in the newspaper, page one was the ultimate reward, being 'briefed' the ultimate put-down short of having the story rejected entirely. Indeed, being briefed was defined by some reporters as the equivalent to 'no story' and hence represented no accomplishment.

Newspaper reporters and editors placed great value in bylines. The granting or withholding of a byline was *the* routine means of reward or punishment. A byline was a shared, public sign of a job well done. Reporters repeatedly expressed satisfaction at being awarded a byline. Editors repeatedly expressed the value of the byline in signifying good work and thereby socializing reporters into their terms of the vocabulary of precedents. One senior editor said in interview that reporters 'certainly see it as something to have and work for.' He stated that 'bylines should be applied to meritorial stories where you think somebody has written either exceptionally or he's done a good job of reporting or done something just a notch above the ordinary and has earned a byline and I agree with that.'

The length, complexity, and importance of the story had bearing on awarding a byline. A short story with primary facts only and without a range of opinion was an unlikely candidate. A longer story that included a range of sources and opinions, and secondary and/or tertiary understanding, was a likely candidate. The longer story was also likely to have involved greater effort and 'digging' by the reporter, which was to be rewarded. Furthermore, from the assignment process onwards it was more likely to be judged as important and thus to be awarded a byline.

Another element in the assessment of quality leading to a byline was how clean the copy was. If substantial copy editing was required, the chances of its receiving a byline decreased. If the comments of additional sources had to be gleaned from other reporters who were not originally working as a team on the story, or from wire material, it was less likely a byline would be awarded because the contribution was no longer that of a single author. Awarding the reporter a byline in this context was seen as no better than giving the pitcher credit for a 'win' in baseball.

A reporter working as a topic specialist was seen by other reporters as having a distinct advantage in the byline stakes. One reward of being assigned to a topic specialization over time was an enhanced likelihood of being more routinely granted a byline. Not surprisingly, it was the management-selected rising stars who were put into topic specializations as a way of giving them public prominence and identification. In the words of one manager, bylines were also used 'as simply identification, so that readers can tend to relate to people whose bylines they come to know, who are writing in fields that they're interested in.'

Another aspect of choice-making in relation to bylines was the relations between the reporter and the decision-makers: the slot editor, assignment editor, desk editor, and managing editors. Reporters attributed instances of not being given a byline to 'crossing' editors, for example, by filing late or after disagreements concerning substantive editing. Several reporters expressed the view that one could not question the decision not to award a byline in a particular instance because it would 'cross' those who had made the decision and harm future relations with them.

The award of a byline was also seen as being related to particular aspects of newspaper layout. If a reporter had two or more stories appear on a page, only one at most would be awarded a byline. There was also a sense of the total number of bylines that could be given for the total items published in the page layout of the desk. It was deemed to be poor appearance to have too many stories with bylines. Again, reporters who were not topic specialists were somewhat disadvantaged in this regard since part of the daily quota of bylined stories was predetermined in favour of the topic specialists.

This byline system was not only a 'top-down' reward structure. During the course of our research reporters initiated a 'byline protest' by agreeing collectively not to have their names included with their filed stories. This protest was intended as a public sign of their concern over delays in completing negotiations for a new contract. It was permissible under a clause in the agreement between the newspaper and the Guild that stated that an employee's byline shall not be used over his protest. It is significant that even for the short period of this protest, some reporters expressed privately to researchers the wish that items they regarded as important, and which received substantial play, had been published with their byline.

Editors' internal criteria of value in play decisions also had to articulate with criteria of value in the wider culture. In this respect editors were especially sensitive to ongoing relations with sources and the hierarchy of credibility. This fact was revealed at news-conference meetings where page-one and other prominent-play decisions were discussed. In this context editors conveyed special pleadings from sources, for example, arguments for coverage because the source believed he had been maligned in the past. The current status and influence of sources were discussed in terms of deciding how much play to accord to a story involving them. The question of organizational status was bound up with these judgments. As mentioned previously, an editor explained to a researcher that he was not promoting a story on habitual offenders for the front page because the study-group report on which the story was based was not conducted by an 'independent group.' At this point he believed the study group consisted of concerned citizens, but he later learned that it had actually been conducted by an 'independent group', namely a provincial corrections association and parole board. The story eventually received front-page coverage on this basis. A researcher asked this editor what type of group he would consider not to be independent in this context. He said, a group concerned with the protection of prisoners' rights, and that that was the sort of group he had thought had released the report. The researcher suggested that the provincial corrections association and parole board could be considered an interest group, and the editor agreed but felt they were 'more independent' than a prisoners' rights group of the type he visualized. He added that the story made the front page because it turned out to be an important one in comparison to other stories for the day.

Editors constantly visualized filed news items in terms of the overall flow and coherence of the newspaper-page layout. On one occasion it seemed fortuitous that a reporter 'fishing' for stories at the annual meeting of the American Society of Criminology (ASC) in Toronto 'hooked' a story that could be juxtaposed with another one to offer consumers a 'reading' not otherwise available in each item singly. The reporter cited an ASC conference delegate claiming that police sell themselves as crime fighters in order to justify their resource expansion. Another delegate was cited reporting research findings on how crime rates are not always substantially different during police strikes. This item concluded with a quotation from the first delegate: 'We can assume that the selling is successful because their budget keeps getting passed, they keep getting stronger and stronger, the empire keeps getting larger and ... the press is, overall, very pro-police.' This item was immediately followed by an item inset by editors, with the headline, 'Police budget will require 7.5% more.'

The main article ran as:

"Crime fighters" as police image called sales pitch

Portraying the police as crime fighters is just a selling technique that doesn't really correspond to reality, says a sociologist with the federal Solicitor-General's office.

The Metropolitan Toronto Police's image as a 'thin blue line' protecting society from chaos is a promotional technique to justify its existence, said Margaret Beare of the Solicitor-General's office. She said that the selling is as calculated as a corporation's, and is 'exaggerated' in times of crisis.

Crime rates from 11 police strikes in the U.S. show that 62 per cent of the figures do not support the notion that criminals would run amuck without police, said professor Erdwin Pfuhl of Arizona State University in a speech.

The two were addressing a workshop at a four-day American Society of Criminology meeting in Toronto that ends tomorrow.

Miss Beare was reading part of a thesis about how the Metro police have promoted themselves for the past 25 years.

She quoted from the book of Toronto The Good, by A.S. Clarke, published in the 1890s, to show that public acceptance was not automatic.

'I can only ascribe the tyranny of the police force to one cause, an overwhelming majority of them, knowing themselves to be the scum they are, are aware that the only chance they have of speaking to a gentleman is to tell him to "move on," or to associate with one is to arrest him ...

'I regret to say that in the report for last year, no deaths occurred in the force, but I have much pleasure in pointing out that two men have been sent to the insane asylum.'

Miss Beare said in a interview: 'Crime fighting is one of (the police's) selling techniques and definitely a very strong one ... and yet, to a large extent, it is very difficult for them because they cannot control crime.'

She said the other selling techniques include isolating a group as dangerous and being seen fighting it, and creating problems that they can combat.

She said she did not mean that the police were deceiving the public but 'in order to maintain their existence ... they have to maintain community suport.

'We can assume that the selling is sucessful because their budget keeps getting passed, they keep getting stronger, the empire keeps getting larger and ... the press is, overall, very pro-police,' she said.

The 'inset' article was:

Police budget will require 7.5% more

A preliminary Metro Toronto Police operating budget of $295 million for 1983 has been approved by Metro Board of Police Commissioners for submission to Metro Council.

The proposed budget, which would require a third of the property tax reve- nue next year, is 7.5 per cent higher than estimates for this year.

The budget maintains an existing force of 4,458 officers and 1,544 civilians and complies with a Metro order for hiring freeze. The commission trimmed $5 million in various areas before accepting the budget.

Metro Chairman Paul Godfrey, a commission member, said the budget comes close to conforming to a Metro objective of a 5 per cent property tax rate increase next year 'but we are not going to place the community in the position of having our streets endangered because of the lack of police.'

Etobicoke Mayor Dennis Flynn, another commission member, said the pub- lic is asking for additional police protection.

The increase in the police budget was largely attributed to a 15 per cent increase in the cost of fuel. 'No one is suggesting that we limit the use of police cars,' said Mr. Godfrey.

Other increases arose from the taking over of the harbor and port police forces to give Metro Police total control over waterfront policing and from the expansion of civilian staff to operate the 911 emergency telephone system.

An estimated 90.2 per cent of the police budget is for salaries and fringe benefits. The budget lists over $225 million for salaries and $35 million for fringe benefits.

In television news the entire show was structured as an inverted pyramid, moving from the most important to least important items where possible. 'Editing is often regarded as the fulcrum of the film art' (Monaco, 1981: 103) because of the way it gives order to a series of statements (syntagma). In television news the ordering of statements is not only within a given item, but in the linking of a series of items as a grouping. Television lineup editors and producers deal in the syntagmatic in grouping items. In the process they introduce a logic or order that is not there 'spontaneously,' or in existence prior to their creative acts. The visualization of these links and groups begins with the assignment process (see chapter 6), but can be enhanced or altered throughout the day and right into the production. The thinking involved is largely a matter of seeing how one type of deviance and control problem is linkable to another under an appropriate rubric.

After several top of the show stories about Eastern-bloc countries, in- cluding the death of Breshnev, and the release of the Solidarity leader Walesa by the Polish authorities, an item was included in the same grouping on a major anti–nuclear-weapon demonstration at a local plant involved in weapon manufacture. What was scripted and filmed by the reporter as a local police- demonstrator public-order scuffle – with all the details of demonstrator num- bers, police numbers, arrest numbers, and visual scenes thereof – was syn- tagmatically linked to the Eastern-bloc stories to make a statement to the viewer beyond the sum of the individual parts. As suggested by this example, problems in deviance and control visualized and linked for the convenience of continuity have a manufactured quality with ideological implications. Regardless of intentions, the effect of giving order to the news is ideological. This is as true of newspaper layout (see Voumvakis and Ericson, 1984: esp. 56–9) as of television groupings in the lineup. As observed by the Glasgow group in their research on industrial reporting in Britain:

> [T]he continuous use of subject matter in a preferred order must in itself provide the elements of a structure of interpretation, aside from language. If the dominant logic of the news is to present fragments of information with no general coherence apart from that of the bulletin structure, this structure cannot be dissociated from a taken-for-granted interpretation of the world above and beyond the 'facts' and events being reported. It cannot simply be justified in terms of professional criteria of reporting and presentation; the placing of stories demonstrated very clearly that this is a structure which mediates in quite specific ways the information which is transmitted ... The close proximity between economic and industrial items suggests that items about particular industrial situations are likely to be juxtaposed with items (usually shorter) on the general state of the economy, with a resultant strong implication of a causal connection. (GUMG, 1976: 118)

The Fact of Fiction

In the 'as if' world of rulebooks it is possible to enunciate values about facts. An example is provided in a policy book given to television reporters: 'The editing process must result in a true reflection of reality of what was originally seen and heard and any terms agreed upon during the preparation of the program ... It would be impractical to expect the whole of reality in an edited program. What in fact results from selection and editing is a compression of reality, a slice of reality – which must nonetheless reflect the essential truth without distortion ... Production techniques may not be used to distort reality nor to have the effect of producing editorial comment.'

A manual for news producers in the same newsroom directed them to treat news as theatre. How can reality be represented, albeit in a compressed and sliced form, and the essential truth conveyed without distortion, using the techniques of fiction and drama as in the theatre? Is this a contradiction in policy terms, or a rather explicit and honest recognition of the fact of fiction in the human production of all texts?

We can begin to address these questions by considering again the nature of fiction. There is a sense in which everything thought of, categorized, and characterized by humans has an element of fiction because it is not the thing itself. As Nietzsche observed, 'What can be thought of must certainly be a fiction.' Fiction is bound up with our ways of imaginatively construing the world, of visualizing what something is to know it and act upon it. Most of organized life is dependent upon acting 'as if' things are as they have been imaginatively construed. The law requires legal fictions to take and justify action (Fuller, 1967). Historians require regulative fictions, 'the imposition of a plot on time' (Kermode, 1966: 43). Social-science ethnographers interpret their materials so that they are something 'made' or 'fashioned' and in that sense are fictive (Geertz, 1973: 15; Van Maanen, 1979). The same holds for the practices of science more generally (Knorr-Cetina and Mulkay, 1983).

In the case of literary fiction, to which news discourse seems most akin, the essence is what Coleridge once termed the 'willing suspension of disbelief' so that the material can be engaged as if it is reality. Literary fictions are 'consciously false' (Varhinger, 1968), and hence not intended to deceive. In this light, perhaps the best analogy for news discourse is that it is like the novel as originally conceived, that is, as fiction whose function was to report facts about the world.

In news discourse, as indeed with all human discourse, fictions are employed to discover and apprehend the world. As such fictions give order to the world and are essential to the creation of an orderly world of fact. We experience events with a sense of randomness, except when we attend to them closely and analyse them for patterns. News discourse provides analysis in this sense, using fictions to order news products and how those products depict the world. '[T]he randomness of events occurring daily around the world is presented by the daily newscasts as a structured, artistically contrived unity' (Pietropaolo, 1982: 53).

Like the novel, news discourse is also a fantasy. As with fiction, fantasy does not mean that it is all made up with whim and fancy, or that it is intended to deceive. Rather, it is grounded in reality, a way in which people both make sense of their experiences and make their social worlds. It is also a methodology for 'the imaginative and creative interpretation of events that fulfills a psychological or rhetorical need. The Greek root is *phantaskikos* and means to be able to present or show to the mind, to make visible. A fantasy theme is a way for people to present or show to the group mind, to make visible (understandable) a common experience and invest it with an emotional tone' (Bormann, 1983: 108).

Metaphor – an 'application of name or descriptive term or phrase to an object or action to which it is imaginatively but not literally applicable,' (*Oxford English Dictionary*) – is one means of accomplishing this imaginative and creative work. It assists in making things visible and understandable. It is a primary vehicle by which news organizations visualize deviance for their audiences. Without the attractions of metaphor, audiences might choose not to see it, and even if they do choose to see it they might not otherwise know what they are looking at.

Recalling some examples from television news cited previously, it is evident that accounts include metaphors to give them a reality they would lack otherwise. Metaphors were strategically placed in the anchorperson's 'roll-up' or 'tease' to an item to secure attention and provide a basis for imaginatively construing the event. A reporter attending the inquest into the death of a person in a highrise-building fire showed his script to a producer. The producer told him to alter the roll-up for the anchorperson to depict it as a '*raging* fire.' A reporter who had interview clips from only three spokes-persons expressing disapproval of a RCMP 'secret' list on ethnic groups (per-taining to security clearances) prepared a roll-up for the anchorperson that visualized a surveyed consensus among a wide range of ethnic groups and citizens that this was bad news: 'News of a secret federal handbook on ethnic groups compiled by the RCMP has sent *waves of anger* and *tremors of fear* through some of Metro's ethnic communities. As [names reporter] reports, the *communities are disgusted*' (emphasis added). A reporter doing a story on efforts to establish a halfway house for federal prisoners in a community where a specially formed pressure group of citizens was opposed to it, in-terviewed a spokesperson for the group and one for the organization trying to estabish and run the house. She also interviewed two citizens 'on the street,' but did not include their comments directly since one had not heard of the matter and the other did not seem to care. The anchorperson's 'tease' for this item before the commercial break read: 'A halfway house for [names area]. Half of the residents don't want it, half of them do, and [names reporter] reports from the *battlefront* when we return' (emphasis added).

Portraying ordinary human negotiations as if the parties were at war was not only a feature of individual items, but used over the course of several items grouped in a segment. For example, producer A and producer B met to prepare a script for the special municipal-election–night show the newsroom was responsible for producing. They tried out their lines aloud, while one producer typed out the snippets they both agreed were good. They quickly visualized an overall boxing metaphor. The proposed lead-up (not verbatim) was 'we have picked the heavyweight battles to highlight,' introducing to their audience the fact that their criteria of values would come into play throughout. Producer A suggested an addition: 'those fights likely to go the distance,' but producer B said most people would not understand that expres-sion and suggested, 'likely to go fifteen rounds,' instead. In response to this latter suggestion, producer A suggested that they include along with this phrase a bell ringing, as at the conclusion of a round in a boxing match. Producer B liked this idea, and then came up with another phrase for the metaphorical sequence. 'By casting your ballot, you're the judges.' Producer A then came up with, 'Sitting at ringside are our colour commentators ...' and producer B added '... to give you a blow-by-blow description.'

In television news, it is not only that one picture is used to say a thousand words. The choice of words itself is a means of visualizing much more than meets the eye. In this sense, the fictions of script metaphors are crucial to news productions. Having quoted Langer (1962: 117) that metaphor is 'the power whereby language, even with a small vocabulary, manages to embrace multi-million things,' Geertz (1973: 210–11) observes:

> In metaphor one has, of course, a stratification of meaning, in which an incongruity of sense on one level produces an influx of significance on another. As Percy [1958] has pointed out, the feature of metaphor that has most troubled philosophers (and, he might have added, scientists) is that it is 'wrong'. The power of a metaphor derives precisely from the interplay between the discordant meanings it symbolically coerces into a unitary conceptual framework and from the degree to which that coercion is successful in overcoming the psychic resistance such semantic tension inevitably generates in anyone in a position to perceive it. When it works, a metaphor transforms a false identification (for example, of the labour policies of the Republican Party and of those of the Bolsheviks) into an apt analogy; when it misfires, it is a mere extravagance.

Metaphors are constructed intentionally to make items recognizable in terms of the presumed common sense. Metaphors thus serve to give meaning and flow to events in the world in the recognizable terms of news discourse. The need to sustain the meaningful narrative means that the meaningful term is employed even if it is known that the term is not altogether justifiable in light of available knowledge.

Again recalling a story cited previously, a reporter wrote the anchorperson roll-up for her story concerning the ongoing research by the Centre for Disease Control in Atlanta into the deaths of babies at a local children's hospital. Her roll-up read, 'Medical experts at the Centre for Disease Control in Atlanta say foul play may not have caused mysterious baby deaths at the [names hospital]. While experts there haven't ruled out foul play – they say they are looking at other reasons for the deaths ... like medical errors and faulty drugs.' The producer rewrote the roll-up as, 'A new probe into the mysterious deaths at [names hospital] says there may not have been foul play – but foul play hasn't been ruled out.' The reporter stated that it was not a new probe, but the producer interjected, 'I'll let you explain that in the story' and left the sense of newness as a key ingredient of the roll-up.

On the day of a bombing at a factory involved in the manufacture of nuclear weapons, several reporters were assigned. One reporter was told to obtain a clip from the company president saying 'it's a terrorist act' (which he had said, but not on camera) and to obtain 'emotional responses' from him and other employees. At the point of the noon newscast, however, this material was not available and the primary coverage of another reporter only was used. The anchorperson introduced the lead-up with a statement that political terrorism had come to Toronto. This led one producer, watching the show in the newsroom, to shudder, asking aloud how 'they' could say that political terrorism had come to Toronto since they did not know who was responsible for planting the bomb. The story had been trademarked as 'terrorism,' with an implication of responsibility to anti-nuclear protesters, without any official evidence or source statement other than the off-camera comment of the president of the victimized company.

Why would there be a desire to describe as 'new' something that was admitted to be old? to describe as 'terrorism' something that was not otherwise confirmed as such? One answer is that fake words were required to invest these matters with significance, to make it apparent to the common sense that what was being visualized was worth attending to. They were important in filling the gap between a random event in the world and what most people find meaningful. They were used as one of several tools to give the items unity.

The need for order, coherence, and unity also motivated other practices commonly referred to in the newsroom as 'fakes.' According to *The Concise Oxford English Dictionary* to fake is to 'make presentable or plausible; alter so as to deceive; contrive out of poor or sham material; feign.' To feign is to '1. Simulate, pretend ... practise simulation. 2. (arch.) Invent (excuse, story, accusation), forge (document); represent in fiction, imagine.' The term 'fake' within the newsroom culture was not used to refer to intentional deception or forging. Rather, it referred to simulation devices, and fictions that would add order, coherence, and unity and thus make their items, segments, and entire newscasts more presentable and plausible.

Something deeply ingrained in the plausibility structure of newscasts is that the outlet's journalists have been 'everywhere' to cull the news and to produce first-hand accounts of their discoveries. Hence, references are dropped in at appropriate places in the script to the effect that the outlet's journalists have overextended themselves to ensure that they are on-the-scene witnesses of reality for their audiences. These references are such an important trademark of the newscast in conveying its sense of purpose that they are used even when the reporter has not been where he might have been or 'dug' as hard as he might. A reporter was assigned to cover a news conference, but he arrived late for work at the newsroom and decided not to attend. However, editors had already sent a cameraman to take visuals at the news conference, and the reporter used the film with his voice-overs to make the story. The anchorperson's roll-up script for this item included the phrase, '[our] specialist [names reporter] reports from their news conference ...'

Being there was also a matter of degree. Often reporters were visualized to be at an event culling the field for the discovery of news, when in fact they had pre-arranged an interview with a source prior to attending the event and undertook no inquiries beyond the pre-formulated frame and the source interview that would fit it. A reporter contacted an acquaintance he had known for a long time, who was in the city for a major conference on criminal corrections. He arranged to meet this person at the conference hotel to do an interview on the specific topic of violence in prisons and how this phenomenon is explained. Apart from talking-head visuals of his source, he had film taken of commercial display booths at the conference that exhibited weapons, electronic doors, barbed wire, surveillance devices, and other hardware paraphernalia of interest to prison adminstrators. These helped the reporter to visualize for the viewer the violent atmosphere that permeates incarceration.

In the on-camera interview the source was asked initially if violence in North American prisons was escalating. The source said violence in North American prisons had been increasing in the last two years and this was *one* of the subjects being discussed at the conference. The reporter did not pursue any of the other subjects and therefore could not give consideration to their relative importance to the delegates. He did not attend any of the dozens of conference sessions on a wide variety of topics or explore any other possible theme or issue salient at the conference. He had predetermined that the theme of prison violence was most salient, since at this time there were continuing news stories on a major riot at a Canadian penitentiary, with reference to two other riots in the previous year. Indeed it was this riot that made his frame newsworthy, and the continuing stories on this subject made it acceptable to base his entire story on the opinions of one source. In spite of this predetermination, the assertion was made in his voice-over script that for *all* delegates, 'their chief preoccupation was the rising level of prison violence and how to deal with it.' The lead of the anchorperson's script also underscored this: 'The rising levels of prison violence was the chief topic of discussion at today's session of the American Correctional Association Conference meeting at the Sheraton Centre. [Our] specialist [names reporter] was there.' While the reporter was able to show that he was physically in the conference building, busy visualizing the signs of the conference for the audience, the entire item was predetermined by his context of the 'increase' in Canadian prison riots (one that year, two the previous year) and the opinions of one expert source. For the sense of 'being there,' and of visualizing a heightened sense of violence in prisons and what was to be done about it, it was significant for the reporter to be on location at the conference. However, for the substance of the story it did not matter.

Producers and editors authorized fakes in relation to visuals. While helping a reporter with a large volume of visuals from a fire-disaster scene, a producer took the visuals and sound slightly out of synchronization to make the editing flow more smoothly. While doing this the producer talked about 'frauds' on television news. The greatest problem in synchronization is the need to have visual deeds accompanied by appropriate words. Good television news has visuals to show what the reporter has visualized in his script. Thus, in this fire-disaster story the script phrase 'Relatives waited anxiously for news of the trapped victims' appeared. In searching for an appropriate visual, the producer and reporter hit upon a shot of a woman in a 'M*A*S*H' T-shirt looking up and putting her hand over her mouth, with the reporter standing beside her. According to the researcher who was present when this shot was taken, the woman did not have a relative in the building, only her cat.

The approach to obtaining visuals is well illustrated in the case of a simple update story where the text said it all but visuals were nevertheless needed. The story was an update on the condition of a lung-transplant patient. Stock pictures were relied upon in the main. One exception was a telephone interview with the patient's father, in which the audio tape-recording was used with a fake shot of the reporter on the telephone (i.e., during the shot she was not actually talking to the father). The other exception was the concluding stand-up, with the reporter being shown in front of the hospital where the patient resided. The reporter insisted on this location, although a producer had suggested that she do it on the street outside the newsroom since 'It's dark out now, it won't make a difference.' This was as close as she got to 'being there.' Otherwise the visuals were stocks, and even these were possibly 'fakes.' One picture used was of a man standing on a farm property. A technician said he believed this was a shot of the patient, but he was uncertain if it actually was. Another stock shot was of a hospital operating room, but this was known not to be a shot of the actual lung-transplant patient's operation. Throughout the item no reference was made to the fact that these were library film clips, let alone to their 'fake' aspects.

Like all fiction, news requires an ending (cf Kermode, 1966). There must be an ending to an individual news item, and to a story continued over successive days. The ending is usually to be an acknowledgment of order, if not otherwise a happy one. Thus, if an incident of deviance or a social problem is reported, the social-control resolution is also required. In a story regarding efforts by a group of citizens to block a halfway house for prisoners in their neighbourhood, the reporter focused on source accounts from a spokesperson for this group and a spokesperson for the private organization trying to set up and operate the home on contract with the federal government. The reporter introduced her item live in the studio, and at the end she was shown back in the studio with the anchorperson. Based on the sample of two sources shown in the item, the anchorperson was prepared to state:

Anchorperson: [reporter's first name], I think *everyone agrees* that these people should be deinstitutionalized. How do you do it in a way that pleases everyone?

Reporter: I think public education is important. Mayor Eggleton has one suggestion, and that's what he calls a community outreach programme that involves teaching people in the community what group homes are like, how they run, taking them on tours, and also detailing in a handbook or pamphlet how operators of these homes could deal better with the public, telling them the steps they could take to educate them.

Anchorperson: So that everybody should become better informed about how it functions?

Reporter: I think so.

Anchorperson: Thank you, |reporter's first name|.

It is hard to visualize a more consensual ending than this. How could anyone – but especially persons watching television news – argue that they would prefer not to be better informed?

There must also be an ending to an overall newscast. Producers order their segments to flow towards an ending which is often a 'brightener' or good news. The flow is often structured from really bad news to less bad news to bad news to good news. Incidentally, this flow is the opposite of at least one scholarly approach to the news (GUMG, 1976, 1980, 1982). The evening television-news shows we studied, designed as they were for the 6:00–7:00 p.m. dinner hour, perhaps adequately captured what Brecht has termed the 'gastronomic.' They reach a happy ending and acknowledge order just in time for the viewer to resume his normal, stable, and orderly routines.

The examples in this chapter illustrate most vividly that editors and producers are compelled to imaginatively construe, alter, and even forego the facts in order to sustain news as a form of fiction. Concerned as they are with news as theatre, it is impossible for them to 'reflect the essential truth without distortion' or to avoid having 'production techniques ... distort reality' with 'the effect of producing editorial comment.' The fact of fiction is too central to the news genre for it to be otherwise.

PART IV

Conclusions

9

Conclusions

In previous chapters we analysed how journalists organize to make news about deviance and control, and we made evident the nature of knowledge-claims in the news. In the process we also made our own claims to knowledge, and we now summarize these and draw conclusions from them.

Our research contributes to knowledge in three general areas. First, it broadens understanding about culture and social organization. Second, it is instructive about the nature of social deviance and control. Third, it illuminates some of the distinctive features of contemporary politics. In delineating the contributions of our research to each of these areas, we show at the same time how aspects of organization, deviance, and politics are interconnected in the news process.

The News Media and Organization

SOCIAL ORGANIZATION AND NEWS TRANSFORMATION

It is the organization of news, not events in the world, that creates news. Organization includes not only that of the news-media institution and particular news operations, but also sources and their apparatus for making news (Blyskal and Blyskal, 1985). As we document and analyse in a subsequent companion volume, (Ericson et al, forthcoming a), source organizations work out, in ongoing relations with journalists, what information they are willing to provide routinely. Sources have to conform to news discourse if they wish access, but they negotiate the terms of communication with journalists.

In reality journalists become entwined with their source organizations, and sources become reporters for news organizations. A fluidity exists in organizational boundaries, because first and foremost all organization is constituted by social relationships among people who have common tasks (Weick, 1979). Through their visualizations and practices, journalists are actively involved in *organizing*: they shape the nature and direction of their own news organization, the news-media institution, and the source organizations and institutions they report on. In *enacting* their environments, journalists are a part of what they report on: often physically, usually in social relations, and always symbolically.

Journalists visualize deviance, control remedies, and political reform in much the same way as the organizations they report on. They are one of the many agencies for policing organizational life, although with a much wider mandate and field than most other agencies. This policing is usually accomplished subtley through choice of topics, sources, frames, and formulations, that transform the matter into how they want it to appear. Occasionally it is more direct, as journalists literally create the procedural irregularity they wish to report on. Regardless, this emphasis upon the policing of organizational life is part of the obsession with bureaucratic procedure in modern society, which provides *the* basis for underpinning or undercutting claims to legitimacy and the attendant authority of organizations within the social structure. News of deviance and control rises to the fore because of this focus on procedure. While it has other values and functions – holding audiences because it is entertaining; fitting with constraints on making news in a predictable way; articulating with news culture values of what is newsworthy; instructing about dominant culture values concerning the nature of social order – news of deviance and control dominates because it contributes to the organizing and enactment of social life.

Interpretive work is necessary as journalists transform activity in source organizations into news events within their own organizational system. Information does not lie around like pebbles in the sand, waiting to be picked up and turned into knowledge. Knowledge is interpretation in context, and all work of journalists involves interpretation in context as they transform the specialized and bureaucratic knowledge of sources into the common sense. What is required to do this is itself common sense, knowledge that seems natural, practical, simple, immethodical, and accessible. The reporter seeks to illuminate, not to search; to borrow, not to burrow. His is the power of news transformation, constructing as part of the common sense what most people do not know otherwise.

Recent academic literature (e.g., Schlesinger, 1978; Tuchman, 1978; Fishman, 1980) has given emphasis to the fact that news is not a veridical account of reality, but a social and cultural construction of journalists and their sources. The journalists we studied recognized that their work is an interpretive enterprise; to repeat the succinct statement of a news executive: 'The whole process of reporting is investing facts with significance.' In valuing facts and putting them into their particular interpretive context, journalists give their stories a fictive character. As fiction, news stories seem unobtrusive enough, but they carry the power to imprint particular versions of reality as acceptable wisdom. '[O]ur media-metaphors classify the world for us, sequence it, frame it, enlarge it, reduce it, color it, argue a case for what our world is like' (Postman, 1985: 10).

A case can be argued that journalists' power of transforming knowledge into the common sense gives them a special place and influence in the contemporary knowledge society. The news worker is not merely 'an information broker to society' and news is not simply 'a library of human activity' (Smith, 1980: 11). Journalism is much more active than this. Journalists are power brokers, and news texts control human activity. Journalists are not only a hub and repository, but are active agents of organized life. As linkers and transformers of knowledge in its most elementary forms, journalists offer perpetual articulations of organized life: its problems and prospects, its excesses and successes, its sense of failure and promise of progress. Thus, journalists and their news products have a central place in the knowledge society. Commentators on the knowledge society have stressed the increasing power of those with specialist knowledge (e.g., Gabel, 1984; Böhme, 1984), but they have ignored the very significant power available to those, such as journalists, who are in a position to transform specialized knowledge into the common sense.

THE SYSTEMIC NOSE FOR NEWS

Our immersion in newsrooms led us to an appreciation that while the news organization has systemic features, it is not tightly rule-bound in the manner suggested by previous researchers. Journalists do experience real organizational constraints, including external influences (e.g., economic, legal regulation, the need to have and hold an audience or readership, the need for a regular supply of material from source bureaucracies); influences within the news-media institution (e.g., provision of story ideas and material; professional-culture values such as fairness and balance); and, the organization of their newsroom (e.g., material and human resources, working-culture expectations, the medium of communication), all within the pervasive requirements of time and space. However, they experience the process of newsmaking in terms of equivocality, change, fluidity, and discovery. Their choices in newsmaking are experienced in terms of an intuitive 'nose for news,' yet their senses are limited by systemic properties of the news organization that yield rather uniform and predictable products.

Journalists feel considerable tension between, on the one hand, the equivocality of their intuitive, interpretive work, and on the other hand, the or-

ganizational constraints on their work. This tension is revealed in the conflicts
that characterize everyday life in the newsroom. Conflicts have a social base
regarding interpersonal relations; a material base regarding personnel and
technological resources, as well as information as a commodity; and, a cultural
base regarding ideological preferences. Contrary to the dominant normative
view in the academic literature that journalism is characterized by consensus
among its practitioners, we found persistent and pervasive differences, divisions, and conflict. Editors struggled to control their own preferences through
who they assigned, the angles they urged, the resources they recommended,
substantive editing, and play. Reporters asserted their autonomy by refusing
assignments, altering angles, adding their own sources, keeping information
to themselves, formulating their stories in appealing ways, filing stories to
avoid disfavoured editors, and so on. This activity ensured that there was real
equivocality, and openings for discovery and alternatives, in their work.

The facts of some openness, considerable equivocality, and extensive
conflict, require explanation. If journalists are not automatons operating in
strict conformity to paths laid down in a normative system, what else provides
the basis for their actions? We discovered an answer by inquiring into the
nature of journalists' knowledgeability and developing the notion of vocabulary of precedents within the working culture.

There is a very real sense in which journalists' judgments are based in
'a nose for news.' Journalists believe something is reportable when they can
visualize it in the terms of news discourse. In particular, when something can
be visualized for its deviance and control possibilities, it becomes a newsworthy topic. The journalist can sense who to approach for information or
comment, and how this can be formulated within the genre capacities of news.
The journalist's sense and sensibilities do not come from consulting definitive
professional texts; indeed there are no such texts available because the craft
cannot be captured and ruled in this form. Rather, a sensitive nose for news
comes from consulting news items, being scrutinized by editors, talking to
more experienced colleagues, and doing the work.

What journalists learn, and use to guide their work, is a vocabulary of
precedents: what previous exemplars tell them should be done in the present
instance. The ongoing articulation of precedent in the working culture of
journalists provides them with recognition knowledge (that this is a story of
a particular type), procedural knowledge (how to get on with contacting and
using human and documentary sources), and accounting knowledge (how to
frame and formulate the story; how to justify the chosen approach to others).
One reporter described the process as analogous to the Eskimo carver who
eventually learns the standards and taste of the urban marketplace and shapes
his products accordingly.

While they work at presenting a dramaturgical model of organized life, journalists themselves organize more in accordance with a game model. As in the game of chess, the rules and other organizational constraints enter into journalists' visualizations of choices and moves in ways not directly visible to those observing the moves themselves, and not always available for articulation if the journalist is asked about them. Like the deviance and control moves within the source organizations they focus on, journalists' moves are visualized as part of a game that is much more complex and sinuous than how it is dramatically actualized in news content.

The way in which these organizational constraints are brought to life in news work, and made accessible to the researcher, is in their relation to journalists' accounting knowledge within the vocabulary of precedents. Organizational constraints are not only limiting on what the journalist can do, but enabling in justification and excuse for the choices he makes. Normative analysts have focused on the norms of obligation created through social and cultural organizational constraints; they have ignored the justifications and excuses available through these same social and cultural considerations (cf Brandt, 1969; Edgerton, 1985). For example, a source can be coaxed into co-operation by saying that it would not be fair to publish allegations of deviance against him without his response. An editor can be told that it is unreasonable to expect the inclusion of material from additional sources, in spite of expectations of fairness, because of time constraints. An assignment can be refused because it might interfere with relations with sources the reporter is trying to sustain regarding other matters. A deadline is not fixed; it can be negotiated in terms of the requirements and importance of the particular story. The space available for an item is not fixed; it can be made flexible by strategies and tactics of interesting source selection, writing, filing, and so on.

The journalist develops an account ability to achieve accountability on the job. Organizational considerations in news judgment are just that, considerations to take into account in deciding how to account for what is being done. They are negotiable features of the newsroom, and hence a source of considerable conflict, as they are used by each journalist in ordering his relations with colleagues, superiors, and sources. Through skilful mobilization of organizational resources the journalist can create some autonomous space in which to practise his craft. The journalist who is articulate in the vocabulary of precedents has the power to turn organizational constraints to advantage. He has acquired the nose for news required to work the system. Indeed, this is what makes the system work.

The vocabulary-of-precedents conception challenges the dominant normative paradigm in the study of news work, and indeed in the study of occupations and organizations generally. Normative analysts have accepted the public-culture values and norms of journalism at face value to explain what journalists do, or have ferreted out norms they perceive to prevail in the working culture as explanations of journalists' choices. A picture emerges of great normative consensus among journalists, who thus appear as automatons in the mass-media production process. To the contrary, we have shown that values and practices are not fixed rigidly, but are worked out in ongoing negotiations and conflicts among newsroom personnel at all levels.

Let us return to the fact of conflict and what explains it. Newsrooms are permeated with culturally based conflict over what is important, who is important, and how they should be made more or less important through news coverage. Newsrooms are also filled with socially based conflict, which focuses on the use of human and material resources in light of cultural criteria of importance. Conflict is manifested in particular in assignment, editing, and feedback exchanges between management and reporters. These are the occasions on which the vocabulary of precedents is revised and tentatively established for future reference. Like the organizations they report on, journalists use conflicts over competing expectations or deviance-defining activity as a means of activating, policing, controlling, and changing their own organizational life.

The vocabulary of precedents or knowledgeability peculiar to any occupation tends to be self-limiting. In journalism, the themes and expectations of news work tend to reinforce the news media's view of themselves and their work more than the events they report on. News comes closer to mirroring the social and cultural reality of its own organization than to mirroring the events it reports on.

With very few exceptions, journalists do not have specialist knowledge in the fields they report on. This is not a matter of low standards for the occupation, but an explicit recognition by newsroom managers that specialist knowledge is not required to get the job done. Specialist knowledge can even be counterproductive, leading the reporter to look for complexity and to qualify his knowledge when what news discourse requires is a simple transformation into the common sense. Assignments in terms of specialist knowledge can also give news managers less flexibility, since the specialist is more confined to a single topic area while the journalist-as-journeyman can be used across topic and beat assignments as the need arises.

Journalists look inward. The prevailing view is that to be knowledgeable one must be up on the latest news. In assignment, extensive reference and deference is made to the reports of other news outlets. In reporting, there is a convergence on the same or similar sources, the same or similar quotations from sources, and using quotations or other information already obtained by reporters from other news outlets. In editing, too, information and quotations published in other news outlets are inserted to round out what the editor visualizes to be the essence of the matter. Editorials and letters to the editor also take their lead from, and feed back into, news items. Finally, the hermeneutic circle of journalism is sealed by the practice of one news outlet not criticizing or even directly correcting another news outlet for publishing material known to be fictive, faulty, or false.

The self-referential nature of journalism means that journalists do not develop their knowledgeability through their general readership or audience. There are no systematic surveys for journalistic purposes whereby the public is asked what they find newsworthy, relevant, or worthwhile. There are surveys and ratings on the marketing side, but these are based on news-business criteria related to having an audience to sell to advertisers, not journalistic criteria related to knowing the audience for the purpose of making better news judgments. At best, knowledge of the audience is derived from each journalist talking independently to friends, associates, and regular news sources. Thus, journalism is concerned primarily with communications among élite authorized knowers. Journalists are oriented to the audience of regular sources-as-reporters who join them in their hermeneutic circle. Everyone else is left to watch, listen to, or read the distant representations that form this symbolic spectacle. For the journalist, the general audience is only imagined as something he represents, not surveyed in a representative manner.

In turning to sources for knowledge there are further limitations on journalists' knowledgeability. Sources are not surveyed in a systematic or random manner, but selected individually to represent their organizational position. Sometimes the opinion of a source or two is fictively said to be representative of the entire organization or community, but is actually only a representation of what the journalist visualizes as fitting the circumstances. Sources who say things that complicate the frame find that the complicating things are omitted, or they end up not being cited at all.

Journalists have limited opportunity for direct observation of the matters they report on. Moreover, when the opportunity for direct observation exists – as in public demonstrations, legislatures, courts, news conferences and other dramatic settings – the context is already highly structured by the source. The journalist is left to reproduce the representations the sources have decided to make of themselves, rather than obtain direct independent evidence which might challenge these public representations.

Source documents routinely available to journalists have a similar performative character. Already tailored for the public face of the bureaucracy in which they are produced, they represent the organization in the image it wishes to be presented in. Journalists can, and very occasionally do, make efforts to obtain other documents, although there is a disinclination to do so because it can actually upset their criteria of objectivity, end a controversy between opposing sides, and therefore exhaust the potential for continuing stories.

In summary, in their relations with sources journalists find their knowledgeability circumscribed even further. Most things are left to their imagination. They are forced to visualize, to make evident to the mind that which is not evident to the eye. They are '*n*th-level' reproducers of knowledge, relying heavily upon sources to provide written or oral constructs that represent their organizational position on a matter. While reporters are sometimes able to penetrate organizations for more direct surveillance, or for scrutiny of more original documents, this form of 'investigation' is rare in practice, although not in myth. Moreover, even on the rare occasions when journalists do get close to the original source of social constructs, they are usually required to obtain a constructed account from an authorized source rather than able to provide their own direct interpretation.

In spite of the fact that the knowledgeability of journalists is severely circumscribed, we see more openness, equivocality, and choice in the news process than do other recent academic analysts. The social and cultural conflict that characterizes newsrooms is testimony to the fact that journalists see the potential for negotiating alternative ideas, approaches, and outcomes. In any dominant culture and newsroom culture at a given point there is a finite number of frames. Nevertheless, the range available is better visualized in terms of the number of windows in a modern multi-story newspaper office building than as '*a* window on the world' (Tuchman, 1978: 1, our emphasis).

Our understanding of journalists' knowledgeability contributes to what Geertz (1983) has termed the ethnography of modern thought. We have emphasized the ways in which the thinking of news workers is a social process, involving active manipulation of the common-sense forms of culture. We have focused on how they acquire their thought models through the vocabulary of precedents; the lack of their division of labour regarding specialist knowledge in favour of the common sense; their processes of intersubjectivity with one another and their sources; and, their attendant framing techniques whereby they translate the bureaucratic and professional knowledge of sources into the common sense. We have shown how they help to socially construct the cultural contours of the knowledge society by representing authorities in the knowledge structure, marking organizational boundaries, and conveying the rhetoric of persuasion. We have stressed that a degree of diversity is evident in this work: while a system is evident, it is subject to the equivocality, controls, and change of those who constitute it.

NEWSPAPER AND BROADCAST-NEWS COMPARISONS

These general features of journalists' knowledgeability, social organization, and news transformation are salient in different news organizations and media. Nevertheless there are many specific features of each news organization and each medium that create considerable variation in social organization, in how the news is put together, and in news products. The fact that the research reported in this book was based on only a few news organizations in television and newspapers, with little sustained research on radio, means that we are limited in what we can say about the origin, nature, and direction of this news-media variation. We offer more data pertinent to questions of variation in subsequent volumes, where we show how different media are suited to the social organization of different news beats and we analyse how news sources access and use the different media for different purposes (Ericson et al, forthcoming a). In addition we provide content survey data on variations in coverage between popular and quality news outlets in each of newspaper, radio, and television (Ericson et al, forthcoming b).

In spite of the limitations of our present data base, we can make some reasonable inferences about the differences between the newspaper and television station and draw some tentative conclusions that are tested more thoroughly in our subsequent research. The most fundamental point to make at this juncture is that each medium has genre capacities peculiar to itself, with attendant capabilities for offering its own version of the truth. As McLuhan argued, the medium itself has ideological features which must be understood in order to appreciate its messages. Form determines content; each medium provides a structure for discourse that both eliminates coverage of some matters and insists upon coverage of other matters. 'The news of the day is a figment of our technological imagination. It is, quite precisely, a media event ... Without a medium to create its form, the news of the day does not exist' (Postman, 1985: 8).

The television newsroom is a more enclosed social organization than the newspaper, and its content more preordained. In the words of a producer we studied, television news is a system of paint-by-numbers. The television newsroom has limited resources and very few journalists. The fact that there is only a handful of journalists means that there is a particular emphasis on general assignment reporting, with very few topic or beat specialists. Time and space restrictions are especially severe. Each 75- to 90-second item typically allows for a short script and the use of three sources or fewer. Thus the reporter gravitates to a point/counterpoint format within the strategic ritual of objectivity. The limited personnel resources also place a special pressure on each reporter to produce a story a day, to pull his weight in filling the show.

In addition to producing a written script and oral statements, the television journalist has to make visual representations. In spite of the fact they give greater believability to the item, visuals do not add any real context. Rather they isolate images from context and make them visible in a different way. There is no such thing as taking a visual out of context because a visual does not require context.

Preoccupied with visualizing in this way, the television journalist is severely limited in the contexts in which he can place his item. The need to obtain the visuals, process film, and edit the material takes most of his time in producing the item. This gives him less time to contact a range of sources and to go into depth with them. Moreover, the contexts for using sources are limited because the predominant orientation is towards how the source's thoughts can be reduced to a clip of a few seconds. Usually the best that can be hoped for is fragmented conversations between two or three talking heads visualized to be representing the facts of the matter.

A concomitant limitation on television journalists is the need to sustain a dramatic narrative that is entertaining enough to hold the audience through an item and over successive items. While most newspapers try to carve out a particular place in the marketplace of ideas, most television stations try to provide the marketplace itself by offering dramatic, entertaining items that will appeal to the broadest possible audience which in turn will be appealing to advertisers. Television 'has made entertainment itself the natural format for the representation of all experience ... Entertainment is the supra-ideology of all discourse on television' (Postman, 1985: 87). This narrows television journalists into the grooves of a few basic themes for continuing stories, and to packaging items into 'wraps' for the dramatic structuring of the news show.

The consequence of all the above for daily life in the newsroom is close supervision and efforts at tight control by editors and producers. Most assignment ideas come from the top down, as the producer and assignment editor decide what items will fit into the continuity of their dramatic structuring. Particular sources and news events are recommended to reporters to go along with this. While the television reporter does enjoy participation in the editing of his item through to the final product, the producer nevertheless scrutinizes and alters his script and sometimes also takes over the film or video editing. Regardless, the assignment editor and producer have been close enough to the story idea and production along the way that the end product is predictable enough for the purpose of slotting it into the show as they wish to structure it.

A related consequence is that television journalists are led to rely heavily on predictable sources of stories in particular bureaucratic settings. This reliance includes that on deviance and control stories, and especially crime-control stories: these are available endlessly, and supply all the drama of good and evil that is so fitting for televised popular culture. Typical is a clip of someone imputing deviance and of the alleged deviant saying it isn't so. Also typical is a clip of the police in pursuit of the villain. These cathected scenarios blur with what is seen on the police detective show that immediately follows the news, a show that has been put in place to enhance the audience ratings for the news show.

The social organization of the newspaper is relatively less closed. The newspaper has more resources, including a far greater number of journalists. These resources allow the newspaper to set up a more decentralized system for routine news work, including a larger number and more diverse range of topic and beat specialists. These specialists, as sub-assignment editors, have relative autonomy to develop their own story ideas, sources, and angles.

Newspaper time and space constraints are less severe. The newspaper has greater overall news space, which allows for more flexibility in the length of items. Longer items allow for the use of more sources, and more and different viewpoints. Since editors have more than enough material to choose from, there is less pressure on the reporter to file a story on a given day, and a greater possibility of exploring further leads and more sources for a better story. The newspaper reporter has much more control over the pacing of his work.

The newspaper reporter is largely free of the need to obtain visual representations. Most stories are not accompanied by still photographs; when they are, the arrangements are usually made by editors. While the newspaper reporter does have some concern for sustaining themes in continuing stories, many items are treated as if they stand on their own. While items are often juxtaposed on a newspaper page to suggest links, this is more casual and *ad hoc* than in television and it is usually the concern of editors rather than reporters.

These elements indicate that the newspaper reporter has more autonomy than his counterpart in television. Where he loses autonomy is in the use of his material by editors. The editor is not so compelled to use his filed story to fill the newspaper because he has more to choose from. Pieces that are badly written, or which the editor is opposed to ideologically, can be dropped without worrying about the need to fill the space. The editor can also make writing style or ideological adjustments by altering the reporter's material, adding other material, and writing a headline, usually without consultation with the reporter who filed the story.

While the newspaper reporter remains heavily reliant on sources for routine supply, he has more opportunity to contact a range of different sources in a variety of contexts. One newspaper we studied did not have a regular police-beat reporter, and focused instead on procedural deviance and control in a range of bureaucracies, including, of course, police deviance. Their emphasis on institutional reporting meant that they downplayed ordinary crime-control stories, and played up particular instances of deviance they found offensive and the control of which they wished to participate in. In contrast to the television newsroom's paint-by-number system, the newspaper news-room offered a collage of a number of paintings.

Our understanding of these differences, and the ideological role of each medium, remains partial. To fill in the picture we require different methodologies and alternative grounds to our knowledge. This task is taken up as a central feature of our subsequent research.

The News Media and Deviance

Journalists are central agents in the social construction of reality about deviance and control. They shape the moral boundaries and contours of social order, providing an ongoing articulation of our senses of propriety and impropriety, stability and change, order and crises. They underpin the authority of certain other control agencies and agents, offering them preferred access and framing events and issues in their terms. They are control agents themselves, using their power of imprinting reality in the public culture to police what is being done in the microcultures of bureaucratic life, including especially the activities of other control agencies. Finally, their own deviance and control processes within the news-media institution play an important part in giving life to their work and shaping how they organize.

As cultural workmen who contribute to the construction of social order, journalists inevitably concentrate on deviance and control, because designating deviance is itself so fundamental to articulations of culture. Our cultural identity, our sense of what we are, derives from pointing to what we are not: that which is bad, wrong, faulty, in error, straying, etc. Bad news provides a barometer of how good our life is. It is at once an abstract vision and practical template for constructing order and managing change.

News is the most common stock of knowledge generated to meet the desire to control and command the environment. Its focus on information about deviance and control, disorder and order, stability and change, is part of the insatiable quest to reduce equivocality in the environment and attain a workable level of certainty. News of deviance and control is able to do this in particular because, like religion, it helps to create a factual basis for commitments, giving values the appearance of objectivity. It provides a reassurance structure as well as a plausibility structure. The feeling of certainty it offers serves in turn as an impetus to organizing, to getting on with the daily chores in one's particular sphere of organized life.

In this light it is not surprising that the news is permeated with talk about procedures that fail. Such talk about wrongs, errors, faults, and cracks in every nook and cranny of organized life gives a sense of how organization can be improved to make things better, to progress. It also provides a reading of the authority of the organization concerned, since obsessive attention to procedural detail is the defining characteristic of legitimacy in modern bureaucratic life. Thus news discourse is saturated with intra- and inter-organizational negotiations, differences and conflicts regarding meaning, power, and moral norms. Procedural deviance prompts discourse, and it is this discourse of deviance that is the essence of news.

At the level of social order, this discourse fits with what we have said about the knowledge or administered society. A society that is economically impelled to material consumption, politically administered according to principles of equality, and culturally rationalized through publicity, is bound to produce bad news. In such a society, source bureaucracies clamour for control over problem definition and solution as a vehicle for assertion of their claims to authority. Modern bureaucracies search constantly for procedural strays as part of the insatiable quest for the more perfectly administered society, and journalists join in this search, bringing to the public culture the talk about tinkering or repair work that can be done to set matters straight. The result is bad news, a rhetoric of failure, a sense that nothing is ever quite as it should be. This bad news offers the citizen a sense of the knowledge-power arrangements in society and where he might fit in it. In being bombarded daily with stories of misfits and who is authorized to designate and deal with them, the citizen is given his sense of place in the administered society. As cultural labourers actively participating in the construction of the administered society, journalists find that processes in deviance and control provide the best building material.

The fact that they have control over the media of communication means that journalists are powerfully located among the deviance-defining élite. Part of their power is the ability to systematically underpin other members of the deviance-defining élite. Only certain organizations and people are given routine access to say who and what is good or bad, and who and what should be given more freedom or less freedom, and what measures seem appropriate to effect the desired control. Traditionally the police have held a strong place in this élite, appearing as legitimacy incarnate. Not only do they have the power to hold that something is not a crime until they say it is a crime, but they are increasingly called upon to comment as experts about the most effective forms of punishment, law reform, urban planning, etc. Journalists routinely underpin police authority as primary definers of social order (e.g., Hall et al, 1978).

Control over the media of communication also gives journalists the power to undermine members of the deviance-defining élite, or to keep aspirants to the élite from entering the membership in the first place. The news media play an active and instrumental role in social and political movements (Gitlin, 1980), underpinning the authorities by giving them preferred access while undermining the organizations in political opposition by giving them unfavourable coverage.

The news media are themselves an agency of social control, and journalists their agents. The news items produced by journalists tangibly impose themselves on the organizations they are about, providing an important ordering impulse as well as impetus for change in those organizations. As is evident from our research, journalists frequently set out to have such social-control effects. Other research shows that, regardless of intentionality, news plays a significant role in the lives of those who are the subject of reports. The process by which journalists act directly as social-control agents, and the effect of this role as experienced by sources, is a central focus of the analyses in a forthcoming companion volume (Ericson et al, forthcoming a).

Finally, our analysis of what occurs inside newsrooms shows the essential contribution of deviance and control to journalists' own organizing activity. What happens inside news organizations and the news-media institution is itself important for understanding processes of deviance and control. As in all other occupations and organizations, journalists are perpetually engaged in imputing deviance to colleagues and making efforts to control them, in order to achieve a workable level of order. This activity is manifested in their conflicts over material resources, ideological differences, and social relationships. We have interpreted these conflicts as part of journalists' efforts to refine their own procedures, to articulate through the vocabulary of precedents their current conception of procedural regularity.

At the institutional level, we have learned that like the source bureaucracies they report on, journalists must publicly traffic in the 'as if' world of procedural propriety to sustain their sense of legitimacy. They must implant fictions in the public culture that their methods are what they seem to be. Thus objectivity, fairness, and balance serve as public-culture legitimations for journalistic practices. This implanting helps to explain the central place of investigative reporting in both the working culture of journalists and public mythology about journalism. The belief is created both within the craft and publicly that 'real reporting' consists of extensive investigation and profound discovery using multiple sources and methods in arriving at the truth. Journalists internalize this 'as if' world, even in face of the fact that it could not be farther from the truth of what their work actually consists of. If they were not committed to these procedural concepts, if these values were not experienced as objectively real, it would prove too difficult to sell the legitimacy of their product publicly, and especially to their regular sources. In keeping with other modern bureaucracies, news organizations often respond more to the myths of their institutional environment than to their actual work situation.

Also in keeping with other modern bureaucracies, the legitimation work of news organizations is only partially successful. The news media themselves have become very much a part of public-culture debate regarding their role in fostering disorder as well as mobilizing consensus. Public inquiries and academic studies have addressed problems ranging from the political economy of excessive concentration of ownership in the newspaper industry to the social psychology of the effects of bad news on children and other apparently vulnerable citizens.

For their part, citizens are relatively sceptical. While the police seem legitimacy incarnate, the news media are legitimacy inchoate. Survey research indicates that a substantial proportion of readers perceive the news as serving particular corporate and special interests, and as lacking in the very values that are supposed to sustain journalism as a craft (Royal Commission on Newspapers [RCN], 1981a). This view suggests that if journalism pushes these values too far it may create an impossible mandate for itself which the public can see through easily and which might have a long-term delegitimating effect. Indeed it is arguable that citizens have already seen through the mythology and treat news accounts with the healthy scepticism they deserve (ibid).

Since citizens consume news voraciously in spite of their scepticism, the basis of news-media legitimacy must be elsewhere. One plausible location is in the fact that the so-called 'legitimate' press and broadcast-news organizations address the perspectives and values of the politically powerful. News organizations ground their own claims to authority in the legitimacy of the authorized knowers they cite regularly. While everyone seems to know how bad the news really is – that it is highly interpretive, speculative, selective, distorted, and partial knowledge – they seem to rest assured that at least the facts are being construed by those they most value in the social hierarchy of credibility. Journalists have the power of other people's authority, and know how to use it for their common good.

The News Media and Politics

JOURNALISM AND REFORM POLITICS

Visualizing deviance is so central to the news because journalists are a part of a system of politics in which they contribute to the policing of organizational life. Especially under conditions of reduced competition and even local monopoly, the corporate power of news outlets allows them to make selective forays into adversarial journalism, especially against government targets. Beyond this, the institutional ties between journalists and their major bureaucratic sources ensure an ongoing policing relationship. This is engaged in terms of both procedural propriety within each bureaucracy, and the efforts of each bureaucracy to impute deviance and effect control in relation to other bureaucracies.

In the contemporary administered society, those in control of the political system turn all existential questions into problems and then mobilize to provide solutions to these problems. This is *the* characteristic of politics in the administered society, its motor force. A discourse of problems and failure is endemic to this politics, reproducing a constant sense of the need for more correction, repair, alteration, improvement, and resources. Always the belief is sustained that more might work where less has not. This discourse of problems, deviance, crisis, failure is necessary to the creation of a sense of progress. Progress sustains the Aristotelian conception that the state, on behalf of the polity, can provide for the good life rather than for life only.

In visualizing their own work, and in their practices of visualizing deviance in the organizations they report on, journalists function as an agency of reform politics. They participate in political developments and conflicts. They are integral to political processes of defining and responding to problems of deviance. As contributors to, and controllers over, problem definition and solution, they are able to assert claims to their own authority. Journalists, news organizations, and the news-media institution are thus significant contributors to knowledge-power-control relations in society.

JOURNALISM AND POLITICAL DISCOURSE

Liberal political theorists have always placed vibrant and diverse media at the forefront of their platform. Thus J.S. Mill saw the universal distribution of basic contemporary knowledge as an important component of citizenship in democracy. He also stated, 'Unity of opinion, unless resulting from the fullest and freest comparison of opposite opinions, is not desirable, and diversity is not an evil, but a good.' News organizations have taken this view seriously, incorporating it into their public statements of justification. To repeat the claims of the Canadian Broadcasting Corporation (CBC) (1978), 'We stake everything – indeed the whole notion of democratic society – on the rational dialogue of an informed public. Only the media can reach the mass of population to provide the information base required for that rational dialogue.'

What is the nature of the political dialogue provided in the news media? It seems much more limited than what classical liberal theorists might have thought possible, and compared to what contemporary media officials say publicly. The nature, extent, and direction of the limits of news are evident in the data we have presented and in our citation of other research. At this juncture we summarize the main limiting features of news on political discourse and suggest why it is so limited.

Journalists and their regular sources in the deviance-defining élite set the terms of political culture. The journalist quickly learns that things can only be grasped if his political reach is restricted, and thereby appreciates that he can only convey partial knowledge. The journalist is partial to going where the power is. He goes to the person who is best placed in an organization to give an authoritative version of what appears to be the case. This person may be the least well placed to know about the matter he is asked to address, but that does not matter for the purposes of news and political discourse. What matters is that the chosen source has been authorized politically and bureaucratically to give an account.

Like journalists themselves, authoritative sources are typically far removed from what they are asked to talk about. As nth-level reproducers of social constructs, they visualize what is going on in terms of the political-bureaucratic values they think should be conveyed. Their bureaucratically valued accounts are presented as fact, and the evaluative differences between them are likewise presented as differences in fact. One can speculate that as a result political consciousness is reduced to a bureaucratic conception of organized life. 'Every time journalists treat bureaucratic accounts ... as plain fact, they help an agency make the reality it wants to make and needs to make in order to legitimate itself. Thus, not only does routine news provide ideological accounts of real people and real happenings, it ends up legitimating institutions of social control by disseminating to the public institutional rationales as facts of the world' (Fishman, 1980: 138).

This is the political consciousness of the administered society. In perpetually referring and deferring to the valued facts of authorized knowers in bureaucratic settings, journalists offer the most visible, common-sense articulation of the knowledge structure of society, and a who's who of its administration. '[N]ews consumers are led to see the world outside their firsthand experience through the eyes of the existing authority structure. Alternative ways of knowing the world are simply not made available. Ultimately, routine news places bounds on political consciousness' (ibid).

For citizens who are not élite members of the knowledge structure, politics is a spectator sport. They are left to consume symbolic spectacles, which tell them what to think about if not what to think. This is a central feature of the knowledge society. 'Physical reality seems to recede in proportion as man's symbolic activity advances. Instead of dealing with the things themselves man is in a sense constantly conversing with himself. He has so enveloped himself in linguistic forms, in artistic images, in mythical symbols or religious rites that he cannot see or know anything except by the interposition of [an] artificial medium' (Cassirer, 1956: 43).

While regular sources who are members of the deviance-defining élite can and do act on news information, other citizens are more limited. News as a form of modern political spectatorship entails consumption of 'fragmented conversations' and 'disconnected facts' which most people have difficulty remembering, let alone using. The fact that the audience has difficulty retaining news, especially television news, has been thoroughly documented (e.g., Stern et al, 1973; Neuman, 1976; Katz et al, 1977; Stauffer et al, 1981). And, even if they do remember it, they may only be able to use it to play on their emotions; or, to display their competence in retaining facts as an end in itself, as in that great Canadian invention, 'Trivial Pursuit' (cf Postman, 1985).

The emotive aspects of modern political discourse are especially salient. Like the contemporary advertisement, political communications in the news say very little about the substance of the products, and a lot about the moral character of leading personalities. They also tell a lot about the character of the people who consume them. These people apparently search for their own values and reassurances through dramatic representations of deviance, control, and moral order. Indeed, given that political parties and governments are among the leading advertisers, it is not just a matter of the advertisement being 'the fundamental metaphor for political discourse' (ibid: 126); the advertisement is simply *the* fundamental form of political discourse, whether paid for directly in commercials, or indirectly through a public-relations apparatus that generates news (Blyskal and Blyskal, 1985).

Whether in the political arena, sports arena, or theatre, spectators can of course be satisfied solely on the basis of amusement. Another feature of the knowledge society is that symbols are used to engage the populace in endless entertainments, including, of course, news as theatre. This fact coexists with the emphasis on policing and reform politics, the administered society. Political discourse in the knowledge society thus incorporates the vision of *both* George Orwell and Aldous Huxley (cf Postman, 1985): Orwell's sense of thrust towards the perfectly administered society, and Huxley's sense of thirst for society as burlesque. In both of these components – the administered society and the entertainment society – the citizen is propelled into spectatorship and indifference.

It is extremely difficult for non-members of the deviance-defining élite to penetrate its hermeneutic circle. As just suggested, many are made indifferent to it. Beyond this, penetration is difficult because those who control the media of public communication, and especially the news media, are part of the central institutions of social control, and join with key sources from the other central institutions of social control to effect hegemony. Their knowledge is inward-looking, self-referential, and partial. As we have emphasized it is this social organization among journalists and their sources rather than the specifics of events in the world, that creates news. Unless this social organization can be penetrated and eventually joined, the citizen at best remains cast as a spectator, or at worst, appears as an agitator.

The news, as *the* form of public political discourse, is a very restricted means by which the truth is fashioned and clothed. While it carries considerable weight·as a form of truth-telling, because of its legitimacy, the news offers only truth reduced to its genre capacities. To understand these genre capacities we have looked inside news organizations. We discovered that journalists are very partial to what is already in the news as it coheres with the other resources at their disposal. This is the news recipe for being a means not to know. In spite of its important station in organized life, in spite of its significant contribution to the knowledge-structure of society, news provides only partial – limited and interested – knowledge.

In spite of how it is circumscribed in its social organization, news is nevertheless successful in providing a way of understanding the world that articulates with the common sense. In seeming natural, news has the essential component of myth as defined by Barthes (1972). It shapes not only our knowledge of the world, but also our knowledge of how to know. In transforming the bureaucratic knowledge of other social controllers into the common sense, journalists are simultaneously providing citizens with a means not to know. In reading the news, consumers experience 'erasure' (O'Neill, 1981), although they are unlikely to know it. If there is any general political sensibility raised by this, it is sympathy for the bureaucratic agents of control, alternating with moral outrage when they are visualized as procedural strays.

More than anything else, news visualizes people and organizations as out of step and disordered, and uses this view to generate discourse on how they may be made to fit with the political-culture template. Erased is any fundamental questioning of the template itself: whether instead of adapting initiatives to the order of things, the order of things might be adapted to meet the initiatives.

In our research we have used the news as a vehicle to question the template. We have sought understanding by getting behind the news appearances of those whose job it is to give official imprint to versions of reality. This is important because the role of the news media in influencing what we see or know, and do not see or know, is rarely subject to analysis. However, this book is only a beginning. Other research, grounded in different ways of knowing, is required to offer a more complete picture. We undertake this task in our research on how sources organize to produce the news and in our systematic survey of news content in different types of news organization and media in forthcoming companion volumes.

Our research has committed us to the importance of establishing links among processes of political power, designating deviance, and the media of communication. Deviance and control have always been central to the public drama of reform politics and claims to political authority, but the media of communication have varied greatly. This is why it is so important to inquire into the social and cultural organization of contemporary media. This inquiry is crucial to understanding more about political discourse and the place of deviance and control talk in it.

Recently political talk has included a concern for control of the news media themselves. There is an apparent yearning for a golden past when newspapers were many and diverse, and 'had in fact the same characteristics as politics itself' (Waite, 1962: 4, quoted in RCN, 1981: 136). The news media still do have the characteristics of politics, but politics has changed along with the media. As we have argued, politics in the knowledge society seeks perfection in administration (the perpetual cleaning up and repairing of flawed procedures) and reflection in entertainment (the perpetual propping up and staging of prefabricated spectacles).

These elements of politics, and news-media entanglements in them, require more extensive examination. One approach is to research how regular sources, politically involved in the deviance-defining élite, organize to benefit through the news media. Some individuals, organizations, and institutions have news access, and they thereby gain power both over and through the news media. Grounded inside the newsroom, the research reported in this book has a tendency to depict news-media power as virtually boundless. Grounded in source organizations, the research reported in a forthcoming volume adjusts this picture. Journalists face the bounds of powerful sources who mobilize strategically to variously avoid and make news. While the news-media institution is effectively closed to most citizens, and a powerful force in society, a limited range of sources can pry it open and sometimes harness its power to advantage.

References

Abercrombie, N. 1980. *Class, Structure and Knowledge: Problems in the Sociology of Knowledge*. New York: New York University Press

Alderson, J. 1982. 'The Mass Media and the Police,' in C. Sumner, ed., *Crime, Justice and the Mass Media*, pp. 7–24. Cambridge: Institute of Criminology, University of Cambridge

Altheide, D., and J. Johnson. 1980. *Bureaucratic Propaganda*. Boston: Allyn and Bacon

Altick, R. 1970. *Victorian Studies in Scarlet*. New York: Norton

Annan, Lord. 1977. *Report of the Committee on the Future of Broadcasting*. London: HMSO

Asquith, S. 1978. 'The Structure, Ownership and Control of the Press, 1780–1855,' in G. Boyce et al, *Newspaper History*, pp. 98–116. London: Constable

Atkinson, M. 1979. *Order in Court: The Organization of Verbal Interaction in Judicial Settings*. Atlantic Highlands, NJ: Humanities Press

Bailey, S. 1983. 'Semiotics and the Study of Occupational and Organizational Cultures,' *Administrative Science Quarterly*, 28: 393–413

Barrile, L. 1980. 'Television and Attitudes about Crime.' PhD dissertation, Department of Sociology, Boston College

Barth, F. 1975. *Ritual and Knowledge among the Baktaman of New Guinea*. New Haven: Yale University Press

Barthes, R. 1972. *Mythologies*. London: Jonathan Cape

Becker, H.S. 1963. *Outsiders: Studies in the Sociology of Deviance*. Glencoe, Ill.: Free Press

– 1967. 'Whose Side Are We On?' *Social Problems*, 14: 239–47

– 1982. 'Cultures: A Sociological View,' *Yale Review*, 71: 513–27

Bell, D. 1973. *The Coming of Post-Industrial Society*. New York: Basic Books

– 1976. *The Cultural Contradictions of Capitalism*. New York: Basic Books

– 1985. 'Gutenberg and the Computer,' *Encounter* (May): 15–20

Bentham, J. 1843. 'On Publicity,' *Essay on Political Tactics* in John Bowring, ed., *The Works of Jeremy Bentham*. vol. 2, pp. 310–17. Edinburgh: W. Tait

Ben-Yehuda, N. 1985. *Deviance and Moral Boundaries*. Chicago: University of Chicago Press

Berger, P. 1977. *Facing up to Modernity*. New York: Basic Books

Berger, P., and H. Kellner. 1964. 'Marriage and the Construction of Reality,' *Diogenes*, 46: 5–22

Berger, P., and T. Luckmann. 1966. *The Social Construction of Reality: A Treatise in the Sociology of Knowledge*. Harmondsworth: Penguin

Bergesen, A. 1977. 'Political Witch-hunts: The Sacred and Subversive in Cross-National Perspective,' *American Sociological Review*, 42: 220–33

– 1978. 'A Durkheimian Theory of Political Witch-hunts and the Chinese Cultural Revolution of 1966–1969 as an Example,' *Journal for the Scientific Study of Religion*, 17: 19–29

Bernstein, R. 1978. *The Restructuring of Social and Political Theory*. Philadelphia: University of Pennsylvania Press

Bishop, J. 1979. 'Institutional and Operational Knowledge in Work: A Sensitizing Framework,' *Sociology of Work and Occupations*, 6: 328–52

Bittner, E. 1970. *The Functions of the Police in Modern Society*. Rockville, Md: National Institute of Mental Health

Black, E. 1982. *Politics and the News: Political Functions of the Mass Media*. Toronto: Butterworth

Bloor, D. 1976. *Knowledge and Social Imagery*. London: Routledge

Blyskal, J., and M. Blyskal. 1985. *PR: How the Public Relations Industry Writes the News*. New York: Macmillan

Böhme, G. 1984. 'The Knowledge-Structure of Society,' in E. Bergendal, ed., *Knowledge Policies and the Traditions of Higher Education*. Stockholm: Almqvist and Wiksell Int.

Bok, S. 1979. *Lying: Moral Choice in Public and Private Life*. New York: Vintage

– 1982. *Secrets: On the Ethics of Concealment and Revelation*. New York: Pantheon

Bourdieu, P., and J.C. Paseron. 1970. *La Reproduction*. Paris: Minuit

Bormann, E. 1983. 'Symbolic Convergence: Organizational Communication and Culture,' in L. Putnam and M. Pacanowsky, eds., *Communication and Organizations: An Interpretive Approach*, pp. 99–122. Beverly Hills: Sage

Box, S. 1971. *Deviance, Reality and Society*. London: Holt, Rinehart, Winston

Boyd-Barrett, O. 1978. 'Market Control and Wholesale News: The Case of Reuters,' in G. Boyce et al, eds., *Newspaper History*, pp. 192–204. London: Constable

Brandt, R. 1969. 'A Utilitarian Theory of Excuses,' *Philosophical Review*, 78: 337– 61

Brannigan, G. 1981. *The Social Basis of Scientific Discoveries*. Cambridge: Cambridge University Press

Breed, W. 1955. 'Social Control in the Newsroom,' *Social Forces*, 33: 326–35

Brodeur, J.-P. 1983. 'High Policing: Remarks about the Policing of Political Activities,' *Social Problems*, 30: 507–20

Brown, R. 1978. 'Bureaucracy as Praxis,' *Administrative Science Quarterly*, 23: 271

Brunsdon, C., and D. Morley. 1978. *Everyday Television: Nationwide*. London: British Film Institute

Burnham, D. 1976. *The Role of the Media in Controlling Corruption*. New York: The John Jay Press

Burns, T. 1977. *The BBC: Public Institution and Private World*. London: Macmillan

– 1979. 'The Organization of Public Opinion,' in J. Curran et al, eds., *Mass Communication and Society*, pp. 44–69. Beverly Hills: Sage

Butcher, H., et al. 1981. 'Images of Women in the Media,' in S. Cohen and J. Young, eds., *The Manufacture of News: Deviance, Social Problems and the Mass Media*, pp. 317–25. London: Constable

Canadian Broadcasting Corporation. 1978. *The C.B.C. – A Perspective*. Submission to the C.R.T.C. in Support of Applications for Renewal of Broadcast Licences. Three volumes. Ottawa: CBC

– 1982. *Journalistic Policy*. Ottawa: CBC Information Centre

Cantor, M. 1971. *The Hollywood Television Producer*. New York: Basic Books

Carey, J. 1979. 'Mass Communication Research and Cultural Studies: An American View,' in J. Curran et al, eds., *Mass Communication and Society*, pp. 409–25. Beverly Hills: Sage

Carnoy, M. 1984. *The State and Political Theory*. Princeton: Princeton University Press

Cassirer, E. 1956. *An Essay on Man*. New York: Doubleday

Carter, R. 1958. 'Newspaper Gatekeepers and Their Sources of News,' *Public Opinion Quarterly*, 22: 133–44

Cayley, D. 1982. 'Making Sense of the News,' *Sources*, Spring: 126–8, 130–3, 136–7

– 1982a. 'The Myth of the Free Press,' *Sources*, Spring: 127, 138–42

Chibnall, S. 1977. *Law-and-Order News*. London: Tavistock

Christie, N. 1977. 'Conflicts as Property,' *British Journal of Criminology*, 17: 1–15

Cirino, R. 1973. 'Bias through Selection and Omission,' in S. Cohen and J. Young, eds., *The Manufacture of News: Deviance, Social Problems and the Mass Media*, pp. 40–62. London: Constable

Clarke, D. 1981. 'Second-hand News: Production and Reproduction at a Major Ontario Television Station,' in L. Salter, ed., *Communication Studies in Canada*, pp. 20–51. Toronto: Butterworths

Clement, W. 1975. *The Canadian Corporate Elite*. Toronto: McClelland and Stewart

Clyde, R. 1968. 'News Readership as a Function of Several Affective Characteristics,' *Journalism Quarterly*, 45: 535–7

Cohen, S. 1972. *Folk Devils and Moral Panics*. London: Paladin

Cohen, S., and J. Young, eds. 1981. *The Manufacture of News: Deviance, Social Problems and the Mass Media*. London: Constable

Connolly, W. 1983. *The Terms of Political Discourse*. Oxford: Martin Robertson

Coon, C.S. 1969. *The Story of Man*. 3rd ed. New York: Knopf

Craven, P. 1983. 'Law and Ideology: The Toronto Police Court 1850–80,' in D.

Flaherty, ed., *Essays in the History of Canadian Law*, pp. 248–307. Toronto: The Osgoode Society

Croll, P. 1974. 'The Deviant Image,' unpublished manuscript

Cumberbatch, G., and A. Beardsworth. 1976. 'Criminals, Victims and Mass Communications,' in E.C. Viano, ed., *Victims and Society*, pp. 72–90. Washington: Visage Press

Curran, J. 1978. 'The Press as an Agency of Social Control,' in G. Boyce et al, eds., *Newspaper History*. London: Arnold

– 1979. 'Capitalism and Control of the Press, 1800–1975,' in J. Curran et al, eds., *Mass Communication and Society*, pp. 195–230. Beverly Hills: Sage

Darnton, R. 1975. 'Writing News and Telling Stories,' *Daedalus*, 104: 175–93

Davey Special Senate Committee on Mass Media. *Report*. 3 vols. Ottawa: Government of Canada

Davis, F. 1973. 'Crime News in Colorado Newspapers,' in S. Cohen and J. Young, eds., *The Manufacture of News*, pp. 127–35. London: Constable

Davis, M. 1971. 'That's Interesting: Toward a Phenomenology of Sociology and a Sociology of Phenomenology,' *Philosophy of Social Science*, 1: 309–44

Ditton, J., and J. Duffy. 1982. *Bias in Newspaper Crime Reports: Selected and Distorted Reporting of Crime News in 6 Scottish Newspapers During March, 1981*. Background Paper Number 3, Department of Sociology, University of Glasgow

Dominick, J. 1973. 'Crime and Law Enforcement on Prime-Time Television,' *Public Opinion Quarterly*, 37: 241–50

– 1978. 'Crime and Law Enforcement in the Mass Media', in C. Winick, ed., *Deviance and Mass Media*, pp. 105–28. Beverly Hills: Sage

Dollard, H. 1937. *Caste and Class in a Southern Town*. New Haven: Yale University Press

Douglas, J. 1971. *American Social Order: Social Rules in a Pluralistic Society*. New York: The Free Press

Douglas, M. 1966. *Purity and Danger: An Analysis of the Concepts of Pollution and Taboo*. New York: Pantheon

Douglas, M., and A. Wildavsky. 1982. *Risk and Culture: An Essay on the Selection of Technological and Environmental Dangers*. Berkeley: University of California Press

Drechsel, R. 1983. *News Media in the Trial Courts*. New York: Longman

Dreir, P. 1982. 'The Position of the Press in the U.S. Power Structure,' *Social Problems*, 29: 298–310

Dunn, D. 1969. *Public Officials and the Press*. Reading, Mass: Addison-Wesley

Durkheim, E. 1933. *The Division of Labor in Society*. New York: Free Press

– 1938. *The Rules of Sociological Method*. New York: Free Press

Dussuyer, I. 1979. *Crime News: A Study of 40 Ontario Newspapers*. Toronto: Centre of Criminology, University of Toronto

Eco, U. 1981. *The Role of the Reader: Explorations in the Semiotics of Texts*. London: Hutchinson

Edelman, M. 1964. *The Symbolic Uses of Politics*. Urbana: University of Illinois Press

–   1971. *Politics as Symbolic Action*. New York: Academic Press
Edgerton, B. 1985. *Rules, Exceptions, and Social Order*. Berkeley: University of
California Press
Elliott, P. 1974. 'Selection and Communication in a Television Production – A
Case Study,' in G. Tuchman, ed., *The TV Establishment: Programming for
Power and Profit*, pp. 72–89. Englewood Cliffs, NJ: Prentice Hall
–   1978. 'Professional Ideology and Organizational Change: The Journalist since
1800,' in G. Boyce, et al, *Newspaper History*. London: Constable
–   1979. 'Media Organizations and Occupations: An Overview,' in J. Curran,
ed., *Mass Communication and Society*, pp. 142–73. Beverly Hills: Sage
Epstein, E. 1974. *News from Nowhere*. New York: Vintage
Ericson, R. 1975. *Criminal Reactions: The Labelling Perspective*. Farnborough:
Saxon House
–   1977 'From Social Theory to Penal Practice: The Liberal Demise of
Criminological Causes,' *Canadian Journal of Criminology and Corrections*,
18: 170–91
–   1981. *Making Crime: A Study of Detective Work*. Toronto: Butterworth
–   1981a. 'Rules for Police Deviance,' in C. Shearing, ed., *Organizational
Police Deviance*, pp. 82–110. Toronto: Butterworth
–   1982. *Reproducing Order: A Study of Police Patrol Work*. Toronto: University
of Toronto Press
–   1985. 'Legal Inequality,' in S. Spitzer and A. Scull, eds., *Research on Law,
Deviance and Social Control*, 7: 31–78. Greenwich, Conn: JAI Press
–   1987. 'The State and Criminal Justice Reform,' in R. Ratner and J.
McMullan, eds., *State Control: Criminal Justice Politics in Canada*.
Vancouver: University of British Columbia Press
Ericson, R., and P. Baranek. 1982. *The Ordering of Justice*. Toronto: University
of Toronto Press
Ericson, R., P. Baranek, and J. Chan. forthcoming a. *Negotiating Control: A Study
of News Sources*
Ericson, R., P. Baranek, and J. Chan. forthcoming b. *Acknowledging Order: A
Study of News Content*
Ericson, R., and C. Shearing. 1986. 'The Scientification of Police Work,' in G.
Böhme and N. Stehr, eds., *The Knowledge Society: The Impact of Scientific
Knowledge on Social Structures*. Dordrecht: Reidel
Erikson, K.T. 1966. *Wayward Puritans: A Study in the Sociology of Deviance*.
New York: Wiley
–   1973. 'Notes on the Sociology of Deviance,' in E. Rubington and M.
Weinberg, eds., *Deviance: The Interactionist Perspective*, pp. 26–30. New
York: Macmillan
Fallers, L. 1961. 'Ideology and Culture in Uganda Nationalism,' *American
Anthropologist*, 63: 677–86
Fishman, M. 1978. 'Crime Waves as Ideology,' *Social Problems*, 25: 531–543.
–   1980. *Manufacturing the News*. Austin: University of Texas Press
Fiske, J., and J. Hartley. 1978. *Reading Television*. London: Methuen
Fleming, T. 1983. 'Mad Dogs, Beasts and Raving Nutters: The Presentation of the

Mentally Disordered in the British Press,' in T. Fleming and L. Visano, eds., *Deviant Designations*, pp. 153–84. Toronto: Butterworth

Foucault, M. 1965. *Madness and Civilization: A History of Insanity in the Age of Reason*. New York: Random House

– 1975. *The Birth of the Clinic: An Archeology of Medical Perception*. New York: Random House

– 1977. *Discipline and Punish: The Birth of the Prison*. New York: Pantheon

– 1980. *Power/Knowledge*. New York: Pantheon

Fox, C. 1978. 'Political Caricature and the Freedom of the Press in Early Nineteenth Century England,' in G. Boyce, ed., *Newspaper History*, pp. 226–46. London: Constable

Fuller, L. 1967. *Legal Fictions*. Stanford: Stanford University Press

Gabel, J. 1984. 'Is Nonideological Thought Possible?' in N. Stehr and V. Meja, eds., *Society and Knowledge: Contemporary Perspectives in the Sociology of Knowledge*, pp. 25–33. New Brunswick, NJ: Transaction Books

Galtung, J., and M. Ruge. 1981. 'Structuring and Selecting News,' in S. Cohen and J. Young, eds., *The Manufacture of News: Deviance, Social Problems and the Mass Media*, pp. 52–63. London: Constable

Gans, H. 1972. 'The Famine in Mass Media Research: Comments on Hirsch, Tuchman and Gecas,' *American Journal of Sociology*, 77: 697–705

– 1980. *Deciding What's News*. New York: Vintage

Garofalo, J. 1981. 'Crime and the Mass Media: A Selective Review of Research,' *Journal of Research in Crime and Delinquency*, 18: 319–50

Garrison, C. 1981. 'The Energy Crisis: A Process of Social Definition,' *Qualitative Sociology*, 4: 312–23

Geach, H. 1982. 'Social Work and the Media,' in C. Sumner, ed., *Crime, Justice and the Mass Media*, pp. 90–100. Cambridge: Institute of Criminology, University of Cambridge

Geertz, C. 1973. *The Interpretation of Cultures*. New York: Basic Books

– 1983. *Local Knowledge*. New York: Basic Books

Giddens, A. 1976. *New Rules of Sociological Method*. London: Hutchinson

– 1979. *Central Problems in Social Theory: Action, Structure, and Contradiction in Social Analysis*. London: Macmillan

– 1982. *Profiles and Critiques in Social Theory*. London: Macmillan

– 1984. *The Constitution of Society*. Cambridge: Polity

Gitlin, T. 1980. *The Whole World Is Watching*. Berkeley: University of California Press

– 1982. 'Television's Screens' in M. Apple, ed., *Cultural and Economic Reproduction in Education*. London: Routledge

– 1983. *Inside Prime Time*. New York: Pantheon

Glasgow University Media Group. 1976. *Bad News*. London: Routledge

– 1980. *More Bad News*. London: Routledge

– 1982. *Really Bad News*. London: Writers and Readers

Goffman, E. 1959. *The Presentation of Self in Everyday Life*. New York: Doubleday

– 1974. *Frame Analysis*. Cambridge, Mass: Harvard University Press

– 1983. 'The Interaction Order,' *American Sociological Review*, 48: 1–17

Golding, P. 1981. 'The Missing Dimension – News Media and the Management of Social Change,' in E. Katz and T. Szecsko, eds., *Mass Media and Social Change*, pp. 63–81. Beverly Hills: Sage

Goodenough, W. 1978. 'Multiculturalism as the Normal Human Experience,' in E. Eddy and W. Partridge, eds., *Applied Anthropology in America*, pp. 79–87. New York: Columbia University Press

Gordon, M., and L. Heath. 1981. 'The News Business, Crime, and Fear,' in D. Lewis, ed., *Reactions to Crime*, pp. 227–50. Beverly Hills: Sage

Gouldner, A. 1976. *The Dialectic of Ideology and Technology*. New York: Seabury
– 1979. *The Future of Intellectuals and the Rise of the New Class*. New York: Macmillan

Graber, D. 1980. *Crime News and the Public*. New York: Praeger

Gramsci, A. 1971. *Selections from the Prison Notebooks of Antonio Gramsci*. New York: International Publishers

Gruneau, R. 1983. *Class, Sports and Social Development*. Amherst: University of Massachusetts Press

Gusfield, J. 1981. *The Culture of Public Problems*. Chicago: University of Chicago Press

Habermas, J. 1970. *Toward a Rational Society*. Boston: Beacon
– 1975. *Legitimation Crisis*. Boston: Beacon

Hall, S. 1979. 'Culture, the Media, and the 'Ideological Effect,'' in J. Curran et al, eds., *Mass Communication and Society*, pp. 314–48. Beverly Hills: Sage

Hall, S., C. Critcher, T. Jefferson, J. Clarke, and B. Roberts. 1978. *Policing the Crisis*. London: Macmillan

Halloran, J., P. Elliott, and G. Murdock. 1970. *Demonstrations and Communications: A Case Study*. Harmondsworth: Penguin

Harre, R., and P. Secord. 1973. *The Explanation of Social Behavior*. Totowa, NJ: Littlefield, Adams

Harris, M. 1974. 'Why a Perfect Knowledge of All Rules One Must Know to Act Like a Native Cannot Lead to the Knowledge of How Natives Act,' *Journal of Anthropological Research*, 30: 242–51

Hartley, J. 1982. *Understanding News*. London: Methuen

Hartmann, P. and C. Husband. 1981. 'The Mass Media and Racial Conflict,' in S. Cohen and J. Young, eds., *The Manufacture of News: Deviance, Social Problems and the Mass Media*, pp. 288–302. London: Constable

Hartung, B., and G. Stone. 1980. 'Time to Stop Singing the "Bad News" Blues,' *Newspaper Research Journal*, 1: 19–26

Hay, D. 1975. 'Property, Authority, and the Criminal Law,' in D. Hay et al, *Albion's Fatal Tree*. Harmondsworth: Penguin

Heath, L., M. Gordon, and R. LeBailly. 1981. 'What Newspapers Tell Us (and Don't Tell Us) about Rape,' *Newspaper Research Journal*, 2(4): 48–55

Heisenberg, W. 1958. *Physics and Philosophy*. New York: Harper

Hepworth, M., and B. Turner. 1982. *Confession: Studies in Deviance and Religion*. London: Routledge

Hirsch, P. 1977. 'Occupational, Organizational and Institutional Models in Mass Media Research: Toward an Integrated Framework,' in P. Hirsch et al, eds., *Strategies for Communication Research*, pp. 13–42. Beverly Hills: Sage

Holy, L., and M. Stuchlik. 1983. *Actions, Norms and Representations: Foundations of Anthropological Inquiry*. Cambridge: Cambridge University Press

Hubbard, J., M. DeFleur, and L. DeFleur. 1975. 'Mass Media Influences on Public Conceptions of Social Problems,' *Social Problems*, 23: 22–35

Hume, D. 1948. 'An Enquiry Concerning the Principles of Morals,' in H. Aiken, ed., *Hume's Moral and Political Philosophy*. New York: Macmillan

Hurd, G. 1979. 'The Television Presentation of the Police,' in S. Holdaway, ed., *The British Police*, pp. 118–34. London: Edward Arnold

Jackson, J. 1981. 'On the Implications of Content and Structural Analysis,' in L. Salter, ed., *Communication Studies in Canada*, pp. 232–49. Toronto: Butterworth

Janis, I. 1972. *Victims of Groupthink: A Psychological Study of Foreign Policy Decisions and Fiascoes*. Boston: Houghton Mifflin

Jefferson, T., and R. Grimshaw. 1984. *Controlling the Constable: Police Accountability in England and Wales*. London: Frederick Muller / The Cobden Trust

Johnson, B. 1982. 'Self-Promotion Ottawa Style: Spend Money,' *Globe and Mail*, 8 May

Jones, E. 1976. 'The Press as Metropolitan Monitor,' *Public Opinion Quarterly*, 40: 239–44

Katz, E., H. Adoni, and P. Parness. 1977. 'Remembering the News: What the Pictures Add to Recall,' *Journalism Quarterly 54*: 233–42

Kazin, A. 1973. *Bright Book of Life*. Boston: Little Brown.

Keillor, M. 1982. 'Interview with Cameron Smith,' *Canadian Lawyer*, March, 14–16, 33– 6

Kermode, F. 1966. *The Sense of an Ending: Studies in the Theory of Fiction*. London: Oxford University Press

Knight, S. 1980. *Form and Ideology in Crime Fiction*. Bloomington: Indiana University Press

Knorr-Cetina, K. 1981. *The Manufacture of Knowledge: An Essay on the Constructivist and Contextual Nature of Science*. Oxford: Pergamon

– 1983. 'New Developments in Science Studies: The Ethnographic Challenge,' *Canadian Journal of Sociology*, 8: 153–77

Knorr-Cetina, K., and A. Cicourel. 1981. *Advances in Social Theory and Methodology: Toward an Integration of Micro- and Macro-Sociologies*. London: Routledge

Knorr-Cetina, K., and M. Mulkay. 1983. *Science Observed: Perspectives on the Social Study of Science*. Beverly Hills: Sage

Konrád, G. and I. Szelényi. 1979. *The Intellectuals on the Road to Class Power*. New York: Harcourt Brace Jonavich

Kuhn, T. 1970. *The Structure of Scientific Revolutions*. Chicago: University of Chicago Press

Langer, S. 1962. *Philosophical Sketches*. New York: New American Library
Lasch, C. 1979. *The Culture of Narcissism*. New York: Norton
Latour, B., and S. Woolgar. 1979. *Laboratory Life: The Social Construction of Scientific Facts*. Beverly Hills: Sage
Lec, S. 1962. *Unkempt Thoughts*, tr. J. Galazka. New York: Funk and Wagnalls
Lemert, E. 1951. *Social Pathology*. New York: McGraw Hill
– 1972. *Human Deviance, Social Problems and Social Control*. Englewood Cliffs, NJ: Prentice-Hall
Lester, M. 1980. 'Generating Newsworthiness: The Interpretive Construction of Public Events,' *American Sociological Review*, 45: 984–94
McDonald Commission. 1981. *Commission of Inquiry Concerning Certain Activities of the Royal Canadian Mounted Police*. 3 vols. Ottawa: Supply and Services Canada
McMahon, M., and R. Ericson. 1987. 'Reforming the Police and Policing Reform,' in R. Ratner and J. McMullan, eds., *State Control: Criminal Justice Politics in Canada*. Vancouver: University of British Columbia Press
McQuail, D. 1979. 'The Influence and Effects of Mass Media,' in J. Curran et al, eds., *Mass Communication and Society*, pp. 70–94. Beverly Hills: Sage
McQuail, D. and S. Windahl. 1981. *Communication Models: For the Study of Mass Communications*. London: Longman
Manning, P. 1977. *Police Work*. Cambridge, Mass: MIT Press
– 1982. 'Organizational Work: Structuration of Environments,' *British Journal of Sociology*, 33: 118–34
– 1986. 'Signwork.' *Human Relations*, 39: 283–308
Marx, G. 1981. 'Ironies of Social Control: Authorities as Contributors to Deviance through Escalation, Non-Enforcement, and Covert Facilitation,' *Social Problems*, 28: 221–46
– 1985. 'I'll be Watching You: Reflections on the New Surveillance,' *Dissent* (Winter): 26–34
Marx, G., and N. Reichman. 1984. 'Routinizing the Discovery of Secrets: Computers as Informants,' *American Behavioural Scientist*, 27: 423–52
Matza, D. 1969. *Becoming Deviant*. Englewood Cliffs, NJ: Prentice-Hall
Mazur, A. 1982. 'Bomb Threats and the Mass Media: Evidence for a Theory of Suggestion,' *American Sociological Review*, 47: 407–11
Mead, G.H. 1918. 'The Psychology of Punitive Justice,' *American Journal of Sociology*, 23: 586–92
Merton, R. 1957. *Social Theory and Social Structure*. Glencoe: Free Press
– 1973. *The Sociology of Science*. Chicago: University of Chicago Press
Meyer, J.W. and B. Rowan. 1977. 'Institutionalized Organizations: Formal Structure as Myth and Ceremony,' *American Journal of Sociology*, 83: 340–63
Miliband, R. 1977. *Marxism and Politics*. London: Oxford University Press
Mill, J.S. 1962. *Considerations on Representative Government*. South Bend, Indiana: Gateway
Mills, C.W. 1940. 'Situated Actions and Vocabularies of Motive,' *American Sociological Review*, 5: 904–13

Minority Press Group. 1980. *The Other Secret Service: Press Distributors and Press Censorship*. London

Molotch, H., and M. Lester. 1974. 'News as Purposive Behavior,' *American Sociological Review*, 39: 101–12

Monaco, J. 1981. *How to Read a Film: The Art, Technology, Language, History, and Theory of Film and Media*. Oxford: Oxford University Press

Moon, P. 1981. 'Designs on Dominica: The Ku Klux Klan, A Mobster's Money and a Failed Coup,' *Globe and Mail*, 13 May

Mulkay, M. 1979. *Science and the Sociology of Knowledge*. London: Allen and Unwin

Mulkay, M., and G.N. Gilbert. 1983. 'Scientists' Theory Talk,' *Canadian Journal of Sociology*, 8: 179–97

Mullan, K. 1982. 'Reporting Northern Ireland: The case of the Bobby Sands hunger strike.' MA dissertation, Centre of Criminology, University of Toronto

Murdock, G. 1982. 'Disorderly Images: Television's Presentation of Crime and Policing,' in C. Sumner, ed., *Crime, Justice and the Mass Media*, pp. 104–21. Cambridge: Institute of Criminology, University of Cambridge

Murdock, G., and P. Golding. 1978. 'The Structure, Ownership and Control of the Press, 1914–1976,' in G. Boyce et al, eds., *Newspaper History*, pp. 130–48. London: Constable

– 1979. 'Capitalism, Communication and Class Relations,' in J. Curran et al, eds., *Mass Communication and Society*, pp. 12–35. Beverly Hills: Sage

Neuman, W. 1976. 'Patterns of Recall among Television News Viewers,' *Public Opinion Quarterly*, 40: 118–25

Ng, Y. 1982. 'Ideology, Media and Moral Panics: An Analysis of the Jacques Murder.' MA dissertation, Centre of Criminology, University of Toronto

Nunnally, J. 1981. 'Mental Illness: What Do Media Present,' in S. Cohen and J. Young, eds., *The Manufacture of News: Deviance, Social Problems and the Mass Media*, pp. 186–96. London: Constable

O'Connor, J. 1973. *The Fiscal Crisis of the State*. New York: St. Martin's

O'Neill, J. 1981. 'The Literary Production of Natural and Social Science Inquiry: Issues and Applications in the Social Organization of Science,' *Canadian Journal of Sociology*, 6: 105–20

– 1981a. 'McLuhan's Loss of Innis-Sense,' *Canadian Forum*, 61 (May): 13–15

Parsons, T. 1937. *The Structure of Social Action*. New York: McGraw-Hill

Pearce, F. 1981. 'The British Press and the 'Placing' of Male Homosexuality,' in S. Cohen and J. Young, eds., *The Manufacture of News: Deviance, Social Problems and the Mass Media*, pp. 303–16. London: Constable

Pearson, G. 1983. *Hooligan: A History of Respectable Fears*. London: Macmillan

Percy, W. 1958. 'Metaphor as Mistake,' *The Sewanee Review*, 66: 79–99

Phillips, B. 1977. 'Approaches to Objectivity: Journalistic versus Social Science Perspectives,' in P. Hirsch, P. Miller, and F. Kline, eds., *Strategies for Communication Research*, pp. 63–77. Beverly Hills: Sage

Pietropaolo, D. 1982. 'Structuring 'Truth': The Uses of Drama in 'Information' Radio,' *Canadian Theatre Review*, 36: 52–6

Pool, I., and I. Shulman. 1959. 'Newsmen's Fantasies, Audiences and Newswriting,' in L. Dexter and D. White, eds., *People, Society and Mass Communications*, pp. 141–59. New York: Free Press

Poole, M., and R. McPhee. 1983. 'A Structural Analysis of Organizational Climate,' in L. Putnam and M. Pacanowsky, eds., *Communication and Organization: An Interpretive Approach*, pp. 195–219. Beverly Hills: Sage

Popper, K. 1972. *Objective Knowledge*. Oxford: The Clarendon Press

Postman, N. 1985. *Amusing Ourselves to Death*. New York: Viking

Punch, M. 1985. *Conduct Unbecoming: The Social Construction of Police Deviance and Control*. London: Tavistock

Putnam, H. 1981. *Reason, Truth and History*. Cambridge: Cambridge University Press

Ratner, R., and J. McMullan. 1987. *State Control: Criminal Justice Politics in Canada*. Vancouver: University of British Columbia Press

Rawls, J. 1971. *A Theory of Justice*. Cambridge, Mass: Harvard University Press

Reiss, A. 1983. 'The Policing of Organizational Life,' in M. Punch, ed., *Control in the Police Organization*, pp. 78–97. Cambridge, Mass: MIT Press

Robertson, S. 1981. *Courts and the Media*. Toronto: Butterworth

Rock, P. 1973. *Deviant Behaviour*. London: Hutchinson

– 1973a. 'News as Eternal Recurrence,' in S. Cohen and J. Young, eds., *The Manufacture of News*, pp. 73–80. London: Constable

– 1986. *A View from the Shadows*. Oxford: Oxford University Press

Roshco, B. 1975. *Newsmaking*. Chicago: University of Chicago Press

Roshier, B. 1973. 'The Selection of Crime News by the Press,' in S. Cohen and J. Young, eds., *The Manufacture of News*, pp. 28–39. London: Constable

Royal Commission on Newspapers. 1981. *Final Report*. Ottawa: Supply and Services Canada

– 1981a. *Newspapers and Their Readers*. Ottawa: Research Studies on the Newspaper Industry, Supply and Services Canada

– 1981b. *The Journalists*. Ottawa: Research Studies on the Newspaper Industry, Supply and Services Canada

– 1981c. *Canadian News Sources*. Ottawa: Research Studies on the Newspaper Industry, Supply and Services Canada

– 1981d. *Newspapers and Computers: An Industry in Transition*. Ottawa: Research Studies on the Newspaper Industry, Supply and Services Canada

– 1981e. *The Newspaper and Public Affairs*. Ottawa: Research Studies on the Newspaper Industry, Supply and Services Canada

– 1981f. *Labour Relations in the Newspaper Industry*. Ottawa: Research Studies on the Newspaper Industry, Supply and Services Canada

Runciman, W. 1982. *A Treatise on Social Theory: Volume One. The Methodology of Social Theory*. Cambridge: Cambridge University Press

Rutherford, P. 1982. *A Victorian Authority: The Daily Press in Late Nineteenth Century Canada*. Toronto: University of Toronto Press

Sandy, P. 1979. 'The Ethnographic Paradigm(s),' *Administrative Science Quarterly*, 24: 527–38

Schiller, D. 1981. *Objectivity and the News: The Public and the Rise of Commercial Journalism*. Philadelphia: Pennsylvania University Press

Schlesinger, P. 1978. *Putting 'Reality' Together: B.B.C. News*. London: Constable

Schlesinger, P., G. Murdock, and P. Elliott. 1983. *Televising 'Terrorism': Political Violence in Popular Culture*. London: Comedia

Schudson, M. 1978. *Discovering the News*. New York: Basic Books

Scott, M., and S. Lyman. 1970. 'Accounts, Deviance and Social Disorder,' in J. Douglas, ed., *Deviance and Respectability: The Social Construction of Moral Meanings*, pp. 89–119. New York: Basic Books

Seaton, J. 1980. 'Politics and Television,' *Economy and Society*, 9: 90–107

Seymour-Ure, C. 1974. *The Political Impact of the Mass Media*. London: Constable

Shapiro, M., ed., 1984. *Language and Politics*. Oxford: Blackwell

Sheley, J., and C. Ashkins. 1981. 'Crime, Crime News and Crime Views,' *Public Opinion Quarterly* 45: 492–506

Sheridan, A. 1980. *Michel Foucault: The Will to Truth*. London: Tavistock

Sherizen, S. 1978. 'Social Creation of Crime News: All the News Fitted to Print,' in C. Winick, ed., *Deviance and Mass Media*, pp. 205–24. Beverly Hills: Sage

Sherman, L. 1978. *Scandal and Reform: Controlling Police Corruption*. Berkeley: University of California Press

– 1983. 'Reducing Police Gun Use: Critical Events, Administrative Policy, and Organizational Change,' in M. Punch, ed., *Control in the Police Organization*, pp. 98–125. Cambridge: MIT Press

Sigal, L. 1973. *Reporters and Officials*. Lexington, Mass: D.C. Heath

Simon, H. 1957. *Models of Man*. New York: Wiley

– 1976. *Administrative Behavior*. New York: Free Press

Singer, B. 1986. *Advertising and Society*. Don Mills: Addison-Wesley

Smircich, L. 1983. 'Concepts of Culture and Organizational Analysis,' *Administrative Science Quarterly* 28: 339–58

Smith, A. 1978. 'The Long Road to Objectivity and Back Again: The Kinds of Truth We Get in Journalism,' in G. Boyce et al, eds., *Newspaper History*, pp. 152–71. London: Constable

– 1979. 'Technology and Control: The Interactive Dimensions of Journalism,' in J. Curran et al, eds., *Mass Communication and Society*, pp. 174–94. Beverly Hills: Sage

– 1980. *Goodbye Gutenberg: The Newspaper Revolution of the 1980s*. New York: Oxford University Press

Smith, D. 1974. 'The Ideological Practice of Sociology,' *Catalyst* 8: 39–54

– 1981. 'On Sociological Description: A Method from Marx,' *Human Studies*, 4: 313–37

– 1984. 'Textually-Mediated Social Organization,' *International Social Science Journal*, 36: 59–75

Stanga, J. 1971. 'The Press and the Criminal Defendant: Newsmen and Criminal Justice in Three Wisconsin Cities.' PhD dissertation, University of Wisconsin

Stauffer, J., R. Frost, and W. Rybolt. 1981. 'Recall and Learning from Broadcast News: Is Print Better?' *Journal of Broadcasting* (Summer 1981): 253–62

Steed, J. 1982. 'The Big Shakers at the Corp,' *Globe and Mail*, 22 May

Stehr, N., and G. Böhme, eds. 1986. *The Knowledge Society: The Impact of Scientific Knowledge on Social Structures*. Dordrecht: Reidel

Stehr, N., and V. Meja. 1984. 'Introduction: The Development of the Sociology of Knowledge,' in N. Stehr and V. Meja , eds., *Society and Knowledge: Contemporary Perspectives in the Sociology of Knowledge*. New Brunswick, NJ: Transaction Books

Stern, A. 1973. 'A Study for the National Association of Broadcasting,' in M. Barret, ed., *The Politics of Broadcasting, 1971–72*. New York: Cromwell

Strauss, A. 1978. *Negotiations*. San Francisco: Jossey-Bass

Sudnow, D. 1965. 'Normal Crimes: Sociological Features of the Penal Code in a Public Defender's Office,' *Social Problems*, 12: 255–72

Sumner, C. 1979. *Reading Ideologies*. London: Academic Press

– 1981. 'Race, Crime and Hegemony,' *Contemporary Crises*, 5: 277–91

– 1982. ''Political Hooliganism' and 'Rampaging Mobs': The National Press Coverage of the Toxteth 'Riots,'' in C. Sumner, ed., *Crime, Justice and the Mass Media*, pp. 25–35. Cambridge: Institute of Criminology, University of Cambridge

Swope, H.B. 1958. 'Statement recalled in obituaries after his death,' cited in R. Tripp, *The International Thesaurus of Quotations*. Harmondsworth: Penguin, 1978

Tompkins, P., and G. Cheney. 1983. 'Account Analysis of Organizations,' in L. Putnam and M. Pacanowsky, eds., *Communication and Organizations*, pp. 123–46. Beverly Hills: Sage

Thompson, J.D. 1967. *Organizations in Action*. New York: McGraw-Hill

Tracey, M. 1978. *The Production of Political Television*. London: Routledge

– 1984. 'Does Arthur Scargill have a Leg to Stand On? – News,' *The Sunday Times*, 28 August

Trujillo, N. 1983. ''Performing' Mintzberg's Roles: The Nature of Managerial Communication,' in L. Putnam and M. Pacanowsky, eds. *Communication and Organizations: An Interpretive Approach*, pp. 73–97. Beverly Hills: Sage

Tuchman, G. 1977. 'The Exception Proves the Rule: The Study of Routine News Practices,' in P. Hirsch, P. Miller, and F. Kline, eds., *Strategies for Communication Research*, pp. 43–62. Beverly Hills: Sage

– 1978. *Making News*. New York: Free Press

– 1981. 'Myth and the Consciousness Industry: A New Look at the Effects of the Mass Media,' in E. Katz and T. Szecsko, eds., *Mass Media and Social Change*, pp. 83–100. Beverly Hills: Sage

– 1981a. 'The Symbolic Annihilation of Women by the Mass Media,' in S. Cohen and J. Young, eds., *The Manufacture of News: Deviance, Social Problems and the Mass Media*, pp. 169–85. London: Constable

Tumber, H. 1982. *Television and the Riots*. London: Broadcasting Research Unit, British Film Institute

Varhinger, H. 1968. *The Philosophy of the As If: A System of the Theoretical, Practical, and Religious Fictions of Mankind*. London: Routledge

Van Maanen, J. 1979. 'The Fact of Fiction in Organizational Ethnography,' *Administrative Science Quarterly*, 24: 539–50

Voumvakis, S., and R. Ericson. 1984. *News Accounts of Attacks on Women: A Comparison of Three Toronto Newspapers*. Toronto: Centre of Criminology, University of Toronto

Waite, P. 1962. *The Life and Times of Confederation*. Toronto: University of Toronto Press

Waller, I., and N. Okihiro. 1978. *Burglary and the Public*. Toronto: University of Toronto Press

Warshett, G. 1981. 'The Information Economy in Late Capitalism,' in L. Salter, ed., *Communication Studies in Canada*, pp. 178–95. Toronto: Butterworths

Weber, M. 1917. 'Parliament and Government,' in G. Roth and C. Wittich, eds., *Max Weber on Economy and Society*. Berkeley: University of California Press

– 1946. *From Max Weber*, H. Gerth and C.W. Mills, eds. New York: Oxford University Press

Weick, K. 1979. *The Social Psychology of Organizing*. 2nd ed. Reading, Mass: Addison-Wesley

– 1983. 'Organizational Communication: Toward a Research Agenda,' in L. Putnam and M. Pacanowsky, eds., *Communication and Organizations*, pp. 13–29. Beverly Hills: Sage

Williams, R. 1974. *Television: Technology and Cultural Form*. London: Fontana

– 1976. *Communications*. 3rd ed. Harmondsworth: Penguin

Willis, P. 1981. *Learning to Labor: How Working Class Kids Get Working Class Jobs*. New York: Columbia University Press

Winter, J., and A. Frizzle. 1979. 'The Treatment of State-owned versus Private Corporations in English Canadian Dailies,' *Canadian Journal of Communication* 6: 1–11

Wittgenstein, L. 1972. *Philosophical Investigations*. Oxford: Blackwell

Wuthnow, R., J. Hunter, A. Bergesen, and E. Kurzweil. 1984. *Cultural Analysis*. London: Routledge

Young, J. 1974. 'Mass Media, Drugs and Deviance,' in P. Rock and M. McIntosh, eds., *Deviance and Social Control*, pp. 229–59. London: Tavistock

– 1981. 'The Manufacture of News: A Critique of the Present Convergence in Mass Media Theory,' in *State Control of Information in the Field of Deviance and Social Control*, pp. 231–60. Leuven: European Group for the Study of Deviance and Social Control. Working Papers in European Criminology, no. 2.

Index

Shearing, C., 21, 119
Sheley, J., 45, 46, 76
Sheridan, A., 14, 35
Sherizen, S., 44, 45, 49
Sherman, L., 68, 69
Shulman, I., 194
Sigal, L., 211, 298
Simon, H., 24, 26
Singer, B., 38
Smircich, L., 42
Smith, A., 13, 15–16, 19, 22, 32, 33,
    37, 44, 52, 107, 120, 121, 137, 240,
    310, 347
Smith, D., 9, 19–20, 24, 66, 87
Source organizations, 73–4; control
    over information, 16, 51, 69, 238–
    40, 274–5, 351–2; difficulty of doing
    investigative journalism in, 118–19;
    ideology and, 9–10, 20–2, 361;
    interdependence between journalists
    and, 9–10, 22–5, 66–7, 69, 245,
    345–6, 351–2; and negotiated order,
    53–6; negotiations with, for
    information, 240–7; as originators of
    ideas for news stories, 182, 186–8;
    and reform politics, 56–9; social-
    control effects of news organizations
    on, 65–70; transformation of
    occurrence into news event, 40–2;
    vetting of journalists, 245; see also
    Authorized knowers; Sources
Sources: choosing, 226–33; documents
    as, 258–64; difficulties in contacting,
    112–13, 203–5, 236–7; and the
    hierarchy of credibility 282–6, 291,
    332, 359; ideology and, 9–10, 20–2,
    361; interviews with, 237–47;
    journalists as, 264–70; negotiating
    with, for information, 240–7; news
    organizations as, 292–3; and 'off the
    record' information, 242–4, 246; and
    point / counterpoint objectivity, 106,

226–9, 259–61, 272–3, 353; practices
    in quoting, 286–93; staging for
    visuals, 274–5; surveys and survey
    data as, 247–56; see also Authorized
    knowers; Source organizations
Southam newspapers, 82
Sports reporting, 170–1
Staging, of visuals, 102, 239, 274–7
Stanga, J., 66, 69
Stauffer, J., 361
Steed, J., 29
Stehr, N., 12, 17, 43
Stern, A., 361
Stocks, 147–8, 278
Stone, G., 196
Strauss, A., 7, 42, 54
Stuchlik, M., 17, 18, 74, 78
Style, news, 311–13; and ideology,
    313–18; 'pyramid,' 325, 327, 334
Sudnow, D., 175
Sumner, C., 14, 26, 53, 58, 68, 77, 80
Sun newspapers, 82
Surveys, 247–56
Swope, H.B., 153
Szelényi, I., 14

Taste, in journalism, 322–5
Techniques, reporting. *See*
    Methodology, reporting
Television: assignment editor, 87, 96–7,
    181–220; dependence on newspapers
    for story ideas, 189–91; entertainment
    requirements in, 50–1, 101–2, 335–
    42, 354; 'fillers' in, 328–9; framing
    news in, 143–7, 200, 327–9, 334–5;
    and government control, 28–9, 32–5;
    knowledge of audience in, 194–7;
    and the law, 318–22; newscripts,
    100, 279–82, 298, 304–8, 309–10,
    311–13; news ratings, 84–6;
    newsrooms, 96–100; production and
    editing process in, 99, 298, 303,